Software Engineering

We work with leading authors to develop the
strongest educational materials in computer science,
bringing cutting-edge thinking and best learning
practice to a global market.

Under a range of well-known imprints, including
Addison Wesley, we craft high quality print and
electronic publications which help readers to
understand and apply their content,
whether studying or at work.

To find out more about the complete range of our
publishing please visit us on the World Wide Web at:
www.pearsoneduc.com

Software Engineering

A Programming Approach

Third Edition

DOUGLAS BELL

An imprint of **Pearson Education**

Harlow, England · London · New York · Reading, Massachusetts · San Francisco
Toronto · Don Mills, Ontario · Sydney · Tokyo · Singapore · Hong Kong · Seoul
Taipei · Cape Town · Madrid · Mexico City · Amsterdam · Munich · Paris · Milan

PEARSON EDUCATION LTD

Edinburgh Gate
Harlow
Essex CM20 2JE
England

and Associated Companies around the World

Visit us on the World Wide Web at:
www.pearsoneduc.com

First published under the Prentice Hall imprint 1987
Second edition 1992
Third edition 2000

© Pearson Education Limited 1987, 1992, 2000

ISBN 0 201 64856 3

British Library Cataloguing-in-Publication Data
A catalogue record for this book can be obtained from the British Library

Library of Congress Cataloging-in-Publication Data
Bell, Doug, 1944-
    Software engineering / Douglas Bell.-- 3rd ed.
        p. cm.
    Includes bibliographical references and index.
    ISBN 0-201-64856-3 (pbk.)
    1. Software engineering. I. Title.

QA76.758 .B45 2000
005.1--dc21   99-053633

10 9 8 7 6 5 4 3 2 1
04 03 02 01 00

Typeset by 42
Printed and bound in Great Britain by Biddles Ltd, www.biddles.co.uk

Contents

Preface   xv

Part A Introduction

1 Software – problems and prospects   3
1.1   Introduction   3
1.2   Meeting users' needs   4
1.3   The cost of software production   5
1.4   Meeting deadlines   10
1.5   Software performance   10
1.6   Portability   11
1.7   Maintenance   12
1.8   Reliability   13
1.9   Human–computer interaction   16
1.10 A software crisis?   16
1.11 A remedy – software engineering?   17
1.12 Summary   18
Exercises   19
Answers to self test questions   20
Further reading   20

2 Process models   21
2.1   Introduction   21
2.2   The components of software development   22
2.3   Validation and verification   24
2.4   The waterfall model   25

2.5 Prototyping   28
2.6 Formal methods – the transform model   36
2.7 The spiral model   37
2.8 Discussion   40
2.9 Summary   41
Exercises   41
Answers to self test questions   42
Further reading   42

Part B Requirements engineering

3 Requirements analysis   45
3.1 Introduction   45
3.2 The notion of a requirement   46
3.3 The process of eliciting requirements   47
3.4 The requirements specification   49
3.5 Summary   52
Exercises   53
Further reading   54

4 Formal specification   55
4.1 Introduction   55
4.2 Formal specification in Z: an example   57
4.3 The role of formal specification   64
4.4 Summary   65
Exercises   66
Answers to self test questions   67
Further reading   67

Part C Design

5 Structured programming   71
5.1 Introduction   71
5.2 Arguments against goto   72
5.3 Arguments in favor of goto   76
5.4 Selecting control structures   77
5.5 What is structured programming?   79
5.6 Summary   82
Exercises   83
Further reading   84

6 Modularity   85
6.1 Introduction   85

6.2   Why modularity?   86
6.3   Module size   88
6.4   Complexity   90
6.5   Global data is harmful   91
6.6   Information hiding and abstract data types   92
6.7   Coupling and cohesion   94
6.8   Coupling   95
6.9   Cohesion   98
6.10 Shaw and Garlan's classification   100
6.11 Object-oriented programming   102
6.12 Summary   103
Exercises   104
Answer to self test question   105
Further reading   105

7 Functional decomposition   106
7.1   Introduction   106
7.2   An example – a video game   107
7.3   More about the method   110
7.4   What about data?   111
7.5   Alternative solutions   112
7.6   The place of functional decomposition   113
7.7   Discussion   113
7.8   Summary   114
Exercises   114
Further reading   115

8 Data structure design: The Michael Jackson
   program design method (JSP)   116
8.1   Introduction   116
8.2   A simple example   117
8.3   Processing input files   122
8.4   Physical and logical structures   124
8.5   Processing several input and output streams   126
8.6   Structure clashes   131
8.7   Discussion and evaluation   135
8.8   Summary   137
Exercises   138
Answer to self test question   139
Further reading   140

9 Data flow design   141
9.1   Introduction   141
9.2   An analogy   142

9.3 First examples 143
9.4 Case study – point-of-sale terminal 146
9.5 Case study – monitoring a plant 150
9.6 Rationale for the method 151
9.7 Discussion 153
9.8 Summary 155
Exercises 155
Further reading 156

10 Object-oriented design 157
10.1 Introduction 157
10.2 The features of OOP 158
10.3 The aims of OO design 163
10.4 Finding the classes 165
10.5 Specifying the responsibilities of the classes 167
10.6 Specifying the collaborators 168
10.7 Other design techniques and notations 169
10.8 Using the class library 169
10.9 Class–responsibility–collaborator (CRC) cards 170
10.10 Use-case analysis 171
10.11 Creating good class hierarchies 172
10.12 Is-a and has-a analysis 175
10.13 Design guidelines 176
10.14 Re-usable design patterns (frameworks) 176
10.15 Object-oriented design methodologies 177
10.16 Discussion 177
10.17 Summary 179
Exercises 179
Answers to self test questions 181
Further reading 181

11 User interface design 183
11.1 Introduction 183
11.2 An interdisciplinary field 184
11.3 Styles of human–computer interface 184
11.4 Different perspectives on HCI 186
11.5 Design principles and guidelines 187
11.6 Human–computer interface design 190
11.7 Task analysis 191
11.8 Design evaluation 193
11.9 Help systems 194
11.10 Implementation tools 195
11.11 Summary 196
Exercises 196

Answers to self test questions 197
Further reading 197

12 Formal development 199

12.1 Introduction 199
12.2 What is a formal method? 200
12.3 Formal development: a case study 201
12.4 The role of formal development 208
12.5 Summary 209
Exercises 210
Answers to self test questions 211
Further reading 211

Part D Programming paradigms

13 The programming language 215

13.1 Introduction 215
13.2 Design principles 216
13.3 Language syntax 218
13.4 Control abstractions 221
13.5 Data types and strong typing 227
13.6 Procedural abstraction 238
13.7 Abstract data types 243
13.8 Programming in the large 249
13.9 The role of programming languages 256
13.10 Summary 258
Exercises 258
Answers to self test questions 260
Further reading 264

14 Object-oriented programming (OOP) 265

14.1 Introduction 265
14.2 Encapsulation 265
14.3 Classes 267
14.4 Creating objects 268
14.5 Constructor methods 269
14.6 Destructor methods 270
14.7 Class or static methods 270
14.8 Inheritance 271
14.9 Single versus multiple inheritance 274
14.10 Polymorphism 274
14.11 Event-driven programming 275
14.12 Case study – a complete Java program 276

14.13 The role of OOP   280
14.14 Summary   281
Exercises   282
Answers to self test questions   284
Further reading   285

15 Concurrent programming   286

15.1   Introduction   286
15.2   Independent threads   288
15.3   Dying and killing   291
15.4   The state of a thread   292
15.5   Scheduling and thread priorities   293
15.6   Mutual exclusion   293
15.7   Thread interaction   296
15.8   The producer–consumer problem   301
15.9   Interruptions   312
15.10 Deadlock   313
15.11 Conclusions   314
15.12 Summary   316
Exercises   316
Answers to self test questions   318
Further reading   320

16 Functional programming   321

16.1   Introduction   321
16.2   Procedural languages   322
16.3   Characteristics of functional programming   324
16.4   Other functional languages   331
16.5   The role of functional programming   333
16.6   Summary   335
Exercises   336
Answers to self test questions   337
Further reading   337

17 Logic programming   338

17.1   Introduction   338
17.2   Facts and rules   340
17.3   Execution mechanisms   342
17.4   Prolog in use   348
17.5   Conclusions   350
17.6   Summary   351
Exercises   352
Further reading   352

Part E Implementation

18 Software tools   355
18.1   Introduction   355
18.2   Tools for programming   356
18.3   Not programming tools   357
18.4   Examples of tools   357
18.5   Discussion   365
18.6   Application development tools   365
18.7   The physical environment   369
18.8   Summary   370
Exercises   371
Answers to self test questions   371
Further reading   371

19 Verification   372
19.1   Introduction   372
19.2   The nature of errors   373
19.3   The problem of testing   374
19.4   Black box (functional) testing   375
19.5   White box (structural) testing   377
19.6   Walkthroughs and inspections   379
19.7   Other testing strategies   382
19.8   Discussion   383
19.9   System (integration) testing   385
19.10 Bottom-up testing   386
19.11 Top-down development   387
19.12 Summary   390
Exercises   391
Answers to self test questions   393
Further reading   395

20 Software fault tolerance and exceptions   396
20.1   Introduction   396
20.2   Fault detection by software   399
20.3   Fault detection by hardware   402
20.4   Dealing with damage   405
20.5   Exceptions and exception handlers   407
20.6   Recovery blocks   410
20.7   N-version programming   413
20.8   The role of fault tolerance   414
20.9   Summary   414
Exercises   415

Answers to self test questions   417
Further reading   417

21 Software metrics and quality assurance   418

21.1   Introduction   418
21.2   Complexity metrics   419
21.3   Faults and reliability – estimating bugs   422
21.4   Software quality   423
21.5   Quality assurance   425
21.6   Process improvement   426
21.7   The capability maturity model (CMM)   426
21.8   Summary   427
Exercises   428
Answers to self test questions   429
Further reading   429

22 Project management   430

22.1   Introduction   430
22.2   The challenge of project management   431
22.3   The ingredients of project management   431
22.4   Cost estimation   432
22.5   Team organization   434
22.6   Selecting tools and methods   441
22.7   Introducing new methods   442
22.8   The project plan   442
22.9   Peopleware   443
22.10   Summary   444
Exercises   444
Further reading   445

Part F   Review

23 Review   449

23.1   Introduction   449
23.2   Assessing and comparing development methods   450
23.3   Software tools   452
23.4   Software re-usability   452
23.5   The current state of methods   452
23.6   A single development method?   453
23.7   The real world of software engineering   454
23.8   The question of skill   457
23.9   The future of software engineering   457
23.10   Summary   458

| | Exercises | 459 |
| | Further reading | 460 |

Appendix:	**An introduction to Java**	**463**
	A.1 Variables and assignment	463
	A.2 Control structures	464
	A.3 Methods	464
	A.4 Summary	465
	Index	467

A COMPANION WEB SITE ACCOMPANIES *SOFTWARE ENGINEERING*, 3E BY DOUGLAS BELL

Visit the *Software Engineering* Companion Web Site at www.booksites.net/bell_se
Here you will find valuable teaching and learning material including:

For Lecturers:

● Suggestions and guidance on how to use the book to accompany your course. Includes proposed chapter plans for varying routes through the text
● Supplementary material will be provided on a chapter by chapter basis to augment the book
● Links to useful resources on the web.

For Students:

● Study material designed to help you improve your results
● Links to resources on the web.

TRADEMARK NOTICE

The following are trademarks or registered trademarks of their respective companies: Ada is a trademark of the US Department of Defense – Ada Joint Program Office; Delphi is a trademark of Borland International, Inc; Eiffel is a trademark of Nonprofit International Consortium for Eiffel (NICE); EMACS is a trademark of Sphinx Limited; IBM is a trademark of International Business Machines Corporation; Interlisp is a trademark of Xerox Corporation; Microsoft, Windows NT, Windows, and Visual Basic are trademarks of Microsoft Corporation; Java and Modula-2 are trademarks of Sun Microsystems, Inc.; Macintosh and Mac OS are trademarks of Apple Computer, Inc; Miranda is a trademark of Research Software Limited; Netscape Navigator is a trademark of Netscape Communications Corporation; PostScript is a trademark of Adobe Systems Incorporated; Simula 67 is a trademark of Simula AS; Smalltalk-80 is a trademark of ParcPlace Systems; UNIX is a trademark licensed through X/Open Company Ltd.

Preface

Software engineering is about the creation of large pieces of software – software that consists of many thousands of lines of code and involves many person months of effort. Equally, software engineering is about imagination and creativity – the process of creating something apparently tangible from nothing.

One of the attractions of software engineering is that there is no one single method for doing it, but instead a whole variety of different approaches. So the software engineer needs a knowledge of many different techniques and tools. This diversity is one of the delights of software engineering. This book celebrates this diversity by presenting the range of current techniques and tools.

Some software engineering methods are well defined while others are ill defined. The processes of software development are under ever-increasing scrutiny – particularly with the advent of quality assurance procedures. Whichever technique is used, software engineering methods have not yet been analyzed and routinized and thus there is still great scope for using imagination and creativity. So the exercise of skill and flair is one of the pleasures of software engineering.

Ideally you, the reader, will have savored the joy of creating an elegant solution to a programming problem. You will also have experienced the intense frustration of trying to find an elusive bug. And you will know the satisfaction of subsequently tracking down the bug and eliminating it.

This book is for people who have experienced the pleasures of writing programs and who want to see how things change in the scale up to large programs and software systems.

This book explains the challenges that large software projects present. It explains the different techniques and tools that are used. It doesn't present ready answers about the value of these techniques. Indeed it asks the reader to make an assessment of each technique. This is what the software engineer has to do – now and in the future – choose the appropriate techniques for the project in hand, from the multiplicity of techniques that are on offer.

This book provides an introduction to software engineering for students in undergraduate programs in computer science, computer studies, information technology, software engineering and related fields at the college or university level. The book is also aimed at practising software developers in industry and commerce who wish to keep abreast of current ideas in software engineering.

The prerequisites for understanding this book are:

● familiarity with a high-level programming language

● some experience with developing a moderately sized program of a few hundred lines.

This book is written in such a way that each chapter can be read on its own, independently of any others, but the book is segmented into parts which each have a theme:

● Introduction

● Requirements engineering

● Design methods

● Programming paradigms

● Implementation

● Review

The introduction sets the scene and looks at models for organizing the process of software development.

The segment on requirements engineering reviews not only requirements elicitation but also specification.

The segment on design methods explains the mainstream approaches to deciding on the structure of a software system.

The segment on programming paradigms reviews not only procedural and object-oriented programming and languages, but also examines alternative paradigms like functional and logic programming. Concurrent programming is also included here.

The segment on implementation examines verification, project management, tools, metrics, quality assurance and fault tolerance.

Finally there is a chapter that reviews and sums up the whole subject.

Throughout the text, UML (Unified Modeling Language) is used as appropriate as a design notation and Java as an illustrative procedural programming language. In the appropriate chapters, Haskell is used as the illustrative functional language and Prolog as the example of a logic programming language.

If you have comments or suggestions on the book, or to see additional material and updates, please visit the Companion Web Site for this book at http://www.booksites.net/bell_se.

Acknowledgments

The author is indebted to current and past colleagues, including Mike Parr, Jawed Siddiqi, Andy Bissett, and John Pugh. Ian Morrey contributed four wonderful chapters, with little reward other than the joy of the subject. Ian, you are a star. Any defects are, of course, the author's.

Introduction

Software – problems and prospects

This chapter:

- describes the difficulties of constructing large-scale software
- analyzes the problems that software engineers face.

1.1 ● Introduction

Software engineering is about methods, tools and techniques used for developing software. This particular chapter is concerned with the reasons for having a field of study called software engineering, and with the problems that are encountered in developing software. This book as a whole explains a variety of techniques that attempt to solve the problems and meet the goals of software engineering.

Software surrounds us everywhere in the industrialized nations – in domestic appliances, communications systems, transportation systems and in businesses. Software comes in different shapes and sizes – from the program in a mobile phone to the software to design a new automobile. In categorizing software, we can distinguish two major types:

- *system software* is the software that acts as tools to help construct or support applications software. Examples are operating systems, databases, nletworking software, and compilers.
- *applications software* is software that helps perform some directly useful or enjoyable task. Examples are games, the software for automatic teller machines (ATMs), the control software in an airplane, e-mail software, word processors, and spreadsheets.

Within the category of applications software, it can be useful to identify the following categories of software:

- games
- information systems – systems that store and access large amounts of data; for example an airline seat reservation system
- real-time systems – in which the computer must respond quickly; for example the control software for a power station
- embedded systems – in which the computer plays a smallish role within a larger system; for example the software in a telephone exchange or a mobile phone; embedded systems are usually also real-time systems.
- office software – word processors, spreadsheets, e-mail
- scientific software – carrying out calculations, modeling, prediction; for example weather forecasting.

Software can either be off-the-shelf (e.g. Microsoft Word) or tailor-made for a particular application (e.g. software for the Apollo moonshots).

All these types of software – except perhaps information systems – fall within the remit of software engineering. Information systems have a different history and, generally, different techniques are used for their development. Often the nature of the data (information) is used to dictate the structure of the software, so that analysis of the data is a prime step, leading to the design of the database for the application. This approach to software development is outside the scope of this book.

Constructing software is a challenging task, essentially because software is complex. The perceived problems in software development and the goals that software development seeks to achieve are:

- meeting users' needs
- low cost of production
- high performance
- portability
- low cost of maintenance
- high reliability
- delivery on time.

We will now look at each of these goals in turn. Each of these goals is also a problem, since software engineering has generally been rather unsuccessful at reaching them. Later we will look at how the goals relate one to another.

In the remainder of this book we shall see that particular types of software require the use of special techniques for their development, but many development techniques have general applicability.

1.2 ● Meeting users' needs

It seems self-evident to remark that a piece of software must do what its users want of it. Thus, logically, the first step in developing some software is to find out what the client,

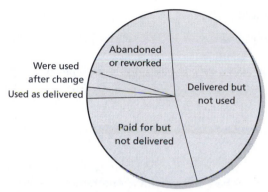

Figure 1.1 Effectiveness of typical large software projects

customer or user needs. This step is often called requirements analysis or requirements engineering. It seems obvious that it should be carried out with some care. There is evidence, however, that this is not always the case. For example, one study of the effectiveness of large-scale software projects, Figure 1.1, found that, of a total budget of $6.2 million, less than 2% were used as delivered.

These figures are one of the few pieces of hard evidence available because (not surprisingly) organizations are rather secretive about this issue. But we might extrapolate from this data and deduce that a large proportion of systems do not meet the needs of their users and are therefore not used as supplied.

We might go further and deduce that the main problem of software development seems to lie in requirements analysis, rather than in any other areas – like reliability and cost discussed below

The task of trying to ensure that software does what its users want is known as *validation*.

1.3 ● The cost of software production

1.3.1 Examples of costs

First of all, let us get some idea of the scale of software costs in the world. In the USA it is estimated that about $500 billion are spent each year on producing software. This amounts to 1% of the gross national product. The estimated figure for the world is $1,000 billion spent each year on software production. These figures have risen and are set to rise by about 15% each year. The operating system that IBM developed for one of its major range of computers (called OS 360) is estimated to have cost $200 million. In the USA, the software costs of the manned space program were $1 billion between 1960 and 1970.

These examples indicate that the amount spent on software in the industrialized nations is very great.

1.3.2 Programmer productivity

The cost of software is determined largely by the salaries paid to the programmers and by the productivity of the programmers. Perhaps surprisingly, the productivity of the average programmer is only about 10–20 programming language statements per day. However, this apparently poor performance does not just reflect the time taken to carry out coding, but also includes the time required to carry out clarifying the problem specification, program design, coding, testing and documentation. It is remarkable that this figure for productivity is independent of the programming language used. It is similar whether a third-generation language like C or a fourth-generation language such as Visual Basic is used. However, this is an average figure that should be qualified in two ways. First, enormous differences between individual programmers – factors of 20 – have been found in studies. Second, the type of software makes a difference; applications software can be written more quickly than systems software. However, to the lay person, a productivity of 20 lines of code per day may well seem disgraceful – but is this a consequence of laziness, poor tools, or inadequate methods?

SELF TEST QUESTION

1.1 A well-known word processor consists of a million lines of code. Calculate how many programmers would be needed to write it, assuming that it has to be completed in five years. Assuming that they are each paid $50,000 per year, what is the cost of development?

1.3.3 Predicting software costs

It is very difficult to predict in advance how long it will take to write a particular piece of software. It is not uncommon for a manager to under-estimate by 50% the timescale, and hence the cost and delivery date, of software.

1.3.4 Hardware versus software costs

The relative costs of hardware and software can be a lively battleground for controversy. In the early days of computers, hardware was costly and software relatively cheap. Nowadays, thanks to mass production and miniaturization, hardware is cheap and software (labor intensive) is expensive. So the costs of hardware and software have been reversed. These changes are reflected in the so-called "S-shaped curve," Figure 1.2, showing the relative costs as they have changed over the years. Whereas in about 1955, software cost typically only about 10% of a project, now it is the hardware that is only 10%.

These proportions should be treated carefully; they hold for certain projects only – not in each and every case. In fact, figures of this kind are derived largely from one-off large-scale projects.

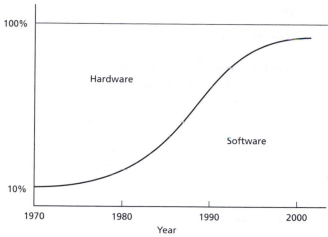

Figure 1.2 Changes in the relative costs of hardware and software

---

SELF TEST QUESTION

1.2 Someone buys a PC, with processor, monitor, hard disk and printer. They also buy an operating system and a word processing package. Calculate the relative costs of hardware and software.

We will now look at a number of issues that affect the popular perception of software and its costs.

1.3.5 The impact of personal computers

Perhaps the greatest influence on popular perceptions of software costs has come about since the advent of the microcomputer and personal computing. Many people buy a PC for their home, and so come to realize very clearly what the costs are.

First is the "rock and roll" factor. If you buy a stereo for $200, you don't expect to pay $2,000 for a CD. Similarly, if you buy a PC for $1,000, you don't expect to pay $10,000 for the software, which is what it would cost if you hired a programmer to write it for you. So, of course, a software package for a PC is priced at about $50 or so. It can be hard to comprehend that something for which you paid $50 has costs millions of dollars to develop.

Second is the "teenager in the bedroom" syndrome. Many school students write programs, either as part of their studies or as a hobby. So a parent might easily think "My kid can write a computer game in two weeks. What's so hard about programming? Why is software so expensive?"

1.3.6 Software packages

There has been another significant reaction to the availability of cheap computers. If you want to computerize accounting or production planning, you can buy a program off the shelf to do it. Such software packages can cost as little as $50. Even compilers for PC's can be bought for this price. The reason for the remarkably low price is, of course, that the producers of the software sell many identical copies – the mass production of software has arrived. The problem with an off-the-shelf package is, of course, that it may not do *exactly* what you want to do and you may have to resort to tailor-made software, adapt your way of life to fit in with the software, or make do with the inadequacies.

Nonetheless, the availability of cheap packages conveys the impression that software is cheap to produce.

1.3.7 Application development tools

If you want to create certain types of applications software very quickly and easily, several development tools are available. Notable examples of these tools are Visual Basic (discussed in a later chapter) and Microsoft Access. These tools enable certain types of program to be constructed very easily and even people who are not programmers can learn to use tools like a spreadsheet (for example Microsoft Excel). Thus a perception is created that programming is easy and, indeed, that programmers may no longer be necessary.

The truth is, of course, that some software is very simple and easy to write, but most commercially used software is large and extremely complex.

1.3.8 The IT revolution

The sophistication of today's software far outstrips that of the past. For example, complex graphical user interfaces (GUIs) are now seen as essential, systems are commonly distributed amongst a network of computers and the sheer size of projects has mushroomed. People and organizations expect ever more facilities from computers. Arguably software costs can only continue to spiral as hardware becomes available to make previously impractical software projects feasible.

In summary, what we see today is that software is expensive:

● relative to the gross national product
● because developers exhibit apparently low productivity
● relative to the cost of hardware
● in popular perception.

1.3.9 How is the cost made up?

It is interesting to see which parts of a software development project cost most money. Figure 1.3 shows typical figures.

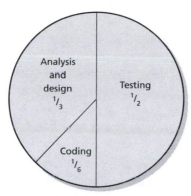

Figure 1.3 Relative costs of the stages of software development

Clearly the cost of testing is enormous, whereas coding constitutes only a small part of software development. One interpretation of this is that if a new magical program development method was devised that ensured the software was correct from the start, then testing would be unnecessary, and therefore only half the usual effort would be needed. Such a method would be a discovery indeed!

If mistakes are a major problem, when are they made? Figure 1.4 shows figures showing the number of errors made at the various stages of a typical project.

However, this data is rather misleading. What matters is how much it costs to *fix* an error. And an error costs more, the longer the error remains undiscovered. So errors made during the earlier stages of a project tend to be more expensive, unless they are discovered almost immediately. Hence Figure 1.5 showing the relative costs of fixing mistakes in a typical project is probably more relevant.

A design flaw made early in the project may not be detected until late on in system testing – and it will certainly involve a whole lot of rework. But, by contrast, a syntax

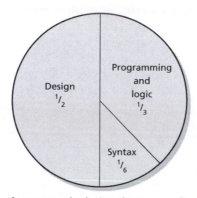

Figure 1.4 Relative numbers of errors made during the stages of software development

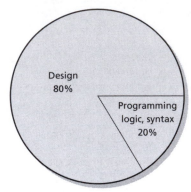

Figure 1.5 Relative cost of fixing different types of error

error in a program made late in the project will be automatically detected on a first compilation and then easily corrected.

1.3.10 Software re-use

One response to the perceived high cost of software is to suggest re-using existing software. But as we shall see later, it is usually enormously difficult to adapt software to fit a
new environment. Another approach is to construct software components that, like electronic components, can be taken off the shelf and linked together to perform the desired
function. Thus while some advances in programming languages and design techniques
are attempting to pursue this route, it is far from being a mature technology.

1.4 ● Meeting deadlines

Meeting deadlines has always been a headache in software production. For example, surveys have consistently shown that this is the worst problem faced by information system
managers. The problem is related to the difficulty of predicting how long it will take to
develop something. If you don't know how long it is going to take, you can't hope to
meet any deadline. It is a common experience for a software project to run late and over-
budget, disappointing the client and causing despair amongst the software team.

Just one example of a major piece of software that was late is Microsoft's first version
of its NT operating system, which was allegedly one year late.

1.5 ● Software performance

Program performance is sometimes called efficiency. This terminology dates from the
days when the cost and speed of hardware meant that every effort was made to use the
hardware – primarily memory and processor – as carefully as possible. More recently a

cultural change has come about due to the increasing speed of computers and the fall in the cost of computers. Nowadays there is more emphasis on meeting people's requirements and consequently we will not spend much time on performance in this book. Not that performance can be neglected – often we are concerned to make sure that:

● an interactive system responds within a reasonably short time
● a control signal is output to a plant in sufficient time
● a game runs sufficiently fast that motion appears smooth
● a batch job is not taking twelve hours when it should take one.

SELF TEST QUESTION

1.3 Identify two further software systems in which speed is an important factor.

The trouble with fast run time and small memory usage is that they are usually mutually contradictory. As an example to help see how this comes about, consider a program to carry out a calculation of tax. We could either carry out a calculation – which would involve using fairly slow machine instructions; alternatively we could use a lookup table – which would involve a fairly fast indexing instruction. So the first case is slow but small, and the second case is fast but large. Generally, of course, it is necessary to make a judgment about what are the particular performance requirements of a piece of software.

1.6 ● Portability

The dream of portability has always been to transfer software from one type of computer to another with the minimum expenditure of effort. With the advent of high-level languages and the establishment of international standards, the prospects looked bright for the complete portability of applications programs.

The reality is that market forces have dominated the situation. A supplier seeks to attract a customer by offering facilities over and above those provided by the standard language. Typically these may lessen the work of software development. An example is an exotic file access method. Once the user has bought the system, he or she is trapped. The user is locked into using the special facilities and is reliant on the supplier for developments in equipment that are fully compatible. The contradiction is, of course, that each and every user is tied to a particular supplier in this way, and can only switch allegiance at a considerable cost in converting software. Only large users, like government agencies, are large and powerful enough to insist that different suppliers adopt standards.

Given this picture of applications software, what are the prospects for systems software, like operating systems and filing systems, with their closer dependence on specific hardware?

1.7 ● Maintenance

Maintenance is the term for any effort that is put into a piece of software after it has been written and put into operation. There are two main types:

- *remedial maintenance* is the time spent correcting faults in the software (fixing bugs)
- *adaptive maintenance* is altering software either because the users needs have changed or because, for example, the computer, operating system or programming language has changed.

Remedial maintenance is, of course, a consequence of inadequate testing. But, as we shall see, effective testing is notoriously difficult and time-consuming and it is an accepted fact of life in software engineering that maintenance is inevitable.

It is often difficult to predict the future uses for a piece of software and so adaptive maintenance is also rarely avoided. But because software is called soft, it is sometimes believed that it can be modified easily. In reality the truth is more accurately described by saying that software is brittle, like ice, and when you try to change it, it snaps rather than bends.

In either case, maintenance is usually regarded as a nuisance – both by managers, who have to make sure that there are sufficient people to do it, and by programmers, who regard it as less interesting than writing new programs.

Some idea of the scale of what has been called the "maintenance burden" can be appreciated by looking at Figure 1.6, showing typical figures for the amount of time spent in the different activities of developing a particular piece of software.

In a project like this, the maintenance effort is clearly overwhelming. It's not unusual for organizations that use well-established computer systems to be spending $^3/_4$ of their programming time on maintenance.

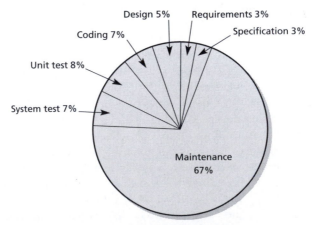

Figure 1.6 Relative costs of the stages of software development

Here are some more estimated figures:

● World-wide, there are 50 billion lines of Cobol in use today.
● In the US, 2% of the GNP is spent on software maintenance.
● In the UK, £1 billion (about $1.5 million) annually are spent on software maintenance.

The millions of lines of program code written in what many people consider to be outdated programming languages (like Cobol) constitute what are known as *legacy systems*. These are software systems that are up to 30 years old, but in full use in organizations today. They are often poorly documented, either because there was no documentation in the first place or because the documentation is useless because it has not been kept up to date as changes have been made. Legacy systems were written using expertise in tools and methods that is rarely available today. For these reasons, it is expensive to update them to meet ever-changing requirements. Equally, it would be expensive to rewrite them from scratch using a contemporary language and methods. Thus legacy systems are a huge liability for organizations.

Another major example of the problems of maintenance is the *millennium bug*. A great deal of software was written when memory was in short supply and expensive. Dates were therefore stored economically using only the last two digits of the year, so that for example, the year 1999 was stored as 99. After 2000, the date value 99 may be treated as 1999, 2099, or even 0099. The problem is that the meaning that is attached to a year differs from one system to another, depending on how the individual programmer decided to design the software. The only way to make sure that a program works correctly after the year 2000 (termed year 2000 compliance) is to examine it line-by-line to find any reference to a date and then to fix the code appropriately. This is an immensely time-consuming, skilled and therefore costly process. The task may need a knowledge of an outdated programming language and certainly needs an accurate understanding of the program's logic. The penalties for not updating software correctly are potentially immense, as modern organizations are totally reliant on computer systems for nearly all of their activities.

1.8 ● Reliability

A piece of software is said to be reliable if it works and continues to work, without crashing and without doing something undesirable. We say that software has a bug or a fault if it does not perform properly. We presume that the developer knew what was required and so the unexpected behavior is not intended. It is common to talk about bugs in software. But it is also useful to define some additional terms more clearly:

● *error* – a wrong decision made during software development
● *fault* – a problem that may cause software to depart from its intended behavior
● *failure* – an event when software departs from its intended behavior.

In this terminology, a fault is the same as a bug. An error is a mistake made by a human being during one of the stages of software development. An error causes one or more faults within the software, its specification or its documentation. In turn, a fault can cause one or more failures. Failures will occur while the system is being tested and after it has been put into use. (Confusingly, some authors use the terms fault and failure differently.) Failures are the symptom that users experience, whereas faults are a problem that the developer has to deal with. A fault may never manifest itself because the conditions that cause it to make the software fail never arise. Conversely a single fault may cause many different and frequent failures.

The job of removing bugs and trying to ensure reliability is called *verification*.

There is a close but distinct relationship between the concept of reliability and that of meeting users needs, mentioned above. Requirements analysis is concerned with establishing clearly what the user wants. *Validation* is a collection of techniques that try to ensure that the software does meet the requirements. On the other hand, reliability is to do with the technical issue of whether there are any faults in the software.

Currently one of the main techniques for trying to ensure that software works correctly is testing. In testing, you run the software and check its behavior against what you expect to happen. But, as we shall see later in this book, there is a fundamental problem with testing: however much you test a piece of software you can never be sure that you have found every last bug. This leads us to assert fairly confidently the unsettling conclusion that every large piece of software contains errors.

One way of gauging the scale of the reliability problem is to look at a series of cautionary tales.

In the early days of computing – the days of batch data processing systems – it used to be part of the folklore that computers were regularly sending out gas bills for (incorrectly) enormous amounts. Although the people who received these bills might have been seriously distressed – particularly the old – the situation was widely regarded as amusing. Reliability was not treated as an important issue.

IBM's major operating system OS 360 had at least 1,000 bugs each and every time it was rereleased. How is this known (after all we would expect that IBM would have corrected all known errors)? The answer is that by the time the next release is issued, 1,000 errors had been found in the previous version.

During the American space program, an unmanned vehicle was sent to look at the planet Venus. Part way on its journey a course correction proved necessary. A computer back at mission control executed the following statement, written in the Fortran language:

```
DO 3 I = 1.3
```

This is a perfectly valid Fortran statement. But the programmer had intended it to be a repetition statement, which is introduced by the word DO. However, a DO statement should contain a comma, rather than the period character actually used. The use of the period makes the statement into an assignment statement, placing a value 1.3 into the variable named DO3I. The space probe turned on the wrong course and was never seen again. Thus small errors can have massive consequences. Note that this program had been compiled successfully without errors – which illustrates how language notation can be important. The program had also been thoroughly tested – which demonstrates the limitations of testing technique.

In March 1979, an error was found in the program that had been used to design the cooling systems of nuclear reactors in the USA. Five plants were shut down, because their safety became questionable.

Some years ago, the American system for warning against enemy missiles reported on its alarms that the USA was being attacked. It turned out to be a false alarm – the result of a computer error. But before the error was discovered, people went a long way into the procedures for retaliating using nuclear weapons. This happened not just once, but three times in a period of one year.

Perhaps the most expensive consequence of a software fault was the crash, 40 seconds after blast off, of the European Space Agency's Ariane 5 launcher in June 1996. The loss was estimated at $500 million, luckily without loss of life.

The incidents related above are just a few in a long catalog of expensive problems caused by software errors over the years, with no indication that the situation is improving.

How does the reliability of software compare with the reliability of hardware? Studies show that where both the hardware and software are at comparable levels of development, hardware fails three times as often as software. Although this is grounds for friendly rivalry between software and hardware designers, it can be no grounds for complacency amongst software people.

Our conclusion is that, generally, software has a poor reputation for reliability.

There are particular applications of computers that demand particularly high reliability. These are known as *safety-critical systems*. Examples are:

- fly-by-wire control of an aircraft
- control of critical processes, such as a power station
- control of medical equipment.

In this book we will look at techniques that can be used in developing systems such as these.

It is not always clear whether a piece of software is safety-related. The example mentioned earlier of the faulty software used in designing a power plant is just one example. Another example is communications software that might play a critical role in summoning help in an emergency.

SELF TEST QUESTION

1.4 Identify three further examples of software systems that are safety-critical and three that are not.

1.9 ● Human–computer interaction

The user interface is what the human user of a software package sees when they need to use the software. There are many examples of computer systems that are not easy to use:

● Many people have difficulty programming a video cassette recorder (VCR).

● Some people find it difficult to divert a telephone call to another user within an organization.

In recent years, many interfaces have become graphical user interfaces (GUIs) that use windows with features like buttons and scroll bars, together with pointing devices like a mouse. Many people saw this as a massive step in improving the user interface. But it is still a challenging problem to design a user interface that is simple and easy to use.

SELF TEST QUESTION

1.5 Think of two computer-based systems that you know of that are difficult to use in some way or another. Alternatively, think of two features of a program you use that are difficult to use.

1.10 ● A software crisis?

We have discussed various perceived problems with software:

● It fails to do what users want it to do.

● It is expensive.

● It isn't always fast enough.

● It cannot be transferred to another machine easily.

● Maintenance is expensive.

● It is unreliable.

● It is often late.

● It is not always easy to use.

Of these, meeting users' needs (validation), reducing software costs, improving reliability (verification), and delivery on-time are probably the four most important present-day problems.

Many people argue that things have been so bad – and continue to be so bad – that there is a continuing real "crisis" in software development. They argue that something must be done about the situation, and the main remedy must be to bring more scientific

Figure 1.7 Complementary and conflicting goals in a software project

principles to bear on the problem – hence the introduction of the term software engineering. Indeed, the very term software engineering conveys that there is a weightier problem than arises in smaller-scale programming.

One of the obstacles to trying to solve the problems of software is that very often they conflict with each other. For example, low cost of construction and high reliability conflict. Again, high performance and portability conflict. Figure 1.7 indicates the situation.

Happily, some goals do not conflict with each other. For example, low cost of maintenance and high reliability are complementary.

1.11 ● A remedy – software engineering?

As we have seen, it is generally recognized that there are big problems with developing software successfully. A number of ideas have been suggested for improving the situation. These methods and tools are collectively known as software engineering. Some of the main ideas are:

● greater emphasis on carrying out all stages of development systematically

● computer assistance for software development – software tools, software development environments, and Computer Aided Software Engineering (CASE)

● an emphasis on finding out exactly what the users of a system really want (requirements engineering and validation)

● formal specification of the requirements of a system

● demonstrating an early version of a system to its customers (prototyping)

● use of new, innovative programming languages

● greater emphasis on trying to ensure that software is free of errors (verification).

We will be looking at all of these ideas in this book. These solutions are not mutually exclusive; indeed they often complement each other.

Formal specification, verification, prototyping, and other such techniques actually address only some of the problems encountered in software development. A large-scale software project will comprise a number of separate related activities – analysis, specification, design, implementation and so on; it may be carried out by a large number of people working to strict deadlines; and the end product usually has to conform to prescribed standards. Clearly, if software projects are to have any chance of successfully delivering correct software on time and within budget, they must be thoroughly planned in advance and effectively managed as they are executed. Thus the aim is to replace ad hoc methods by an organized discipline.

One term that is used a lot these days in connection with software is the word *quality*. One might argue that any product (from a cream bun to a washing machine) that fulfills the purpose for which it was produced could be considered to be a quality product. In the context of software, if a package meets, and continues to meet, a customer's expectations, then it too can be considered to be a quality product. In this perspective, quality can be attained only if effective standards, techniques, and procedures exist to be applied, and are seen to be properly employed and monitored. Thus, not only do good methods have to be applied, but they have to be seen to be applied. Such procedures are central to the activity called "quality assurance."

The problem of producing "correct" software can be addressed by using appropriate specification and verification techniques (formal or informal). But correctness is just one aspect of quality; the explicit use of a project management discipline is a key factor in achieving high-quality software.

1.12 ● Summary

We have considered a number of goals and problem areas in software development. Generally software developers have a bad image, a reputation for producing software that is:

● late
● over budget
● unreliable
● inflexible
● hard to use.

Because the problems are so great there has been widespread talk of a crisis in software production. The general response to these problems has been the creation of a number of systematic approaches, novel techniques, and notations to address the software development task. The different methods, tools, and languages fit within a plan of action (called a process model). This book is about these approaches. Now read on.

EXERCISES

These exercises ask you to carry out an analysis and come to some view of a situation. Often there is not a unique "right answer." Sometimes you will have to make reasonable assumptions or conjectures. The aim of the exercises is to clarify your understanding of the goals of software engineering and some of the problems that lie in the path of achieving these goals.

1.1 Write down a list of all of the different items of software that you know about. Then categorize them within types.

1.2 What are your own personal goals when you develop a piece of software? Why? Do you need to re-examine these?

1.3 Is software expensive? What criteria did you use in arriving at your conclusion?

1.4 Is programming/software development easy? Justify your answer.

1.5 The evidence suggests that there are enormous differences between programmers in terms of productivity. Why do you think this is? Does it matter that there are differences?

1.6 Consider the following cases:

(a) a microcomputer-controlled washing machine
(b) a system to control a power station
(c) software to calculate and print an organization's payroll
(d) a general-purpose operating system or database management system
(e) a system to monitor and control medical equipment
(f) a general-purpose mathematical routine
(g) a computer game.

For each of these situations analyze the importance of the various goals identified in this chapter. Rank them in order, for each situation.

1.7 What would you expect the relative costs of hardware and software development to be in each of the cases above?

1.8 How do you personally feel about software maintenance? Would you enjoy doing it?

1.9 Think of an example of a program in which the aims of minimizing run time and memory occupancy are mutually contradictory. Think of an example where these two are in harmony.

1.10 Analyze the conflicts and consistencies between the various goals of software engineering.

1.11 In addition to the goals described in this chapter, are there any other goals that software engineering should strive for? What about making sure that it is fun doing it?

ANSWERS TO SELF TEST QUESTIONS

1.1 50 people at a cost of $12.5 million.

1.2 Hardware: $1000
Software: $100
To buy, the hardware is approximately 10 times the cost of the software.

1.3 Examples are: a Web browser, a telephone switching system.

1.4 Examples of safety critical systems: an ABS braking system on a car, a fire alarm system, a patient record system in a health center.
Examples of systems that are not safety critical are a payroll system, a word processor, a game program.

1.5 Some well-known word processor programs incorporate the facility to search for a file. This facility is not always easy to use – especially when it fails to find a file that you know is there somewhere.

The DOS operating system provides a command-line command to delete a file or any number of files. Coupled with the "wild card" feature, denoted by an asterisk, it is easy to delete more files than you plan, for example:

```
del *.*
```

FURTHER READING

Accounts of failed projects are given in: Stephen Flowers, *Software Failure: Management Failure: Amazing Stories and Cautionary Tales*, John Wiley, 1996; and in Robert Glass, *Software Runaways*, Prentice Hall, 1998.

A very readable and classic account of the problems of developing large-scale software is given in the following book, written by the man in charge of the development of the software for an IBM mainframe range of computers. It has been republished as a celebratory second edition with additional essays: Frederick P. Brooks, *The Mythical Man-Month*, Addison-Wesley, 2nd edition, 1995.

A compelling account of the arguments for portable software is given in: Peter Van Der Linden, *Not Just Java*, Sun Microsystems Press and Prentice Hall, 1997.

Analyses of the costs of the different stages of software development are given in the classic book, which is still relevant despite its age: B. W. Boehm, *Software Engineering Economics*, Prentice Hall, 1981.

A fascinating review of disasters caused by computer malfunctions (hardware, software, and human error) is given in: Peter G. Neumann, *Computer-Related Risks*, Addison-Wesley/ACM Press, 1995.

In conjunction with the ACM, Peter Neumann also moderates a USENET newsgroup called comp.risks which documents incidents of computer-related risks. Archives are available at: ftp.sri.com/risks

For an up-to-date look at how software professionals see their role, look at the newsletter of the ACM Special Interest Group in Software Engineering, called *Software Engineering Notes* (SEN), published bimonthly. Its web address is at: http://www.acm.org/sigs/sigsoft/SEN/

The equivalent periodical from the IEEE is simply called *Software*. This is produced by and for practitioners, reflecting their current concerns and interests, such as software costs.

2

Process models

This chapter:

- identifies the activities within software development
- distinguishes between validation and verification
- explains the stages in the waterfall model
- explains how to carry out prototyping
- distinguishes between throwaway and evolutionary prototyping
- explains the advantages and disadvantages of prototyping.

2.1 ● Introduction

We have seen (Chapter 1) that software systems are often large and complex. There is a clear need to be organized when embarking on a development. What do you need when you set about a software project? You need:

- a clear statement of what is required (this is the subject of Chapter 3)
- a package of methods and tools (this is the subject of most of this book)
- a plan.

The plan of action is known as a *process model*. It is a plan of what steps are going to be taken as the development proceeds. This term is derived as follows: a process is a step or a series of steps. A process model is a model in the sense that it is a representation of reality. Like any model, a model is only an approximation of reality. A process model has two distinct uses:

- It can be used as a basis for the plan for a project. Here the aim is to predict what will be done.
- It is used to analyze what actually happens during a project. Here the aim is to improve the process for the current and for future projects.

There are several mainstream process models:

- seat-of-the-pants, do-it-yourself, or ad hoc
- waterfall
- prototyping
- formal methods
- spiral.

Each of these approaches will be discussed later in this chapter.

The first of these is no plan at all, and no organization would admit to using such an approach. A software development project can take several years and involve tens or even hundreds of people. Moreover, software development is a complex task. To avoid catastrophe, some way of organizing a project must be established. Most approaches identify a series of distinct stages within a project.

First we identify some of the significant elements of software development. Then we clarify the nature of two essential activities that take place throughout software development – validation and verification.

2.2 ● The components of software development

During the development of a software system there are several activities that *must* be carried out at some time. These include:

- requirements engineering
- architectural or large-scale design
- small-scale design
- coding
- system integration
- validation
- verification
- maintenance.

All these ingredients are contained within the various process models in one guise or another. Some elements, such as verification, are performed again and again during development.

We now examine each of these activities, leaving validation and verification to a later section.

2.2.1 Requirements engineering (specification)

At the start of a project, the developer finds out what the user (client or customer) wants the software to do and records the requirements as clearly as possible. This stage is addressed in Chapter 3.

The product is a requirements specification.

2.2.2 Architectural (large-scale) design

A software system may be large and complex. It is usually too large to be written as one single program. The software must be constructed from modules or components. Architectural, or large-scale design, breaks the overall system down into a number of simpler modules.

The products of this activity are an architectural design and module specifications.

2.2.3 Detailed Design

The design of each module, or component, is carried out.

The products are detailed designs of each module.

2.2.4 Coding

The detailed designs are converted into instructions written in the programming language.

The product is the code.

2.2.5 System integration

The individual components of the software are combined together.

The product is the complete system.

2.2.6 Maintenance

The software is put into use. Sooner or later it will probably need fixing or enhancing. Fixing faults is part of maintenance. At some future time the users may want some enhancement made to the program. Making this change also constitutes maintenance. Software maintenance often goes on for years after the software is first constructed.

The product is the modified software.

In some process models, all of these stages are visible; in other process models some of these stages vanish or become part of some other stage.

SELF TEST QUESTION

2.1 Which stages of software development, if any, can be omitted if the software being developed is only a small program?

This chapter explains some of the mainstream process models for software development. We will see that, in dividing the work into a series of distinct stages, it may appear that work is carried out strictly in sequence. However it is usual, particularly on large projects, for many activities to take place in parallel. In particular, this happens once the large-scale (or architectural) design is complete. It is at this stage that the major software components have been identified. Work on developing each of these components can now proceed in parallel, often undertaken by different individuals.

2.3 ● Validation and verification

Validation and verification are ways of checking that development has been done properly. Two of the major challenges of software development are:

● making sure that the software meets its users' needs

● producing reliable software.

The terms "validation" and "verification" describe these two problems. The terms are sometimes confused or used interchangeably. One of the gurus of software engineering, Boehm, describes the difference like this:

● verification: "Are we building the product right?"

● validation: "Are we building the right product?"

One way of understanding the difference is that validation is to do with the clients' view of the system, while verification is concerned with the developers' view. Another way of understanding the difference is that validation is to do with the external view of a system, while verification is concerned with the internal consistencies within the system.

As is to be expected, both validation and verification are carried out continuously during software development.

A significant example of validation is *acceptance testing*. The software is apparently complete and is demonstrated to its client and accepted by them as satisfactory. The inputs to acceptance testing are the client and the apparently completed software. The products are a sign-off document and an accepted system. The outcome is that the system complies with the requirements of the client.

Two examples of verification are *unit testing* and *system testing*.

2.3.1 Unit testing

Each module of the software is tested in isolation. The inputs to unit testing are:

1. the unit specification
2. the unit code
3. a list of expected test results.

The products of unit testing are the test results. Unit testing verifies that the behavior of the coding conforms to its unit specification. Methods for doing this are discussed in Chapter 19.

2.3.2 System testing or integration testing

The modules are linked together and the complete system tested. The inputs to system testing are the system specification and the code for the complete system. The outcome of system testing is the completed, tested software. System testing verifies that the system meets its specification. This process is described in Chapter 19.

Verification is carried out after every stage of software development, except the first (requirements analysis). It is the way in which the correctness of each stage is checked.

Current evidence suggests that many computer systems do not meet the needs of their users, and that therefore successful validation is a major problem in software engineering today. It is a common experience that users think they have articulated their needs to the software engineer. Then the engineer will spend months or even years developing the software only to find, when it is demonstrated, that it was not what the user wanted. This is not only demoralizing for both users and developers, it is often massively costly in terms of the effort needed to correct the deficiencies. Or the system is abandoned.

It is too easy to blame the requirements analysis stage of development, because the basic problem is one of the quality of the communication between users and developers. Users do not know (and usually do not care) about technicalities, whereas the software engineer is often from a different culture. Worst of all is the problem of some common language for accurately describing what the user wants. The users are probably happiest with natural language (e.g. English), whereas the software engineer would probably prefer some more rigorous language that would be incomprehensible to the users. There is a cultural gap.

As we shall see, a major problem with one of the main process models, the waterfall model, is that users do not see what the system does until very late in the development process. If the system does not meet their needs, an enormous amount of work may have to be redone.

The essential problem with validation is that, given that there are difficulties with accurately describing users needs, developers need some way of demonstrating a working version of the software – a prototype – as early as possible. This chapter describes techniques for achieving this.

2.4 ● The waterfall model

The *waterfall* approach, Figure 2.1, has dominated software development for a number of years. Software development is split up into a number of independent steps that are carried out in sequence one after the other. Each stage produces a product, which is the input into the next stage.

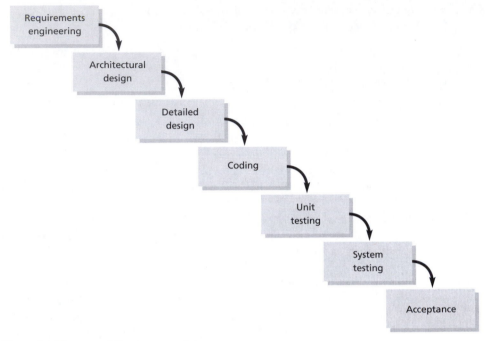

Figure 2.1 The waterfall process model

The waterfall model makes no stipulations about what methods are used at any of its stages, nor does it stipulate what notations are used for the products at each stage. (This whole book is about the different methods and notations that are available.)

Different people and authors have slightly different ideas about what exactly the steps should be, but the principles of the waterfall model are:

● it is a series of steps (like a production line)
● each step is well defined
● each step creates a definite product (this is often a piece of paper)
● each product forms the basis for the next step
● the correctness of each step can be checked (verification or validation).

The waterfall model has its name because each stage produces a product, like a stream of water, that passes on to the next stage. So the complete development process is like a series of small waterfalls, the way in which Figure 2.1 has the appearance of a series of small cascades.

The strengths of the waterfall model are that:

● it divides a complex task into smaller, more manageable tasks
● each task produces a well-defined deliverable.

2.4.1 Feedback in the waterfall model

One of the drawbacks of a strict waterfall model is that the water cannot flow upwards – if a problem is found at a particular stage in development, there is no way of influencing an earlier stage in order to rectify the problem. Examples are:

● during coding, an error in the design (the previous stage) is discovered
● during unit testing, a detailed design fault is revealed.

To overcome this drawback, a variant of the waterfall model provides for feedback between stages, so that a problem uncovered at one stage can cause remedial action to be taken at the previous stage. Thus the waterfall model with feedback between stages is as shown in Figure 2.2.

You will see, however, that this approach only provides for feedback to the immediately preceding step; and in reality, any step may necessitate changes in any of the preceding stages. For example:

● during system testing, an architectural design fault is revealed
● during user acceptance, a problem with the specification becomes evident.

So the reality of the waterfall model is that development does not proceed linearly, step-by-step. Instead there is commonly frequent feedback to earlier stages, requiring rework (which can seriously disrupt the timescale of a project). To be more realistic, Figure 2.2

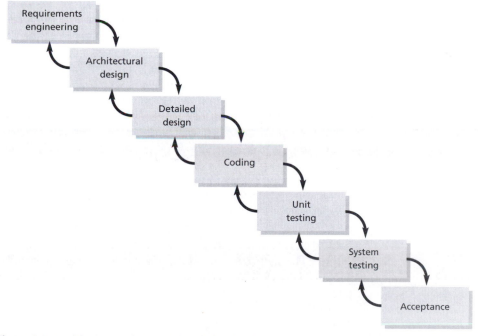

Figure 2.2 Modified waterfall model with feedback

should show arrows leading backwards from every activity to every preceding activity. The designers of the waterfall model clearly and wrongly perceived software development to be simple and straightforward, with development proceeding smoothly onwards from stage to stage without disruption. So there is a fundamental problem with using the waterfall model as a basis for a project plan. Nonetheless, it is common to do just that.

2.4.2 Validation in the waterfall model

Perhaps the most serious problem with the waterfall model is that the client only gets to see the product at the very end of the development – and if it is not what they want, it is too late! The problem is the huge gap between requirements analysis at an early stage in a project and acceptance testing near the end. There is no opportunity to validate the user requirements at an early stage in development. This is a major problem with the waterfall model.

2.5 ● Prototyping

Prototyping presents one solution to the problem of ensuring that the customer gets what they want. In prototyping, the customer is presented at a very early stage with a working version of the system. (It may not be a complete system, but it is at least part of the system and it works.) They can check that it does what they want, or specify modifications. The developer amends the system and demonstrates it again and again until it does what the customer wants. Thus the main purpose of prototyping is usually ensuring that the users needs are satisfied. (There are, however, sometimes other goals of prototyping.)

When a new car is being developed, one or more prototypes will be built. These prototypes are tested intensively before a real production line is set up. It is possible to follow a similar approach with software development. Prototyping is the practice of building an early version of a system which does not necessarily reflect all the features of the final system, but rather those which are of interest. Prototyping is sometimes called rapid prototyping and, as the name suggests, a rapid prototype should cost very little and take very little time to develop. The emphasis is on using whatever methods are available to produce a system that can be demonstrated to the user. Typically the only noticeable difference between the prototype and the desired system is its performance, or in the volumes of data that it handles.

Prototyping seems to contradict current ideas of using systematic, careful methods during development; a prototype is produced in as quick (and perhaps as dirty) a manner as possible. So why do it ? The purpose is to aid the analysis and design stages of a project by enabling users to see very early what the system will do – that is to facilitate validation. Users seldom have a clear, concise understanding of their needs. The conventional specification is a narrative description of a system that may be technical and time-consuming to read. The larger the development team, including user representatives, the more difficult communication becomes. Prototyping is one technique that attempts to address these problems and provide possible solutions. The benefits of developing a prototype early in the software process are:

● misunderstandings between software developers and users may be identified as the system functions are demonstrated
● missing facilities may be detected
● difficult-to-use or confusing facilities may be identified and refined
● software developers may find incomplete and/or inconsistent requirements as the prototype is developed.

There are sometimes other objectives:

● a working, albeit limited, system is available quickly to demonstrate the feasibility and usefulness of the application to management
● user training – a prototype system can be used for training users before the final system has been delivered
● to establish that some new technology will provide the facilities needed (for example, does Java provide sufficient security for electronic transfer of funds?)

2.5.1 Evolutionary or throwaway?

A prototype is one of two types:

● *throwaway* (the final system is implemented in some different way), or
● *evolutionary* (the prototype becomes the final system).

For example, a throwaway prototype might be written in LISP so as to demonstrate the essential functions that a system will carry out. But then the software might be re-written in C++ so that the system provides the user-friendly interface that the users expect.

Alternatively, an evolutionary prototype might be implemented in Ada to demonstrate to the user the main features of the system. Having checked that the system does what is required, new features and facilities could be added to the prototype, gradually transforming it into its complete form.

In evolutionary prototyping, the first priority is to incorporate well-understood requirements into the prototype, then move on to those requirements which are unclear. In throwaway prototyping, the priority is to understand requirements that are unclear and therefore requirements which are straightforward may never need to be prototyped.

In summary:

● The product of a throwaway prototype is a specification.
● The product of an evolutionary prototype is a system.

2.5.2 Throwaway prototyping

The starting point for throwaway prototyping is an outline specification for the software. A throwaway prototype implements only those requirements that are poorly understood.

It is discarded after the desired information is learned. After the prototype is complete, the developer writes a full specification, incorporating what was learned, and constructs a full-scale system based on that specification. Thus the purpose of throwaway prototyping is the formulation of a validated specification.

Again, to be effective, throwaway prototyping is carried out within a systematic framework. A process model for prototype development is shown in Figure 2.3.

The stages of throwaway prototyping are:

1. *Outline specification*: The first step in throwaway prototyping is the creation of an initial, often partial, specification. This contains areas of uncertainty.

2. *Establishment of objectives*: What is the prototype to be used for? What aspects of the proposed system should it reflect? What can be learned from the prototype? The objective may be to develop a system to prototype the user interface, to validate functional requirements, to explore uncertain new technologies, or to demonstrate the feasibility of the application to management. The same prototype cannot meet all objectives. The areas that are most often prototyped are the user interface, and uncertain or vague functions

3. *Selection of functions*: The next stage is to decide what to put into and what to leave out of the prototype. This is determined by the objectives of the system. If the purpose of prototyping is to clarify users requirements, then the uncertain areas are the candidates for prototyping. The development of a working model allows the developers to make sure that the solution they are proposing will satisfy the requirements and perform effectively. Depending on the objectives, it may be decided to prototype all system functions but at reduced level. Alternatively a subset of system functions may be included in the prototype.

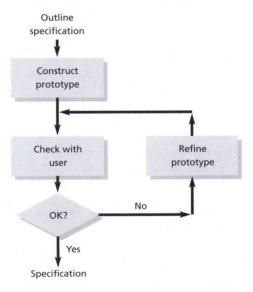

Figure 2.3 Throwaway prototyping

4. *Prototype construction*: Speed and cost of construction of the prototype is crucial. Fast, low-cost construction is normally achieved by ignoring the normal quality requirements for the final product (a "quick and dirty" approach), unless this is in conflict with the objectives.

5. *Evaluation (check with the user)*: The users interact with the prototype. During evaluation, inconsistencies and shortcomings in the developer's perception of the customer requirements are uncovered. The prototype becomes an effective communication medium between the developer and customer.

6. *Iteration (refinement)*: The prototype is rapidly modified, evaluation is carried out and the process repeated until the prototype meets the objectives (usually an agreed specification).

7. *Completion (specification)*: The product of the prototyping process is a specification that meets the users' requirements. Since the working prototype has been validated through interaction with the client, it is reasonable to expect that the resultant specification document will be correct. When the requirements are clearly established, the prototype is thrown away. At this stage, a different software process model, such as the waterfall model, is undertaken.

Users should resist the temptation to turn a throwaway prototype into a delivered system that is put into use. The reasons for this are:

1. Important system characteristics such as performance, security, and reliability will probably have been ignored during prototype development.

2. During the prototype development, the prototype will have been changed to reflect user needs. It is likely that these changes will have been made in an uncontrolled way and not properly documented other than in the prototype code.

3. The changes made during prototype development will probably have degraded the structure of the software. The software will be difficult and expensive to maintain.

2.5.3 Evolutionary prototyping

Evolutionary prototyping is based on the idea of developing an initial implementation, exposing this to user comment and refining this through repeated stages until an adequate system has been developed.

To be effective, evolutionary prototyping is carried out within a systematic framework. A process model for evolutionary prototype development is shown in Figure 2.4. The stages are:

1. *Requirements definition (initial specification)*: a stage of thorough analysis is used to create an initial specification for the software.

2. *Prototype construction*: A prototype is built in a quality manner, including design, documentation, and thorough verification.

3. *Evaluation (check with the user)*: During evaluation, problems in the developer's perception of the customer requirements are uncovered. The prototypes are the

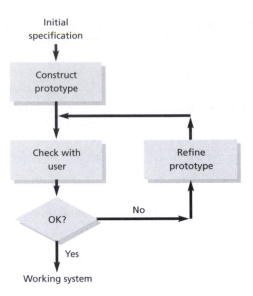

Figure 2.4 Evolutionary prototyping

communication medium which enables the developer and customer to communicate with each other.

4. *Iteration (refine the prototype)*: Evaluation is carried out repeatedly until the prototype meets the objectives. The specification is updated with every iteration. The product is a fully working system.

SELF TEST QUESTION

2.2 What are the differences between throwaway and evolutionary prototyping?

2.5.4 Prototyping tools and techniques

A prototype needs to be created quickly so that users can comment on it at an early stage. A prototype also needs to be altered quickly, to incorporate the users' views as the prototype changes to meet their requirements. But how can software be created any more quickly than usual? There is no magic here – whatever tools and methods that are suitable are put into use. A number of tools can be used, including executable specification languages, very high level languages, application generators, fourth-generation languages, and re-usable components.

If a specification is expressed in a formal, mathematical language, it may be possible to animate the specification to provide a prototype. Animation means the direct execution of the specification. However, the drawbacks of this approach are: graphical user interfaces cannot be prototyped using this technique; the executable system is usually slow and inefficient; executable specifications only test functional requirements.

Very high-level languages include many facilities which normally have to be built from more primitive constructs in languages like C++, Java, or Ada. Smalltalk is a language that can be used to prototype adventurous graphical user interfaces (GUIs) with very little programmer effort. A drawback of Smalltalk is that it can be a massive consumer of processor time and memory, so that after prototyping it may be necessary to rewrite the system in some other language. So Smalltalk may only be useable for throwaway prototyping.

Another choice of prototyping tool is a logic programming language such as Prolog (Chapter 17). This supports easy specification of many problems, but without a friendly user interface. A Prolog-based system would probably run too slowly for a final production system.

Evolutionary prototyping is now fairly commonly used for developing business applications using a fourth-generation language (4GL). Fourth-generation languages are successful because there is a great deal of commonality across data processing applications. In essence, many business applications are concerned with updating a database and producing reports from the information held in the database. At their simplest, 4GLs are database query languages such as SQL. Fourth-generation languages are generally used, often in conjunction with CASE tools, for the development of small-to-medium-sized systems. The end users may be involved in the development or may even act as developers.

Visual Basic (Chapter 18) is a tool with many high-level features for rapid software development, including creating a graphical user interface by using drag-and-drop from a palette.

The time needed to develop software can be reduced if many parts of that system can be re-used rather than designed and implemented. Prototypes can be constructed quickly if there is a library of re-usable components and some mechanism to combine the components into systems. The re-usable components may also be used in the final system thus reducing its development cost. An example of this approach to prototyping is found in the Unix operating system (see Chapter 18 on tools). The success of Smalltalk and LISP as prototyping languages is as much due to their re-usable component libraries as to the inbuilt language facilities.

So much for tools. What about techniques for constructing prototypes?

It is often possible to construct a system that appears realistic, but is in fact massively incomplete. For example, if software for a network of computers is to be developed, a prototype running on a stand-alone computer is created. This simulates the complete system for the purpose of validation. But the developer is freed from considerations of networking, large data volumes, and possible performance problems that would need to be considered in the production version of the system.

Some other major ingredients required in the production version of a software system can be omitted from a prototype. In many systems as much as one-half of the software is concerned with error handling. This includes:

● validation of user data input from keyboards

● handling input–output device errors

● fault-tolerant software (see Chapter 20) that copes with faults in the software.

These components of a production-quality system can be significantly costly in development effort and so their omission makes construction of a prototype quicker.

Another type of prototype is one which actually does nothing at all, but merely gives a superficial appearance on the computer screen. For example, suppose we were setting out to develop a new text editor. We could, very quickly, create a mock-up of what would appear on the screen, while the actual functions of the editor are simply not implemented. This type of prototype is often used during the design of the human–computer interface (Chapter 11).

Finally, for some applications, the user may well be satisfied with a working demonstration of a system that only has a crude user interface, so long as they are convinced that the system carries out the desired functions.

2.5.5 Advantages

What are the advantages of prototyping? During requirements specification, the developer can show the user a suggested working system at a very early stage. Users are not always certain what they want a system to do. It is difficult for users to properly understand and be able to state detailed functional requirements unambiguously before they have an opportunity to experiment interactively with the options. A prototype gives the user a very clear picture of what the system will look like and what it will do. By examining options in the various versions of the prototype, the users are stimulated to discover requirements that they might not have thought of until after full implementation using any other method. The user is able to tell the developer their views about the system, and modifications can be made. The value lies in better communication between user and analyst, and validation is carried out early in the life of the project. Thus prototyping eliminates many of the design errors in the very early stages of a project. The greatest savings in time and effort stem from avoiding the work in changing a system that does not do what the user really wanted.

Prototyping promotes a participatory approach to development and when users are involved, they often gain confidence in a system. They see first hand the problems and errors, but they also see the mistakes getting resolved quickly.

The advantages of prototyping can be that:

● it enables developers to cope with lack of clarity in requirements

● it gives the user the opportunity to change his/her mind before commitment to the final system

● user requirements are easier to determine

● systems are developed faster

● development effort is reduced because the resultant system is the right system

- maintenance effort is reduced because the system meets the users needs
- end-user involvement is facilitated
- user-developer communication is enhanced
- users are not frustrated while they wait for the final system, because they can see a working system
- there is an increased chance that a system will be more user friendly
- systems are easier for end-users to learn and use because users know what to expect
- it enables a system to be gradually introduced into an organization
- it facilitates user training while development is going on
- there is increased customer satisfaction with the delivered software.

The question about prototyping is whether the cost of constructing the prototypes is off-set by the savings.

2.5.6 Pitfalls

For users, the problems of prototyping are:

- Because prototyping is carried out in an artificial environment, users may miss some of the shortcomings.
- Undue user expectations – the ability of the developers to create a prototype so quickly may raise undue expectations that the final system will soon be complete. They see a partial system and may not understand that it is not the finished system.
- Inconsistencies between a prototype and the final system – if the prototype is a throw-away, the end-product may not be exactly like the prototype. In other words, what the user sees may not be what the user gets.
- Users may never be satisfied because they are given too much opportunity to change the development of the system.

For software engineers, the problems can be:

- Incomplete analysis – because prototypes are produced quickly, developers may be tempted to plunge into prototyping before sufficient requirements analysis has taken place. This may result in a system that has a good user interface but that is not properly functional. This is how the reputation of prototypes which are quick but dirty came about.
- Iteration is not easily accepted by some designers, because it necessitates discarding their own work.
- Non-functional requirements may be omitted, since a prototype focuses only on functionality.

The managerial problems of using prototyping may be:

- Estimating, planning and managing a prototyping project can be difficult because it can be hard to predict how many iterations of prototyping will take place.

● Procedures for change and configuration management may be unsuitable for controlling the rapid change inherent in prototyping.

● Many project management structures are set up assuming a process model, like the waterfall model, that generates regular deliverables to assess progress. But prototypes usually evolve so quickly that it is not cost effective to keep pace with the documentation.

Maintenance of a system constructed using evolutionary prototyping can be difficult and costly because continual change tends to corrupt the structure of the prototype.

Prototyping may not always be an appropriate technique, for example in:

● embedded software

● real-time control software

● scientific numerical software.

SELF TEST QUESTION

2.3 Identify one advantage and one disadvantage of prototyping.

2.6 ● Formal methods – the transform model

In this model of software development, the formality and rigor of mathematics are used. First a mathematical specification is constructed (Chapter 4). Two alternative notations for specification are widely used – VDM and Z. The specification is then transformed stage-by-stage into the working software. This approach is described in Chapter 12. This transformation can sometimes be partially carried out automatically. Even when it cannot be carried out automatically, the aim is to preserve the correctness of the initial specification. Mathematical proving techniques are used as necessary at each stage to ensure that the new product is consistent with the previous description.

Formal software development is a radical departure from other, traditional approaches. The only stage in common is a specification stage, but even this is very different from a traditional specification phase. The step of verification, usually a distinct stage in other software development approaches, is incorporated within each refinement stage of the process. Some stages disappear altogether – architectural design, detailed design, and coding – although the final stage of transformation is effectively coding.

The appeal of formal methods is:

● the precision of a formal specification

● preservation of the correctness during transformation, leading to verification of the final product

● that they afford many opportunities for automation (for example, automated coding, verification, validation, test case generation)

● that they afford the possibility for early animation of the specification (direct execution of the specification as an aid to validation).

The problems with the formal approach to software development can be:

● A formal specification is a barrier to communication with the client or user.
● Automatic transformation tools are not yet widely available.
● Considerable time and skill is required to carry out manual transformation.

This method is described in greater detail in Chapter 12.

One new approach uses the animation of a formal specification to demonstrate the software functionality to a client as a prototype.

SELF TEST QUESTION

2.4 Identify one advantage and one disadvantage of a formal development method.

2.7 ● The spiral model

The *spiral model* attempts to solve some of the problems of the waterfall model, while incorporating its best features – planning, phases, intermediate products. It also incorporates prototyping as necessary. The main feature of the spiral model is the recognition that there is often enormous uncertainty at many stages during a software development project. It therefore incorporates periodic risk analysis. The spiral model therefore offers greater flexibility than the waterfall model.

In common with other approaches, the spiral model recognizes that software development must consist of a series of major steps:

1. feasibility study
2. requirements analysis
3. architectural software design
4. implementation (including detailed design, coding, unit testing, integration, and acceptance).

However, the distinctive feature of the spiral model is that it makes explicit the idea of risk. We have seen (Chapter 1) that during software development there are difficult problems to be overcome. The spiral model explicitly recognizes that there are uncertainties associated with software development and that they should be dealt with as carefully as possible. Examples of risks are:

● During a long development, the users requirements are neglected.
● A competitor launches a rival package on to the market.

- Someone leaves the development team.
- One of the component tasks of the development goes beyond its deadline.
- It is discovered that the software performs much too slowly.
- The software occupies too much main memory.
- A new software development tool becomes available.
- A user requirement was misunderstood.
- The user changes one of the requirements.
- The target hardware configuration changes.

The spiral model makes explicit provision for dealing with areas of uncertainty like these and thereby minimizes the risk to the software project. A notable feature of the spiral model is that risks are addressed repeatedly at each stage of the project.

The spiral model also recognizes that the major steps have a number of activities in common with each other. Thus each major step consists of:

1. taking stock (identifying objectives, alternatives, and constraints)
2. dealing with risks (risk analysis and resolution)
3. development activities peculiar to this step – for example, requirements analysis, design, or coding
4. validation and verification, as appropriate
5. planning the next stage
6. review.

The first stage, taking stock, consists of:

1. establishing the objectives of the product of this stage (performance, functionality, ease of change)
2. identifying the constraints that affect this stage (cost, deadlines, interfaces with other software components)
3. identifying the alternative ways of implementing this stage (buying it, re-using something else, developing it one way, developing it another way).

The second stage, dealing with risks (risk analysis and resolution) consists of:

1. evaluating the alternative implementation schemes against the criteria set by the objectives and the constraints
2. identifying areas of risk
3. deciding how to overcome the risk
4. carrying out activity to reduce the risk.

For example, if meeting user requirements is identified as a potential problem, then the decision might be taken to carry out some prototyping to clarify the users needs.

It is at this stage in each phase of the project that considerable flexibility can be exercised. In effect, the whole of the progress of the project is reviewed and options for continuing are investigated. Use is made of whatever method is appropriate at that stage of the project. This might be prototyping, the waterfall approach, or a formal method.

Next, validation and/or verification is carried out, depending on the nature of the development step.

Planning consists of establishing deadlines for the next stage of the project and deciding how many people will be involved. Finally, a review is used to establish that the project is on track and that all the participants are happy with the plans.

In summary, the spiral model consists of a series of major steps. Each major step consists of a series of minor steps which are similar for all major steps. A single cycle of the spiral model is shown in Figure 2.5 and the complete spiral model is usually shown

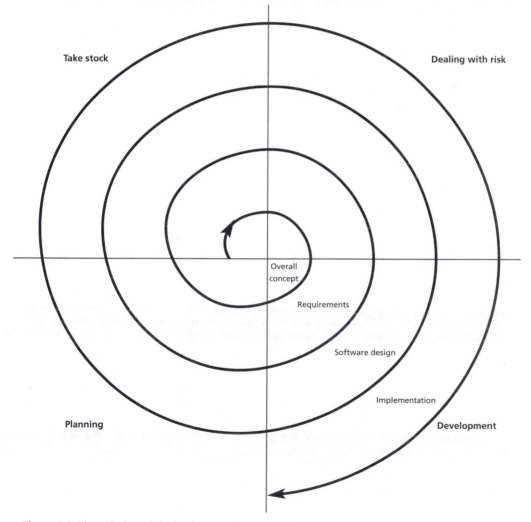

Figure 2.5 The spiral model of software development

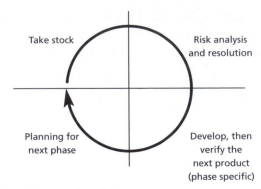

Figure 2.6 A single cycle of the spiral model

as in Figure 2.6. The similarity between stages is emphasized by the cycle that each stage performs. The progress of a project spirals outwards from the center of the diagram to convey the increasing expenditure of time and effort.

The spiral model is essentially a cautious and robust approach to development. At every stage, any risks to the successful progress of the project are assessed. Then an appropriate method is selected in order to minimize that risk.

SELF TEST QUESTION

2.5 Identify one advantage and one disadvantage of the spiral model.

2.8 ● Discussion

As we have seen, the various process models are often combined. For example, the spiral model uses prototyping, when appropriate. Again, throwaway prototyping can lead to a waterfall model, once the specification has been established. During integration testing, incremental development can be used in conjunction with any other model.

Later in this book we shall see that some development approaches need a variation of one of these process models. Object-oriented development, for example, requires a stage that identifies re-usable software components.

Which process model is best? The advice is to choose the model which is most appropriate to the circumstances. For example:

● The best model for the creation of a small information system in an office will probably be different from the model for constructing the computer system for a national lottery.

● If the requirements for the system are well understood, prototyping is unnecessary.

● If the project appears to involve a number of risks, use the spiral model.

● For a system that is safety-critical, it is worth considering using formal development, provided that expertise is available

2.9 ● Summary

There is a variety of process models to choose from, including:

● waterfall

● prototyping

● formal methods

● spiral.

The waterfall model consists of a series of stages carried out one after the other, with very little feedback between stages.

The waterfall process model suffers from the major problem that user acceptance is a long way from requirements analysis. Thus the wrong system may be built. Prototyping can reduce this gap and hence avoids the massive reconstruction arising from failing to meet the users needs.

The spiral model consists of a repeated cycle of small steps, designed to assess and cope with risks at every cycle.

EXERCISES

2.1 Discussion question on validation and verification: what do these mean, what is the difference between them, and which is better:

● a program that works (but doesn't meet the specification)
● a program that meets the specification (but doesn't work).

2.2 Discussion question on validation and verification: what do the following terms mean and how do they relate to one another (if at all):

● correctness
● working properly
● error-free
● fault
● tested
● reliable
● meet the requirements.

2.3 Draw up a process model for preparing a meal, including buying the ingredients and washing up afterwards. Don't forget to identify the product at each stage.

2.4 Draw up a process model for a large civil engineering project, such as building a road bridge across the channel between England and France. Identify similarities and differences between this project and a large software development project.

2.5 Which process models are a sequential series of stages and which involve repetition or iteration of steps?

2.6 Compare and contrast the process models introduced in this chapter.

2.7 Validation and verification are clearly important. For each process model, identify where validation is carried out and where verification is carried out.

2.8 "The waterfall model is useless." Discuss.

2.9 Compare and contrast throwaway with evolutionary prototyping.

2.10 Review the advantages of prototyping.

2.11 Review the software tools that are available for constructing a prototype easily and quickly.

2.12 Assess whether and how prototyping might be used in the development of embedded systems such as a car braking system.

ANSWERS TO SELF TEST QUESTIONS

2.1 Architectural design, unit testing.

2.2

	Throwaway	Evolutionary
Product	Specification	System
Starting point	Unclear requirements	Outline specification
Construction	Quick and dirty	Quality

2.3 Advantage: early validation of user requirements.
Disadvantage: need for suitable tools.

2.4 Advantage: mathematical verification.
Disadvantage: large effort and skill requirement.

2.5 Advantage: flexibility in the face of risks.
Disadvantage: lack of a early fixed plan.

FURTHER READING

For a review of process models and an explanation of the spiral model see: Barry W. Boehm, A Spiral Model of Software Development and Enhancement, *IEEE Computer*, 21 (5), (May 1988), pp. 61–72.

For a discussion of evolutionary development see: Felix Redmill, *Software Projects: Evolutionary vs Big-Bang Delivery*, John Wiley, 1997.

Requirements
engineering

· ·

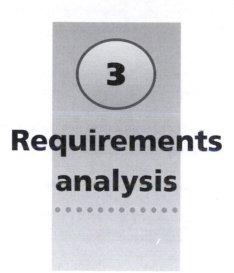

3

Requirements analysis

This chapter:

- explains the difference between functional and nonfunctional requirements
- explains how to analyze the requirements for a software system.

3.1 ● Introduction

Logically the first stage of software development is to establish precisely what the users of the system want. The dominant part of this stage is the communication between the users and the software developer or engineer. When engineers are dealing with requirements, they are normally referred to as requirements engineers, systems analysts or, simply, analysts. The term we shall use is "analyst." As far as the users are concerned, they are sometimes known as clients or customers. There is, of course, often a difference between a user and the customer. For example, an organization (the customer) will often buy a computer system for its employees (the end-users) to use. We will use the term user.

The story begins when a user has an idea for a new (or enhanced) system. He or she summons the analyst and thereafter they collaborate on drawing up the requirements specification. The user's initial idea may be very vague and ill defined, sometimes clear and well defined.

Arguably, establishing the requirements is the single most important activity in software development. If we cannot accurately specify what is needed, it is futile to implement it. Conversely we could implement the most beautiful software in the world, but if it is not what is needed, we have failed. In the real world of software development there are strong indications that many systems do not meet their users' needs, precisely because the needs were not accurately specified in the first place. (It is not easy to collect evidence of problems of this sort, since people are not keen to publicize their failures.)

Establishing the requirements for a software system is the first step in trying to ensure that a system does what its prospective users want. This endeavor continues throughout the software development and is called validation.

The requirements specification has a second vital role. It is the yardstick for assessing whether the software works correctly. The job of striving to ensure that software has the minimum number of errors is a time-consuming and difficult process that takes place throughout development. It is called verification.

3.2 ● The notion of a requirement

The task of analyzing and defining the requirements for a system is not new or peculiar to software. For generations engineers have been carrying out these activities. For example, the following is part of the requirements specification for a railway locomotive:

On a dry track, the locomotive must be able to start a train of up to 100 tonnes on an incline of up to 5% with an acceleration of at least 30 km/h/h.

This requirement serves to emphasize that a requirement tells us *what* the user (in this case the railway company) requires. It says nothing about *how* the locomotive should be built. Thus, it does not state whether the locomotive is diesel, coal or nuclear powered. It says nothing about the shape or the wheel arrangements.

One of the great controversies in computing is whether it is desirable (or even possible) to specify what a system should do without considering how the system will do it. This is the relationship between specification and implementation. We will now look at both sides of this argument.

On the one hand, there are several reasons why the requirements specification should avoid implementation issues. The prime reason is that the user cannot reasonably be expected to understand the technical issues of implementation and cannot therefore be expected to *agree* such elements of the specification. To emphasize the point, how many users of a word processor really understand the nature of software? A second reason for minimizing implementation considerations is to avoid unduly constraining the implementation.

On the other hand, some people argue that it is impossible to divorce specification and implementation. Indeed in several major approaches to specification they are intermixed. In such a method the first task is to understand and to document the workings of an existing system. (This might be a manual or a computer-based system, or some combination.) This investigation serves as the prelude to the development of a new computer system. Thus the implementation of one system (the old) acts as a major ingredient in the specification for the new system. For example, suppose we wished to develop a computer system for a library – one that currently does not use computers. One approach would be to investigate and document all the current, manual, procedures for buying books, cataloging, shelving, loaning, etc. Having accomplished this task, the next step is to decide which areas of activity are to be computerized (for example, the loans system). Finally, the specification of the new system is derived from the design (implementation) of the old system. This approach to development seems very appealing and logical. However, it does mean that implementation and specification are intertwined.

There are several additional and powerful reasons why the analyst must think about implementation during specification. First, he or she must check that a requirement is technically possible. For example, is it possible to achieve a response time of 0.1 seconds? Second, it is vital to consider implementation in order to estimate the cost and delivery date of the software. In order to estimate figures for performance and cost it will almost certainly be necessary to carry out some development at least as far as architectural design.

Another feature of a requirements specification is that it should provide clear guidance as to how to check that the system meets its users' needs. In the specification for the loco-motive, there is plenty of quantitative information that would allow an objective judg-ment of the success of the locomotive by using measuring instruments like stopwatches.

We have seen that the locomotive specification has the following characteristics:

1. It specifies requirements, not implementation.

2. It is testable.

3. It is clear.

However, the specification suffers from at least one deficiency: it is *incomplete*. There is no mention of, for example, cost or a deadline.

Let us now look at the requirements specification for a simple piece of software:

> Write a Pascal program to provide a personal telephone directory. It should imple-ment functions to look up a number and to enter a new telephone number. The program should provide a friendly user interface.

In deciding whether this is a good specification, we should ask ourselves:

● Does it say *what* and not *how*?

● Is it clear?

● Is it sufficiently detailed?

● Is it complete?

On the first question, the specification stipulates that the program is to be written in Pascal, which is definitely to do with the "how" of implementation. Second, the specifi-cation gives no detail about the nature of the two functions – it is entirely vague. Third, the requirement to provide a user-friendly interface is hopelessly vague.

It is easy to write poor requirements specifications for software; it is difficult to write good specifications. We will examine guidelines for writing specifications in some detail later in this chapter.

3.3 ● The process of eliciting requirements

The activity of eliciting requirements involves the analysts and users talking together, with the former trying to understand the latter. It necessitates the clearest form of communication. The skills involved on the part of the analyst are not the usual, technical skills that are associated with developing software. It is beyond the scope of this book to explore the issues of human communication that are involved, and we shall largely concentrate on the notations and format of specifications. We will, however, touch on the issue of viewpoints.

We can distinguish three activities that lead to a requirements specification:

1. listening (or requirements elicitation)
2. thinking (or requirements analysis)
3. writing (or requirements definition).

Elicitation involves listening to users' needs or requirements, asking questions that assist the users in clarifying their goals and constraints, and finally recording the users' viewpoint of the system requirements.

Requirements analysis is the stage where the software engineer simply thinks about the information obtained during the first stage. He or she transforms the users' view of the system into an organized representation of the system as seen by the analyst. And this may be complicated by the fact that there may be a number of different users with different views of what is wanted.

Requirements definition is the writing of a clear statement, often in natural language, of what the system is expected to provide for its users. This information is called the requirements specification.

As in any complex process of communication and negotiation, these three activities will usually take place repetitively and sporadically.

The conversation between clients and analysts will often be long and complicated. There is primarily the need to communicate clearly and then to record the requirements clearly. But then there is also the negotiating ingredient, during which the user may balk at the price quoted for a particular feature. Eventually, we hope, agreement can be reached on the final requirement specification.

From the outset of any project there are at least two viewpoints – that of the users and that of the developers. As we shall see, there are cultural differences between these two groups. But also there will often be differences of view within the group of users. For example, consider a computer system that is to be used by cashiers in a bank. The cashiers may be concerned with giving good customer service, with job satisfaction, with enriching their jobs. They may resent any attempt to speed up or intensify their work. They may object to any facilities in the system to monitor their work rate. The management in the bank, however, will probably be concerned with costs, with performance and effectiveness. There may very well be a conflict of interest between the cashiers and the managers. This paints an extreme picture, but illustrates that the users will not necessarily present a single, uniform view.

Another example of a potential gulf between users and analysts is to do with the level of expectation of users. Some users have seen the science fiction films and have come to believe that computers can do anything – or at least can offer a high level of artificial intelligence. Others, perhaps, are naive in the opposite direction – they believe that computers can carry out only the most mundane tasks.

To sum up, the role of the analyst is:

1. to elicit and clarify the requirements from the users
2. to help resolve possible differences of view amongst the users and clients
3. to advise users on what is technically possible and impossible
4. to document the requirements (see the next section)
5. to negotiate and to gain the agreement of the users and clients to a (final) requirements specification.

From the users' initial idea to an agreed requirements specification will often be a long and tortuous journey.

3.4 ● The requirements specification

The end-product of requirements elicitation and analysis is the requirements specification. It is a vital piece of documentation that is crucial to the success of any software development project. If we cannot precisely state what the system should do, how can we develop the software with any confidence, and how can we hope to check that the end-product meets its needs? The specification is the reference document against which all subsequent development is assessed. It is also often a major element of a legally binding contract.

Three important factors to be considered are:

● the level of detail
● to whom the document is addressed
● the notation used.

The first factor is about the need to restrict the specification as much as possible to specify *what* the system should do rather than *how* it should do it. As we have seen, the specification should ideally be the users' view of the system rather than say anything about how the system is to be implemented.

The second problem arises because the specification has to be understood by two different sets of people – the users and the developers. The people in these two sets have different backgrounds, expertise, and jargon. They share the common aim of clearly describing what the system should do, but they will be inclined to use a different language. The users will have a preference for non-technical descriptions expressed in natural language. Unfortunately while natural language is excellent for poetry and love letters, it is a poor vehicle for achieving a precise, consistent, and unambiguous specification. On the other hand, the analysts, being of a technical orientation, will probably wish to use precise (perhaps mathematical) notation in order to specify a system. This brings us to the question of the notation.

Several notations are available for writing specifications:

informal, writing in natural language, used as clearly and carefully as possible.
In this chapter we will concentrate on this approach.

formal, using mathematical notation, with rigor and conciseness. We will examine this approach in the next chapter.

semiformal, using a combination of natural language together with various diagrammatic and tabular notations. Most of these notations have their origins in methods for software design – that is, in methods for the implementation of software. These notations are discussed later in this book and include pseudocode, data flow diagrams, and structure charts.

At the present time, most requirements specifications are written in natural language. Semiformal notations, such as the data flow diagrams described later in this book, are sometimes used to clarify the natural language text.

One modern approach is to draw up two documents:

1. a requirements specification written primarily for users, describing the users view of the system, expressed in natural language. This is the substance of the contract between the users and the developers.

2. a technical specification that is used primarily by developers, expressed in some more formal notation, and describing only a part of the information in the full requirements specification.

If this approach is adopted, there is then the problem of ensuring that the two documents are compatible.

Given that a requirements specification will usually be written in natural language, it is useful to plan the overall structure of the specification and to identify its component parts. We can also identify those ingredients that, perhaps, should not be included at all, because they are concerned with the implementation rather than the requirement. The remainder of this section presents one way of structuring specifications.

One approach to giving a clear structure to a specification is to partition it into parts. Programs essentially consist of the combination of data and actions. In specifications, the corresponding elements are called functional and data requirements. One of the major debates in computing is about which of these two main elements – data or function – is primary. In software engineering approaches to development, much greater emphasis tends to be placed upon actions. This reflects what used to be the primary application areas – process control systems (for example controlling a power station). In information systems engineering approaches to development, data plays a far greater role. This reflects what used to be the prime application areas – banks, libraries, retailing. Some modern approaches to development, notably the object-oriented approach, are rather more holistic and attempt to treat function and data with equal importance. But our concern here is with specification, not with development approaches. However, the format of a specification will tend to reflect the system development method being employed.

A checklist of the contents of a requirements specification might look like this:

1. the functional requirements
2. the data requirements

3. constraints

4. guidelines.

We shall now look at these in turn.

3.4.1 Functional requirements

The functional requirements are the real essence of a requirements specification. They state what the system should *do*. Examples are:

The system will display the titles of all the books written by the specified author.

The system will continuously display the temperatures of all the machines.

Functional requirements are characterized by verbs that perform actions.

3.4.2 Data requirements

Data requirements have two components:

1. data that is input to or output from the system, for example, the layout of VDU screens;

2. data that is stored within the system, usually in files on disks; for example information about the books held in a public library.

3.4.3 Constraints

These are influences on the implementation of a system. Examples are:

The system must be written in Ada.

The system will respond to user requests within 1 second.

Constraints deal with items like:

1. cost

2. delivery date

3. the computer hardware that is to be used

4. the amount of memory available

5. the amount of backing store available

6. response times

7. the programming language to be used

8. data volumes (e.g. the system must be able to store information on 10,000 employees)

9. loading levels to be coped with (e.g. the system must be able to cope with 100 transactions per minute from the point-of-sale terminals)

10. reliability requirements (e.g. the system must have a mean time between failure of 6 months).

Constraints often address implementation (for example, the specification of the programming language) and therefore should be assessed with caution. For example, this might be unnecessarily constraining:

The algorithm must use a binary chop search method.

3.4.4 Guidelines

A guideline provides useful guidance for the implementation in a situation where there may be more than one implementation strategy. For example:

The response times of the system to keyboard requests should be minimized.

Or, as an alternative:

The usage of main memory should be as small as possible.

Now that we have identified a suitable partitioning of a specification, we will examine some common deficiencies in specifications.

Vagueness is a common problem. For example:

The interface will be user-friendly

Sometimes requirements contradict each other, as in these two:

The data will be stored on magnetic tape.

The system will respond in less than 1 second.

Omissions or incompleteness can be difficult to identify. A typical area of specification that is omitted is that of how to deal with input errors from a user of the system. Many specifications mix up the areas identified above, so that, for example, design guidelines are confused with functional items.

Sometimes a requirement is simply unclear or susceptible to alternative interpretations, and this, of course, may well be due to the use of natural language in the specification.

All in all, constructing a successful specification is a demanding activity that requires the clearest of thinking and review of the specification by a number of people.

3.5 ● Summary

The ideal characteristics of a requirements specification are that it:

1. specifies requirements (what) and not implementation (how)
2. is clear and unambiguous to all parties involved
3. can be used for validation and verification

4. is consistent within itself

5. is complete (free of omissions).

A multitude of notations and approaches are available to carry out requirement specification. The notations range from informal (natural language) through semiformal (e.g. data flow diagrams) to formal (mathematics).

One useful checklist for the ingredients of a specification is:

1. functional requirements

2. data requirements

3. constraints

4. guidelines.

EXERCISES

3.1 Group exercise. One way of understanding more clearly the difficulties of carrying out requirements elicitation is to carry out a role-playing exercise. Students can split up into groups of four people, in which two act as users (or clients), while the other two act as software analysts.

The users spend ten minutes in deciding together what they want. Meanwhile the analysts spend the ten minutes deciding how they are going to go about eliciting the requirements from the users.

The users and analysts then spend 15 minutes together, during which the analysts try to elicit requirements. At the end of this period an attempt is made for all parties to sign the requirements specification.

After the role-play is complete, everyone discusses what has been learned from the exercise.

A possible scenario for the above role play is where a multiscreen cinema complex has decided that it is time to replace its current ticket issue system with a new state-of-the-art computer system.

3.2 Discussion: who should be consulted when collecting the requirements of a computer-based system to replace an existing information system?

3.3 Discussion: Who should be consulted when collecting the requirements for a process control system or an embedded system?

3.4 Discussion: Define the terms "completeness" and "consistency" in a specification. How can we achieve them?

3.5 What are the skills required to collect and record software requirements?

3.6 Explain the difficulties in using natural language for describing requirements.

3.7 Given below is the specification for a small information system. Identify the functional and data components of the system. Identify problems with the specification such as ambiguities, inconsistencies, and vagueness.

s1   Software is required to maintain information about books held in a small departmental library.

s2   The software must run on a standard PC with a 10 gigabyte hard disk.

s3   For each book, the following information is held in the computer:
title
author
ISBN
year
borrower (if on loan)
date of issue (if on loan).

s4   The computer should be able to store information on up to 1,000 books.

s5   The computer system should respond to commands from the keyboard to:

(a) issue a book to a borrower

(b) receive a book back from a borrower

(c) create information about a newly acquired book.

s6   The commands should be accessible via cursor selection from a menu.

s7   The computer must respond within 1 second to any request.

s8   The system should be capable of printing the entire catalogue on continuous fanfold paper, with suitable headings. It should do this while any other commands are simultaneously being handled.

s9   With suitable security precautions, the system will initialize the library information so that it contains zero books.

s10 When a book becomes overdue, the system should display appropriate information.

s11 The software must be delivered by such-and-such a date and cost no more than $50,000. It must be fully documented and easy to maintain.

FURTHER READING

This is a clearly-written book on how to write requirements specifications that is a joy to read: Benjamin L. Kovitz, *Practical Software Requirements: A Manual of Content and Style*, Manning Publications Company, 1998.

This book is a good blend of theory, guidelines and practical advice: Ian Sommerville, Pete Sawyer and Allan Sommerville, *Requirements Engineering: A Good Practice Guide*, John Wiley, 1997.

This is written in distinctive thought-provoking style. Well worth reading: Michael Jackson, *Software Requirements and Specifications: A Lexicon of Practice, Principles and Prejudices* (Acm Press Books), Addison-Wesley, 1995.

A comprehensive collection of papers is presented in: Richard H. Thayer, M. Dorfman and Sidney C. Bailin (editors), *Software Requirements Engineering*, IEEE Computer Society, 1997.

4

Formal specification

This chapter:

- explains the differences between a specification, realization and verification
- outlines how to use one notation, Z, for formal specification
- explains the role of formal specification in software development.

4.1 ● Introduction

This chapter is about understanding and writing formal (mathematical) specifications. We have to be able to interpret specifications in many aspects of everyday life. For example, before buying a car we would probably be interested in knowing its performance figures – acceleration, turning circle, top speed, petrol consumption, and so on. Similarly, we would expect to see figures for power output, distortion levels, and frequency response in a specification for a hi-fi amplifier. Such a specification is a description of the characteristics of the product we're buying. These are in fact the same characteristics that the designer saw before embarking on the design of the car or amplifier – except that then the specification represented a proposal which the completed design had to fulfill. The important thing is that the specification said nothing to the designer about how the components of the specification should be achieved. Realizing the specification (that is, building the car, or constructing the amplifier), subject to additional constraints such as cost, manpower, etc., draws on the skill and experience of the designer. The specification said what had to be built, and the designer stated how it could be done.

Our concern is with the writing of specifications for programs, but the principle is just the same. We want to be able to state what task the program is supposed to accomplish, but not how the programmer should structure the program in order to perform that task. The dividing line between these two notions is a narrow one. It is always tempting to state, or at least hint, how a task should be performed, rather than leaving that to the discretion of the programmer, particularly when the specifier is an experienced implementer. Any notation for writing formal program specifications should facilitate abstraction, that is, it should only admit a statement of *what*, and discourage or prevent any hint as to *how*. Chapter 3 described the requirements analysis phase of software development, whose task is to turn a statement of a user's needs (which is often vague and unclear) into an unambiguous document devoid of errors. The output of requirements analysis is a requirements specification which contains both functional and nonfunctional requirements, that is, it details precisely what the software should do as well as any practical constraints that the developer should take into account (such as response times). We shall refer to the functional component of the requirements specification as the *software* specification. It is the latter which will concern us for the rest of this chapter.

Every working program performs some task correctly. What is of interest to a potential user is whether the program performs its intended task, or exhibits the behavior required by its sponsor. The latter is especially influenced by three specific phases in the software development process: specification, implementation, and verification. A conventional approach is to specify in English, program in Java (say), and verify by testing. It has been argued that such an approach is prone to all sorts of misunderstandings and errors, and can lead ultimately to incorrect software.

Using this conventional approach, how and why do incorrect programs get written? There are essentially three reasons:

- The specification is wrong – it may be ambiguous, vague, inconsistent, and/or incomplete.
- The program is wrong – it doesn't do what the specifier intended.
- The verification is incomplete – the testing isn't exhaustive. More than likely, it *can't* be exhaustive.

So what are the three phases of software development really for?

1. The specification is a *description* – it says *what* the problem is.
2. The program is a *realization* of the specification – it says *how* the problem can be solved.
3. The verification is a *justification* – it says *why* the realization satisfies the specification.

If this three-phase development process is so fraught with potential pitfalls, what can be done to improve it? Specifying in a formal notation rather than English holds the promise of bringing the most immediate benefits. ("Formal" means written entirely in a language with an explicitly and precisely defined syntax and semantics. Mathematics is an appropriate basis for such a language.) The advantages of using a formal notation can be summarized as follows:

- Formal specifications can be studied mathematically – in other words, a specification can be reasoned about using mathematical techniques. For example, certain forms of inconsistency or incompleteness in the specification can be detected automatically.

● Formal specifications are easier to maintain than those written in a natural language. That is, a specification can be safely enhanced, while ensuring strict control of the possible consequences of change.

● The notation used for expressing formal specifications is extensible. That is, if it doesn't exhibit a feature we need, we can extend the notation to include it. An analogous extension in English would, for example, involve augmenting the vocabulary and grammar of English sentences – an unrealistic and potentially dangerous activity for anyone who is not an expert in linguistics. In a mathematical notation, the underlying formality ensures that the meaning and use of such extensions can be unambiguously defined. (We are not here advocating arbitrary extensions made by the *user*, since these could be idiosyncratic and uncontrolled. Rather, extensions can be made by the notation's *designers* so as to incorporate extensions – following the usual rules of version control – which would benefit all users.)

Using a formal specification language also gives us the possibility of mechanizing the transformation of specifications into programs. Prototype systems (generally inefficient) can be automatically generated from specifications, and used for establishing the appropriateness of the specification, and the viability of the proposed system. Most importantly, we have the potential to *prove* programs correct with respect to their specifications.

4.2 ● Formal specification in Z: an example

The Z specification language was first introduced by Jean-Raymond Abrial in 1979, with subsequent development centered on the Programming Research Group at Oxford University. A powerful feature of Z is that structured specifications can be achieved using the *schema calculus*: this enables specifications to be built from smaller building blocks, much as programs can be designed top-down or bottom-up from their component procedures. Z is a large and complex notation. It is interesting (and perhaps comforting) to note that a relatively small set of Z constructs enables a large collection of typical problems to be specified quite easily.

First, a gentle review of some simple mathematics. In order to understand the example which follows, we shall need to clarify the mathematical notion of *sets*. A set is a collection of objects, normally expressed by enumerating its elements enclosed in curly brackets. For example,

```
{Bob, Carol, Ted, Alice}
```

is a set of names. We can test for set membership using the $\in$ *(is a member of)* and $\notin$ *(is not a member of)* operators. Thus

```
Carol ∈ {Bob, Carol, Ted, Alice}
```

but

```
Rupert ∉ {Bob, Carol, Ted, Alice}
```

The *union* of two sets A and B (written A ∪ B) is the set of elements which are contained in either A or B or both. Thus

```
{Bob, Carol, Ted} ∪ {Ted, Alice} = {Bob, Carol, Ted, Alice}
```

Note that sets cannot have repeated elements. The *intersection* of two sets A and B (written A ∩ B) is the set of elements which are contained in both A and B. Thus

```
{Bob, Carol, Ted} ∩ {Ted, Alice} = {Ted}
```

A set A is a subset of a set B (written A ⊆ B) if every element of A is also in B. Thus

```
{Bob, Ted} ⊆ {Bob, Carol, Ted}
```

The *difference* between two sets A and B (written A \ B) is the set of elements which remain when the elements contained in B are removed from A. Thus

```
{Bob, Carol, Ted} \ {Ted, Alice} = {Bob, Carol}
```

Now that we have the basics for expressing simple formal specifications, we shall use Z (which is founded on such basic mathematical concepts) to specify a very simple library system. The proposed system will maintain a database of those books which are shelved and therefore available, and those which are on loan. Our specification will describe the operations of borrowing and returning a book.

Our first task is to establish an appropriate mathematical model of the proposed system. We shall assume that all books owned by the library can be identified by a unique catalog number, and we therefore introduce a new data type called CATNO using the Z "given type" notation:

```
[CATNO]
```

A type in Z is also a set, so CATNO can be viewed as the set of all possible catalog numbers which can be used by the library. We shall take a sufficiently high-level view of the system that the precise membership of CATNO is immaterial for an understanding of the specification.

The library can be modeled as two sets of books (or catalog numbers of books) which we shall call shelved and loaned. Clearly a given book cannot be in both of these sets, because it cannot be shelved and on loan at the same time. We shall record this description of our chosen library model in a Z *schema* called Library:

```
┌─Library─────────────────────────────────
│
│ shelved, loaned : ℙ CATNO
│──────────────────────────────────────────
│ shelved ∩ loaned = ∅
│
└──────────────────────────────────────────
```

Z is described as a graphical notation, although all this really means is that schema definitions are enclosed in a box-like structure. The Library schema describes the *system state* (i.e. the library model), and the *data invariant* (i.e. a statement about the model). The top half of the schema (the text above the middle line) declares the state components – in this case the variables shelved and loaned – to be of type ℙ CATNO. This is the *power set* of CATNO – that is, the set of all sets of catalog numbers. Thus the variables shelved and loaned could have as value any set of catalog numbers taken from the set CATNO. The bottom half of the schema contains a predicate (an expression having the value true or false) which expresses an *invariant* – an assertion about the components of the mathematical model upon which the specification is based. The invariant must always hold whatever operations we may perform on the state. So here we are recording our earlier assertion that shelved and loaned will never have any common elements. ($\emptyset$ stands for the empty set {}).

Suppose CATNO was the potentially infinite set {c1, c2, c3, c4, c5, ... }. Then typical values of shelved and loaned which satisfied the invariant might be

```
shelved = {c1, c2, c4}
loaned = {c3, c5}
```

Conversely, we would say that the values

```
shelved = {c1, c2, c4}
loaned = {c2, c3, c5}
```

were *in conflict* with the invariant because c2 is both shelved and on loan at the same time.

(These examples describe a library owning a total of five books, which illustrates the principle if not the reality of a typical library stock!)

We now have to formally specify the operations which are to be performed on the system modeled. Invariants provide a valuable tool for ensuring consistency over the operations which make up a specification. We must ensure that if the invariant holds before any of the operations we specify, it must also hold after that operation is completed.

Here is a specification of the Borrow operation:

```
┌─Borrow ──────────────────────────────────
│ Δ Library
│ book? : CATNO
├──────────────────────────────────────────
│ book? ∈ shelved
│ shelved' = shelved \ {book?}
│ loaned' = loaned ∪ {book?}
│
```

Because we have already defined a schema called Library, by default we also have access to a schema called ΔLibrary, which looks like this:

```
┌─ΔLibrary ────────────────────────────────
│ shelved, shelved' : ℙ CATNO
│ loaned, loaned' : ℙ CATNO
├──────────────────────────────────────────
│ shelved ∩ loaned = ∅
│ shelved' ∩ loaned' = ∅
│
```

A convention in Z is that schema names beginning with the Greek character Δ denote schemas whose purpose is to describe before and after states, where the after state differs from the before state. Z also uses the convention of using unprimed names to denote the state before, and primed names to denote the state after an operation. So, for example, `shelved` represents the state of the shelved books before an operation such as `Borrow` has been invoked, and `shelved'` the state after. So ΔLibrary is the same as `Library`, but additionally contains declarations of the after state components and the corresponding invariant predicate for those components.

The `Borrow` schema refers to the ΔLibrary schema in its definition, using a technique known as *schema inclusion*. (Schema inclusion is just one example of the *schema calculus* mentioned earlier. It enables us to build specifications from smaller components, thus taking a modular approach and accruing all the usual benefits that entails). This is what the `Borrow` schema would look like if we were to write it out in full:

```
┌─Borrow1 ─────────────────────────────────────
│ shelved, shelved'  :  ℙ CATNO
│ loaned, loaned'  :  ℙ CATNO
│ book?  :  CATNO
├──────────────────────────────────────────────
│ book? ∈ shelved
│ shelved ∩ loaned = ∅
│ shelved' ∩ loaned' = ∅
│ shelved' = shelved \ {book?}
│ loaned' = loaned ∪ {book?}
└──────────────────────────────────────────────
```

In constructing `Borrow1`, the declarations from ΔLibrary have been merged with those of `Borrow`, and the predicate from ΔLibrary has been conjoined ("anded") with the `Borrow` predicate. Thus, after a `Borrow1` operation is complete, all five lines of the predicate must be true. In fact, `Borrow1` is completely equivalent to `Borrow`, so long as `Library` is defined. The attraction of the latter approach is that the `Library` schema can be re-used in other schema definitions, thus leading to more concise specifications.

The `Borrow` operation needs as input the catalog number of the book being borrowed – this is held in the input variable `book?` (another convention in Z is to give each input variable a name ending in ?).

The first line of the predicate describes the condition which must hold for the operation to be applicable (the *precondition*). In this case, the precondition is that the book being borrowed must currently be shelved, and therefore available.

The last two lines of the predicate express the relationship between the state of the system before and the state of the system after the operation (the *postcondition*). They state that the new shelved set will be decremented by the borrowed book, and the new loaned set will be similarly augmented.

So if we start with the library in this state:

```
shelved = {c1, c2, c4}
loaned = {c3, c5}
```

and `book? = c2`, the new state of the library will be

```
shelved' = {c1, c4}
loaned' = {c2, c3, c5}
```

Here is a specification of the `Return` operation:

```
┌─ Return ──────────────────────────────────
│ ΔLibrary
│ book?  : CATNO
├───────────────────────────────────────────
│ book? ∈ loaned
│ loaned' = loaned \ {book?}
│ shelved' = shelved ∪ {book?}
└───────────────────────────────────────────
```

SELF TEST QUESTION

4.1 If, once again, we start with the library in this state:

```
shelved = {c1, c2, c4}
loaned = {c3, c5}
```

and book? = c3, what will be the new state of the library after a `Return`?

As a specification (or model) of a real library, the above is obviously inadequate in many respects. For example, it would be nice to know who the borrower is when a book is issued. So let's extend the specification to include a representation of library card holders, and a representation of the relationship between a book and its borrower.

If we assume that every library member is identified by a unique membership number, we'll need another given type (which we'll call MEMNO), which contains all possible membership numbers. So MEMNO might be the potentially infinite set {m1, m2, m3, ... }.

In order to model the idea of a relationship between a book and a member, we need to look at another feature of Z – *functions*. A function expresses a relationship between the elements of two sets. For example, the function loans might associate catalog numbers (CATNO) with membership numbers (MEMNO). We would describe loans like this:

```
[CATNO, MEMNO]
loans : CATNO ↦ MEMNO
```

We say that loans is of type CATNO ↦ MEMNO. CATNO is called the *source* of the function, and MEMNO is the *target*. Any function of this type can take as its argument a member of CATNO, and return as its result a member of MEMNO. However, our particular loans is *partial* in the sense that it is only defined for some of the elements of CATNO, since not every book will be on loan. The subset of CATNO for which loans is defined is called the *domain* of the function.

For example, suppose CATNO is the set {c1, c2, c3, ... }, and MEMNO is the set {m1, m2, m3, ... }. Then loans might be defined explicitly as follows:

```
loans(c2) = m1
loans(c4) = m3
```

That is, if we apply loans to c2, m1 is returned, and applying it to c4 returns m3. Our interpretation of these loans applications is that m1 has borrowed c2, and m3 has borrowed c4. Nobody else has borrowed anything, so loans(c1), loans(c3), etc. are undefined. The domain of loans (written dom loans) is the set {c2, c4}, which is clearly a subset of CATNO. Similarly, the *range* of loans (written ran loans) is the set {m1, m3}, a subset of MEMNO.

Alternatively, the loans function can be defined by explicitly enumerating (as a set of *maplets*) how elements of CATNO are mapped to elements of MEMNO:

```
loans = {c2 ↦ m1, c4 ↦ m3}
```

Functions express "many to one" relationships. That is, if we model loans as a function, then several books can be borrowed by one member, but one book can have no more than one borrower. A function is called *total* (rather than partial) if its domain is equal to its source. For example, consider the square function, which squares its integer argument. The type of square could be described thus:

```
square : ℕ → ℕ
```

$\mathbb{N}$ is the set {0, 1, 2, 3, ... } of *natural numbers*, and is one of several basic types provided by Z. square is *total* (indicated by the arrow without the bar) because it can be applied to any element of $\mathbb{N}$, not just a subset.

Now we'll update our original library model to include the new components:

```
┌─Library1────────────────────────────────────
│ Library
│ members :  ℙ MEMNO
│ loans : CATNO  ⇸  MEMNO
├─────────────────────────────────────────────
│ loaned = dom loans
│ ran loans ⊆ members
└─────────────────────────────────────────────
```

Note that the inclusion of the schema Library in the definition of Library1 ensures that the original components of the model (shelved and loaned) are implicitly included, together with the original invariant from Library, which stated that the intersection of shelved and loaned is empty.

Typical values of shelved, loaned, member, and loans might be:

```
shelved = {c1, c2, c4}
loaned = {c3, c5}
members = {m1, m2, m3}
loans = {c3 ↦ m1, c5 ↦ m2}
```

The first line of the explicit predicate in `Library1` documents the relationship which must hold between `loaned` and `loans`. That is, we must know the borrowers of all books that are loaned. The second line states that only members (that is, library card holders) can borrow books.

Now let's write the borrow operation for this new library model:

```
┌─Borrow2 ─────────────────────────────────────
│ ΔLibrary1
│ book?  :  CATNO
│ person?  :  MEMNO
├──────────────────────────────────────────────
│ book? ∈ shelved
│ person? ∈ members
│ shelved' = shelved \ {book?}
│ loans' = loans ∪ {book? ↦ person?}
│ members' = members
└──────────────────────────────────────────────
```

This time, there are two inputs to the operation – the book to be borrowed, and the person borrowing it. For example, suppose we start with the library in this state:

```
shelved = {c1, c2, c4}
loaned = {c3, c5}
members = {m1, m2, m3}
loans = {c3 ↦ m1, c5 ↦ m2}
```

and `m1` brings the book `c1` to the issue desk. Line 1 of the `Borrow2` predicate ensures that the book is currently shelved (`c1 ∈ shelved`). Line 2 ensures that `m1` is a legitimate borrower (`m1 ∈ members`). Line 3 removes `c1` from the shelved set. Line 4 updates `loans` so that it contains the new maplet documenting the new loan, so that

```
loans' = {c3 ↦ m1, c5 ↦ m2, c1 ↦ m1}
```

Finally, line 5 states that the `members` set is unchanged by the operation. It is usual in operation definitions to record the components of the state model that don't change as well as those that do.

SELF TEST QUESTION

4.2 Specify the `Return` operation for this new library model.

Note that the `Borrow2` operation does not explicitly state what happens to the `loaned` set when a book is borrowed. We would of course expect that `loaned` would be augmented by the catalog number of the book being issued. In fact, this is implicit in the schema definition, because the included schema `ΔLibrary1` contains the predicate

```
loaned' = dom loans'
```

and `Borrow2` contains the predicate

```
loans' = loans ∪ {book? ↦ person?}
```

So by implication, if `dom loans` gets augmented by `book?`, then so does `loaned`.

Answering questions like this is part of the *validation* of a specification. We'll have more to say about this in Chapter 12.

4.3 ● The role of formal specification

A formal specification, such as that explained above, describes only the functional requirements of a system. The ingredients of a specification that are not normally addressed within a formal specification are:

● the user interface

● nonfunctional requirements.

While nonfunctional requirements are not normally part of a formal specification, it is possible to describe *some* nonfunctional requirements formally. For example, stipulating that some software must occupy less than 4 megabytes of RAM is a nonfunctional requirement which is expressed (semi-)formally.

What are the benefits to be gained from expressing the library specification mathematically rather than in English?

The first thing to note is that the specification makes no recommendations as to appropriate data structures for the implementation. For example, although the library has been modeled using partial functions and sets, the programmer may choose to implement it using a sequential or random access file, as a collection of arrays, or in some other way. The choice is open and unconstrained. In this respect, the notation has forced abstraction upon us; this is an important aspect of formal specification.

In addition, formal specifications provide a sound basis for examination and analysis during regular walkthroughs or inspections of a design. Some devotees also argue that formality releases a specifier from any emotional attachment to his or her work, and this relaxes participants who are called upon to defend their designs.

We can think of the specification as a contract between those who wish to use the software and those who have to construct it. For the user, the contract states the properties that he or she would like the software to exhibit; for the implementer, it states the behavior of the software which must be built. In addition, a validator may act as the representative of potential users – his or her concern is that the specification properly embodies the requirements; and a verifier's task would be to show the correctness of the implementation with respect to the specification.

A formal specification is more precise – less open to misunderstandings – than one written in a natural language. One of the great strengths of formal specification is that it uses the power and rigor of mathematics. It uses concepts and notations that are old, well-established, respectable, and backed by a vast edifice of proofs and techniques. The respectability of mathematics as a precise notation with a long and well-established underlying theory inevitably inspires confidence in its rigor and expressive power.

Taking the view that a formal specification merely replaces the traditional natural language specification, the developer's task is the same as it always was: to use the specification as a description of the problem (a statement as to *what* is required) and to construct a realization (an implementation prescribing *how* it should be solved). The software which implements the specification may then be constructed in the usual way by relying on the programmer's skill, experience, and understanding of the specification. Alternatively, it may be systematically generated from the specification using a procedure known as *refinement*. We'll examine this procedure in some detail in Chapter 12.

To summarize: the typical ingredients for a software component developed using formal methods are as follows:

● a formal specification, backed up by an informal description to aid understanding

● a prototype (however slow) which can be demonstrated to the client to enable validation

● the software, written from the specification

● a proof that the software is correct with respect to the specification.

In this chapter we have concentrated on the first of these phases. Formal specification has now been established in the computing industry as a viable and productive way to improve the effectiveness of the software development process, and to increase a user's confidence in the correctness of the software produced. The development of integrated software tools to support each phase is considered vital to the eventual acceptance of such a scenario.

4.4 ● Summary

● Software specifications should include only a statement of what the problem is, not how to solve it.

● A specification is a description; a program is a realization; a verification is a justification.

● Formal specifications allow the possibility of proving programs correct.

● Z takes a model-based approach to formal specification.

● Ideally, integrated tools should support the phases of formal specification, prototyping, implementation, and proof.

● Formal specification has been established as a viable and productive way to improve the effectiveness of the software development process.

EXERCISES

4.1 Write down (in English) some functional requirements of a computer system to control the borrowing of books from a public library, in addition to those considered in this chapter. List some nonfunctional requirements of an implementation of the library system. For example, how many library members should it be able to accommodate?

4.2 Write a Z specification to maintain information about the ages of a group of people. Specify operations to find the age of a given person, and to add 1 to a given person's age.

4.3 Extend the library specification to include the operations of joining the library, and canceling a library membership. If someone cancels their membership, what happens to the books they have on loan?

4.4 Specify the operation to buy a new book for the library. You'll need to update your model of the library to include a record of how much money the library currently has to spend, and perhaps model a book price catalog. Now specify the operation to sell a book which is old stock.

4.5 Add date stamping of books. When a book is issued, it gets stamped with the date it's due to be returned (assume dates are just natural numbers). When it's returned, the date on the book is compared with today's date. Refine your library model appropriately and respecify the issue and return operations in terms of this new model.

4.6 A library member should be able to reserve as many books as they like, and a particular book may be reserved by several members. Update your library model to capture book reservations. Specify the operation which allows a member to reserve a book which is currently on loan to another reader. Once a book is reserved, it can only be issued to the person who reserved it, so your issue operation will need to be respecified to reflect the new library model, as will your return operation. (Hint: it is perfectly valid to define functions that, given an argument, return a set of values as result.)

4.7 Write a Z specification of the requirements for a simple database system to be used by a marriage bureau. The bureau wishes to record in the database the clients who wish to be introduced to suitable partners, and must be able to update their records when existing clients benefit from the service by marrying. So you'll need to maintain a set of married and unmarried clients (including their gender), and specify operations for registering a new (unmarried) client and adding them to the database; marrying two existing clients, updating the database accordingly; and allowing two (now married) clients to end their registration with the bureau.

4.8 "Write a sorting program." In what way is this inadequate as a specification?

4.9 A necessary aspect of specifications is discussing them with potential users. The average user may not understand mathematics. Isn't this a disadvantage? Why might a formal specification still be worth producing?

4.10 What would you say were the most important attributes a specification should have for a programmer who has to implement it?

ANSWERS TO SELF TEST QUESTIONS

4.1 shelved = {c1, c2, c4, c3}

loaned = {c5}

4.2

```
┌─Return2 ─────────────────────────────────────────
│ ΔLibrary1
│ book? : CATNO
│ person? : MEMNO
├───────────────────────────────────────────────────
│ book? ∈ loaned
│ person? ∈ members
│ shelved' = shelved ∪ {book?}
│ loans' = loans \ {book? ↦ person?}
│ members' = members
└───────────────────────────────────────────────────
```

FURTHER READING

A readable introduction to the mathematics needed for an understanding of formal methods is given in: J. Woodcock and M. Loomes, *Software Engineering Mathematics*, Pitman, 1988.

An introductory guide to Z is: D. Rann, J. Turner and J. Whitworth, *Z: A Beginner's Guide*, Chapman and Hall, 1994.

A more thorough coverage of Z is given in: B. Potter, J. Sinclair and D. Till, *An Introduction to Formal Specification and Z*, Prentice Hall, 1991.

This book describes and compares the two most popular formal specification notations, Z and VDM: A. Harry, *Formal Methods Fact File: VDM and Z*, Wiley, 1996.

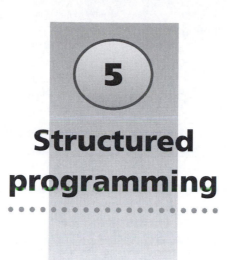

5

Structured programming

This chapter explains

- the principles of structured programming
- the arguments surrounding the `goto` statement.

5.1 ● Introduction

Structured programming is now part and parcel of most approaches to programming. It is widely accepted that it is not only the best, but the only way to carry out programming. This was not always the case. At one time there was a great debate about structured programming – what it meant and whether it was a good idea. This chapter reviews the principles and practice surrounding structured programming. It seeks to answer questions like: what is the essence of structured programming? What is the role of the `goto` statement? Why are certain control structures favored?

One view of structured programming is that it holds that programs should only be built from three components – sequences (normally written in the order in which the statements are to be executed), selections (normally written as `if...then...else`), and repetitions (written as `while...do`). The `goto` statement is, by implication, banned. In this chapter we begin by examining the controversy about the `goto` statement. The outcome of the argument is that `goto`'s are an irrelevancy; the argument is about something else – good program structure. We go on to explore the significant principles of structured programming.

There are various subsidiary questions. If the three structures of structured programming are diagrammed as flowcharts (Figure 5.1), the following characteristics become clear:

1. they have only one entry and exit
2. none of the constructs consists of more than three boxes.

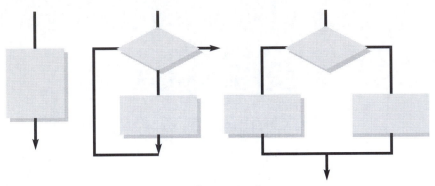

Figure 5.1 The three structures of structured programming

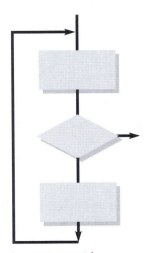

Figure 5.2 A control structure that is not structured

If we visualize any one of the three constructs as they are used, then a third characteristic is evident:

3. the entry is at the start and the exit is at the end.

Why is it that these characteristics are important? Why are other constructs that have the same characteristics (Figure 5.2) ruled out? We now go on to look at these questions.

5.2 ● Arguments against goto

5.2.1 goto's are unnecessary

Fortunately there is a mathematical theorem guaranteeing that any program written using goto statements can be transformed into an equivalent program that uses only the structured constructs. The converted program will, in general, need additional data items that are used as flags to control the actions of the program. Indeed the new program may look rather contrived; nonetheless, it can be done. On the face of it, therefore, there is no need for programs with goto's in them.

Note, as an interesting side issue, that the theorem does not tell us how to transform the unstructured program; only that it can be done.

5.2.2 Experimental evidence

Structured programming is well established and widely regarded as the best approach to programming. You might think, therefore, that there would be clear evidence from real software projects that it is beneficial. But this is not so; there are no convincing results from real projects – largely because a carefully controlled experiment would be difficult and expensive to mount. It would be necessary to develop a particular piece of software two ways – once using structured programming and again using "unstructured" programming. All other variables, like the expertise of the programmers, would have to be held constant. The two versions of the software could be compared according to criteria like development time and number of errors. Regrettably, there are no results of this type.

However, experimenters have carried out small-scale studies comparing how easily people can understand and debug small structured programs compared with unstructured ones. In a typical experiment, each of a group of subjects is presented with the listing of a program, written in a structured way, and asked a series of questions that are designed to assess their comprehension of the program. The accuracy of the replies and the time taken to reply are both measured. These are measures of the ease with which the program could be debugged or changed. A second group of subjects is given copies of the same program, rewritten in an unstructured way. The accuracy and response times of the two groups are compared. The results of these experiments generally indicate that structured programs are superior to unstructured ones.

The results of empirical studies are reviewed in the literature given at the end of the chapter. In a review published in 1984, long after the dust had settled on the structured programming debate, Vessey and Weber concluded that "the evidence supporting [structured programming] is weak." This conclusion largely stems from the difficulty of carrying out experiments that give trustworthy results.

5.2.3 Clarity and expressive power

Compare the following two equivalent program fragments:

```
      ------                    ------
      ------                    ------
 label:                    while a > 0 do
      ------                    ------
      ------                    ------
      if a > 0 goto label       endwhile
      ------                    ------
      ------                    ------
```

As we read down the first program fragment, we are not immediately sure what are the roles of the `label` and `goto`. It could take us some time to read and study the program in order to discover that they are being used to create the repetition of a piece of code. This is made immediately obvious by the `while` statement in the second program. Worse still, there is a remaining doubt in the first program, that there may be another `goto`, aimed at this same `label` from some other point in the program.

The facilities of a programming language should allow people to describe what they want to do in a meaningful way. If we examine a typical program written using `goto`'s we see that the `goto`'s are used for a variety of purposes, for example:

● to avoid a piece of code (which is to be executed in different circumstances)
● to perform repetition
● to exit from the middle of a loop
● to invoke a shared piece of code.

When we see a `goto`, there are few clues that allow us to decide the purpose for which the `goto` is being used. The alternative is, of course, a unique language construct for use in each of these different circumstances. These are, respectively:

● `if...then...else`
● `while...do` or `repeat...until`
● `exit`
● procedure call.

It is as if the `goto` is too primitive an instruction – like a machine instruction to load a register – that can be used in a whole variety of circumstances, but does not clearly convey its meaning in any of them.

In summary, the `goto` lacks expressive power and it is therefore difficult to understand the logic of a program that is written using a lot of `goto`'s. When we look at a piece of coding, words like `while` and `if` give us a strong clue as to what is intended; `goto`'s do not.

5.2.4 How many pencils?

Suppose we want to read a program in order to understand it, by tracing through it as if we were a computer executing it. Suppose we have available a supply of pencils (or fingers) to help us. The pencils will be used as markers, to be placed on the program listing to point to places of interest.

If we are following a simple sequence, then we will only need one pencil to keep track of our position. If we encounter a procedure call, we need two pencils – one to leave at the point of the call (in order to know where to return) and another to proceed into the procedure.

If we encounter a `while` statement or a `for` loop, then we need an integer, a counter, to keep count of the number of times we have repeated the loop.

To summarize, if the program has been written in a structured way, we need:

1. one pencil to point to the current position
2. one pencil to point to each procedure call that has been executed but not returned from
3. a counter for every uncompleted loop.

This may seem like a lot of equipment, but consider the alternative of a program that contains a lot of goto's. As before, we will need to indicate the position of the current statement. Next, we need a pencil to point at every goto that has been executed. But now, whereas in the structured program we can remove a pencil whenever we return from a procedure, finish a loop, or complete an if statement, we can never dispense with pencils; instead we need ever more. The increased number of pencils reflects the increased complexity of the goto program.

The real problem becomes evident when we want to refresh our memory about what happened *before* we arrived at the current point in the program. In the program without goto's we simply look back up the program text. In the unstructured program, when we look backwards we are defeated as soon as we reach a label, because we have no way of knowing how we reached it.

5.2.5 Ease of reading (static and dynamic structures)

In the Western world we are used to reading left to right and top to bottom. To have to begin by reading forwards and then to have to go backwards in the text is rather unnatural; it is simpler if we can always continue onwards. This is an important feature of a structured program; it can always be read from top to bottom – provided it has no procedures. The exception to this rule arises in comprehending a while loop, during which repeated references back to the terminating condition at the start of the loop are necessary.

Programs are essentially dynamic beings that exhibit a flow of control, while the program listing is a static piece of text. To ease understanding, the problem is to bring the two into harmony – to have the static text closely reflect the dynamic execution. In a structured program, the flow of control is always down the page, which exactly corresponds to the way that text is normally read.

5.2.6 Proving programs correct

To formally prove all programs correct is not a practical proposition with present-day techniques. Nonetheless there are some lessons that can be learned from proving.

In one technique of program proving, assertions are made at strategic points in the program. An assertion is a statement of what things are true at that point in the program. More exactly, an assertion describes the relationships that hold between data items that the program acts upon. An assertion at the start and end of a piece of program code are called the input and output assertions respectively. Proving consists of rigorously demonstrating that if the input assertion is true, then the action of the program will lead to the output assertion being true.

A structured program consists solely of components that have a single entry and a single exit point. This considerably aids the process of reasoning about the effect of the program. In contrast, it is usually impossible to isolate single-entry, single-exit structures within a program with goto's in it.

Even when formal proof techniques are not being used, but where an informal study of the program is being made, the single-entry and single-exit character of programs aids checking and understanding.

5.3 ● Arguments in favor of goto

5.3.1 Deskilling

The goto statement is one tool amongst many provided by the programming language. To take it away from the programmer is to deprive him or her of a tool that can be validly used in certain circumstances.

Consider a craftsperson who is an expert at making delicate objects from wood. Suppose that we remove from that person a tool that we consider to be inappropriate, say an ax. The skill of making a discriminating selection amongst the available tools is reduced, because the choice is narrower. Furthermore, the skill in using the tool is no longer required. (Remember, however, that there may be occasional circumstances in which an ax is the most suitable tool.)

5.3.2 Exceptions

Often a program is required to detect an error and to take some special action to deal with it. Suppose that such an error is detected many levels down in a chain of procedure calls. One way of handling the error is to create an additional parameter associated with each procedure call. This approach can become very unwieldy as procedures receive and merely pass on parameters that they do not need to act on.

An alternative is for the procedure detecting the error to simply goto a suitable place in the program where the error can be dealt with. This can result in a significant simplification to the program. The essence of the argument is that an exceptional situation in the program demands an exceptional solution – a goto.

Some programming languages, such as Java, have solved this problem using a special mechanism for handling exceptional situations.

5.3.3 Program performance

On occasions it is possible to write a program that will run more quickly using goto statements. An example is a program to search a table a for an item x:

```
for i := 1 to tableSize do
    if a(i) = x then goto found endif
endfor

notfound:
    ------
    ------
found:
    ------
    ------
```

The nearest we can get to writing this as a structured program is to write:

```
i := 1
while i <= tableSize and a(i) not = x do
    i := i+1
endwhile
if i > m then
    ------
    ------
else
    ------
    ------
endif
```

which requires an additional test. Although both programs achieve the same end – finding (or not finding) the desired item – the steps taken by the two programs differ. The first (unstructured) program takes fewer steps, and there is no way of writing a structured program that works in the same way. Thus it is possible to write `goto` programs that run more quickly than structured ones.

5.3.4 Naturalness

Take the table searching program above. Arguably the unstructured solution is the best in the sense that it is the solution that solves the problem most naturally. Any transformation of this program, or any other solution, is a distortion of the natural solution. In other words, getting rid of `goto`'s in existing programs (as can always be done), will sometimes needlessly destroy a good program.

The trouble is deciding what is "natural." It surely differs from person to person, depending on individual psychology and cultural experiences. So it is a rather subjective judgment.

5.4 ● Selecting control structures

Rather than take part in a parochial debate about the merits of a particular control structure, let us take a constructive approach. If we had a free choice and a blank piece of paper, what control structures would we choose to use in programming? Perhaps our first consideration should be to establish the principles that govern the selection. Let us examine the following criteria:

- standardization
- abstraction
- expressive power
- orthogonality
- minimality.

We shall see that some of these conflict with each other. Note also that in our examination we are confining ourselves to sequential, imperative programming, in contrast to concurrent or declarative programming (as in logic or functional programming).

5.4.1 Standardization

Domestic appliances exhibit enormous variety, and yet all plug into a standard electrical socket. Similarly, it is desirable to build software from components that all exhibit the same external interface.

The simplest interface comprises one entry point, at the start, and one exit point at the end. This has the strength of being consistent with the essence of sequential programming. It also conforms with the important idea of calling a procedure. We are used to the idea of calling a procedure as a sequential step and returning from it to the next instruction in sequence. (We do not, for example, expect to supply a label as a parameter to which control is returned.)

5.4.2 Abstraction

Abstraction is probably the most important idea in structured programming. The human mind cannot devise or understand the whole of a complex system. Instead we can only understand one part of the system at a time. Nonetheless it is vital to understand the whole system. The only way to resolve these contradictory statements is to be able to perceive the overall structure in a digestible way. The solution is to use *abstraction*; the system must be described in a notation that allows subsystems to be seen as black boxes whose task is readily understood, but whose detail is invisible. In programming, the procedure has long been a mechanism that fulfills this role.

Other constructs that possess the same single-entry at the start, single-exit at the end property, are `if...then...else` and `while...do`.

5.4.3 Expressive power

In discussing the arguments against the `goto` statement, we saw that the `goto` is too primitive. It has more to do with describing what a machine will do than what a programmer intends. Instead we look at the range of structures on offer, tempted on the one hand to seize every mechanism available, while at the same time conscious of the need for minimality.

Certainly we need some mechanism for repetition, and either a `while` statement or recursion are sufficient to provide this facility. Many languages provide both a `while` statement and a `repeat...until` statement. Most languages also support recursion.

Arguably we also require a statement to carry out a choice of actions following a test. The `if...then...else` fulfills this requirement, but others are equally valid, including the `case` statement. Again, we are torn between expressive power and minimality.

5.4.4 Orthogonality

When designing a set of facilities, a good design principle is to create features that are each as different from each other as possible. If this is so, we can more easily satisfy the goal of a minimum number of functions, while at the same time ensuring that the facilities are sufficiently powerful for all our needs.

5.4.5 Minimality

The principle of minimality curbs our tendency to include too many facilities. One of the uses of the Bohm–Jacopini theorem is that we know that the three control structures are sufficient. (Strictly, a construct for iteration, such as a `while`, is also unnecessary, because any loop that can be written iteratively can also, in theory, be achieved using only recursion.) Consider the flowcharts of various control structures. A sequence has one box, `while` has two, and `if` has three boxes. There are other control structures that involve only three or less boxes; but from amongst them all, this is the minimal feasible set.

5.5 ● What is structured programming?

It is easy to become engrossed in the arguments about the `goto` statement, but is this the central issue of structured programming?

Can a program that is written using only the three structures claim to be well structured? The answer is no; it is possible to create a bad program structure using the three structures, just as it is possible (with greater difficulty) to create a good structure that uses `goto` statements. To illustrate why this is so, consider a badly structured program that has been written using many `goto`'s. If we now transform this into a program that uses the three structures, we still have a badly structured program, since we have done nothing significant to improve it.

As a second example, consider a program to search a table for a required item. Two alternative solutions, one structured, the other not, were compared earlier. However, arguably, neither of these is the best solution. Here is another, in which the item being sought is first placed at the end of the table:

```
a(tableSize + 1) := x
i := 1
while a(i) not = x do
    i := i + 1
endwhile

if i = tableSize + 1
then

    ----

else

    ----

endif
```

This is arguably the best of the solutions because it is less complex (the condition in the while statement is simpler) and would execute more quickly on a conventional computer (for the same reason that there is only one condition to test.) This example illustrates that the use of the approved structures does not necessarily guarantee the best design.

A structured program is essentially one that can be understood easily, and the most useful tool in understanding is abstraction. Abstraction is concerned with identifying the major elements of what is being studied, and ignoring detail. Such is the complexity of software that we have to do this in order to stand a chance of understanding it.

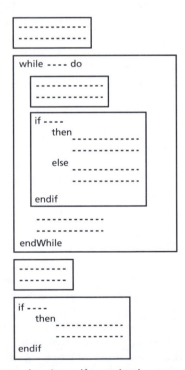

Figure 5.3 A structured program, showing self-contained components

Abstraction can only be achieved if the control flow constructs are used in a disciplined way, so that part of structured programming is the avoidance of goto's. For example, consider the program in Figure 5.3.

We can draw boxes around components as shown. Because it is built from limited control structures, we can view the program at all levels of detail as consisting of abstract components that have only one entry and one exit. If we examine any subsystem of the program, it is totally contained – the boxes do not overlap. If we look in detail at its contents, it does not suddenly sprout connections with other subsystems. When we uncover the nested contents of a traditional Russian wooden doll we do not expect suddenly to encounter a doll that affects any of those we have already seen. (Structured programs are, of course, more complex than these dolls; it is as if, when we open a doll, not just one, but several more are revealed.)

Suppose that in the above program we inserted a goto as shown in Figure 5.4.

We have now ruined the structure, since we can no longer view the program at different levels of abstraction.

As an analogy compare the problems of understanding a plate of spaghetti as compared with a plate of lasagna. In order to understand the spaghetti, we have to understand it all; we cannot employ abstraction. With the lasagna, we can peel off layers, one by one, uncovering the interesting detail of successive layers and understanding each separately from the others.

Notice, though, that throughout our discussion we have concentrated almost exclusively on *control* structures and have neglected references to data. Although a program

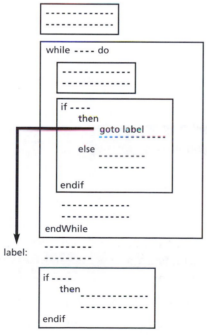

Figure 5.4 An unstructured program

that uses the three structures may have abstraction of control, it may well have global data. This seriously weakens the abstraction, since at any level of detail all of the data have to be considered. Thus control abstraction is only one side of the coin; the other side is data abstraction – an important theme that is developed in the chapters on modularity, object-oriented design and object-oriented programming later in this book.

The idea of abstraction is a powerful tool in constructing software that is understandable. But, by itself, it is inadequate. In order to create programs that are well structured, we need a systematic *method* that takes us from the statement of the problem to the structure of the program. There are a variety of methods, discussed in later chapters. Most modern methods are top-down. They exploit the idea of abstraction in the following way. Initially an overall, abstract description of the problem is constructed. This is refined or broken down into several more detailed components. These, in turn, are refined again, and so on until the level of detail is adequate.

5.6 ● Summary

We have recounted the arguments about the pros and cons of goto's. The arguments against the goto are:

1. it is unnecessary
2. the experimental evidence
3. the lack of expressive power of goto's
4. the difficulty of finding out where you came from in a program constructed using goto's
5. the need to read backwards in a program with goto's in it
6. the difficulty of proving the correctness of programs that use goto's.

The arguments for goto's are:

1. to ban them is to deskill programming
2. they have a use in exceptional circumstances
3. goto's are sometimes necessary in order to make programs perform well
4. it is sometimes "natural" to use goto's.

Much of the debate about structured programming has been conducted in this way. Throughout the arguments, the need for clarity in programs is the dominant idea.

The avoidance of goto's does not necessarily lead to a structured program. The central idea of structured programming is abstraction. Indeed, we can define structured programming as:

"the systematic use of (control) abstraction in programming."

(Abstraction can be applied not just to control, but to data as well. This is the subject of other chapters.)

Abstraction requires not only the use of suitable control structures but also a systematic design method.

EXERCISES

5.1 Review the arguments for and against goto statements and criticize their validity.

5.2 State in your own words what structured programming is. Imagine that you meet a friend who has their own personal computer and is used to programming using goto's. Explain in simple clear language what structured programming is.

5.3 A while statement can be used instead of an if statement, because the statement:

```
if bool then s endif
```

can be rewritten as:

```
while bool do s bool := false endwhile
```

Show how an if...then...else statement can similarly be rewritten using while statements. If the if statement is superfluous, why have it?

5.4 Convert the following into a structured program.

```
i := start
loop:
if x = a[i] then goto found endif
if i = end then goto notFound endif
i := i + 1
goto loop

notFound:
  write 'not found'
  action1
  goto end

found:
  write 'found'
  action2
end:
```

Compare and contrast the two programs.

5.5 Recursion can be used to accomplish repetition, as in the following example of a procedure to skip spaces in a stream of input information:

```
procedure skipSpaces
read (char)
if char = space then skipSpaces endif
endprocedure
```

Convert this example to a procedure that uses a `while` statement for repetition. Compare and contrast the two solutions. What is the role of recursion in the programmer's toolkit?

5.6 Argue for and against providing the following constructs in a programming language:

● `case`

● `repeat...until`

● `until...do`

FURTHER READING

The famous article that launched the debate about structured programming is: E. W. Dijkstra, Go To Statement Considered Harmful, *Communications of the ACM*, 11 (3), (March 1968), pp. 147–148.

It is widely agreed that structured programming is a vital ingredient of software development. For a review of the (inconclusive) experimental evidence about the effectiveness of structured programming, see: I. Vessey and R. Weber, Research on Structured Programming: An Empiricist's Evaluation, *IEEE Trans on Software Engineering*, 10 (4), (1984), pp. 397–407.

A vigorous exposition of the argument that structured programming is deskilling is given in: P. Kraft, *Programmers and Managers*, Springer-Verlag, New York, 1977.

6

Modularity

This chapter explains:

- the nature of modularity
- the argument against global data
- information hiding and encapsulation
- coupling and cohesion
- Shaw and Garlan's classification
- an outline of objects.

6.1 ● Introduction

This book describes a number of methods for software design. Several methods contend for the role of the single ideal method but no method can claim to lead the designer to an ideal structure. Given this situation, a number of important guidelines have emerged. Their role is to supplement some or all of the design methods in providing guidance during the process of design. In addition, they enable us to make judgments on the quality of a piece of software that has been designed. These guidelines are largely independent of particular design methods.

Many of the guidelines described in this chapter center around the idea of modularity. Modularity is one of the key issues in program design. It is the unobtainable Holy Grail. Modularity is to do with the structure of software. This structure is the end-product of all of the major current design methods such as functional decomposition, object-oriented design, and data structure design.

If we were asked to design an automobile, we would probably design it in terms of several subsystems – engine, transmission, brakes, chassis, etc. Let us call these subsystems modules. In identifying these particular components for an automobile we have selected items that are as independent of each other as possible. This is the essence of good modularity.

The guidelines we shall describe in this chapter help to answer questions like:

● how big should a module be?

● how complex is this module?

● how can we minimize interactions between modules?

Before we embark on these questions, we should identify what a "module" and "modularity" are. Usually this is dictated by practical considerations, such as the facilities provided in the available programming language and operating system. There is a variety of mechanisms for splitting software into independent modules, or, expressed another way, grouping together items that have some mutual affinity. In various programming languages, a module is as follows:

    Cobol – paragraph, subprogram
    BASIC – subroutine
    Fortran – subroutine
    Pascal – procedure or function
    Modula-2 – module
    C – function
    C++ – function, object, or class
    Ada – procedure or package
    Java – method, class or package.

Java is a typical modern language. At the finest level of granularity, a number of statements and variable declarations can be placed in a procedure (termed a method). A set of procedures can be grouped together, along with some shared variables, into a class. A number of classes can be grouped into a package. Thus a module is a fairly independent piece of program that has a name, some instructions, and some data of its own. A module is used, or called, by some other module and, similarly, uses (calls) other modules.

In this chapter we use the term "module" in the most general way to encompass any current or future mechanism for dividing software into manageable portions.

6.2 ● Why modularity?

The scenario is that of software that consists of thousands or even hundreds of thousands of lines of code. The complexity of such systems can easily be overwhelming. Some means of coping with the complexity are essential. In essence, the desire for modularity is about trying to construct software from pieces that are as independent of each other as possible. Ideally, each module should be self-contained, and have as few references as possible to other modules. This aim has consequences for nearly all stages of software development.

6.2.1 Architectural design

This is the step during which the large-scale structure of software is determined. It is therefore critical for creating good modularity. A design approach that leads to poor modularity will lead to dire consequences later on.

6.2.2 Module design

If the architectural design is modular, then the design of individual modules will be easy. Each module will have a single well-defined purpose, with few, clear connections with other modules.

6.2.3 Debugging

It is during debugging that modularity comes into its own. If the structure is modular, it should be easier to identify which particular module is responsible for the observed fault. Similarly, the correction to a single module should not produce "knock-on" effects, provided that the interfaces to and from the module are not affected.

6.2.4 Testing

Testing a large system made up of a large number of modules is a difficult and time-consuming task. It is virtually impossible to test an individual module in detail once it has been integrated into the system. Therefore testing is carried out in a piecemeal fashion – one module at a time. (See Chapter 19 on verification.) Thus the substructure of the system is crucial.

6.2.5 Maintenance

Maintenance means fixing bugs and enhancing a system to meet changed user needs. This activity consumes enormous amounts of software developers' time. Again, modularity is crucial. The ideal would be to make a change to a single module, with total confidence that no other modules will be affected. However, too often it happens that obvious or subtle interconnections between modules make the process of maintenance a nightmare.

There are two other important aspects of modularity.

6.2.6 Independent development

Most pieces of software are implemented by a team of people, often over months or years. Normally each module is developed by a single person. It is therefore vital that interfaces between modules are clear and few.

6.2.7 Software re-use

A major current technique is to re-use software from a library or from an earlier project. This avoids re-inventing the wheel, and can potentially save enormous effort. However, a module cannot easily be re-used if it is connected in some complex way to other modules in the previous system. A heart transplant from one human being to another would be impossible if there were too many arteries, veins, nerves, etc. to be severed and reconnected. There are therefore two important requirements for a re-useable module:

- It performs a single useful function.
- It has the minimum of connections to other modules.

6.3 ● Module size

How big should a software module be? Take any piece of software. It can always be constructed in two radically different ways – once with small modules and again with large modules. As an illustration, Figure 6.1 shows two alternative structures for the same software. One consists of many small modules; the other a few large modules. (This software has a hierarchical structure, so that the diagrams are trees. However, the following arguments are the same, whatever the structure.)

If the modules are large, there will only be a few of them, and therefore there will tend to be only a few connections between them. We have a structure which is a tree with few branches and a few very big leaves. The complexity of the interconnections is minimal, but the complexity of each module is high.

If the modules are small, there will be many modules and therefore there will be many connections between them in total. The structure is a tree with many branches and many small leaves. The smaller the modules, the easier an individual module should be to comprehend. But if the modules are small, we run the risk of being overwhelmed by the proliferation of interconnections between them.

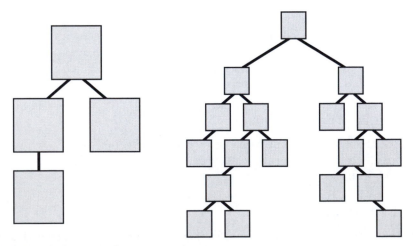

Figure 6.1 Two alternative software structures

The question is: which of the two structures is the better? The alternatives are large modules with few connections, or small modules with many connections. But, as we shall see, the dilemma is not usually as simple as this.

A common point of view is that a module should occupy no more than a page of coding (about 40–50 lines). This suggestion takes account of the difficulty of understanding logic that spills over from one page of listing (or one screen) to another.

A more extreme view is that a module should normally take up about seven lines or less of code, and in no circumstances more than nine. Those who argue for the "magic number" seven do so on the basis of experimental results from psychology. Research indicates that the human brain is capable of comprehending only about seven things (or concepts) at once. This does not mean that we can remember only seven things; clearly we can remember many more. But we can only retain in short-term memory and study as a complete, related set of objects, a few things. The number of objects ranges from about five to nine, depending on the individual and the objects under study. The implication is that if we wish to understand completely a piece of program or a piece of pseudocode it should be no more than about seven statements in length. Relating lines of code to concepts may be oversimplifying the psychological basis for these ideas, but the analogy can be helpful. We shall pursue this further later in the chapter.

Clearly a count of the number of lines is too crude a measure of the size of a module. A seven-line module containing several `if` statements is more complex than seven sequential statements. The next section pursues this question.

We have already met an objection to the idea of having only a few statements in a module. By having a few statements we are only increasing the number of modules. So all we are doing is to decrease complexity in one way (the number of statements in a module) at the cost of increased complexity in another way (the number of modules). So we gain nothing overall.

The argument for small modules is as follows. We pose the question of how a piece of software should be studied. Studying a program is necessary during design, during verification, during debugging, and during maintenance – and it is therefore a vital activity. When studying a program we do not look at the whole program at once, because (for a program of any practical length) it is too complex to comprehend as a whole. Instead we focus attention on only a single module at a time. If the software has been well designed, we can study the logic of an individual module in isolation from any others. As part of the task of studying a module we need to know something about any modules it uses. For this purpose we use the power of abstraction, so that while we understand *what* other modules do, we do not need to understand *how* they do it. When we have completed an examination of one module we turn our attention to another. So we never need to comprehend more than one module at a time. Therefore, we conclude, it is the complexity of individual modules that matters.

Of course this argument assumes that the software has been well constructed. This means that abstraction can be applied in understanding an individual module. However, if the function of a module is not obvious from its outward appearance, then we need to delve into it in order to understand what it does. Similarly, if the module is closely connected to other modules, it will be difficult to understand in isolation. We discuss these issues later.

Small modules can give rise to slower programs because of the increased overhead of procedure calls. But nowadays a programmer's time can cost significantly more than a computer's time. The question here is whether it is more important for a program to be easy to understand or whether it is more important for it to run quickly. These requirements may well conflict and only individual circumstances can resolve the issue. It may well be better, however, first to design, code, and test a piece of software using small modules. Then, if performance is important, particular procedures that are invoked frequently can be rewritten in the bodies of those modules that use them. It is, however, unlikely that procedure calls will adversely affect the performance of a program. Similarly, it is unlikely that encoding procedures in-line will give rise to significant improvement. Rather, studies have shown that programs spend most of their time (about 50%) executing a small fraction (about 10%) of the code. It is the optimization of these small parts that will give rise to the best results.

6.4 ● Complexity

In the early days of programming, main memory was small and processors were slow. It was considered normal to try hard to make programs efficient. One effect of this was that programmers often used tricks. Nowadays the situation is rather different – the pressure is on to reduce the development time of programs and ease the burden of maintenance. So the emphasis is on writing programs that are clear and simple, and therefore easy to check, understand, and modify.

What are the arguments for simplicity?

● It is quicker to debug a simple program.
● It is quicker to test a simple program.
● A simple program is more likely to be reliable.
● It is quicker to modify a simple program.

If we look at the world of design engineering, a good engineer insists on maintaining a complete understanding and control over every aspect of the project. The more difficult the project the more firmly the insistence on simplicity – without it no-one can understand what is going on. Software designers and programmers have frequently been accused of exhibiting the exact opposite characteristic; they deliberately avoid simple solutions and gain satisfaction from the complexities of their designs. Perhaps programmers should try to emulate the approach of traditional engineers.

Many software designers and programmers today strive to make their software as clear and simple as possible. A programmer finishes a program and is satisfied both that it works correctly and that it is clearly written. But how do we know that it is clear? Is a shorter program necessarily simpler than a longer one (that achieves the same end), or is a heavily nested program simpler than an equivalent program without nesting? People tend to hold strong opinions on questions like these; hard evidence and objective argument are rare.

Arguably what we perceive as clarity or complexity is an issue for psychology. It is concerned with how the brain works. We cannot establish a measure of complexity – for example, the number of statements in a program – without investigating how such a measure corresponds with programmers' perceptions and experiences. We now describe one attempt to establish a meaningful measure of complexity. An aim of such work is to guide programmers in selecting clear program structures and rejecting unclear structures, either during design or afterwards.

The approach taken is to hypothesize about what factors affect program complexity. For example, we might conjecture that program length, the number of alternative paths through the program and the number of references to data might all affect complexity. We could perhaps invent a formula that allows us to calculate the overall complexity of a program from these constituent factors. The next step is to verify the hypothesis. How well does the formula match up with reality? What correlation is there between the complexity as computed from the formula and, for example, the time it takes to write or to understand the program?

6.5 ● Global data is harmful

Just as the infamous `goto` statement was discredited in the 1960s, so later ideas of software engineering came to regard global data as harmful. Before we discuss the arguments, let us define some terms. By *global data* we mean data that can be widely used throughout a piece of software, and is accessible to a number of modules in the system. By the term *local data*, we mean data that can only be used within a specific module; access is closely controlled.

For any particular piece of software, the designer has the choice of making data global or local. If the decision is made to use local data, data can, of course, be shared by passing appropriate pieces of data around the program as parameters.

Here is the argument against global data. Suppose that three modules named A, B, C access some global data as shown in Figure 6.2. Suppose that we have to study module A in order, say, to make a change to it. Suppose that modules A and B both access a piece of global data named X. Then in order to understand A we have to understand the role of X. But, now, in order to understand X we have to examine B. So we end up having

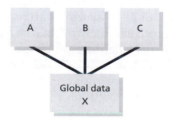

Figure 6.2 Global data

to study a second module (B), when we only wanted to understand one. But the story gets worse. Suppose that modules B and C share data. Then to fully understand B we have to understand C. Therefore in order to understand module A, we have to understand not only module B but also module C. We see that in order to comprehend *any* module that uses global data we have to understand *all* the modules that use it.

In general, local data is preferable because:

● it is easier to study an individual module because it is clear what data the module is using

● it is easier to remove a module to use in a new program, because it is a self-contained package.

● the global data (if any) is easier to read and understand, because it has been reduced in size.

So, in general, the amount of global data should be minimized (or preferably abolished) and the local data maximized. Nowadays most programming languages provide good support for local data and some do not allow global data at all.

Most modern programming languages provide a facility to group procedures and data into a module (called variously a module, class, or package). Within such a module, the procedures access the data, which is therefore global within the module.

6.6 ● Information hiding and abstract data types

Information hiding, *data hiding*, or *encapsulation* is an approach to structuring software in a highly modular fashion. The idea is that for each data structure (or file structure), all of the following:

● the structure itself

● the statements that access the structure

● the statements that modify the structure

should be part of just a single module. A piece of data encapsulated like this cannot be accessed directly. It can only be accessed via one of the procedures associated with the data. Such a collection of data and procedures is called an abstract data type, or (in object-oriented programming) a class or an object.

The classic illustration of the use of information hiding is the stack. Procedures are provided to initialize the stack, to push an item on to the stack top and to pop an item from the top. (Optionally, a procedure is provided in order to test whether the stack is empty.) Access to the stack is only via these procedures. Given this specification, the implementor of the stack has freedom to store it as an array, a linked list, or whatever. The user of the stack need neither know, nor care, how the stack is implemented. Any change to the representation of the stack has no effect on the users (apart, perhaps, from its performance). The procedures that act upon the stack are conceptually, but not necessarily textually, grouped together with the stack itself.

Information hiding meets three aims:

(a) *Changeability*

If a design decision is changed, such as a file structure, changes are confined to as few modules as possible and, preferably, to just a single module.

(b) *Independent development*

When a system is being implemented by a team of programmers, the interfaces between the modules should be as simple as possible. Information hiding means that the interfaces are calls on procedures which, it is argued, are simpler than accesses to shared data or file structures.

(c) *Comprehensibility*

For the purposes of design, checking, testing, and maintenance it is vital to understand individual modules independently of others. As we have seen, global and shared data weaken our ability to understand software. Information hiding simply eliminates this problem.

As another example, suppose that we have to write a text formatting program. Suppose we find it necessary to assemble a line to be printed by placing in it characters, one by one, until the line is full. We could allow the program to access a buffer directly, for example when it needed to place characters in the buffer. We might well end up with a program in which pieces of code are dotted around everywhere. Remembering that putting a character in a buffer will involve updating an index or counter, we might have many references to the same collection of data items. There is plenty of scope for error; a classic mistake would be to reverse the actions of incrementing the index and inserting a character.

An alternative structure would be to create three procedures:

1. initialize the buffer
2. place a character in the buffer (printing if it is full)
3. termination (print any remaining line).

Now none of the information about the line – its length, name, associated index – need be referred to anywhere else in the program. Any change to the representation of the buffer, or to the length of the line, is totally confined to the three procedures.

Some programming languages (Ada, C++, Modula 2, Java) support information hiding by preventing any references to a module other than calls to those procedures declared to be public. (The programmer is also allowed to declare data as publicly accessible, but this facility is only used in special circumstances because it subverts information hiding.) Clearly the facilities of the programming language can greatly help structuring software according to information hiding. An additional facility (not provided in all programming languages) enables a module to initialize itself, thus eliminating the need for calling the first procedure in the above example.

As a further example, consider an information system, e.g. an airline seat reservation system, that responds to inputs from an interactive terminal. The commands might be:

- reserve a seat
- cancel a reservation
- inquire about availability.

One view of the program structure would be to see it as two modules:

1. one that interacts with the user via the terminal, and
2. one that stores and retrieves information from the database.

Each can be seen as a module that encapsulates data, providing access to that data via procedure calls. We might go on to conceive of a third, controlling, module that makes calls on each of the other two, one after the other.

In summary, the principle of information hiding means that, at the end of the design process, any data structure or file is accessed only via certain well-defined, specific paragraphs, procedures, or subprograms. Some programming languages support information hiding, while others do not. This is discussed in Chapter 13, on programming languages.

The principle of information hiding has become a major concept in program design and software engineering. It has not only affected language design (see Chapter 13 on programming languages), but led to completely different views of programming, such as object-oriented programming (see below and Chapter 14). In object-oriented programming, data and actions that are strongly related are grouped together into entities called objects. Normally access to data is permitted only via particular procedures. Thus information hiding is implemented and supported by the programming language. Global data is entirely eliminated.

6.7 ● Coupling and cohesion

The ideas of coupling and cohesion are a terminology and a classification scheme for describing the interactions between modules and within modules. Ideally a piece of software should be constructed from modules in such a way that there is a minimum of interaction between modules (low coupling) and, conversely, a high degree of interaction within a module (high cohesion). If this can be achieved, then an individual module can be designed, coded, tested, or amended without the undue complications of having to deal with other modules. Another beneficial effect is that when an error occurs in a module, the spread of damage to other modules may be limited.

Figure 6.3 illustrates the ideas. Each diagram shows the structure of a piece of software, in each case built from four modules. Within each program there are 20 interactions – these could be procedure calls or accesses to data items. In the left-hand diagram there are many interactions between modules, but comparatively few within modules. In contrast, in the right-hand diagram, there are few interactions between modules and many interactions within modules. The left-hand program has strong coupling and weak cohesion. The right-hand program has weak coupling and strong cohesion.

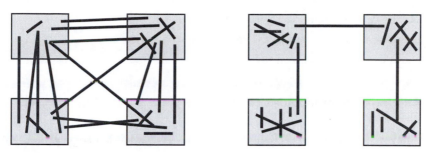

Figure 6.3 Coupling and cohesion in two software systems

Coupling and cohesion are opposite sides of the same coin, in that strong cohesion will tend to create weak coupling, and vice versa.

The ideas of coupling and cohesion were suggested in the 1970s by Yourdon and Constantine. They date from a time when most programming languages allowed the programmer much more freedom than modern languages permit. Thus the programmer had enormous power, but equally had the freedom to write code that would nowadays be considered dangerous. In spite of their age, the terminology of coupling and cohesion is still very much alive and is widely used to describe interactions between software components.

6.8 ● Coupling

We are familiar with the idea of one module making a procedure call on another, but what other types of interaction (coupling) are there between modules? Which types are good and which bad?

First, an important aspect of the interaction between modules is its "size." The fewer the number of objects that connect modules, the better. If modules share common data, it should be minimized. Few parameters should be passed between modules in procedure calls. It has been suggested that no more than about two to four parameters should be used. Deceit should not be practiced by grouping together several parameters into a record and then using the record as a single parameter.

What about the *nature* of the interaction between modules? We can distinguish the following ways in which modules interact. They are listed in an order that goes from strongly coupled (least desirable) to weakly coupled (most desirable):

1. altering another module's code
2. branching to or calling a place other than at the normal entry point
3. accessing data within another module
4. shared or global data
5. procedure call with a switch as a parameter

6. procedure call with pure data parameters

7. passing a serial data stream from one module to another.

We now examine each of these in turn.

6.8.1 Altering another module's code

This is a rather weird type of interaction and the only programming language that normally allows it is assembler. However, in Cobol the `alter` statement allows a program to essentially modify its own code. The problem with this form of interaction is that a bug in one module, the modifying module, appears as a symptom in another, the one being modified.

6.8.2 Entering at the side door

In this type of interaction, one module calls or branches to another at a place other than the normal entry point of the module. Again, this is impossible in most languages, except assembler and Basic. In Cobol, however, a program can be constructed from sections, within which are paragraphs. There is nothing to prevent one section from performing or going to a paragraph within another section. Again, in some dialects of Fortran, a module can be made to have several entry points by the use of the `entry` statement.

The objection to this type of interaction is part of the argument in favor of structured programming. It is only by using modules that have a single entry (at the start) and one exit (at the end) that we can use the power of abstraction to design and understand large programs.

6.8.3 Modifying data within another module

Allowing one module to alter another module's data seems rather less harmful than changing another module's code. However, the objection is the same and the coupling is strong because a fault that appears in one module may be caused by another.

6.8.4 Shared or global data

Shared data is any data that two or more modules have access to. Global data is usually used to mean a collection of data that is accessible to a large number of, perhaps all, modules. The facility to access data in this way is present in nearly all widely used programming languages.

There are several reasons why it is undesirable. First, adding new data to the shared data may cause a name clash with an existing private (local) data item within any one of the modules. Second, if the shared data is used to hold parameters then such items will be subject to the arguments above about altering data within another module.

But the main argument against shared and global data has been discussed above – it makes software much more difficult to understand.

6.8.5 A procedure call with a parameter that is a switch

We have seen that both shared data and unusual transfers of control result in strong coupling between modules. The solution is, of course, to use procedure calls with their attendant parameters. Even so, it is possible to worsen the coupling by passing as a parameter not pure data but an element of control. An example is where a module is passed an indicator telling the procedure which action to take from amongst a number of available actions. (This indicator is sometimes called a switch.) Here is an example of a procedure call on a general-purpose input–output procedure:

```
call io(command, device, buffer, length)
```

The parameter `command` has values 0, 1, 2, etc. that specify whether the operation is a read, write, open, etc. This is undesirable simply because it is unnecessarily complicated. Such a module can be split into several modules, each carrying out a single action. As an alternative to calling a single module and passing it a switch, we can instead call the individual appropriate module, like this:

```
call read(device, buffer, length)
```

We have eliminated a parameter from the interaction and at the same time created well-defined modules, each with a specific function. This contrasts with a single, multipurpose module. Arguably this modularization is easier to understand and maintain.

6.8.6 Procedure calls with parameters that are pure data

Here we have a form of coupling that is nearly ideal. The modules interact in a well-defined manner, suffering none of the weaknesses discussed in the schemes described above. In particular, it is quite clear what information is being communicated between modules. Remember though, that for weak coupling, the number of parameters should be few.

6.8.7 Passing a serial data stream

The weakest (best) coupling is achieved without any transfer of control between modules. This is where one module passes a serial stream of data to another. We can visualize this by imagining that one module outputs information as if to a serial file, and the second module reads it, again as if from a file. The important ingredient is that the outputting module has no access to the data, once it has released it.

This type of interaction is available in some programming languages and most operating systems. Within the core Java API, the classes `java.io.PipedInputStream` and `java.io.PipedOutputStream` allow a producer object (data source) to send a serial stream of data to a consumer object (data sink). Ada allows software to be constructed from concurrent tasks that communicate by message passing. In the Unix system, programs called filters can communicate via "pipes" which again are serial data streams.

Passing a serial data stream is one of the standard design patterns called the filter pattern.

That this form of coupling is best can be shown using information theory.

6.8.8 Conclusion

The conclusion from this review of the types of coupling is that the weakest (best) coupling is to be achieved by using modules that communicate by either

(a) procedure calls with a small number of data parameters, or

(b) passing a serial stream of data from one to the other.

One of the problems of this analysis of types of coupling between modules is that, while it gives us a good qualitative feel for interaction between modules, it gives us no quantitative measure of the interaction.

6.9 ● Cohesion

Cohesion is about unity. How do we group actions together in the best way? How do we group data together in the best way? In the marriage between data and actions, which is dominant and which is subservient, or are they equal partners? Cohesion describes the nature of the interactions *within* a software module. A scheme has been drawn up for classifying the various types of cohesion. These range from low cohesion (undesirable) at the top of the list, to high cohesion (desirable) at the bottom of the list. Some of these types of cohesion are now only of historical interest; current design methods ensure that they just don't arise. The list of categories is:

1. coincidental
2. logical
3. temporal
4. communicational
5. functional.

We will now look in turn at each of the different types of cohesion. In each case our analysis will be based on a statement of what a module will do. We will see that if a module does a mixture of things, then it has poor cohesion. On the other hand, if a module carries out one specific action, then it has good cohesion.

6.9.1 Coincidental cohesion

In coincidental cohesion the components are in the module purely by coincidence. There is no relationship between the components; their coexistence is purely arbitrary. This type of modularity would arise if someone had taken an existing module and arbitrarily chopped it up into modules, say each of one page in length. It would then be impossible to write down a meaningful statement of what each module accomplishes.

6.9.2 Logical cohesion

In logical cohesion the module performs a set of logically similar functions. As an example, we could during the design of a piece of software identify all of the output activities of the system and then combine them into a single module whose function could be described as

```
output anything
```

Such a module is clearly multifunctional. It performs any of a range of (output) operations such as:

- `output text to screen`
- `output line to printer`
- `output record to file`

On the face of it such a module is rational, even logical. It seems like an act of housekeeping has been carried out to collect together logically related activities.

Another example of a logically cohesive module is one that is described by:

```
calculate
```

and which carries out any of a range of mathematical calculations (log, sine, cosine, etc.).

The problem with a logically cohesive module is that it is multifunctional; it carries out any of a menu of actions, rather than one single well-defined action. It is unnecessarily complex. If we need to modify any one ingredient within the module, we will find it hard to ignore the other elements.

6.9.3 Temporal cohesion

In temporal cohesion the module performs a set of actions whose only relationship is that they have to be carried out at the same time. The classic example is a set of initialization operations. Thus a module that carried out the following collection of actions:

```
clear screen
open file
initialize total
```

would exhibit temporal cohesion.

A sequence of initialization actions like this is such a common feature of most programs and systems that it is hard to see how to avoid it. But as we can see in our example, the ingredients are not related to each other at all. The solution is to make the initialization module call other, specialized modules. In the above example the initialization module would be improved if it consisted of the sequence of calls:

```
initialize terminal
initialize files
initialize calculation
```

Initialization plays a role in object-oriented programming. Whenever a new object is created, a constructor procedure is executed to carry out any initialization of the object. A constructor procedure is written as part of the class to which it belongs and has a very specific remit.

6.9.4 Communicational cohesion

In communicational cohesion, functions that act on the same data are grouped together. For example, a module that displays and logs temperature is carrying out two different actions on the temperature data. A similar example is a module that formats and prints total price.

Thus a communicationally cohesive module is described by several verbs and one noun. The weakness of such a module is, again, that it is unnecessarily complex – too many things are being grouped together. The actions can be distinguished and designed as separate modules.

6.9.5 Functional cohesion

Functional cohesion is the best type of cohesion. A module with functional cohesion performs a single, well-defined action on a single subject. Thus a sentence that accurately describes the purpose of the module will have only one verb and a single object that is acted upon by the verb. Here are examples of descriptions of such modules:

- `calculate average`
- `print result`
- `input transaction`
- `open valve`
- `obtain date`

As with the ideas of coupling, if we find that the modules in our software exhibit poor cohesion, the concepts of cohesion do not provide us with a systematic method for improving our structure – they merely tell us how poor our structure is. Another problem with the classification scheme is that it is sometimes very difficult to identify which type of cohesion is present – after all, there does seem to be a very fine line dividing communicational and sequential cohesion. Finally, cohesion is a qualitative assessment of quality – rather than a quantitative measure or metric.

6.10 ● Shaw and Garlan's classification

More recent than the ideas of coupling and cohesion are Shaw and Garlan's ideas on modularity. Their analysis of common software structures suggest that modules typically perform one of the following roles:

- computation only
- memory
- manager
- controller
- link.

A computation-only module retains no data between subsequent uses. Examples are maths routines, and a filter in a Unix filter and pipe scheme.

A memory module maintains a collection of persistent data such as a database or a file system. (Persistent data is data that exists beyond the life of a particular program or module and is normally stored on a backing store medium such as a disk.)

A manager module is an abstract data type, maintaining data and the operations that can be used on it. The classical examples are a stack or a queue.

A controller module controls when other modules are activated or how they interact.

A link module transfers information between other modules. Examples are a user interface (which transfers information between the user of a system and one or more modules) and communication software.

This is a crude and general classification, but it does provide a language for talking about modules. It is part of the move to use design ideas, called design patterns, that are well-established in software engineering, rather than re-inventing the wheel every time that you design a new piece of software.

Shaw and Garlan also analyzed the types of interaction between modules (in a manner reminiscent of the classification scheme for coupling). Their classification for commonly occurring types of interaction between modules is:

● procedure call
● data flow
● implicit invocation
● message passing
● shared data
● instantiation.

This classification system allows for the interacting modules to be running concurrently in a multiprocessing or a multithreading system. Two or more modules can be visualized as running completely simultaneously. In practice, of course, a single processor may be shared amongst the modules. This is the subject of Chapter 15 on parallelism.

The procedure-call mechanism is the obvious one, except that it encompasses remote procedure calling (sometimes called remote method invocation, or RMI). Remote procedure calling occurs when the caller is in a completely different program (or even computer) from the caller.

Data flow connection is where one module sends a serial stream of data to another. The first module writes the data; the second reads it. This is the pipe mechanism of the Unix pipe and filter scheme.

Implicit invocation is event-driven programming; a module is brought to life when some event occurs. This could be an external event, such as the user clicking on a GUI button or an internal event, such as a timer. In implicit invocation, although one module invokes another, the connection is loose and sometimes almost invisible.

In message passing one module sends a message to another. There may be a queue in between the two modules, so that one may continue without waiting for the other.

Shared data has the usual meaning, but the modules may run concurrently with the consequent need for control over access.

Instantiation occurs in object-oriented systems when a module creates a new module (object) as an instance of a class.

SELF TEST QUESTION

6.1 What is the difference between data flow and message passing types of interaction?

6.11 ● Object-oriented programming

In object-oriented programming, procedures and data that are strongly related are grouped together into an object. This matches exactly the ideas of information hiding and encapsulation discussed above. The items within an object are strongly coupled and the object as a whole possesses high cohesion. A well-designed object presents a few, simple interfaces to its clients. The interfaces are those public procedures that are declared to be accessible outside of the object. Thus a well-designed object displays loose coupling. An object can allow clients access to its variables, but this is regarded as poor practice and heavily discouraged.

Object-oriented languages encourage the programmer to describe classes, rather than individual objects. For example, here is the description, in Java, of a graphical object, a ball, which has x and y screen coordinates:

```
class Ball {

    protected int x, y;
    private int radius;
    public void setRadius(int newRadius) {
        radius = newRadius;
    }
    public void setX(int newX) {
        x = newX;
    }
    public void setY(int newY) {
        y = newY;
    }

}
```

Here the private and public elements are clearly distinguished. A third description, pro-tected, means that the item is not accessible to clients but is accessible to subclasses, as we shall see shortly. Not shown in this example are private procedures that are used by a class as necessary to carry out its work.

It is of course possible to miss-use objects, by grouping ingredients that are not related. However it is the purpose of a good design approach to ensure that this does not arise (see Chapter 10).

Object-oriented programming (OOP) completely eliminates global data; all data is encapsulated within objects.

6.11.1 The open-closed principle

If you need to modify a class (or object), there is no need to make a separate edited copy. Instead you can use the inheritance mechanism of OOP. So the original copy of the class remains intact, but is re-used with additional or changed procedures. This is called the open-closed principle. Using the example above, we can create a new class called MovingBall, with additional procedures that cause the ball to move left and right:

```
class MovingBall extends Ball {

    public void moveLeft(int distance) )
        x = x - distance;
    }

    public void moveRight(int distance) {
        x = x + distance;
    }
}
```

The new class MovingBall has all the features of the class Ball, but with two additional procedures. The variables x and y in the superclass are accessible in this subclass because they were declared as protected. MovingBall makes use of Ball without altering it. Thus the modularity and integrity of the original module remain intact. However, inheritance creates an additional type of coupling between a class and its superclasses.

6.12 ● Summary

In this chapter we have discussed a range of considerations that can be taken into account during the design of software. These guidelines help us in three ways:

1. They help us decide what to do during the act of design, guiding us to software that is clear, simple, and flexible.
2. They provide us with criteria for assessing the structure of some completed software.
3. They assist us in restructuring software in order to improve it.

Restricting module size is one crude way of reducing complexity. An extreme view is to restrict all modules to no more than seven statements.

The principle of information hiding holds that data should be inaccessible other than by means of the procedures that are specially provided for accessing the data.

Coupling and cohesion are terms that describe the character of the interaction between modules and within modules, respectively. Coupling and cohesion are complementary. Strong coupling and weak cohesion are bad; weak coupling and strong cohesion are good. Coupling can be categorized into a number of types, ranging from one module altering another module's code to modules communicating by exchanging serial data streams. Types of cohesion can be classified within six categories. Thus coupling and cohesion provide a terminology and a qualitative analysis of modularity.

Object-oriented programming explicitly supports information hiding by the provision of classes and objects.

The ideas in this chapter can be grouped into two areas:

● those that deal with interactions within modules – length, cyclomatic complexity, cohesion

● those that deal with interactions between modules – information hiding, coupling, shared modules.

EXERCISES

6.1   What is modularity and why is it important?

6.2   Argue for and against restricting modules to about seven statements.

Look at the way that the library procedures are called within a library available to you – say the Java library. Assess what forms of coupling are demonstrated by the procedures.

6.3   Write down two different programs to search a table for a desired element. Calculate the cyclomatic complexity of each and hence compare them from the point of view of clarity.

6.4   Examine any software or software design that you have around. How are the modules coupled? What forms of coupling and cohesion are present? Categorize the module types and interconnections according to Shaw and Garlan's schemes. Is information hiding in use? Can the structure be improved?

6.5   Compare and contrast the ideas of coupling and cohesion with Shaw and Garlan's ideas on module types and interconnection.

6.6   Is there any correspondence between:

(a) any one form of cohesion and information hiding?

(b) any form of coupling and information hiding?

6.7   Does functional decomposition tend to lead to modules of a particular form of cohesion? If so, which?

6.8   In functional decomposition (Chapter 7), the modules are functionally independent but they may act upon shared data. Is functional decomposition compatible with information hiding?

6.9 Does the Michael Jackson method (Chapter 8) lead to a program structure that exhibits any particular types of coupling and cohesion? How does information hiding relate to, or contrast with, the Michael Jackson method?

6.10 Does data flow design (Chapter 9) create a program structure that exhibits any particular types of coupling and cohesion?

6.11 Does object-oriented design create software structures that exhibits any particular types of coupling and cohesion?

6.12 Consider a procedural programming language with which you are familiar. What types of coupling are allowed? What types are not permitted?

6.13 Compare and contrast the features for modularity provided by C++, Ada, Java, and Unix.

6.14 What kinds of coupling and cohesion are supported or prevented by declarative programming languages such as functional languages and logic programming languages?

ANSWER TO SELF TEST QUESTION

6.1 Data flow connection normally implies a long stream of serial data with a distinct ending. Message passing is usually intermittent and does not necessarily involve an ending.

FURTHER READING

This is the paper that suggests the small capacity of the human brain when comprehending a set of items as a complete whole. G. A. Miller, The Magical Number Seven, Plus or Minus Two: Limits on our Capacity for Processing Information, *The Psychological Review*, 63 (2), (March 1956), pp. 81–97.

This classic paper introduced the idea of information hiding. D. L. Parnas, On the Criteria to be Used in Decomposing Systems into Modules, *Communications of ACM*, 15 (December 1972), pp. 1053–8. This paper is reprinted in P. Freemen and A. I. Wasserman, *Tutorial on Software Design Techniques*, IEEE, 4th edition, 1983.

This is the book that first introduced the ideas of coupling and cohesion. There is also a treatment of the issue of the optimal size of a module: Edward Yourdon and Larry L. Constantine, *Structured Design*, Prentice Hall, 1979.

This gives a more recent presentation of the ideas of coupling and cohesion: M. Page-Jones, *The Practical Guide to Structured Systems Design*, Yourdon Press, 1980.

Mary Shaw and David Garlan, *Software Architectures. Perspectives on an Emerging Discipline*, Prentice Hall, 1996. This is one of the first books on design patterns (architectures) – general software structures that can be applied to a whole number of software systems. The book also analyses the different mechanisms available for connecting modules.

The filter and pipe form of coupling described in this chapter is cataloged along with others, in: Mark Grand, *Patterns in Java*, vol. 1, John Wiley, 1998.

The ideas of coupling and cohesion have been incorporated into the catalogues of design patterns, as explained in: Mark Grand, *Patterns in Java*, vol. 2, John Wiley, 1999.

Functional decomposition

This chapter explains the method of design known as functional decomposition.

7.1 ● Introduction

Functional decomposition is a method for designing the detailed structure of individual programs or modules. It is also a method for designing the large-scale (architecture) structure of software. As its name suggests, functional decomposition is a method that focuses on the functions, or actions that the software has to carry out. To use the method we first write down, in English, a single-line statement of what the software has to do. For example, suppose we want to write a program to direct a robot to make a cup of instant coffee. We could begin by writing:

```
make a cup of coffee
```

Then we express the problem solution in terms of a sequence of simpler actions:

```
boil water
get a cup
put coffee in cup
add water
add milk
add sugar to taste
```

Next we take each of these statements and write down what it does in greater detail. This process of decomposition or refinement is continued until the solution is expressed in sufficient detail. Usually this is when the solution corresponds to the statements provided in the programming language to be used.

A statement that is to be broken down may be regarded as a call on a procedure (paragraph, subroutine). The set of more elementary steps into which it is decomposed can be viewed as the body of the procedure.

The language that is used to express the solution is called pseudocode (because it is similar in some ways to programming language code), or program design language (PDL). It consists of sequences of (English) sentences, each beginning with a verb. It also involves the approved constructs of structured programming – **if... then... else** for selection or comparison and `while` for repetition. For example, the statement `boil water` above might be refined to:

```
switch on kettle
while water not boiling do
     whistle a tune
endwhile
switch off kettle
```

Again we might refine `add sugar to taste` as:

```
if sugar required
then put sugar in cup
     stir
endif
```

We can restrict ourselves just to `while` and `if` or we can make use of the `repeat`, `for` and `case` constructs.

7.2 ● An example – a video game

In order to illustrate the use of functional decomposition we will design the software for a simple video game, called Breakout. This account can be skipped by the reader who feels that they have a grasp of the method. The game makes use of a screen display and mouse. The screen looks like Figure 7.1.

The screen displays a wall of bricks, a bat (the black rectangle), a ball, and a boundary. The ball bounces around the screen, moving up, down or diagonally, changing direction conventionally when it hits the wall, the boundary, or the bat. The player can move the bat left or right by moving the mouse left or right. The objective is to make the ball hit a brick in the wall. When a brick is struck, it vanishes. When a gap allows the ball to escape the ball breaks out and the player wins the game.

The ball goes out of play when it passes below the bat and the player loses the game. The player is supplied with a succession of four balls. When these have been used, the best score ever attained is displayed.

This completes the specification of the game.

Places on the screen are specified by a pair of (x, y) coordinates. We assume that the software can draw a graphical object at any position on the screen. Similarly a value at

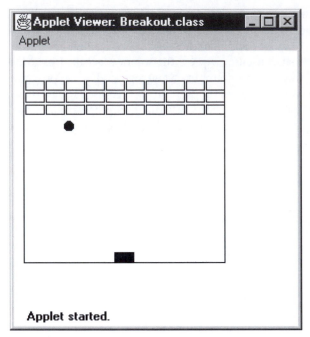

Figure 7.1 Screen for Breakout

any position can be tested using a statement like:

```
if object at (x, y) = brick then ...
```

We will refer to the coordinates of the ball as **xball** and **yball**. We begin with the over-all logic:

```
video game
    draw sides
    draw bat at home position
    while someone wants to play
    do
        draw wall
        play a game
        display biggest score
    endwhile
```

We have delegated detail to statements like:

```
draw sides
```

and we can study and check the design without worrying about detail. We would probably realize that essential steps are missing so that we might amend the above to:

```
video game
    draw sides
    draw bat at home position
    best score := 0
    while someone wants to play
    do
        score := 0
        play a game
        if score > best score
        then best score := score
        endif
        display best score
    endwhile
```

Now that we are satisfied with this, we choose one of the statements and write down what it does in more detail. An obvious candidate is:

```
play a game
    balls left := 4
    while balls left > 0 do
        play a ball
        subtract one from balls left
    endwhile
```

and then:

```
play a ball
    draw wall
    create a new ball
    while ball is in play
    do
        check ball position
        move ball
    endwhile
```

Let us now work on some detail of moving the bat in response to a mouse movement:

```
move bat
    if mouse moved left then move left endif
    if mouse moved right then move right endif
```

which requires:

```
move left
    erase old bat
    if bat position > left wall + 1
    then bat position := bat position - step size
    endif
    draw bat
```

and similarly for move right.

This completes a fair amount of the detail concerned with moving the bat. We can leave further detail for the time being and turn to consider more of the detail of moving the ball.

If we now turn our attention to moving the ball:

```
move ball
      erase ball
      Xball := Xball + Xstep
      Yball := Yball + Ystep
      draw ball at (Xball, Yball)
```

but we have to be careful to check whether it has impacted with something:

```
check ball position
      check out of play
      check sides
      check bat
      check brick
```

We complete the account of this development with just two more pieces:

```
check sides
      if ball at either side
      then Xstep := - Xstep
      endif
      if ball at end boundary
      then Ystep := - Ystep
      endif
check brick
      if object at (Xball+Xstep, Yball+Ystep) is a brick
      then
            erase brick at screen (Xball+Xstep, Yball+Ystep)
            add one to score
            Ystep := - Ystep
            subtract one from bricks left
      endif
```

There is still some way to go with this particular design, but this much gives the flavor of the design and of the method. Notice how the design is refined again and again. Notice how, throughout, we can check the design without having to take account of a lot of unnecessary detail. Notice the informality of the statements used; we can simply make up new actions as necessary, but still within the discipline of the control structures – sequence, `if` and `while`.

7.3 ● More about the method

One way of visualizing this method is to see that at any stage of decomposition the solution is expressed in terms of operations that are assumed to be available and provided by an abstract (or virtual) machine, like a very high-level programming language. This is the idea of "levels of abstraction." In order to design and understand a solution at any one level of detail it is not necessary to understand anything about how the levels beneath work. We know *what* they do, but not *how* they do it. Thus the human mind has a much better chance of understanding the solution and therefore of getting it right.

One approach to functional decomposition is to refine the software design level-by-level. The software structure can be visualized as an upside-down tree – always with a very flat top that grows downwards uniformly. This is the *breadth-first* approach to design; it matches the strict, abstract-machine view of software design, described above.

An alternative approach is to pursue one of the branches of the tree, leaving the others stunted until later. (This is called *depth first*.) Our motive for doing this might be to explore what seems to be a difficult part of the software. We might thereby hope to gain insights that guide us in refining the rest of the structure.

The informality of a pseudocode design makes it impractical to verify its correctness in a formal way. However, the use of abstraction facilitates informal checking. Have all the right steps been included and in the right order? Is the algorithm complete, or is something missing? Because each piece of pseudocode is written according to structured programming, it has only one entry and exit. It is therefore easier to check.

This idea of trying to ignore the detail of lower levels of the design is easier said than done and takes some nerve. In a sense it is a real test of whether we believe software design is worthwhile and whether we can resist the temptation to rush on to coding pieces of the software. During problem solving, the human mind undoubtedly makes wide-ranging leaps over lots of aspects of a problem. So it is debatable whether people can actually think strictly in this manner. Whatever the design method that they claim to use, it is more likely, perhaps, that people design software using some personal, semi-intuitive method and afterwards tidy up the design so that it looks as though it was created in a systematic way.

7.4 ● What about data?

What is the role of data in the method? It does rather play second fiddle to the actions that have to be taken. The making of the cup of coffee illustrates that by concentrating on what the software should do, considerations of data are ignored, or rather postponed. The idea is that the data emerges during the decomposition as it becomes evident what is necessary and what needs to be done with it. We defer decisions about pieces of data and the structure of information until we have a very clear knowledge of what operations have to be performed on them. When that stage is reached we can design data which is tailored precisely to the operations.

There is a possible problem here. Suppose a program is written in this way and later needs modifying. What happens if some new operation on the data is required? Remember that the data was designed with the old operations in mind, so it may not be in a convenient form for the new.

Another question about functional decomposition is whether it is actually possible to delay thinking about data in this way.

7.5 ● Alternative solutions

A major characteristic of functional decomposition is its flexibility, or (put another way) its lack of guidance. This can be seen by looking at an example. Consider a program that is to input 80 character lines of text, consisting of words and spaces, and is required to convert them into 120 character lines, containing as many words as will fit. We might begin like this:

```
initialize
while more input lines
do
     input a line
     process a line
endwhile
clean up
```

Or we could start:

```
initialize
while more input information
do
     assemble an output line
     output the line
endwhile
clean up
```

Or a third start might be:

```
initialize
extract first word
while more words
do
     dispose of word
     extract next word
endwhile
clean up
```

Each of these three solutions could be refined to arrive at a different program. According to functional decomposition they are all reasonable. The method gives us no guidance as to which of the three is best. The only way to find out is to refine all three solutions (along with any others) to a level of detail at which we can make a reasoned choice between them. The choice might be made on the basis of clarity and simplicity, performance, or some other criteria. But functional decomposition, by itself, gives no guidance for selecting the best solution.

Because there is always more than one solution to a problem – more than one design that meets the specification – the user of functional decomposition is duty bound to find not just one solution, but to find the best solution. The criteria for the "best" solution will differ from program to program – sometimes it will be maximum clarity, sometimes it will be optimum performance. If in pursuing one design it turns out to be unsatisfactory, we can retrace the design level-by-level, considering alternatives at each level. It will often prove desirable to replace whole subtrees in this manner. This process is largely under control because we know which part of the structure we are looking at, and it has only one entry and exit point.

7.6 ● The place of functional decomposition

Arguably functional decomposition was the first truly systematic method for software design. It is associated with the names Dijkstra and Wirth. It evolved hand-in-hand with the ideas of structured programming in the 1960s. Since then other methods that claim to involve structured programming have been devised, so that nowadays functional decomposition is just one variety of structured programming.

There is often a lot of confusion about the terminology surrounding structured programming and top-down methods. Let us try to clarify the situation. Functional decomposition is a top-down method, since it starts with the overall task of the software. But it is not unique in this respect. Functional decomposition is also called *stepwise refinement*, though it is, of course, refinement of function.

Unlike some other methods, this one has not been packaged and marketed. Perhaps this is because it originated in academic circles and perhaps because it is a method that is not so well defined as others. There is little hard evidence of how much it is used, though it may well be widely used under different names.

7.7 ● Discussion

Functional decomposition concentrates almost exclusively on defining the functions (the actions) that software must take. The flexibility of functional decomposition means that it can be used in the design of software for any type of application; it is generally applicable. But because it concentrates on the actions that the software has to take, it is perhaps most useful for problems in which the procedural steps are clearly evident. One such area is numerical computation, like a program to calculate a square root. Another is the control of a sequential process, like a washing machine.

Functional decomposition can be used to design the detailed, low-level structure of a program. It can also be used to design the high-level or architectural structure of software. Thus it is applicable to both small and large-scale software.

Overall, how good is this method? If we want a completely well-defined method that we can use almost without thinking, then it is inadequate, since its use requires considerable skill. On the other hand it is an excellent approach if we want a method that guides our thinking but allows us plenty of scope for creativity. In a sense, therefore, the method is not as advanced as some. For example, Jackson's method takes the programmer from a description of the structure of the data or files that the program is to act upon, via a number of fairly precise steps to the program design. By contrast, the use of functional decomposition encourages (some would say necessitates) the use of creativity and imagination in devising software structures. Its use also needs careful judgment in selecting the best structure from amongst any alternatives found. In other words it tends to foster interest in and enjoyment of programming.

In summary, functional decomposition is a general-purpose method for software design, based around structured programming, but in allowing the development of alternative designs for the same problem it poses several unanswered questions:

1. Where do we get the inspiration for alternative designs?
2. How do we choose between designs?
3. How do we know that we have arrived at the best possible design?

We have to look to other sources of ideas to answer these questions. These issues have led some to say that functional decomposition is not really a serious method.

7.8 ● Summary

Functional decomposition proceeds by starting with a single, grand statement of what the piece of software is to do. This is next rewritten as a series of simpler steps using pseudocode (program design language) as a notation. Pseudocode consists of English imperative sentences written as sequences, with `if` statements or with `while` statements. The designs are refined (rewritten as more primitive steps) until the required level of detail is achieved.

The method makes direct use of the power of abstraction provided by structured programming, while requiring significant creativity and judgment to be employed. It is applicable to the full range of computer application areas.

EXERCISES

7.1 Complete the design of the video game program.

7.2 Use functional decomposition to design the software for each of the following:

   (a) a microcomputer-controlled washing machine

   (b) a system to control a power station

   (c) software to calculate and print an organization's payroll

   (d) a general-purpose operating system or database management system

   (e) a system to monitor and control medical equipment

   (f) a mathematical calculation.

7.3 What characteristics should a good software design method have? Does the functional decomposition exhibit them?

FURTHER READING

Arguably the most important book about structured programming is: O. J. Dahl, E. W. Dijkstra and C. A. R. Hoare, *Structured Programming*, Academic Press, London, 1972.

8

Data structure design: The Michael Jackson program design method (JSP)

This chapter explains how to use the Michael Jackson (data structure design) method for program design.

8.1 ● Introduction

Starting with the specification of a program, this method, via a series of steps, leads to a detailed design, expressed in pseudocode. The method is variously called the Michael Jackson program design method (after the name of its inventor), Jackson Structured Programming (JSP), and data structure design.

The basic idea behind the Michael Jackson method is that the structure of a program should match the structure of the information that the program is going to act on. To get a feel for how this can be done, let us look at a few simple examples.

First, suppose we want a program to add a set of numbers held in an array, and terminated by a negative number. Here's some sample data:

```
29 67 93 55 -10
```

With experience of programming, we can, of course, immediately visualize the structure of this program. Its main feature is a `while` loop. But a more rigorous way of looking at the design is to realize that because there is a repetition in the data, there must be a corresponding repetition in the program. Thus we have gone from the data structure to the program structure.

Consider a program that is to print a bank statement. The bank statement will be printed on a number of pages. Each page has a heading, a series of ordinary lines (representing transactions) and a summary line. Ignore, for the time being, the structure of any input data. Again with some experience of programming, we can visualize that we will need statements to print a heading, print a transaction line, and so on. But we can also see that we will need:

- a loop to print a number of pages
- a loop to print the set of transaction lines on each page.

You can see that this description of the program structure matches the structure of the report. What we have done is to derive the structure of the program from what we know about the structure of the report.

These small examples show how it is possible to approach program design using the structure of data. We will return to these examples later, showing exactly how the Jackson method treats them.

8.2 ● A simple example

Let us consider the design of a program to draw the following pattern on a VDU screen. We will assume that, in drawing this pattern, the only possible cursor movements are across the screen from left to right, and down to the beginning of a new line.

```
    *
   * * *
  * * * * *
  * * * * *
   * * *
    *
```

The first step in the method is to analyze and describe the structure of the information that the program is to process (in this case produce). The product of this step is called a data structure diagram. The diagram for the picture is given in Figure 8.1.

In English, this reads:

- The picture consists of the top half followed by the middle, followed by the bottom half
- The top half consists of a line of asterisks, which is repeated. The bottom half also consists of a line of asterisks which is repeated.

In general, the diagrammatic notation has the following meaning.

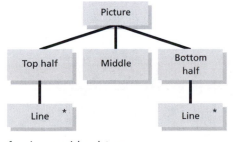

Figure 8.1 Structure chart for the asterisks picture

Figure 8.2 A consists of B

Consists of

A line drawn downwards below a box means "consists of." Thus Figure 8.2 shows that A consists of B.

Sequence

Boxes at the same level denote a sequence. Figure 8.3 shows that A consists of B followed by C.

Repetition

A "*" in a box signifies zero or more occurrences of the component. Figure 8.4 shows that A consists of B repeated zero or more times.

Notice that the data structure is described (decomposed or refined) in a top-down, hierarchical fashion.

Having now described the data structure, the next step is to convert it into a program structure. This is easy because, remember, the program structure must correspond to the data structure. So all we have to do is to write "process" in every box of the data structure diagram. We thereby obtain a "program structure diagram." For our program this is shown in Figure 8.5.

A program structure diagram like this is interpreted as follows:

● The program as a whole (represented by the box at the top) consists of (lines leading downwards) a sequence of operations (boxes alongside one another).

● Sometimes a program component is to be repeatedly executed (a "*" in the box).

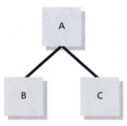

Figure 8.3 A consists of B followed by C

Figure 8.4 A consists of B repeated

The next step is to write down (in any order) a list of all the elementary operations that the program will have to carry out. This is probably the least well-defined part of the method – it does not tell us how to determine what these actions should be. For the program we are working on they are:

1. display n asterisks
2. display blank line
3. display s spaces
4. increment s
5. decrement s
6. increment n
7. decrement n
8. initialize n and s
9. new line.

For later reference, we number the operations, but the ordering is not significant.

Next each of these operations is placed in its appropriate position in the program structure diagram. For example, operation 2 needs to be done once, for the middle of the picture. It is therefore associated with the box labeled "process middle." Similarly, operation 1 is associated with the component "process line" (Figure 8.6).

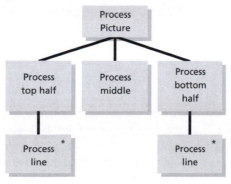

Figure 8.5 Program structure diagram for the asterisks picture program

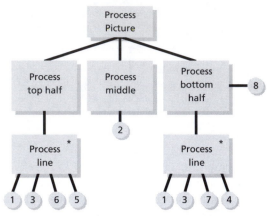

Figure 8.6 Annotated program structure diagram

This act of associating operations with positions is not automatic; instead, as indicated, judgment has to be employed.

Now comes the final step of transforming the program structure diagram into pseudocode. The method has its own notation for pseudocode, called *schematic logic*, which is essentially the same as other program design languages. Expressed in our notation, the structure of our example program is:

```
initialize n and s
while more lines do
    display s spaces
    display n asterisks
    new line
    decrement s
    increment n
endwhile

display blank line
initialize n and s
while more lines do
    display s spaces
    display n asterisks
    new line
    decrement n
    increment s
endwhile
```

To derive this pseudocode from the diagram, start with the box at the top of the diagram and write down its elementary operations. Then indent the code across the page and go down a level on the diagram. Now write down the operations and structures present at this level. Repeatedly go down a level, indenting the code for each new level. This transformation is straightforward and mechanical.

We have now arrived at a program design, capable of being readily translated into most conventional programming languages.

To sum up, the steps we have taken are:

1. Draw a diagram showing the structure of the file.
2. Derive the corresponding program structure diagram.
3. Write down the elementary operations that the program will have to carry out.
4. Place the operations on the program structure diagram.
5. Derive the schematic logic of the program.

Exercises

1. Design a program to draw a pine tree like this:

```
  *
 ***
*****
  *
```

2. Design a program to display a multiplication table, such as young children use. For example, the table for numbers up to 6 is:

	1	2	3	4	5	6
1	1	2	3	4	5	6
2	2	4	6	8	10	12
3	3	6	9	12	15	18
4	4	8	12	16	20	24
5	5	10	15	20	25	30
6	6	12	18	24	30	36

The program should produce a table of any size, specified by an integer input from the keyboard.

3. Design a program to create this pattern of asterisks:

```
*
**
***
****
*
**
***
****
*
**
***
****
```

with the number of repetitions input initially from the keyboard.

4. Design a program to create the following pattern on a VDU screen:

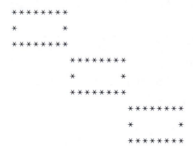

```
********
*      *
********
        ********
        *      *
        ********
                ********
                *      *
                ********
```

with a number of repetitions input as an integer from the keyboard.

5. JSP only makes use of `while`; it ignores `for`. Discussion: why do you think this might be?

8.3 ● Processing input files

To understand how to input and process information from a file, consider the following problem:

Design a program to add up a series of numbers, held in a serial file and ending with a negative number.

The data structure diagram is given in Figure 8.7. And the corresponding program structure diagram is given in Figure 8.8.

We can write down the elementary operations as:

1. get next number
2. add number to sum
3. initialize sum
4. display sum

attach them to the program structure diagram, and derive the pseudocode design:

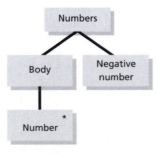

Figure 8.7

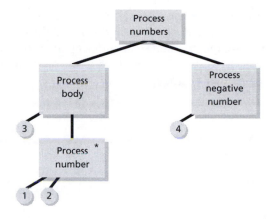

Figure 8.8

```
sum := 0
get first number
while number not negative
do
    add number to sum
    get next number
endwhile
display sum
```

So far there is nothing new here; we have used the method as before. There is just one small point to note. JSP did not help us to realize that we would need an initial operation before the loop, followed by another operation at the end of each loop. JSP gave us the structure or skeleton in which we could place the elementary operations – it did not give us the fine detail.

Here now is a new ingredient of JSP, illustrated by this problem:

A serial file consists of records. Each record describes a person. Design a program to count the number of males and the number of females.

The data structure diagram is given in Figure 8.9.

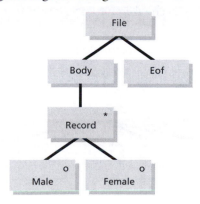

Figure 8.9

What is new here is the boxes with the letter "o" in them (short for or) to indicate alternatives. Such boxes are written alongside each other, and there may be any number of alternatives. We now derive the program structure diagram as before.

After writing down operations and assigning them to the program structure diagram, we arrive at the following pseudocode design:

```
open file
initialize counts
while not end of file
do
    read record
    if record = male
    then increment male-count
    else increment female-count
    endif
endwhile
display counts
close file
```

realizing that the boxes with alternatives in them become `if...then...else` statements.

We have now considered and used all the notations used by the Jackson method. They are: sequence, selection, repetition, and hierarchy.

8.4 ● Physical and logical structures

When we go about describing data we don't always necessarily describe it exactly as it first looks. Sometimes we take a view that is different from its actual (physical) structure in order to view the data according to how we need to process it (the logical structure).

The physical structure of the data describes the structure without considering the processing requirements of the problem (i.e. without considering the particular use to which the data may be put).

The logical structure of the data describes the structure of the data in which the processing requirements have been taken into consideration.

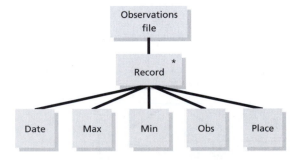

Figure 8.10

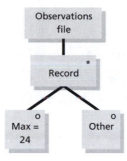

Figure 8.11

The following example is used to illustrate the difference between physical and logical structures.

A file consists of a series of weather observation records; each record contains the following information:

```
date max-temp min-temp observer place
```

The data structure diagram in Figure 8.10 describes the data as specified above – the physical structure.

Suppose that we want to extract information from the file and that we need:

(a) to count the number of days with a max-temp of 24 degrees

(b) to count the number of days the max-temp observed by someone called Jones lies in the range from 18 to 25 degrees.

The data structure diagrams for each of these different processing requirements are shown in Figures 8.11 and 8.12. These describe the different logical views, relevant to the information required.

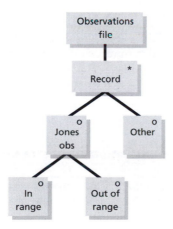

Figure 8.12

SELF TEST QUESTION

8.1 Draw the data structure diagram for the data as seen by a program that needs to extract records describing observations made in Los Angeles during 2002.

Exercises

1. Complete the designs of the three data analysis programs, using the data structure diagrams given above.

2. Design a program to count the number of words in a piece of text which ends with the word "amen." Assume the existence of a procedure to input the next word. Do not count the word "amen" in the total.

3. Design a program to calculate the average word length in a piece of text. The text ends with an asterisk.

4. Design a program to count the percentage occurrence of the letter "e" in a piece of text. The text ends with an asterisk. Assume the existence of a procedure to input the next character.

5. Design a program that acts as a calculator by accepting strings like this:

   ```
   34 + 234 - 71 * 6
   ```

   and outputting the answer. The strings consist of any number of integers and operators (+, -, *, /), evaluated left to right. Assume a perfect typist, who makes no mistakes. (This is similar to a formula entered into a spreadsheet cell.)

6. A file describes issues and receipts of stock. Each record describes either an issue or a receipt and includes the stock number and amount. The file is sorted so that transactions describing the same stock item are grouped together. Count the number of stock items and the number of receipts in the file.

7. Design a program to count the number of blocks of information received down a communication line. The program reads one character or byte of information at a time. A block starts with the character F4 (hex), followed by any number of data bytes, followed by F2 (hex). The stream of blocks is terminated by the character F1 (hex).

8.5 ● Processing several input and output streams

So far we have just looked at programs that process a single input or a single output stream. Now we turn to the more common situation of multiple streams. The method is basically the same, except that we will have to describe all of the streams, and make the program structure reflect them all.

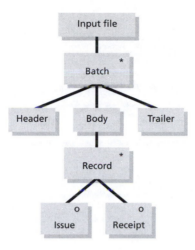

Figure 8.13

The basic principle, as always with the Jackson method, is that the program structure should reflect the structures of all the input and output streams. So we draw a data structure diagram for each input and output file, and then devise a program structure that incorporates all aspects of all of the data structure diagrams.

Consider the following problem.

A serial file describes issues and receipts of stock. Transactions are grouped into batches. A batch consists of transactions describing the same stock item. Each transaction describes either an issue or a receipt of stock. A batch starts with a header record and ends with a trailer record. Design a program to create a summary report showing the overall change in each item. Ignore headings, new pages, etc. in the report.

The data structure diagrams are given in Figures 8.13 and 8.14.

We now look for correspondences between the two diagrams. In our example, the report (as a whole) corresponds to the input file (as a whole). Each summary line in the report matches a batch in the input file. So we can draw a single, composite program structure diagram as in Figure 8.15.

Writing down operations, attaching them to the program structure diagram, and translating into pseudocode, gives:

Figure 8.14

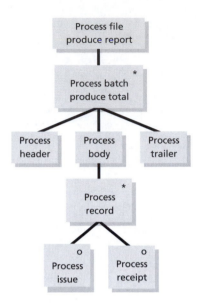

Figure 8.15

```
open files
read header record
while not end of file
do
     total := 0
     read record
     while not end of batch
     do
          update total
          read record
     endwhile
     display total
     read header record
endwhile
close files
```

Thus we have seen that, where a program processes more than one file, the method is essentially unchanged – the important step is to see the correspondences between the file structures and hence derive a compatible program structure.

Here is another example in order to emphasize the point.

The firm of Cheetham and Diddlum keeps a file of its employees. Each record in the file corresponds to an employee and has the following format:

```
employee name age skill1 skill2 skill3
```

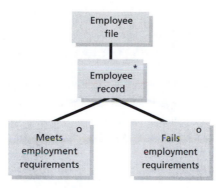

Figure 8.16

The firm decides on a rationalization program (i.e. to sack some of its workers). The basis on which it retains workers is as follows:

EITHER
the worker must be under the age of 25 and possess 2 of the 3 required skills
OR
the worker must be 25 or older and possess all three skills.

The firm requires a program to process the input file to produce an output report. The report consists of a header and a list of names of the sacked workers. At the end of the report, the program must also print the total number of workers who have been sacked.
    As before the initial steps of the Jackson method are to:

1. Draw structure charts to reflect the logical structure of the employee file and the report.
2. State the correspondences.
3. Derive an outline program structure chart.

    The program structure charts are shown in Figures 8.16–8.18 and it is left as an exercise for the reader to complete the program design.

Figure 8.17

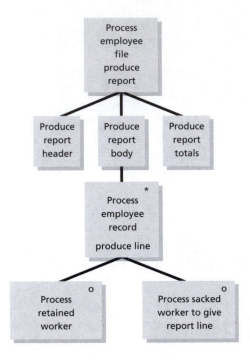

Figure 8.18

Exercises

1. A serial file consists of batches of records. Each record in a batch has the same key value. There are no batch headers and trailers. Design a program to create a report giving a count of the number of records in each batch.

2. A data transmission from a remote computer consists of a series of messages. Each message consists of:

   ● a header, which is any number of SYN bytes

   ● a control block, starting with an F4 (hexadecimal) byte, and ending with F5 (hexadecimal); it contains any number of bytes (which might be control information, e.g. to open an input–output device)

   ● any number of data bytes, starting with F1 (hexadecimal), and ending with F2 (hexadecimal).

   Any of the above three sections can be missing.

   Messages must be processed in this way:

   ● Store any control bytes in an array. When the block is complete, call an already-written procedure called `obey-control`.

   ● Every data byte should be displayed on a VDU.

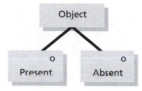

Figure 8.19

Assume that a `read-byte` operation is available to obtain a byte from the remote computer. (Hint: if an object may or may not be present, it can be diagrammed as in Figure 8.19.)

3. Complete the program design for the Cheetham and Diddlum system, by writing down the elementary operations, assigning them to the program structure chart and deriving the pseudocode.

8.6 ● Structure clashes

In a minority of problems, the two or more data structures involved cannot be mapped on to a single program structure. This situation is termed by Jackson a "structure clash." It happens if we try to use the method to design a program to solve the following problem.

Design a program that inputs records consisting of 80-character lines of words and spaces. The output is to be lines of 47 characters, with just one space between words.

This problem looks innocuous enough. But it is more complex than it looks. (Have a go if you don't agree!) A problem arises in trying to fit words from the input file neatly into lines in the output file. Figures 8.20 and 8.21 show the data structure diagrams for the input and output files. Superficially they look the same. But a line in the input file does not correspond to a line in the output file. The two structures are fundamentally irreconcilable and we cannot derive a single program structure. This situation is called a *structure clash*.

Although it is difficult to derive a single program structure from the data structure diagrams, we can instead visualize two programs:

● Program 1, the `breaker`, that reads the input file, recognizes words, and produces a file that consists just of words.

Figure 8.20

Figure 8.21

● Program 2, the **builder**, that takes the file of words created by program 1 and builds it into lines of the required width.

We now have two programs together with a file that acts as an intermediary between the programs.

As seen by the **breaker**, Figure 8.22 shows the data structure diagram for the intermediate file, and it is straightforward to derive the program structure diagram (Figure 8.23).

Similarly, Figure 8.24 shows the structure of the intermediate file as seen by the second program, the **builder**, and again it is easy to derive the program structure diagram for program 2, the **builder** (Figure 8.25).

Thus by introducing the intermediate file we have eradicated the structure clash. There is now a clear correspondence both between the input file and the intermediate file and between the intermediate file and the output file. You can see that choosing a suitable intermediate file is a crucial decision.

From the program structure diagrams we can derive the pseudocode for each of the two programs.

Program 1 (the breaker)

```
open files
read line
while not end of file do
    while not end of line do
        extract next word
        write word
    endwhile
    read next line
endwhile
close files
```

Figure 8.22

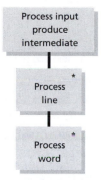

Figure 8.23 Program structure diagram for the breaker program

Figure 8.24

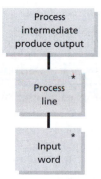

Figure 8.25 Program structure diagram for the builder program

To avoid being distracted by the detail, we have left the pseudocode with operations like `extract next word` in it. Operations like this would probably involve detailed actions on array subscripts.

Program 2 (the builder)

```
open files
read word
while more words
do
    while line not full
            and more words
    do
        insert word into line
        read word
    endwhile
    output line
endwhile
close files
```

We began with the need to construct a single program. In order to eliminate the structure clash, we have instead created two programs, plus an intermediate file. But, at least, we have solved the problem in a fairly systematic manner.

Let us review the situation so far. We drew the data structure diagrams, but then saw the clash between the structures. We resolved the situation by identifying two separate programs that together perform the required task. What method do we use to do this? Jackson says that we examine the two file structures and identify a component that is common to both. (In the example program, this is a word of the text.) This common element is the substance of the intermediate file and is the key to dealing with a structure clash.

What do we do next ? We have three options open to us.

First, we might decide that we can live with the situation – two programs with an intermediate file. Perhaps the overhead of additional input–output operations on the intermediate file is tolerable. (On the other hand, the effect on machine performance might be unacceptable.)

The second option requires special operating system or programming language facilities. In Unix, the facility is provided to construct software as collections of programs, called *filters*, that pass data to and from each other as serial streams called *pipes*. There is minimal performance penalty in doing this and the bonus is high modularity. DOS also supports a kind of pipe facility, but the performance of the mechanism is degraded because of the use of temporary intermediate files.

For the above problem, we write each of the two programs and then run them with a pipe in between, using the Unix command:

```
breaker < InputFile | builder > OutputFile
```

or the DOS command:

```
InputFile | breaker | builder > OutputFile
```

in which the symbol | means that the output from the filter (program) `breaker` is used as input to the program (filter) `builder`.

Another approach is to use a programming language, like Ada or Java, in which a program can be written as a collection of tasks that execute in parallel, communicating by means of serial streams of messages.

The third and final option is to take the two programs and convert them back into a single program, eliminating the intermediate file. To do this, we take either one and transform it into a subroutine of the other. This process is known as *inversion*. We will not pursue this interesting technique within this book.

On the face of it, structure clashes and program inversion seem to be very complicated. So why bother? Jackson argues that structure clashes are not an invention of his, but a characteristic inherent in certain problems. Whichever method that was used to design this program, the same essential characteristic of the problem has to be overcome. The Jackson method has therefore enabled us to gain a fundamental insight into problem solving.

In summary, the Jackson method accommodates structure clashes like this. Try to identify an element of data that is common to both the input file and the output file. In the example problem it is a word of text. Split the required program into two programs – one that converts the input file into an intermediate file that consists of the common data items (words in our example) and the second that converts the intermediate file into the required output. Now each of the two programs can be designed according to the normal Jackson method, since there is no structure clash in either of them. We have now ended up with two programs, where we wanted only one. From here there are three options open to us:

1. Tolerate the performance penalties.

2. Use an operating system or programming language that provides the facility for programs to exchange serial streams of data.

3. Transform one program into a subroutine of the other (inversion).

Exercise

A serial file consists of batches of transactions. Each batch begins with a batch header record and ends with a batch trailer record. Within each batch is a number of transaction records. A report is required. For each batch, the report looks like this:

> a blank line
> batch header
> formatted transaction lines
> blank line
> batch summary line.

Each page of the report is to have a heading consisting of the report name and a page number. Each page should also have a page footing. A page can accommodate 40 lines.

8.7 ● Discussion and evaluation

8.7.1 Theoretical perspective

The basis of the Jackson method is this. What a program is to do, its specification, is completely defined by the nature of its input and output data. In other words, the problem being solved is determined by this data. This is particularly evident in data processing. It is a short step to say that the *structure* of a program should be dictated by the structure of its inputs and outputs. Specification determines design. This is the reasoning behind the method.

The hypothesis that program structure and data structure can, and indeed should, match constitutes a strong statement about the symbiotic relationship between actions and data within programs. Jackson even goes so far as to say that his method not only produces the best design for a program but that it creates the *right* program.

The correspondence between the problem to be solved (in this case the structure of the input and output files) and the structure of the program is termed *proximity*. It has an important implication. If there is a small change to the structure of the data, there should only need to be a correspondingly small change to the program, and vice versa – if there is a large change to the structure of the data. This means that in maintenance, the amount of effort needed should match the extent of the changes to the data that are requested. This makes a lot of sense to a client who has no understanding of the trials involved in modifying programs. Sadly it is often the case that someone (a user) requests what they perceive as a small change to a program, only to be told by the developer that it will take a long time (and cost a lot).

8.7.2 Degree of systematization

The Jackson method can reasonably claim to be the most systematic program design method currently available. It consists of a number of distinct steps, each of which produces a definite piece of paper. The following claims have been made of the method:

● noninspirational – use of the method depends little or not at all on invention or insight

● rational – it is based on reasoned principles (structured programming and program structure based on data structure)

● teachable – people can be taught the method, because it consists of well-defined steps

● consistent – given a single program specification, two different people will come up with the same program design.

● simple and easy to use

● produces designs that can be implemented in any programming language.

While these characteristics can be regarded as advantages, they can also be seen as a challenge to the traditional skills associated with programming. It is also highly contentious to say that the Jackson method is completely noninspirational and rational. In particular, some of the steps arguably require a good deal of insight and creativity – for example, drawing the data structure diagram, identifying the elementary operations, and placing the operations on the program structure diagram.

Because some of the steps in the Jackson method are well defined, tools to support the method are easy to produce (see Further Reading).

8.7.3 Applicability

Jackson claims that his method is generally applicable to all types of problems, including process control and scientific programs. But most of the literature on the method concentrates on serial file processing (batch data processing); few examples are given of the use of the method in other situations.

We can assess how useful this method is for designing computational programs by considering an example. If we think about a program to calculate the square root of a number, then the input has a very simple structure and so has the output. They are both merely single numbers. There is very little information upon which to base a program structure and no guidance for devising some iterative algorithm that calculates successively better and better approximations to the solution. Thus it is unlikely that the Jackson method can be used to solve problems of this type.

8.7.4 The role of JSP

JSP was born in the era of punched cards, when serial files were the norm, whereas we now live in an era of on-line systems, where random access files are more common. Therefore perhaps this method is not as important as it once was. But this ignores the tremendous importance of serial files to hold important information like graphics (for example JPEG and GIF formats), sound files (for example MIDI), files sent to printers (for example PostScript format), Web pages involving HTML, spreadsheet files, and word processor files. Gunter Born's book (see Further Reading) lists hundreds of (serial) file types that need the system programmer's attention. So, for example, if you needed to write a program to convert a file in Microsoft format to an Apple Macintosh format, JSP would probably be of help. But perhaps the ultimate tribute to the method is the use of an approach used in compiler writing called *recursive descent*. In recursive descent the algorithm is designed so as to match the structure of the programming language and thus the structure of the input data that is being analyzed.

Surveys indicate that in the UK and Western Europe, the Jackson method is widely used. In North America, it is used rather less widely.

In a radical development of his program design method, Jackson has proposed a method for the complete process of system development, not just program design. The approach, called Jackson System Development (JSD), completely denies the classical "life cycle" approach to development – analysis, followed by design, followed by module design. The method is based on building a model of the system that the software is to interact with. A model consists of parallel processes that interact by exchanging data. A discussion of the method is outside the scope of this book.

8.8 ● Summary

The basis of the Michael Jackson method is that the structure of a program can be derived from the structure of the files that the program acts upon or creates. The method uses a diagrammatic notation for file and program structures and its own version of pseudocode (PDL). Using these notations as documentation, the method proceeds step-by-step from descriptions of the file structures to a design for the program structure.

The steps are:

1. Draw a diagram (a data structure diagram) describing the structure of each of the files that the program uses.
2. Derive a single program structure diagram from the set of data structure diagrams.
3. Write down the elementary operations that the program will have to carry out.
4. Associate the elementary operations with their appropriate positions in the program structure diagram.
5. Transform the program structure diagram into schematic logic.

The notation for diagramming provides for:

● selection (alternatives)
● iteration (repetition)
● sequence
● hierarchical structure.

In a minority of cases, a problem will exhibit an incompatibility between the structures of two of its inputs or outputs. This is known as a structure clash. The method incorporates a scheme for dealing with structure clashes.

The main advantages of the method are:

(a) There is high "proximity" between the structure of the program and the structure of the files. Hence a minor change to a file structure will lead only to a minor change in the program.

(b) There is a series of well-defined steps leading from the specification to the design. Each stage creates a well-defined product.

EXERCISES

Note that the exercises that ask the reader to use the Jackson method are dispersed throughout the text at appropriate points. The following questions address more general issues.

8.1 Consider the design of a program to compute the square root of a number that is input as data. Try to draw the data structure diagrams for the input and output and therefore to use JSP. What difficulties do you meet? What is the implication for the scope of use of JSP?

8.2 What are the differences between JSP and the other software design methods described in this book?

8.3 What characteristics should a good program design method have? Does the Michael Jackson method exhibit these characteristics?

8.4 Some proponents of the Michael Jackson method claim that it is "noninspirational." How much inspiration do you think is required in using the method?

8.5 What are the advantages and disadvantages of JSP?

8.6 Jackson diagrams allow the specification of sequence, selection, and iteration. What other control structures do you know of? Why do you think JSP doesn't provide for them? Alternatively, how could it provide for them? (Hint: what about recursion?)

8.7 Suggest facilities for a software tool that could assist in using JSP.

8.8 Evaluate Data Structure Design under the following headings:

● Special features and strengths
● Weaknesses
● Philosophy/perspective?
● Systematic?
● Appropriate applications
● Inappropriate applications
● Is the method top-down, bottom-up, or something else?
● Good for large-scale design?
● Good for small-scale design?
● Can tools assist in using the method?

ANSWER TO SELF TEST QUESTION

8.1

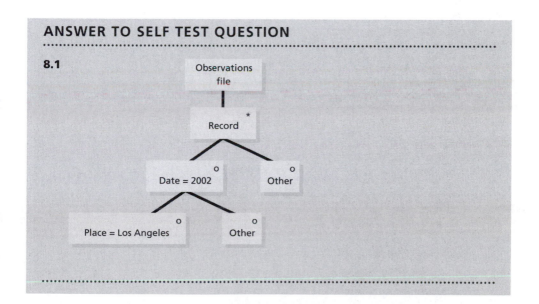

FURTHER READING

The main reference on this method is: M. J. Jackson, *Principles of Program Design*, Academic Press, 1975.

There is another, very readable account of the method in slightly simpler form in: M. J. King and J. P. Pardoe, *Program Design Using JSP – A Practical Introduction*, Macmillan, 1985.

Another account is in: D. King, *Creating Effective Software: Computer Program Design using the Michael Jackson Method*, Prentice Hall, 1988.

The use of the method to design an application program to access a database is described in: R. S. Burgess, Designing Codasyl Database Programs using JSP, *Information and Software Technology*, 29 (3) (April 1987).

A software development environment that is tailored to the Jackson method is described in: A. G. Sutcliffe and C. G. Davies, MAJIC – An Integrated Program Support Environment, *Information and Software Technology*, 29 (3) (April 1987).

Jackson System Development (JSD) is described in: M. Jackson, *System Development*, Prentice Hall International, 1983.

Another, much more concise, explanation is given in: J. R. Cameron, An Overview of JSD, *IEEE Trans on Software Engineering*, SE-12 (2) (Feb 1986), pp. 222–40.

There is another program design method that derives program structure from data structure. It is associated with the names Warnier and Orr and is described in J. D. Warnier, *Logical Construction of Programs*, Van Nostrand Reinhold, 1974.

Read all about the many serial file formats in mainstream use in: Gunter Born, *The File Formats Handbook*, International Thomson Publishing, 1995.

9

Data flow design

This chapter explains how to use the data flow method for software design.

9.1 ● Introduction

Data flow design is a method for carrying out the architectural (large-scale) design of software. It is therefore most useful in designing medium-to-large programs. Data flow design depends on identifying the flows of data through the intended software, together with the transformations on the flows of data. The method leads from a specification of the software to a large-scale structure for the software expressed in terms of:

● the constituent modules of which the software is made
● the interrelationships between the modules.

What is a module? A module is a collection of lines of code, usually involving variables (descriptions of data) and actions. A module is usually self-contained; it is somewhat separate from any other module or modules. A module is invoked, or called, from some other module and, similarly, uses (calls) other modules. Ideally, a module is as independent as it can be. One of the goals of software design is to create software structures in which all of the modules are as independent as possible. Chapter 6 discusses various general aspects of modularity.

Programming languages (nearly) always provide facilities for modularity. Some typical facilities include:

Cobol – subprogram
Fortran – subroutine
Pascal – procedure or function
Modula-2 – module

C – function
Ada – procedure or package
C++ – class
Java – class.

9.2 ● An analogy

We begin exploring the data flow design method using an analogy. Suppose a chef works in a kitchen all day preparing plates of spaghetti bolognese. The principal inputs to the system are:

● spaghetti

● meat.

The output from the system is:

● plates of spaghetti bolognese.

We can draw a diagram (Figure 9.1) to describe what is to happen in the kitchen.

In essence, data flows into the system, is transformed by actions (functions) and data then flows out of the system.

The diagram is called a *data flow diagram*. Each line with an arrow on it represents a stream of data flowing through the system. In this example there are three – spaghetti, meat, and plates of spaghetti. Each bubble represents a transformation, an activity or a process that converts an input flow into an output flow. In this example there is only one transformation – prepare food. Note that the diagram shows data flows (which are dynamic), and does not show files (which are static objects).

We can now explore the detail that lies within the single bubble. We redraw it as Figure 9.2 so as to show more clearly the steps that are involved.

Notice again the essential components – data flows (lines) and functions (bubbles). Each line is labeled to describe exactly what data it is. Each bubble is labeled with a verb to describe what it does.

We could go on redrawing our data flow diagram for the chef in the kitchen, adding more and more detail. There are, for example, other ingredients like tomatoes to consider (data flows) and more, detailed actions (bubbles), like mixing-in the various ingredients.

Figure 9.1 Data flow diagram for making spaghetti bolognese

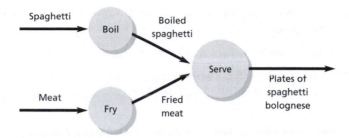

Figure 9.2 More detailed data flow diagram for making spaghetti bolognese

We started with a single, high-level diagram in which all the detail was hidden. We end up with a richer, more detailed diagram in which the components of the system (and their interrelationships) are revealed. In a computer system, the bubbles correspond to the software modules. We have created a design for the kitchen system, expressed in terms of modules and the flows of data between the modules.

9.3 ● First examples

We now turn to looking at the design of a small program. Suppose we want to write a program that converts a temperature measured in Centigrade into the same temperature measured in Fahrenheit. This is a simple enough program, but it will further illustrate the data flow method.

We begin with a data flow diagram showing the flow of data through the intended program and the transformations that will act on the flows of data, Figure 9.3.

A number, representing a temperature in Centigrade, is first input from the keyboard. It is next converted into another number, the temperature in degrees Fahrenheit. Finally the desired number is output to the screen. This program has the three archetypal components of many programs:

● input

● processing

● output

and these are represented by the three bubbles in the data flow diagram.

The main stage of data flow design for this program is now complete, since data flow design concerns itself only with the large-scale structure of programs. However, to

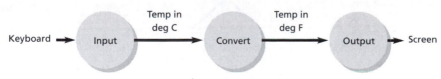

Figure 9.3 Data flow diagram for temperature conversion program

clarify the reader's understanding of the modules in this program, here is what they must do. The input bubble must:

- Carry out a dialogue with the user, requesting the input of the temperature from the keyboard.
- Check the input data, to ensure that it is numeric.
- Take remedial action if the input is invalid.
- Convert the data into internal representation, say floating point.

The processing bubble must:

- Convert the temperature from Centigrade to Fahrenheit, ensuring that the appropriate precision of the number is maintained.

The output bubble must:

- Display the converted temperature on the screen in the required format.

The first and most crucial step of data flow design – drawing the data flow diagram – is now complete. Such a diagram shows the transformations and the flows of data between them. The next step is to convert the data flow diagram into a structure chart or structure diagram. A structure chart shows the modules that comprise a program and how they call each other. Suppose, for example, that a program consists of three modules named A, B, and C. Suppose that module A calls module B and also module C. The structure chart for these components is shown in Figure 9.4.

A structure chart is thus a hierarchical diagram that shows modules at the higher levels calling modules at lower levels. A structure chart is a tree, with one single root at the top of the chart. Notice by contrast that a data flow diagram is not hierarchical. We shall see several structure charts later in this chapter.

Let us now consider the temperature conversion program and see how to convert the data flow diagram into its equivalent structure chart. In the data flow diagram, arguably the central and most important bubble is the processing bubble. We take this to be the main, most important module. Imagine that we can touch and move the objects within the diagram. Suppose that the bubbles are joined by pieces of string. Grasp the central module and lift it into the air. Let the other bubbles dangle beneath. Next change the bubbles into rectangles. We now have a structure chart that looks like Figure 9.5.

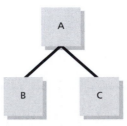

Figure 9.4 Structure chart in which module A calls B and C

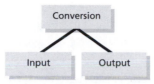

Figure 9.5 Structure chart for temperature conversion program

Each box is a program module. The modules communicate by calls from higher modules to lower modules. The data that flowed along lines in the data flow diagram is now passed as parameters to and from the various modules.

The processing module calls the input module to obtain data from the keyboard. Then it calls the output module to present the output on the screen.

As we have illustrated, the way of converting a data flow diagram into a structure chart is as follows:

1. Identify the most important bubble (transformation).
2. Convert this into the top-level module in the structure chart.
3. Allow the other components to dangle beneath the top-level module, creating a hierarchical tree.
4. Convert the bubbles into rectangles and the data flows into lines representing calls.

There is another possible structure chart for the temperature conversion program. We could create a supervisory module from which the others descend, see Figure 9.6.

The main module calls the input module to obtain the data from the user. It then calls the processing module to carry out the temperature conversion. Finally it calls the output module to display the result.

What he have done here is to create an additional module that was not present in the structure chart. Instead of the data flowing directly from one module to another, it is routed via the supervisory module. This sometimes serves to simplify the design. We still used the data flow design, but used it creatively to derive a structure diagram.

The above example introduces two of the prime notations of data flow design – the data flow diagram and the structure chart. There is one additional feature of structure charts that will be introduced using the following example.

Suppose we need to design a program to act as a simple telephone directory. The task of the program is to input someone's name and provide their telephone number. The data flow diagram is shown in Figure 9.7.

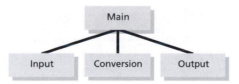

Figure 9.6 Alternate structure chart for temperature conversion program

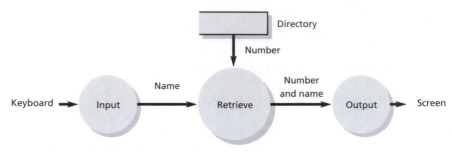

Figure 9.7 Data flow diagram for a telephone directory program

The new ingredient here is the open box notation, which represents a data store. This is normally a file or a database, held on disk. The difference between a data store and data flow is that a data store is static (it does not move).

9.4 ● Case study – point-of-sale terminal

Drawing the data flow diagram for a proposed piece of software is a vital step in the method. How do we do it? There are three alternative approaches.

Method 1 is to start with a single bubble like Figure 9.8 that shows the overall function of the software and its input and output data flows. We then refine the bubble, or break it down, into a set of smaller bubbles like Figure 9.9. We continue redrawing bubbles as sets of smaller ones until we can't do it any more.

Now let us look at an example. A point-of-sale terminal in a supermarket:

● reads bar codes from items moved past the laser reader
● looks up the price of an item
● displays the item price.

The initial data flow diagram is shown in Figure 9.10.

And we can refine it to Figure 9.11.

In method 2, we start with the output data flow from the system and try to identify the final transformation that has to be done to it. Then we try to identify the transformation before that, and so on, until we have a complete diagram.

Method 3 is the same as method 2, except that we start from the input flow to the system and work out the sequence of transformations that should be applied to it.

Figure 9.8 Initial data flow diagram

Figure 9.9 Refined data flow diagram

Figure 9.10 Initial data flow diagram for point-of-sale terminal

Figure 9.11 Refined data flow diagram for point-of-sale terminal

There is no definite, systematic way of drawing these diagrams. Lots of paper, pencil, and erasers (or a software tool) are needed – together with a lot of creativity.

Having obtained the data flow diagram using one of these methods, what do we do with it? One option is to regard each bubble as a program that inputs a serial stream of data from one bubble and outputs a serial stream to another. If we have a language, like Java or Ada, that provides multithreading (or parallelism), we can implement each of these programs as a thread (or task) that receives and transmits information to other threads. Similarly, if we have a system, like Unix (Chapter 18 on Tools), that allows programs to communicate using pipes, we can directly implement a data flow diagram as a series of filters and pipes. However, if neither multithreading or Unix is available, a data flow diagram must be transformed into a structure for a single sequential program.

To transform the data flow diagram into a structure for a single program we proceed as follows. We first identify which bubble is the most important, central bubble. To do this, we start with the input to the system and follow the arrows into the system until we judge that the data has ceased to flow inwards. In the example above, this is at the lookup bubble. As a check we also start at the output from the system and work backwards to find out where it originates. In the point-of-sale terminal system, we arrive again at the lookup bubble. So this is the center of the diagram, the most important bubble.

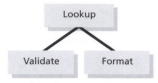

Figure 9.12 Data structure diagram for point-of-sale software

As we did earlier, we now imagine that the bubbles are golf balls, linked together with data flows made of string. We grasp the central bubble and lift it into the air, leaving the others dangling. The result is a hierarchical diagram, with the central bubble at the top. Simply redrawing the bubbles as rectangular boxes, we get the program structure diagram shown in Figure 9.12.

In this diagram each box represents a program module and each line a call from one module to another. The lookup module is the main module. It calls the validate module whenever it needs a bar code. It calls the format module to generate the required display. We have at last arrived at a design for the structure of the program. It is an architectural (large-scale) structure for the program, showing the major components and how they relate to each other.

This simple example illustrates how to use the data flow design method. But the example chosen is very simple and we have deliberately avoided drawing attention to complications. Data flow diagrams typically have tens of bubbles and can be quite complex. Often there are several input and output data flows. In more complex diagrams, it can be difficult to identify a single center of the diagram.

If a data flow diagram seems to have two or three equally important and central bubbles, the way to deal with the situation is to create a single supervisory module that does very little other than call them. In the point-of-sale system, there is clearly one central bubble, so the problem doesn't arise. But for the purposes of illustration we could if we wanted redraw the structure chart as in Figure 9.13. This has a new main module with the three submodules beneath it. The main module only acts as a coordinator, calling the others, supplying and receiving the data to and from them.

Let us complicate the problem of the point-of-sale terminal with additional data flows and transformations. We now add the requirements that the system should display the item price on a second terminal (for the customer), and we further complicate the specification by requiring that the system should transmit item codes to another, central computer whose purpose is to maintain records of stock. The new data flow diagram is Figure 9.14, and the corresponding diagram showing the module structure is Figure 9.15.

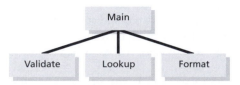

Figure 9.13 Alternate data structure diagram for point-of-sale software

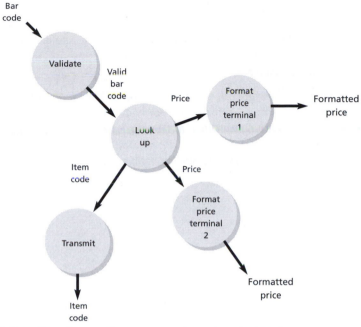

Figure 9.14 Data flow diagram for more complex point-of-sale software

Notice that although the method leads us to a structure for a piece of software that is expressed in terms of well-defined, independent modules, we still have to design the insides of each and every module; we have to carry out the low level or detailed design. In the case of the point-of-sale system, for example, each module is not necessarily trivial. The module that reads bar codes may have to cope with the translation of exotic bit patterns into an item number. It will have to carry out error detection. When there is an error, it will need to correct it by communicating with the shop assistant. This emphasizes that data flow design is only a method for high-level or architectural design. The method gives us no guidance on how to carry out this detailed design, so we might use the Michael Jackson method, functional decomposition, or some other method to accomplish this last step.

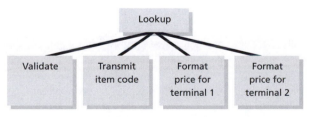

Figure 9.15 Structure chart for more complex point-of-sale software

9.5 ● Case study – monitoring a plant

This next example shows how data flow design can be applied to the design of a process control system. It also shows the importance of correctly selecting the central transform. The specification for the software is:

A computer is being used to monitor an industrial plant. The computer periodically inputs readings from instruments in the plant. Some of the readings require conversion to normal units of measurement (e.g. microvolts into degrees Centigrade). The computer checks each of the readings against permissible values. Alarm reports are displayed on a screen when a value is outside its valid range.

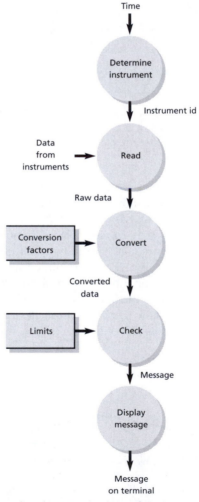

Figure 9.16 Data flow diagram for plant monitoring software

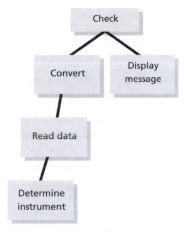

Figure 9.17 Structure chart for plant monitoring software

The data flow diagram for this problem is shown in Figure 9.16. It is almost possible to draw it simply by closely reading the specification and picking out the functional steps that have to be carried out. There is a single, major flow of data through the system. It is relatively clear that the central transform in the system is the bubble that checks the values. Hence we can derive the program structure diagram, Figure 9.17 – assuming of course that we want to create a structure for a single serial program.

9.6 ● Rationale for the method

Why does the data flow method prescribe these steps? There are two main ideas behind the method:

- the connection between data flows and modularity
- the idea of an idealized software structure.

The first concerns the data flow diagram. Why exactly do we draw a data flow diagram and what is its significance? The answer is that the central aim of the method is to create a design with the best possible modularity. As described in Chapter 6, the different types of modularity have been analyzed and classified in an attempt to identify which is the best sort of modularity. Perfect modularity would mean that an individual module could be designed, tested, understood, and changed when necessary, without having to understand anything at all about any other module. The result of the analysis is that out of all the types of relationships, the most independent modules are those that communicate with each other only by inputting and outputting serial streams of data – just like the bubbles in a data flow diagram. This type of interaction is termed data coupling.

The second idea behind the data flow design method is the observation that many software systems have a similar overall structure. Most software carries out some input, performs some action on the input data, and then outputs some information. The most

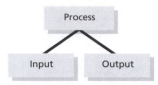

Figure 9.18 Idealized structure for software

important of these three is the action or transformation on the data. Therefore, in general, the ideal structure for any software is as shown in Figure 9.18.

To clarify our understanding of why this should be so, consider an alternative, poor structure shown in Figure 9.19.

Here the input module is the major component of the software. It calls the processing module, which in turn calls the output module. This looks rather illogical because the most vital function is not at the top.

We have seen that the module that does the main processing should be at the top. If we now look at what the input module does, it is likely that it can be broken down into two modules – one that inputs some raw data and another that converts it into a more convenient form. The corresponding structure diagram is shown in Figure 9.20.

In general, a piece of software will require that several transformations are carried out on its input data streams and that, after the main processing, several transformations are carried out on its output data streams.

We can use an analogy from outside computing. To make wine, we have first to grow vines, pick the grapes, transport them to the farm, and then wash them (hopefully). Only then can we carry out the central task of fermentation. After this we have to pour the wine into bottles, store the bottles for some time, and finally transport them to the shop. The (software) structure that corresponds to these steps is shown in Figure 9.21.

Data flow design recognizes this as the archetypal structure for software systems.

As we have seen, data flow design concentrates on modeling the flows of data within software. The essential ingredient is any application in which the flows of data are important and can be identified easily. Data flows are significant because nearly every software system involves data flows. In all computer systems information enters the computer as a serial stream of data, simply because time flows serially. Similarly any component within a software system is only capable of carrying out one task at any time. Thus the

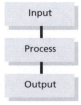

Figure 9.19 Inferior structure for software

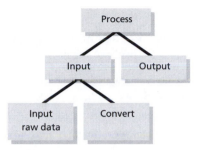

Figure 9.20 Converting raw data for input

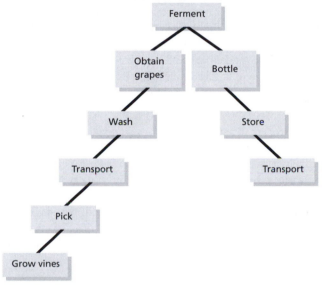

Figure 9.21 Producing wine

demands placed on any component are a serial data stream. Therefore data flows constitute a fundamental concept within software.

9.7 ● Discussion

9.7.1 History

Data flow design had its origins in the era of modular programming in the 1970s. In those days everyone agreed that modularity was a good idea, but there were no generally accepted, clear views on how to go about achieving it. What the proponents of data flow design did was to suggest a definite procedure by which the structure of a large program or software system could be expressed in terms of constituent modules.

9.7.2 The role of data flow design

Data flow design is associated with the names Constantine, Myers, Stevens, and Yourdon. It forms a major part of a package of methods, usually known as "Structured Design." This package includes:

1. Data flow design as described above.

2. Various notations. Structured design uses the data flow diagram and the program structure chart, described above. As used in the method, however, a structure chart is embellished with information describing both the parameters passed between modules and the circumstances in which a module is called – repetitively or conditionally.

3. The ideas of coupling and cohesion. Structured design aims to bring about systems that exhibit high modularity. The concepts of coupling and cohesion are a terminology and a classification scheme for describing modularity, described in Chapter 6. These ideas are used to assess a design that has been produced by data flow design and, where necessary, provide guidance for its improvement. Thus the method does not automatically lead to a unique, ideal solution; instead alternative designs are possible. Coupling and cohesion provide criteria for choosing from amongst them.

Structured design closely relates to a method called "Structured Analysis." Structured analysis is a method for analyzing the activities, typically the clerical procedures, in an organization. (Indeed, analyzing office work is the origin of the data flow diagram technique.) The product of the analysis is a data flow diagram which describes the flow of data in the organization and the operations performed upon the data. Appropriate parts of this diagram may then be selected for computerization. Thus if structured analysis is used, followed by structured design, as it often is, the bubble diagram is already drawn and all that needs to be done is to implement it, as described above. This close relationship with this important method of structured analysis is one reason why structured design is widely used throughout the world.

Data flow design is an essential ingredient in several major software development methods now in use. One major example we have already mentioned – structured design. Another is SSADM (Structured Systems Analysis and Design).

9.7.3 Applicability

As the examples above have indicated, the application of data flow design is not limited to data processing or information systems – see for example the plant monitoring program above.

However, in some problem domains, such as many computational problems, the data flows may not be important or obvious.

9.7.4 UML (Unified Modeling Language)

UML is now the established notation for describing and documenting software. A structure chart corresponds to a UML object diagram. There is no notation within UML for describing data flow, indicating that in the UML view data flow has no significance. However, UML sequence and collaboration diagrams can be used for this purpose in some cases.

9.8 ● Summary

Data flow design proceeds by initially analyzing the data flows and transformations within a software system. The first task is to draw the data flow diagram (bubble diagram), consisting of arcs (data flows) and bubbles (transformations). This diagram can be arrived at by using any one of the following three methods:

1. Starting with a single, large bubble, break it up into smaller bubbles.
2. Start with the output data stream from the software and trace it backwards.
3. Start with the input data stream to the system and trace it forwards.

During the second stage of data flow design, the data flow diagram is transformed into a structure chart, showing the constituent modules of the program and their inter-relationships, by:

1. identifying the most important or central transformation in the data flow diagram
2. lifting this transformation into the air, leaving the others dangling beneath it. This creates a hierarchical or tree-shaped structure for the program.

Arguably data flow design leads to the most modular structure for the software, since the design is based on "data coupling" (the best type) between the modules.

EXERCISES

9.1 Complete the development of the first program given in this chapter, the program that inputs a temperature and converts it to Fahrenheit.

9.2 Design a program that inputs data on sunshine hours during each month of a 12-month period. The program calculates the total hours, average hours and finds the month with the maximum hours. It also draws a histogram showing for each month the sunshine hours as a chart made up of asterisks.

9.3 Use data flow design to design a program to solve the following problem. A program is to input 80-character lines of text, consisting of words and spaces, and is required to convert them into 120-character lines, containing as many words as will fit. (Hint: one of the bubbles inputs lines and outputs words.)

9.4 Suppose that in the point-of-sale system described above, an additional requirement is added – that the system should transmit each item code to a remote stock control computer. Enhance the data flow diagram. Derive the new module structure.

9.5 Use data flow design to design software or a program to:

(a) play a video game like space invaders

(b) implement an on-line interactive system, like a stock control system

(c) calculate some mathematical quantity, like the first 100 prime numbers.

9.6 What characteristics should a good software design method have? Does data flow design exhibit them?

9.7 Suggest the facilities of a software tool that could assist in using data flow design.

9.8 Evaluate data flow design under the following headings:

● Special features and strengths
● Weaknesses
● Philosophy/perspective?
● Systematic?
● Appropriate applications
● Inappropriate applications
● Is the method top-down, bottom-up, or something else?
● Good for large-scale design?
● Good for small-scale design?

9.9 Suggest a toolkit to assist in using data flow design.

FURTHER READING

Data flow design is described in a series of books that have been published over a number of years, starting with: E. Yourdon and L. L. Constantine, *Structured Design*, Prentice Hall International, 1979 and continuing with: W. P. Stevens, *Using Structured Design*, John Wiley, 1981.

Perhaps the most clear explanation of the method is given in: M. Page-Jones, *The Practical Guide to Structured Systems Design*, Yourdon Press, 1980.

The technique of structured analysis (the analysis method that complements structured design) is described in: T. DeMarco, *Structured Analysis and System Specification*, Yourdon Press/Prentice Hall, 1978.

The most recent version of this approach is described in: E. Yourdon, *Modern Structured Analysis*, Yourdon Press/Prentice Hall, 1989.

10

Object-oriented design

This chapter:

- explains how to use one major approach to designing OOP's
- explains how an initial OO design can be improved
- outlines the re-usable design pattern approach to design.

10.1 ● Introduction

We begin this chapter by reviewing the distinctive features and principles of object-oriented programming (OOP). This sets the scene as to what an OO design seeks to exploit. Later we will look at how to go about designing OO programs.

We need to know what OO languages provide so that we can produce designs that exploit their capabilities. We would like any OO design to be implementable in any language – whether OO or not – but that is an unrealistic aim. More achieveably, we would like an OO design to be translatable into any OO language. So, first of all, we review the significant features of OO languages. The widely agreed principles of OOP are:

- encapsulation
- inheritance
- polymorphism.

The advantages of these features is that they promote the re-usability of software components. Encapsulation allows a class to be re-used without knowing how it works – thus modularity and abstraction are provided. Inheritance allows a class to be re-used by using some of the existing facilities, while adding new facilities in a secure manner. Polymorphism further promotes encapsulation by allowing general-purpose classes to be written that will work successfully with many different types of object. Object-oriented languages are usually accompanied by a large and comprehensive library of classes. Members of such a library can either be used directly or re-used by employing inheritance. Thus the process of programming involves using existing library classes, extending the library classes, and (more rarely) designing brand new classes.

10.2 ● The features of OOP

10.2.1 Encapsulation

Encapsulation means collecting together related software ingredients to make highly modular units that can be designed, implemented, debugged, tested, and maintained one-by-one. Unlike traditional languages in which procedures and data are considered as separate entities, object-oriented languages adopt the view that a single indivisible entity, an *object*, should be used to encapsulate those data and procedures that are strongly related. The data contained within an object may only be modified by the procedures (more commonly called *methods*) that are part of that object. Each object can be thought of as a small virtual processor whose behavior is defined solely by how it responds to a method call. In summary, an object-oriented system can be thought of as a collection of objects communicating (co-operating) to achieve some result.

Objects adhere to an important fundamental principle for structuring software systems – *information hiding*. The idea behind information hiding is that users of an object need not (and should not) have access to either the representation or the implementation of the operations. It is useful to think of objects as providing two views of themselves: one to potential users or clients of the object and another to implementers of the object. Users of the object may modify its state but only indirectly by calling one of the methods in the object. A major advantage of this approach is that it allows an implementor to modify the implementation of an object in a manner that is transparent (invisible) to users. Users or clients of the object do not have to be notified of the change. This separation of the object's user interface from its implementation is essential for the production of maintainable and re-usable software.

In OOP, the *class* is the abstraction that captures the attributes and operations common to a set of objects. A class describes the variables and methods followed by each of the members, or in OOP terminology, the *instances*, of the class. In Smalltalk, C++, Ada 95, Java, and in most OO languages, every object is an instance of some class. To summarize, a class is a description of a set of objects with similar characteristics, attributes, and behaviors. An instance is an individual object that is both described by and a member of a particular class.

Real-world systems depend on our ability to classify and categorize. Elephants, tigers, polar bears, horses, and cows are all mammals; lead, silver, and platinum are metals; savings, current, and term deposits are types of bank accounts; and so on. Through classification, we are able to associate characteristics common to all members of a class.

All mammals are vertebrates (have backbones), are warm-blooded, and have hair on their bodies; all metals have atomic weights; and all bank accounts have balances.

In summary, a class is:

- a general description of any number of objects
- a repository for methods (operations) understood by all instances (objects) belonging to that class
- a code-sharing mechanism
- an abstraction of an object
- a data type.

In contrast, an instance of an object is a particular instance of a class, created at run time.

We have seen that an object (or class) consists of both variables and methods. However, the principle of information hiding dictates that data should not be directly accessible, but only accessed via method calls. Thus it is only rarely that an object (or class) is designed so as to permit direct access to data. Throughout this chapter we shall speak as though the only visible (public) items supported by a class are its methods, while the data (variables) are private.

Encapsulation offers the designer (almost) the ultimate in modularity. A system can be designed as a collection of objects, each of which can be regarded as an abstraction, and that have minimal interconnections. In addition, the class system allows as many new objects to be constructed from a class as are necessary for the application.

10.2.2 Inheritance

We often think of objects as *specializations* of other objects. Precious metals are specializations of metals, sports cars are specializations of cars, romance novels are specializations of books, and so on. All precious metals are metals but not all metals are precious metals. Similarly, all sports cars are cars and all romance novels are books, but the reverse is not true. Extending this notion, we can view one class of objects as a *subclass* of another. We can also talk about one class being a *superclass* of another. Similarly, quadrilaterals and triangles are polygons, and squares and rectangles are special kinds of quadrilaterals. Furthermore, a square is a special kind of rectangle. These types of relationships can be described in a diagram called (for obvious reasons) a *class diagram*. A class diagram is a tree-structured chart that shows which classes are subclasses of others. For example, Figure 10.1 shows the class diagram for geometrical shapes.

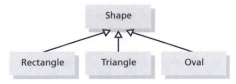

Figure 10.1 A class diagram for geometrical shapes

As a second example, Figure 10.2, shows in an oversimplified way the relationships between some of the Java library classes for GUI widgets. The supreme object at the top of the hierarchy tree in Java is called `object`; it is the ultimate superclass of all classes in Java.

The class diagram is a tree provided that the programming language supports only *single inheritance*. Such languages are Smalltalk, Ada 95, and Java. However, if *multiple inheritance* is supported by the programming language (as in C++), the class diagram becomes a directed graph. We will largely confine ourselves to single inheritance in this chapter.

What does it mean to say that one class is a subclass of another? Intuitively, we mean that the subclass has all the characteristics of the more general class but extends it in some way. Precious metals have all the characteristics of metals but, in addition, they can be distinguished from some metals on the basis of monetary value. Similarly, quadrilaterals are specializations of polygons with four sides. Polygons can have any number of sides. Squares are specializations of quadrilaterals where all four sides have equal length, and adjacent sides are perpendicular to one another. Applying these arguments in reverse, we can describe the superclass of a class as being a generalization of the class.

One of the best ways to describe something new to someone else is to describe it in terms of something that is similar; i.e., by describing how it differs from something known. An example is that a zebra is a horse with stripes! This concise definition conveys a substantial amount of information to someone familiar with horses but not with zebras.

Object-oriented programming languages embody these notions of specialization and differential description. Classes are hierarchically organized in subclassing relationships. When one class is a subclass of another, it is said to assume or *inherit* the representation and behavior of its superclass. Because of the sharing achieved through inheritance, the new class has to describe only how it is different from the superclass. Logically, a brevity of expression is achieved. Physically, this permits a sharing of operations – an operation provided in one class is applicable to each and every subclass. To summarize:

● *Subclass* A class that inherits methods and representation from an existing class.

● *Superclass* A class from which another class inherits representation and methods.

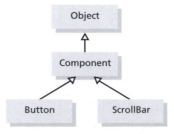

Figure 10.2 Class diagram for some of the classes in the Java class library (simplified)

In summary, a new class may differentiate itself from its superclass in a number of ways. It may:

- support additional operations other than those inherited
- support new implementations of operations that could otherwise be inherited
- contain only a restricted subset of the instances of the original class
- add additional data.

The advantages of inheritance and subclassing are:

- at the design level, concise definitions – subclasses are described only in terms of how they are different from their superclass
- at the implementation level, code re-use – rather than duplicate code, subclasses reuse existing code from their superclasses.

10.2.3 Libraries

Encapsulation means that classes held in a library can be re-used easily, because all the user needs to know is what the class provides (not how it does it). So it is common in OO programming to make extensive use of libraries, just as it is common in non-OO languages. However the additional power of inheritance means that library classes can be used much more flexibly. An existing class in a library can be re-used by inheriting some of its properties (the methods it provides) and extending it by adding new methods. The original module remains intact. Thus the best use can be made of existing tried-and-tested software components.

Most current OO languages provide comprehensive libraries which often form the basis of any new software to be constructed. For example, the Smalltalk class library contains of the order of 150 classes. This is both an advantage and a disadvantage. It is an advantage because new applications can lever off this library and avoid reinventing the wheel. Initially, however, it is a disadvantage as the programmer must learn the contents of the library and, in particular, distinguish between related sets of classes which seemingly provide almost identical functionality. The Smalltalk library, for example, provides many different kinds of collection classes.

The Smalltalk class library has served as the model for many libraries for object-oriented programming languages. The most important classes can be broadly categorized as follows:

Foundation Classes Object, Boolean, Character, Integer, Float, Fraction, Date, Time, etc.

Collection Classes Dictionary, Array, String, Symbol, Set, OrderedCollection, SortedCollection, etc.

Graphical Classes Point, Rectangle, Bitmap, Pen, etc. Classes which provide access to platform-specific graphics routines.

User Interface Classes Classes which support windows, dialog boxes, menus, buttons, text editing, etc.

Tools Classes which navigate through the class library, inspection of objects, source code debugging, change management, etc.

In summary, object-oriented languages encourage the use of class libraries. Many current libraries focus on providing support for data types, graphics, and user interface classes, and programming support tools. But increasingly we are seeing the emergence of application domain specific libraries. One example is the Java library for programming small embedded systems, like mobile phones.

During OO design, the designer must be aware of the wealth of useful classes available in the libraries. To ignore them would be to risk wasting massive design, programming, and testing time. It is common experience for someone setting out to write a new OO program to find that nearly all of the program already exists within the library. OO development is therefore often regarded as (merely) extending library classes. This, of course, requires a discipline – the initial investment in the time to explore and learn about what might be a large library set against the benefits that accrue later.

10.2.4 Polymorphism

Imagine writing a sort program to sort a table of integers into ascending order. Then imagine having to write a new version that deals with real numbers. Using most conventional programming languages a completely different version of the program would be needed. However, using polymorphism, only a single version of the program would be required – and this version would be applicable (unchanged) to arrays of double length integers, double length real numbers, strings, or whatever.

Polymorphism, the third feature of object-oriented programming, means that the interpretation of a method call is in the hands of the receiver; i.e., the same method call can be interpreted in different ways by different objects. Operations exhibiting this property are said to be *polymorphic*. Method calls can be thought of as late-bound procedure calls, where the actual method or procedure to be invoked is not determined until the method is actually applied to a specific object. This process of delaying the determination of the actual method to be invoked until run-time is termed *dynamic binding*. In a non-OO language a series of `if` statements are needed to distinguish between the different cases. In an OO language, these `if` statements are simply not needed, so the software is smaller and simpler. Moreover, it is no longer the programmer's responsibility to determine the correct method to invoke.

A further consequence is that some kinds of updates to programs are very simple; thus an object-oriented solution is more adaptable to change and re-use. In conventional programming, for every new situation, a new `if` statement must be added. But in a large system, this kind of change is extremely error-prone and the chances are that we will fail to make one or more of the necessary changes. By contrast in an OO language, as we have seen, the introduction of an additional object will not need an additional `if` statement.

In summary, the concepts of polymorphism and dynamic binding permit the design of generic re-usable code – code which is independent of the objects involved. This reduces development and maintenance costs.

10.3 ● The aims of OO design

We have seen that OO programming provides the designer with a powerful set of concepts and tools. The designer of an OO program has the task of establishing:

- what classes are appropriate for the program
- what methods each class provides as services to its users
- what other classes each class uses.

In identifying the classes, the designer hopes to make maximum use of:

- classes provided by libraries
- encapsulation
- inheritance
- polymorphism.

At one extreme the designer has the option of creating a design that consists only of one single class. This is always possible, and corresponds to a non-OO program. An example of such a program is the Safe program given in Chapter 14 on OO programming. At the other extreme, the designer might create an unnecessarily large number of classes, with many interconnections. Thus design is a matter of judgment in order to arrive at the optimal classes for the problem.

In recent years, a number of object-oriented programming languages have received widespread use. They can be divided into two groups – pure OOP languages (e.g., Smalltalk, and Eiffel) and hybrid languages (e.g. C++ and Ada 95). Hybrid languages provide extensions to traditional languages and thus support programming in both a traditional and an OOP style, whereas pure languages have been specifically designed to support the OOP paradigm. Java was designed to support OOP, but is not entirely pure, since it supports a group of non-OO data types.

In some programming languages a class can inherit from only one superclass – a class chart is always a tree. This is called *single inheritance*, and is the scheme supported by Smalltalk, Ada 95, and Java. Some languages, like C++, permit *multiple inheritance*, in which a class can inherit from two or more super classes. Multiple inheritance is obviously more complicated, but more flexible. There is considerable debate in OO circles about the desirability of multiple inheritance and one major recent language, Java, does not support it. If we assume, during design, that multiple inheritance is available, we will produce a design that embodies this assumption and that cannot be easily implemented in a single-inheritance language. However, if we create a design that assumes single inheritance, it can be readily implemented using a multiple inheritance language. In this book we largely restrict our outlook to single inheritance, for simplicity.

Now while ideally the implementation programming language for an OO design should support OO features, it is possible (just) to design software in an OO way and then implement it in a non-OO language. However, while it may be possible to simulate some features, such as encapsulation, it is almost impossible to simulate features like inheritance using a non-OO language.

We will explain several approaches and notations for design. We will use the design of two programs for illustration – the calculator and the Breakout game. (Breakout was also used in Chapter 7 as an example of using functional decomposition in design.) Here are the specifications for these programs. The reader might like to carry out the design of these programs before reading further.

10.3.1 The Breakout game

A ball is released from the paddle, with random direction. It bounces between the wall, the paddle, and the sides. When it strikes a brick in the wall, the brick is destroyed, and vanishes. If the ball finds a route through the broken wall to the space beyond, the player wins. If the ball misses the paddle and strikes the wall behind the paddle, the player loses. The player controls the position of the paddle (which can only move left to right) using the mouse. A typical display for the game is shown in Figure 10.3.

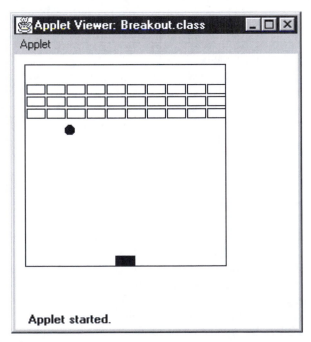

Figure 10.3 The Breakout game

Figure 10.4 The Calculator

10.3.2 The Calculator

The calculator consists of a number of buttons and a display (Figure 10.4). There is a button for each digit (0 to 9) which allows numbers to be entered. Such a number is displayed on the display. There are buttons to request that a calculation be carried out – add, or subtract. The result of a calculation is displayed on the display. The clear button clears the display

10.4 ● Finding the classes

Object-oriented design and programming is most easily described as programming by simulation. Applications are designed and implemented as a simulation or animation. Objects model entities in the real world. This style of programming is often referred to as *programming by personification* or *anthropomorphic programming*. The metaphor is based on personifying the physical or conceptual objects from some real-world domain into objects in the program domain; e.g., objects are clients in a business, foods in a produce store, or parts in a factory. We try to reincarnate objects from the problem domain into our computer models, giving the objects in our program the same characteristics and capabilities as their real-world counterparts. Thus we build a model or a simulation of the problem to be solved. When implementation objects have a direct mapping to problem objects, the resulting software is far easier to understand and use. This process is often referred to as anthropomorphic programming or programming by personification.

The identification of classes is the key to object-oriented design. A common method for initially identifying classes is to examine the specification. A design normally starts from some relatively detailed specification of a problem. The specification is important for any design, but it is crucial in OO design. Scan the specification, identifying nouns. These are likely to be good candidates for the objects in the program.

The process of naming classes is very important; generally class names should be nouns or qualified nouns and the terminology in common usage within the problem should be used.

There is no prescribed formula for finding the right set of objects to model some problem. Moreover, the process is exploratory and iterative; it is common for classes to be initially proposed during a design but subsequently be discarded as the design progresses. Similarly, the need for some classes will not emerge until the implementation (coding) stage. Identifying the classes (and objects) requires insight into the problem.

Using an object-oriented approach to this problem, our first step is to identify, not the functions, but the objects involved in the problem domain. The easiest objects to identify are those with real-world counterparts. In the case of our game example, looking at the screen display leads us to identify objects such as the `bricks`, the `wall`, the `sides`, the `paddle`, the `ball`, and the `game` itself, as shown in Figure 10.5.

Rather than "finding the objects" in a problem domain, it is more usual to talk of "finding the classes," since classes are the fundamental abstraction mechanism in object-oriented design. The concept of a class recognizes the fact that sets of related objects share common characteristics and behavior. For example, we would expect that all the bricks in the wall in the game example would exhibit identical behavior. So individual bricks are said to be instances of class `Brick`. All instances follow the common structure and behavior for all bricks as described by the class. Instances maintain their own state. Each brick, for example, keeps track of its position in the wall.

It is sometimes easier, particularly for novices to OOD, to think about objects rather than classes. After all, objects are more concrete (less abstract) than classes. There is no problem with taking this approach, provided of course that you turn all the objects into classes once you have identified them.

For the calculator program, the classes `Calculator`, `Display`, and `Button` can be identified by analyzing the specification, looking for nouns. We can draw an initial class diagram, Figure 10.6.

It is important in the initial stages of a design not to overelaborate or overcomplicate the design. Now is not the time to start considering different types of buttons; e.g., digit buttons or operator buttons. This is an important issue but should be considered later. Classes should be 'user' classes as seen directly in the problem to be solved. Hidden

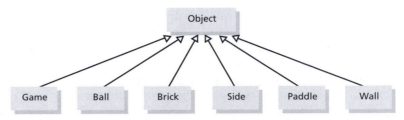

Figure 10.5 Object-oriented decomposition of the game

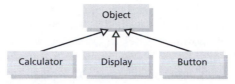

Figure 10.6 Class diagram for the calculator

classes concerned with the implementation such as stacks for keeping track of any partial results of the calculation, or an arithmetic unit for computing, are definitely not appropriate at this stage.

Notice that we have used the term "find the classes" rather than "design the classes." This is because we regard design as the simulation of the real-world problem to be solved, rather than as the creation of entirely new abstractions. Thus we look for or search for the classes present in the problem.

10.5 ● Specifying the responsibilities of the classes

Having identified the classes within a program, a second step in OOD is to determine what the classes are supposed to do; i.e., what are their behaviors – the methods they support? The objective is to define the role and responsibility of each class within the system in one or two short English sentences. Whereas classes were nouns, responsibilities are verb phrases. Again we scrutinize the specification to find them. For each of the classes that we identified, we produce a list of actions. These correspond to the methods that will be provided as part of the classes. For the calculator program, we identify the following.

The `Calculator` class provides methods to:

● draw itself and everything else on it by relaying the request to the buttons and the display;
● compute the sums or differences between two numbers;
● display the results of a computation by asking the display to do it.

The `Display` class provides methods to:
Display anything it is asked to display but cannot compute anything.
The `Button` class provides methods to:
Inform the calculator whenever it is pushed.
Keep track of the digit or operation it stands for.
Display itself.

The next step is to identify the variables and methods associated with each of the objects. Objects have *states* (variables) and *behavior* (methods). A ball might be represented by a radius and a position. A paddle, side, or brick might be described by position, width, and height. Similarly the state of a game might consist of a ball, a paddle, a wall of bricks, and a set of sides. Objects also support behavior – operations that may be applied to modify or interrogate their state. For example, a ball responds to requests to report its position and to modify its position. Similarly, a ball can be asked whether it is located behind the game paddle or whether it is colliding with any of the other components in the game. We could perform similar analyses on the other objects in the game. The end-product of this step is a list of the variables and methods associated with each of the objects in the program. This now determines the structure of the program in terms of its constituent objects and their properties.

10.6 ● Specifying the collaborators

Having identified the classes and their methods, we need to specify (for each class) what their collaborators are; i.e. those classes without whose assistance it would not be possible for the class to carry out its responsibilities. Collaboration suggests a two-way relationship but most often the relationship is one way. A class requests a collaborating class to perform some task by making a method call on an instance of the class. You may wish to substitute the word 'helpers' for collaborators. Components of a class are very often helpers.

The collaborators of a class are those classes that it uses (by making method calls). For the calculator program, the collaborators for each class are as follows.

> The `Calculator` class collaborates with classes `Display` and `Button`. A calculator knows about the display and the buttons (all of them), since it needs to be able to tell them to draw themselves.

> The `Button` class collaborates with the `Calculator` class. A button must know about the calculator since it must tell it that it has been pushed. Each button must also have a label so that it can be distinguished from other buttons and the button label will be a string. However, collaboration with class `string` is minimal and we therefore do not list it as a collaborator. (In most OO languages, `string` is a library class which can be regarded almost as part of the language.)

> The `Display` class collaborates with no other classes; it works independently when provided with a result to display.

Specification of the collaborators gives some initial insight into how objects of the classes communicate with each other to achieve some task and begins to provide a feel for the calls between objects. We can already envisage a button calling a method informing the calculator that it has been pressed and the calculator calling a method in the display as a result of this.

Let us analyze collaborations in the game program. The paddle and the ball in the game are clearly interrelated because when the paddle strikes the ball, the ball will change direction. Similarly there is a relationship between the wall and the ball. Another type of relationship that can be identified is the component or *part-of* relationship. For example this kind of relationship exists between individual bricks and the wall. The wall is made up of bricks. In this way, we can build up a picture of how the game objects interact with each other to achieve a simulation of the game. (Remember, an object-oriented design views an application as a collection of collaborating objects.)

10.7 ● Other design techniques and notations

We have completed an OO design for the calculator program and the game. At this stage in the design, we know:

● the classes that the program consists of
● what each class provides – the set of methods it supports
● how the classes interrelate

and thus we have a complete picture of the design.

This approach to OO design provides good information about the classes and methods and identifies potential ways in which a problem may be partitioned into classes and methods. However, design does not usually proceed in a straightforward, linear manner. Most often, design tends to be a very iterative process. Firstly, candidate classes are identified. Then some will be accepted while others will be rejected – perhaps because they have no responsibilities or because their responsibilities are subsumed by some other class. Responsibilities tend to migrate from one class of object to another as a better understanding of the objects and their role within the problem emerges. This process is known as *refactoring*. Refactoring is the transformation of a correct program structure (for example a class diagram) into an improved structure. Thus iteration is a common feature of OO design.

The design process we have presented is an exploratory process which can form the foundation for an object-oriented design. In this section we look at a number of techniques which go beyond an initial design to allow a designer to further analyze, clarify, and refine a design. They are:

● using the class library
● class–responsibility–collaborator (CRC) cards
● use case analysis
● creating good class hierarchies
● is-a and has-a analysis.

10.8 ● Using the class library

OO programming is often called programming by extending the library because the libraries provided along with OO languages are so rich and so re-usable. There are two distinct ways of using classes in a library:

- creating objects from classes in the library
- defining new classes by extending (inheriting from) classes in the library.

For example in designing the calculator program, the Java library provides classes that implement buttons and text fields – along with classes that support the event-handling associated with these widgets. One approach is to use the `Button` class in the Java library directly, by creating button objects as instances of the `Button` class:

```
Button sumButton = new Button("+");
```

Alternatively, the `Button` class can be extended to create a `SumButton` class that carries out the action associated with the calculator + button:

```
class SumButton extends Button {
    SumButton() {
        super("+");
    }
    public void pressed() {
    etc.
    }
}
```

Then we can create the particular button from this class:

```
SumButton sumButton = new SumButton();
```

In the game program, the Java library provides classes that draw the graphical objects – circles and squares that the program uses. In addition, the game program requires multithreading for its implementation, and the Java library classes provide plenty of support for this facility.

If library classes are being used by inheritance, the classes are usually incorporated into the class diagram for the software.

It is worthwhile looking in the library at the outset of design and then again at every stage of design, in case something useful can be incorporated into the design.

10.9 ● Class–responsibility–collaborator (CRC) cards

To document the design and to restrict the amount of detail that can be introduced, information can be recorded on what are known as class–responsibility–collaborator (CRC) cards to document each class. Each card has a layout as shown in Figure 10.7. Standard 4 inch by 6 inch index cards are used for the convenience of being able to lay them out on a table, see a largish number of them at once, and visualize their interrelationships. Alternatively a software tool is used to maintain and edit this information.

Class name: Button	
Responsibilities	Collaborators
Informs the calculator when it is pushed Remembers the digit or operation it stands for Displays itself	Calculator

Figure 10.7 A Sample CRC card for the class Button in the calculator program

10.10 ● Use-case analysis

An initial design describes the outline responsibilities of the classes. These responsibilities must be refined so we can accurately describe the services which each class provides. For each class, we must identify the state (data) which instances of a class must maintain and the method calls that instances of the class respond to. *Use-case analysis* (sometimes called *walkthroughs* or *execution scenarios*) is a simple mechanism for learning more about how the objects in a design interact and communicate with one another. The notion is to choose some representative examples of using the software – hence the term use-cases. For each use-case, we follow the flow of the method calls from one class to another. The end-product of such an exercise is:

1. clarification of the specification of the program
2. clarification of what methods are needed
3. identification and clarification of what variables are needed within the various classes.

For example, for the calculator, a sample use-case is the user entering the sequence:

$$10 + 2 =$$

using the various buttons. The sequence is:

1. First, press 1. The 1 button tells the calculator "1 has been pressed." The calculator stores the 1 and tells the display "display 1."
2. Next, press 0. The 0 button tells the calculator "0 has been pressed." The calculator stores the 0 by appending it to the previous digit to get 10 and tells the display "append 0 to your display."
3. Next, press +. The + button tells the calculator "+ has been pressed." The calculator stores the +. (It cannot carry out the addition yet because the second operand is not yet available.)
4. Next, press 2. The 2 button tells the calculator "2 has been pressed." The calculator stores the 2 in an area different from where the 10 is stored. (Clearly, we need names – call them operand1, operator, and operand2. So far, operand1 is 10, operator is +, and operand2 is 2.) Next the calculator tells the display "display 2."

5. Finally, press =. The = button tells the calculator "= has been pressed." The calculator executes "operand1 operator operand2," and tells the display to "display the answer."

What was learned from such a use-case analysis? The variables that must be maintained by the calculator have become clearer – they are operand1, operator, and operand2. Also the methods associated with various objects has also been identified. The `Display class`, for example, must support methods:

```
display(int number)
append(String digit)
```

Also, we realize that it would be exceedingly messy to have the calculator respond to each of 10 digit buttons with a unique method; instead we need a generic method in which the label of a digit button pressed is passed as the parameter:

```
pressed(String label)
```

Use-case analysis is continued by choosing other representative examples to expose further details of the variables and methods of the classes involved in an application.

SELF TEST QUESTION

10.1 Identify another use-case for the calculator program.

In summary, use-cases help define the variables and methods of classes in the application and provide a better picture of how the objects in an application interact with one another.

10.11 ● Creating good class hierarchies

It bears repeating that one of the major goals of the object-oriented paradigm is to produce generic, re-usable software components – components which can be re-used both within the application in which they were generated and also in future applications. The concepts of inheritance and subclassing supported by object-oriented languages allow:

● new classes of objects to be described as extensions or specializations of existing classes; i.e. a new class can be defined as a subclass of an existing class;

● subclasses to inherit the behavior and state of their superclasses.

These concepts add extra dimensions to the design process. Taking into account inheritance means that a major design goal is to factor the responsibilities within a hierarchy of classes so that a responsibility attached to a superclass can be shared by all subclasses.

To explore these ideas, we will return to the game example. Our initial design yielded the initial class shown in Figure 10.8. We will assume a single inheritance model (i.e.

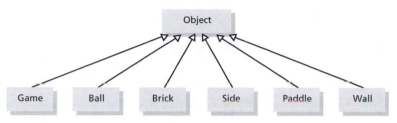

Figure 10.8 Initial class diagram for the Breakout game

classes can have only a single superclass) and the existence of a class `Object` – a class from which all classes inherit. We can see that, for the moment, the classes that constitute the game program are essentially independent of each other. We shall see shortly how we can identify commonality and therefore inheritance. What we do is to see whether any of the classes have anything in common. This means checking to see whether there is a method that is common to two or more classes.

As our first attempt, we see that all of the objects (and therefore the classes) that make up the game have a position (an *x* and a *y* coordinate on the screen) and a size. There is potential therefore for introducing a new class, `Component`, which will deal with these responsibilities on behalf of all its subclasses. However, we must first generalize the notion of size – the ball has a radius while the other components have width and height. We will therefore generalize the size to be a rectangle enclosing an object; this will allow the same notion to be used for all the components.

The class `Component` will hold as variables the coordinates of an object, together with its size, measured as an enclosing rectangle. It will also provide methods to access and change these values. These are methods that are inherited by all the subclasses `Ball`, `Brick`, etc. thus reducing their size and complexity.

SELF TEST QUESTION

10.2 Draw the class diagram for the game program, incorporating the class `Component`

The class `Component` is called an *abstract* class. We will never create instances of this class – its role is to capture the position and size abstraction and take care of that responsibility. (There will, of course, be other responsibilities which are specific to each of the subclasses.) An abstract class does not correspond to anything in the real world – or in the problem to be solved. It is merely a convenient way of grouping together methods and variables that can be used by subclasses. This makes for a shorter, neater program. Some languages, including Java, allow a class to be explicitly described as `abstract` in order to emphasize its role in a design.

Can we further improve the design? What other classes might be useful? There are at least two ideas that we might explore. Firstly, it is clear that some of the game components move (the ball and the paddle), while others remain stationary (the bricks and the sides). Should we therefore introduce classes `MovingComponent` and `StaticComponent`? How do we evaluate whether these are good abstractions or not? Clearly, if very few responsibilities (variables and methods) can be migrated from the individual classes to these new abstract classes, little has been gained and therefore it is not worthwhile.

Let us examine a second possible class structure. We observe that the class `Wall` has bricks as components, and similarly class `Sides` has the three sides as components. This suggests an organization based on whether classes have parts, `CompositeObjects`, or not, `BasicObjects`.

We are faced with a choice of two different abstractions – the composite–basic and the moving–static classifications. Are they worth using, and (if they are both worth using) how do we choose between them? Comparing the designs based on the two different abstractions, it turns out that the parts vs. no-parts abstraction is preferable. The final class diagram is given in Figure 10.9. The judgment as to whether to use an abstraction is normally based on:

● the number and size of the shared methods (do we get value for money from using the abstract class?)

● the potential of the design to accommodate change (does the abstract class facilitate re-use?)

The only way to assess whether a class provides economy of code is to look ahead to the coding phase, sketch out the code, and measure its size. This means, of course, that we are guilty of intermingling two stages of development – design and programming – which are often considered separate activities. But this is a common feature of OO design and programming.

As an example of assessing adaptability, what would be the effect of introducing a new kind of object into the game – an island of bricks in the middle of the screen, for example? The new object could easily inherit the responsibilities provided by the classes `Component` and `CompositeObjects`. All that would be necessary is to provide the specific behavior the new object requires.

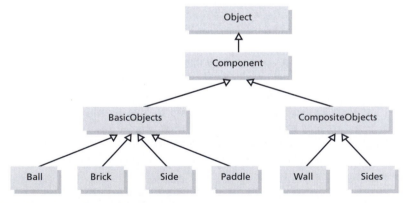

Figure 10.9 Final class diagram for game

Of course if we had multiple inheritance, we could incorporate both structures – both the inheritance structure that supports composite objects and the structure that supports static and moving objects.

10.12 ● Is-a and has-a analysis

As we have seen, a major activity in the refinement of an object-oriented design involves identifying interrelationships between classes and allocating behavior to the appropriate class within a hierarchically organized set of related classes. Identification of the correct interclass relationships is critical to the production of a quality object-oriented design. The technique of is-a and has-a analysis helps the designer to clarify what kind of relationship exists between classes. To use the technique, try to describe the relationship between the classes. The important class relationships to look out for are:

● *is-a* or *is-kind-of* relationships. This relationship manifests itself as a superclass–subclass relationship. For example in the game program, a ball is-a `BasicObject`. Similarly bricks, paddles, and sides are all `BasicObjects`. This type of relationship is shown explicitly in the class diagram.

● *has-a*, *is-part-of*, or *component* relationships. For example a game has-a ball. Similarly the paddle and bricks are components of the game. Furthermore, the wall is made up of bricks. This type of relationship has no role in the class diagram.

● *is-like* or *is-similar-to* relationships. This relationship recognizes that objects such as balls, bricks, paddles, etc. all have position and size attributes. This leads to the introduction of the abstract class `Component`. This type of relationship is shown as an additional class in the class diagram.

It is necessary to exercise a little care during design to identify the precise relationship between classes. Beginners, and sometimes even the more experienced, have a tendency to confuse "is-a" relationships with "is-part-of" relationships. For example in the game example, it might be natural to say that the wall is-a set of bricks – which would imply (mistakenly) that `Wall` is a subclass of `Brick`. However, the correct description is that a brick is-part-of a wall or alternatively that a wall has-a brick.

SELF TEST QUESTION 10.3

Identify the relationships between the following pairs of objects (or classes):

1. piston and engine
2. circle and point
3. cow and animal
4. cow and leg.

Another way to remind ourselves of the two major kinds of relationship between classes is to recognize that subclassing relationships (is-a) are relationships between *classes* while parts or component relationships (has-a) are relationships between *objects*.

10.13 ● Design guidelines

Use of the techniques described above does not necessarily lead to the best design. To assist in identifying weak areas of design, a number of guidelines are useful. These incorporate the guidelines for good modularity discussed in Chapter 6:

● Classes should have minimal coupling with other classes in has-a relationships.
● The magic number seven should be used as a guideline in monitoring the complexity of a class diagram. That is, the number of direct subclasses should probably be limited to about seven.
● A class should have maximum cohesion.
● Classes should not have an excessive number of methods (a maximum of seven public methods is a guideline). This limits complexity and promotes re-use.
● Methods should have no more than three parameters (to promote simplicity).
● A method that uses many `if` statements may be making poor use of polymorphism.

10.14 ● Re-usable design patterns (frameworks)

We have seen how re-usability can be achieved through three mechanisms: instantiating library classes, extending library classes, and using inheritance within the programmer's own classes. These are valuable aspects of OO design. These approaches constitute fine-grain re-use – the re-use of an individual class. Another approach is to re-use successful relationships between classes. These are termed re-usable design frameworks – types of interaction between classes which can be re-used for some particular task, for part of a task, or for some particular application domain. These relationships have been given useful names and cataloged in a number of reference books.

One of the commonest design patterns is exhibited in the Java model for GUI event handling. It is called the *delegation* design pattern. In a Java program, a GUI component such as a button is created in like this:

```
Button button = new Button("Press Me");
```

The button can then be added to the display window using the call:

```
add(button);
```

However, this leaves the question of what happens when the user clicks on the button – an event occurs. In Java, the programmer tells the system which object to call when an event arises. For example:

```
button.addActionListener(this);
```

tells the event handler to call a method `actionPerformed` within the current object (`this`). However, the programmer can easily specify that some other object will handle the event. Thus the mechanism allows the programmer complete freedom to choose which object handles the event. The benefit of using this pattern is that different objects can respond to different events, rather than having a single centralized switch which has to handle every event. Thus the use of the delegation design pattern results in good modularity.

A number of re-usable frameworks have been identified, given names, cataloged, and documented in books. They are available for domains such as user interfaces, file systems, and multithreading. These patterns are available for off-the-shelf use, just as classes are available in class libraries. However, in order to use design patterns the programmer needs considerable experience and understanding of OO design and programming.

10.15 • Object-oriented design methodologies

A considerable number of object-oriented design methodologies have appeared and are used. This diversity reflects the relative immaturity of the area as compared to data flow design (Chapter 9), for example. Each of the methodologies introduces graphical notations for documenting object-oriented designs.

The approach to design described in this chapter is most closely based on the methodology known as *responsibility-driven design*. It involves the three steps explained above:

1. Find the classes; i.e. determine the objects involved and their classes.
2. Specify what they are responsible for; i.e. what they do (behavior).
3. Specify their collaborators; i.e. other classes they need to get their jobs done.

Other well-known methodologies include *object-oriented design* by Grady Booch, *HOOD* which was developed for the European Space Agency, and *OOSD* (object-oriented structured design) which retains aspects of structured design methodologies.

The methodologies differ in:

• their degree of formality

• which features of the problem they choose to model (and not model)

• the types of application for which they tend to be most suited (for example, information systems versus real-time control systems).

Most recently, UML (Universal Modeling Language) became the *de facto* standard for OO design notation. This is the notation used as appropriate in this chapter.

10.16 • Discussion

OO design and programming has become the dominant approach to software development. This is assisted by the availability and widespread use of programming languages that fully support OOP – languages such as C++, Ada, Smalltalk, and Java. The OO approach has also spread to encompass the analysis stage of development; OO analysis is widespread.

The strengths of the OO approach are:

- the intuitive appeal of directly modeling the application as objects, classes, and methods
- the high modularity (information hiding) provided by the object and class concepts
- the ease of re-use of software components (classes) using the inheritance facility.

OO methods look set to dominate software development during the first decades of the new millennium.

10.16.1 Designing is programming and programming is designing

As we have seen, object-oriented design is an iterative process. During each iteration, the design is refined and re-analyzed continuously. Indeed, whereas design and implementation are considered largely distinct activities in traditional software development, using the object-oriented paradigm, the two activities are often indistinguishable. There are a number of reasons for this but perhaps the three most important are:

- Prototyping is seen as an integral part of the object-oriented software design and implementation process. Prototyping recognizes that in most cases the requirements for a system are at best vague or not well understood. It is an exploratory process providing early validation (or otherwise) of analysis, design, and user interface alternatives. Prototyping dictates that design and implementation proceed in at least large-grain iterative steps.
- The activities which take place and concerns which are addressed during the refinement of an object-oriented design are identical whether it is the design or a working prototype that is being refined. Moreover, activities such as re-organizing the class to reflect some newly recognized abstraction are just as likely to take place during the implementation of a prototype as during the design. The design must now be updated to reflect this change – design and implementation are now proceeding in small-grain iterative steps.
- Designers must be far more aware of the implementation environment than previously because of the impact that a large re-usable class library can have on a design. Designers must not only be aware of the classes but subsystems of classes and supporting design frameworks.

In reality, as noted by Meyer, one of the gurus of OO development, OO design and implementation are instances of the same activity – programming.

10.16.2 Detailed design

OO design addresses the large-scale, architectural structure of software. What about the detail? In some (non-OO) approaches to design, some different, complementary technique is used for detailed design. In OO design, it is not usual to use any technique for detailed design. The reason is that the product of OO design is already fairly detailed – a design specifies what classes and methods make up the desired software. Moreover if the design is good, the methods will often be small and simple – easy to implement directly in the programming language.

However, should it be necessary to use a method for detailed design, functional decomposition (Chapter 7) is ideal, using psuedocode as the notation.

10.17 ● Summary

Object-oriented design can be characterized as a three-stage process:

1. Find the classes; i.e. determine the objects involved and their classes.
2. Specify what the classes are responsible for; i.e. what they do (behavior).
3. Specify their collaborators; i.e. other classes they need to get their jobs done.

The following techniques and notations can help clarify and improve an initial design:

● Using the library. At every stage during design it is worthwhile looking in the library for classes that can either be used directly or else extended by inheritance.

● CRC cards. A means of documenting the responsibilities (methods provided) and collaborator classes of each of the classes in a program.

● Use-case analysis. This is a way of learning more about how the objects in a design interact and communicate with one another through the use of sample execution scenarios or role playing. Use-cases capture the dynamics of an object-oriented system – the method calls between the objects

● Identifying relationships between classes (is-a and has-a analysis). Clarifying a design through the identification of the relationships between classes (e.g. is-a, is-like, and has-a).

● Creating good class hierarchies. Identifying commonalities between classes. Translating commonality into class hierarchies and creating abstract classes to maximize code re-use. Migrating behavior from one class to another so as to achieve implementations of behavior which may be shared by subclasses.

● Design guidelines to check the success of a design.

Another major approach to design is using re-usable design frameworks. A number of generic subsystems of collaborating classes have been identified through experience of using OOD. One or more of these can often be used to structure the architecture of a new system or program. These re-usable designs have been given names and cataloged with examples so that they can be referenced and employed easily.

EXERCISES

10.1 Complete the design of the calculator presented in this chapter. In particular, design further use-cases and factor the classes into a class hierarchy.

10.2 Complete the design of the game presented in this chapter. In particular, design use-cases and identify the methods associated with each class.

10.3 Can object-oriented design be characterized as a top-down, a bottom-up, or some other process?

10.4 If programming and design are really two aspects of the same process (as object-oriented design suggests), does this mean that all designers must also be programmers?

10.5 To what extent is an object-oriented design influenced by the class library of re-usable components that is available? To what extent must designers be knowledgable about available components?

10.6 What features or indicators might you use to help identify potential flaws in an object-oriented design? For example, what might be the problem with a class that has an excessive number of methods? What could be done about this class? Again, is there a problem with a class that only calls other classes and provides no methods that are used by other classes? What might be done about this situation?.

10.7 Design a program that allows two-dimensional shapes to be drawn on the screen. A square, circle, triangle, or rectangle can be selected from a list of options and positioned at a place on the screen using a mouse. A shape can be repositioned, deleted, or its size changed using the usual mouse operations.

10.8 Suggest features for a software tool that would support the creation, storage, and editing of class diagrams.

10.9 Suggest features for a software tool that would support the creation, storage, and editing of CRC (Class-Responsibility-Collaborators) cards. Suggest features for checking the consistency of a collection of such cards.

10.10 Evaluate OO design under the following headings:

- Special features and strengths
- Weaknesses
- Philosophy/perspective?
- Systematic?
- Appropriate applications
- Inappropriate applications
- Is the method top-down, bottom-up, or something else?
- Good for large-scale design?
- Good for small-scale design?
- Can tools assist in using the method?

ANSWERS TO SELF TEST QUESTIONS

10.1 There are several possibilities. One is simply pressing the clear button. Another is a simple calculation involving subtracting two numbers.

10.2 The class diagram is now:

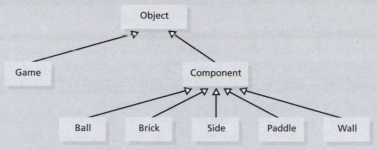

10.3 1. an engine has-a piston

2. circle and point have no obvious relationship at all

3. a cow is-an animal

4. a cow has-a leg

FURTHER READING

Object-oriented design

An excellent book which presents the author's view of the process and notation of object-oriented design and also contains five extensive design case studies. Widely regarded as the definitive book on OO design: G. Booch, *Object-Oriented Design with Applications*, Benjamin Cummings, 1990 and 1991.

A wide-ranging survey of approaches and notations. Very readable. An excellent overview of the different methods and notations: Edward Yourden, *Object-Oriented Systems Design: An Integrated Approach*, Prentice Hall International, 1994.

This describes the method of use-case analysis: I. Jacobson, M. Christerson, P. Johnsson and G. Overgaard, *Object-Oriented Software Engineering*, Addison-Wesley, 1992.

The manual for the HOOD design methodology: *HOOD Manual*, CISI Ingéniére, CRI A/S, Matra Espace, European Space Agency, Noordwijk, Netherlands, 1988.

This describes the OMT (Object Modeling Technique) method for OO design: Mark Priestley, *Practical Object-Oriented Design*, McGraw-Hill, 1997.

This book provides many valuable insights into the design and implementation of object-oriented software. The early chapters provide an excellent and most readable explanation of the principles of OOP. Examples are given using the programming language Eiffel: B. Meyer, *Object-Oriented Software Construction*, Prentice Hall, 2nd edition, 1997.

This excellent book provides a coherent language-independent methodology for object-oriented design known as "responsibility-driven design": R. J. Wirfs-Brock, B. Wilkerson and L. Weiner, *Designing Object-Oriented Software*, Prentice Hall, 1990.

Unified modeling language (UML)

Some of the books on UML are large and formidable. Here are two introductory and easy-to-read books: Perdita Stevens with Rob Pooley, *Using UML: Software Engineering with Objects and Components*, Addison-Wesley, Updated Edition, 1999. Martin Fowler with Kendall Scott, *UML Distilled: A Brief Guide to the Standard Object Modeling Language*, Addison-Wesley, 2nd Edition, 1999.

Object-oriented development

William Brown, Raphael Malveau, Hays McCormick and Thomas Mowbray, *Anti Patterns*, John Wiley, 1998. Explores what can go wrong (calling them antipatterns) during software development, particularly OO development, and explains how to recover from these situations. Easy to read, enjoyable, and refreshing. (The use of the term antipatterns means the opposite of desirable re-useable design patterns, see the references below.)

Tom Love, *Object Lessons. Lessons Learned in OO Development Projects*, SIGS Books, 1993. Written by a consultant who has seen many successful and unsuccessful projects, Tom Love gives the results of his very practical experience. The book begins by identifying the problems of software engineering. As part of this he suggests that successful pieces of software have been written by just two people, young, and without using respectable methods. He goes on to look at the expected benefits of OO. The main part of the book is about practical OO methods including management, "software component foundries," and how to bring about change.

Grady Booch, *Object Solutions: Managing the OO Project*, Addison-Wesley, 1996. This book complements Booch's book about the technical aspects of design with this companion book about the down-to-earth practical aspects of development. Very readable.

Design patterns

Erich Gamma, Richard Helm, Ralph Johnson and John Vlissides, *Design Patterns. Elements of Reusable Object-Oriented Software*, Addison-Wesley, 1995. The first and most significant of the books about re-usable design patterns. Written by authors now referred to as the Gang of Four, it presents a number of OO patterns, each with a name, a rationale, and examples. (The examples of use are mainly in C++, but the designs are more widely applicable.)

Mark Grand, *Patterns in Java, A Catalog of Reusable Design Patterns illustrated with UML*, vol. 1, John Wiley, 1998, and Mark Grand, *Patterns in Java, A Catalog of Reusable Design Patterns illustrated with UML*, vol. 2, John Wiley, 1999. A development of the Gamma book, with examples in Java. Invaluable for anyone using Java for a significant project.

11

User interface design

This chapter explains the techniques, principles, and guidelines for designing a human–computer interface

11.1 ● Introduction

The interface that the user sees when they use the computer is the single, paramount aspect of the system. The interface is the packaging for software. The user does not know and probably does not care how the system works (provided that it is reliable and fast). But they do care what it does and how to use it. If it is easy to learn, simple to use, straightforward and forgiving, the user will be encouraged to make good use of what's inside. If not, they won't. The user interface is often the yardstick by which a system is judged. Interfaces can be hard to learn, difficult to use, unforgiving, and sometimes totally confusing. An interface which is difficult to use will, at best, result in a high level of user errors. At worst, it will cause the software to be discarded, irrespective of its functionality. These are the challenges of Human–Computer Interface, HCI, design.

HCI offers the software engineer:

● some principles to guide interface design (e.g. simplicity, learnability)
● some guidelines for good interfaces
● a process for developing good interfaces, based on prototyping
● a design approach to the user interface (task analysis)
● methods for evaluating interfaces.

Today prototyping is considered essential for user interface development – a prototype is made available to users and the resulting feedback used to improve the interface design. Prototyping normally fits within the requirements analysis stage of software development as discussed in Chapter 2 on process models.

It is common in HCI design to distinguish between principles and guidelines (or rules):

- Principles are high-level and general. An example of a principle is: maintain consistency throughout the interface.

- Guidelines are specific and detailed. An example of a guideline is: black text on a white background is clearer than white text on a black background.

Guidelines are direct, immediate, and therefore easy to apply, but principles have to be interpreted and applied to the specific system.

11.2 ● An interdisciplinary field

HCI is very much an interdisciplinary subject, with contributions from computer science, cognitive psychology, sociology, and ergonomics. Cognitive scientists are concerned with how human beings perceive the world, think, and behave at an individual level. Sociologists study groups of people and their interactions. Ergonomics is about designing systems that are easy to use. Software engineers must often take responsibility for user interface design as well as the design of the software to implement that interface. These different disciplines bring different perspectives to bear on designing the human–computer interface.

User interface design has as much to do with the study of people as it does with technology. Who is the user? How does the user learn to interact with a new system? How does the user interpret information produced by the system? What will the user expect of the system? These are just a few of the questions that must be answered as part of user interface design. User interface design must take into account the needs, experience, and capabilities of the user. It is nowadays considered important that potential users should be involved in the design process.

The different specialisms reflect different views about the interaction between people and computers. At one level it is possible to view HCI as the interaction between one individual and the computer. At this level, the concerns are about such things as the amount of information displayed on the screen and the colors chosen. In the workplace, however, the computer system is often part of the wider context of the work being carried out. Usually, also, other people are involved in the work, so that the sociology of the workplace has a role. The questions here may be: Who does what? How can person A and person B communicate most effectively?

11.3 ● Styles of human–computer interface

The manner in which users tell the computer what they want to do has changed dramatically over the last 10 years. Broadly, there have been three types of interface – command line, menu, and GUI (graphical user interface).

In the early days of computing, the only mode of HCI was the *command line interface*. Communication was purely textual and was driven either via commands or by responses to system-generated queries. If we take as an example the instruction to delete a file, the command to do it typically looks like this:

```
del c:\file.txt
```

where the user has to key in this text (accurately), following a prompt from the system. This type of command is associated with operating systems such as Unix. This kind of interaction is error-prone, very unforgiving if an error occurs, and relatively difficult to learn. Clearly, command line interfaces are not suitable for casual and inexperienced users. On the other hand, experienced users often prefer a command line interface.

A development of the command line is the *menu* interface. The user is offered a choice of commands, like this:

```
To delete the file, key D
To display the file, key L
To open a file, key O
To save the file, key S
```

after which the user makes their selection by pressing the appropriate key.

Menu-based systems have several advantages over a command line interface:

- Users do not need to remember what is on offer.
- Users do not need to know command names.
- Typing effort is minimal.
- Some kinds of user error are avoided (e.g. invalid menu options can be disabled).
- Syntax errors are prevented.
- Context-dependent help can be provided.

Developments in user interfaces have been largely enabled by more sophisticated technology – early computers only had facilities for text input and output, whereas modern computers have high-resolution bit-mapped displays and pointing devices. As hardware became more sophisticated, and software engineers learned more about human factors and their impact on interface design, the modern *window-oriented, point and pick* interface evolved – with a GUI (graphical user interface) or WIMP (windows, icons, menus, and pointing devices). Such an interface presents the user with a set of controls or *widgets* (window gadgets) such as buttons, scroll bars, and text boxes. Instead of typing an option the user makes a selection using the mouse and mouse button.

The advantages of GUIs include:

- They are relatively easy to learn and use.
- The user can use multiple windows for system interaction.
- Fast, full-screen interaction is possible with immediate access to anywhere on the screen.

● Different types of information can be displayed simultaneously, enabling the user to switch contexts.

● The use of graphical icons, pull-down menus, buttons, and scrolling techniques reduce the amount of typing.

One way of helping to achieve interface consistency is to define a consistent model or metaphor for user-computer interaction, which is analogous to some real-world domain that the user understands. A *direct manipulation* interface presents users with a visual model of their information space. The best known of these is the *desktop metaphor*, familiar to users of Microsoft and Apple Macintosh operating systems. Another example is a WYSIWYG (what you see is what you get) word processor.

While there is a massive trend towards multitasking, window-oriented, point and pick interfaces which can make HCI easier, this only happens if careful design of the interface is conducted. Using a GUI is, in itself, no guarantee of a good interface.

11.4 ● Different perspectives on HCI

In designing a user interface it is as well to realize that there are several potentially different viewpoints. The perspectives are:

● the end-user who will eventually get to use the software

● different end-users with different personalities

● the novice or occasional user

● the experienced or power user

● users with different types of skill

● the software developer who designs and implements the system.

Most people do not apply any formal reasoning when confronted with a problem such as understanding what a computer is displaying. Rather, they apply a set of guidelines, rules, and strategies based on their understanding of similar problems. These are called heuristics. These heuristics tend to be domain specific – an identical problem, encountered in entirely different contexts, might be solved by applying different heuristics. An HCI should be developed in a manner that enables the human to develop heuristics for interaction.

The problem is that different people often have different perspectives of the HCI; they also have different skills, culture, and personalities. Each person has some model of how the system works and what it does. These different perspectives are sometimes called *mental models*.

An interface used by two individuals with the same education and background, but entirely different personalities, may seem friendly to one and unfriendly to the other. Therefore, the ideal HCI would be designed to accommodate differences in personality, or, alternatively, would be designed to accommodate for a typical personality among a class of end-users. A third possibility is to create an interface that is flexible and can be used in different ways according to personality differences.

A novice user or an occasional user is not likely to remember much about how to use the system. Thus a direct manipulation interface may be the most suitable approach. But an experienced and frequent user may be frustrated by an interface designed for novices and may prefer shortcut commands and/or a command line interface. A growing number of applications provide a *macro facility*, in which a series of commands can be grouped together, parameterized, and invoked as a single command. Again the need for flexibility in the interface becomes apparent.

The skill level of the end-user has a significant impact on the ability to extract meaningful information from the HCI, respond efficiently to tasks that are demanded by the interaction, and effectively apply heuristics that create a rhythm of interaction. It seems that context- or domain-specific knowledge is more important than overall education or intelligence. For example, an engineer who uses a computer-based diagnostic system to find faults in automobiles understands the problem domain and can interact effectively through an interface specifically designed to accommodate users with an engineer's background. This same interface might confuse a physician, even though the physician has considerable experience with using a computer for diagnosing illnesses in patients.

The software developer may unconsciously incorporate into the HCI some assumptions about the implementation that are irrelevant or even confusing for the users. Take a word processor for example. What the user wants is to create and edit documents, and they know that documents reside in files on a disk. The user probably understands the concept of opening a file, because this is a familiar concept in using manual files. But the idea of saving a file may well be completely mysterious to the user. The reason is that the concept of saving a file derives from the developer's mental model of how a word processor works, i.e. it keeps all or part of the document in main memory. This example illustrates how the designer can get it wrong and therefore the importance of the involvement of the user in design.

In conclusion, there are a number of different viewpoints taken by the users and developers of a user interface. There is scope for either conflict or harmony between these views. Conflict between the user's perception and the developer's concepts can make for a system that is difficult to use. But involving the users in the design can assist in recognizing users' views, and flexibility in the interface can help cater for different users.

11.5 ● Design principles and guidelines

Design principles are high-level principles that can guide the design of an HCI. Three overall principles are:

- learnability – how easily can new users learn to use the system?
- flexibility – does the interface support a variety of interaction styles? (We have already seen why this is an important consideration.)
- robustness – how much feedback does the system give the user to confirm what is going on?

Each of these qualities can be specified in greater detail as follows:
Learnability involves:

- Predictability – is the effect of any of the user actions predictable? A user should never be surprised by the behavior of a system.

- Synthesizability – can the user see the effect of their actions? A counterexample of this characteristic is some Unix commands, which give the user no information or even a confirmation of what they have accomplished.

- Familiarity – are the facilities familiar to the user from their previous experience? The interface should use terms and concepts which are drawn from the anticipated class of user. This attribute will clearly be more easily achieved with a direct manipulation interface.

- Generalizability – can the user safely assume that the same operation in different circumstances gives the same outcome? For example, does clicking the left mouse button on a folder icon have the same effect as clicking on a file icon?

- Consistency – are comparable operations activated in the same way? For example, in a word processor, is the selection of a single character, a word, a line, or a paragraph achieved in a consistent manner?

Flexibility involves:

- User initiative – can the user initiate any valid task whenever they desire? This is an issue of who is in control – the user or the machine.

- Multithreading – can several tasks be carried out concurrently? For example, carrying out text editing while printing is in progress?

- Task migratability – can particular tasks be undertaken either by the user or the system, or some combination of the two? For example, some e-mail systems provide for automatic response to e-mail while the user is on vacation.

- Substitutivity – can a facility be used in different ways? For example, selecting font size either from a menu or by typing font size explicitly.

- Customizability – can the user change the user interface? For example, hiding an unwanted tool bar, adding macros or scripts.

Robustness involves:

- Observability – does the system display information that allows the user to fully know what is going on? Again, this attribute will clearly be more easily achieved with a direct manipulation interface.

- Recoverability – does the system allow the user to recover from an unintended situation? For example, the provision of an undo button can help rectify certain user mistakes.

- Responsiveness – does the system respond in a reasonable time? Response time has two characteristics – length and variability. Variability refers to the deviation from average response time, and is in some ways more important than length, because it can affect the user's rhythm. So it is sometimes better to have equal-length response times (even if they are long) in preference to response times that are unpredictable.

● Task conformance – does the system do everything that the user needs to do? Is some facility missing?

It should be emphasized that this list of principles, useful though it is, constitutes just one of several possible categorizations of desirable attributes. This particular list is taken from Dix (see the reading list at the end of the chapter). Alternative factors that might be considered equally important include user error prevention, minimizing user memory requirements, and productivity.

Principles like these are distilled from practical experience, controlled experiments, and an understanding of human psychology and perception. They serve as goals to aim for during development. They can also act as quality factors (see Chapter 21 on metrics and quality assurance) that can be used to assess the quality of a completed design. For example, if recoverability is important for a particular development, an assessment of this quality can be made in order to evaluate the success of the product.

Let us see how a principle, such as those above, differs from a guideline. The principle of task conformance, for example, tells us what to look for, what to aim for, but not how to achieve it – and it can sometimes be difficult to identify something that is missing. By contrast, a guideline such as "black text on a white background is easier to read than the opposite" is immediately useful and applicable.

SELF TEST QUESTION

11.1 Distinguish between HCI guidelines and principles.

The drawback of principles is that they are not immediately applicable, but have to be interpreted and applied (as with real-life principles). The last example of a principle, task conformance, illustrates a major problem with using these principles for HCI design – it is not always obvious how or when to use them. The designer could post the principles up above their desk, so that they can see them and use them while they carry out design. But there is no explicit way of using the principles as part of a well-defined design methodology. Thus they are more akin to goals than principles.

Design guidelines or rules give the designer more detailed and specific advice during the process of designing an interface. There are many long lists of guidelines in the literature and we give here only a sample of typical guidelines. If you were asked to design an interface for an application running under Microsoft Windows, for example, you would be provided with a comprehensive manual of guidelines specific to the look and feel of Windows applications. Among many guidelines this would stipulate, for example, that the icon to close an application must be displayed at the top right of the window as a cross. Using guidelines such as these promotes the principle of consistency mentioned above.

Here, for illustration, are some examples of guidelines for designing GUI-type interfaces:

- Ask the user for confirmation of any non-trivial destructive action (for example, deleting a file).
- Reduce the amount of information that must be memorized in between actions.
- Minimize the number of input actions required of the user, e.g. reduce the amount of typing and mouse travel that is required.
- Categorize activities by function and group related controls together.
- Deactivate commands that are inappropriate in the context of current actions.
- Display only the information that is relevant to the current context.
- Use a presentation format that enables rapid assimilation of information, e.g. graphs and charts to present trends.
- Use upper and lower case, indentation, and text grouping to aid understanding.
- Use windows to compartmentalize different types of activity.
- Consider the available geography of the display screen and use it efficiently.
- Use color sparingly. (Designers should take account of the fact that a significant number of people are color-blind.)

These guidelines are more detailed and specific than the rather more generalized principles given earlier.

11.6 ● Human–computer interface design

The process for designing a user interface begins with the analysis of the tasks that the user needs to carry out. The human- and computer-oriented tasks are then delineated, general design principles and guidelines are considered, tools are used to prototype a system, and the result is evaluated for quality. Then the prototype is refined repeatedly until it is judged satisfactory.

This can be visualized as a flowchart – see Figure 11.1.

SELF TEST QUESTION

11.2 What problems can you see with this approach to design?

In Chapter 3 we identified requirements analysis as an important early part of any software development project. The process of HCI design, described above, is similar to the requirements analysis phase. In HCI, the user of a system plays a central role and thus user evaluation of prototypes is considered essential.

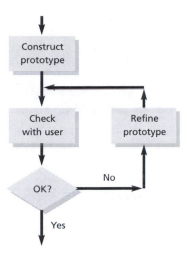

Figure 11.1

11.7 ● Task analysis

Task analysis is concerned with recording and analyzing the tasks that users undertake. One type of task analysis is known as *hierarchical task analysis*, because it breaks an overall task down into subtasks. It uses as a notation either pseudocode or structure charts. Information about what users do is obtained from a variety of sources:

- observation
- interviews
- manuals.

Observation of users is carried out while they use the current system, which may be either manual or computer-assisted.

The purposes of task analysis are twofold:

- to assist in requirements elicitation
- to guide design.

In clarifying requirements, hierarchical task analysis helps to clarify the functions that a new system should provide. In guiding the design process, hierarchical task analysis suggests the actions that the system will provide. It also identifies tasks that are carried out frequently; these can then be provided as quick and easy features. An example of how task analysis might lead to identifying frequent tasks is the finding that selecting a word of text is a common operation in word processing. The design of this task can then be made easy, e.g. double mouse clicking within the required word.

Consider the task of editing text, with or without the aid of a word processor. This task can be diagrammed as a structure chart as shown in Figure 11.2. This shows the overall task (edit text) broken down into subtasks – hence the use of the word hierarchical as part of the name of the technique. A box with an asterisk in the top-right

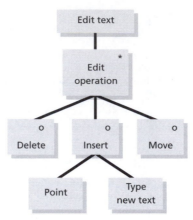

Figure 11.2 Hierarchical task analysis structure chart of editing text

corner means that the task is repeated. Thus an individual edit operation is performed a number of times. A box with the letter O in the top-right corner means that it is one of two or more alternatives. Thus deletion, insertion, and movement of text are alternative tasks. Boxes alongside each other are tasks that are performed in sequence, one after the other. Thus insertion involves pointing, followed by entering new text.

Note that task analysis models the user's view of activities – not the structure of software. For example, in a full study of word processing, a hierarchical task analysis would include specifying activities such as inserting floppy disks and switching-on a printer. However, for the majority of the activities represented in a task analysis diagram, software support will be provided.

SELF TEST QUESTION

11.3 The design of the HCI for a desk calculator is under consideration. One of the tasks being analyzed is the conversion of a list of sums of money from US dollars to Yen. Carry out hierarchical task analysis for this task.

Task analysis helps clarify requirements, but it also provides information that can be used for architectural design. For example, if we were to use object-oriented design for the word processor example, task analysis might lead us to model `text` as an object and `select` as a method.

As we have seen, hierarchical task analysis models the tasks or functions that users carry out. Task analysis can also be carried out using other techniques described elsewhere in this book to model other aspects of the user:

● Functional decomposition, using pseudocode, models tasks using an alternative notation from the graphical notation shown above.

● Data flow diagramming models data flows (in fact data flow design was originally created as a notation for modeling manual procedures in an office).

● Object-oriented techniques model both actions and objects.

But remember that task analysis is applied to modeling human activities, not computer activities. Task analysis puts the user and their actions at the center of design. It does not record their thinking (the reasons for their actions) – just what they need to do.

Once task analysis has been carried out, a decision must be made about which tasks are to be carried out by the computer and which by the user. This is not always obvious. In command and control or process control systems, a large amount of responsibility can be assigned to the computer. Knowledge-based systems and intelligent agents are capable of undertaking many tasks formerly the preserve of humans. Judgment is needed to decide how much is subject to automation. Even in a simple word processor, decisions need to be made about who carries out spell correcting or formatting.

In summary, the steps involved in task analysis are:

1. Model the user tasks.
2. Identify the tasks to be performed by computer.
3. Create the functional specification.
4. Use the model to devise the software architectural design.

The drawback with task analysis is that, because design is based on the current way of working, it is unlikely to lead to a markedly innovative design.

11.8 ● Design evaluation

Once a user interface prototype has been created, it is evaluated to determine whether it meets the needs of the user. Evaluation can range from an informal test drive to formally designed studies that use statistical methods for the evaluation of questionnaires completed by a population of end-users.

The evaluation cycle proceeds as follows. After a preliminary design has been completed, a first prototype is created. The prototype is evaluated by the user or users, who provide the designer with comments about the efficacy of the interface. Design modifications based on the user comments are then made, and the next prototype is created. The cycle continues until no further modifications to the interface design are necessary.

An HCI evaluation is concerned with assessing the usability of the interface and checking that it meets user requirements. Ideally, an evaluation is conducted against a usability specification – the specification of a system should include, wherever possible, quantitative values for usability attributes. Possible usability attributes are:

● learnability – the time taken to achieve a specified level performance

● throughput – the speed at which the user can carry out tasks

● robustness when confronted with user errors

● recoverability from user errors
● adaptability – the extent to which the system can accommodate tasks that were not envisaged during design.

Metrics for each of these usability attributes can be devised. For example, a learnability metric might state "a user who is familiar with the work supported by the system will be able to use 80% of the system functionality after a three-hour training session." A recoverability metric might state that "a user who is familiar with the computer system will be able to recover from an error that they made in less than 2 seconds."

There are a number of techniques for user interface evaluation. Some involve directly monitoring users as they use the system. There are several techniques:

● observation – someone watches users as they use the system
● video recording – users are video recorded as they use the system
● software monitoring – the inclusion of monitoring software which collects information as the system is used
● verbalizing – the user speaks aloud as they use the system, relating what they are doing and what they are thinking.

Most large software development organizations maintain dedicated usability laboratories, in which numbers of users are monitored while using prototypes of software products under development.

An alternative approach is to use questionnaires or rating sheets to elicit views after people have used the system. Questions may ask for:

● a simple yes or no response, for example "Is the clear button easy to use?"
● numeric response on a scale, say 1 to 10, for example "How easy is the clear button to use?"

If desired the designer can extract quantitative feedback from this information, for example "70% of users found the clear button easy to use."

11.9 ● Help systems

Help systems are just one aspect of user guidance, which deals with three areas:

● the messages produced by the system in response to user actions
● the on-line help system
● the documentation provided with the system.

The design of useful and informative information for users should be taken seriously and should be subject to the same quality process as designs or programs. Error messages should always be polite, concise, consistent, and constructive. They must not be abusive and should not have associated beeps or other noises which might embarrass the user.

Error messages should:

● describe the problem in jargon the user can understand
● provide constructive advice for recovering from the error
● spell out any negative consequences of the error
● be accompanied by a visual cue
● not blame the user.

Help facilities may be either *integrated* or *add-on*. An integrated help facility is designed into the software from the beginning. It is usually context-sensitive, providing information relevant to what the user is doing. An add-on help facility is added to the software after the system has been built. It is often merely an on-line manual with query capability. A number of design issues should be considered when a help facility is considered:

● Will help be available for all system functions at all times?
● How will the user request help – help menu, function key, HELP command?
● How will help be represented – separate window, reference to printed document, one-line suggestion in a fixed screen location?
● How will the user return to normal interaction – return button, function key, control sequence?
● How will the information be structured – flat, layered, hypertext?

Some help systems provide a network structure in which each frame of help information may refer to several other information frames like those in Web pages. Ideally a help frame should not simply be a reproduction of the user manual, since people read paper and screens in different ways.

11.10 ● Implementation tools

As we have seen, the process of user interface design is iterative. A design model is created, implemented as a prototype, examined by users, and modified based on their comments. To make the task of construction and modification easier, interface design and prototyping tools have evolved. Called *user-interface toolkits* or *user-interface development systems* (UIDS), these tools provide software modules or objects that facilitate creation of windows, menus, event handling, error messages, commands, and many other elements of an interactive environment.

Other useful tools are Visual Basic (see Chapter 18 on tools) and its Pascal equivalent Delphi, which are widely used software tools that support the rapid development of applications. The advantage of these tools for HCI design is that they support the direct design of a user interface, allowing the designer to select buttons, text boxes, scroll bars, and all the usual widgets using convenient drop and drag. A new interface can be constructed in minutes, shown to a user and then easily modified to meet requirements.

It is good design practice to keep the software required for information presentation separate from the information itself. The representation on the user's screen can then be changed without having to change the underlying software. So for example the time remaining to complete some task can be displayed as a number, as a bar, an egg timer, or as a stop watch. The particular choice can be decided when the interface is constructed, rather than when the application is implemented.

Object-oriented languages and development systems such as Smalltalk are ideal tools for creating GUI interfaces because the inheritance mechanism means that complex interfaces can be constructed fairly simply.

11.11 ● Summary

- There are a number of different views of the HCI – the software engineer, the user, the psychologist, the sociologist.
- A number of design guidelines and principles are available to assist in HCI design.
- Prototyping is currently the most effective method for HCI design.
- Prototyping is accompanied by repeated evaluation of an interface until it meets usability standards
- Task analysis is a major method for clarifying requirements and guiding what the user interface should provide.
- A set of guidelines is available to assist in the design of help systems.

EXERCISES

11.1 Continue hierarchical task analysis for the word processor. Hence identify a set of functions that might be provided by a word processor. Design an interface. Suggest how the interface could be evaluated.

11.2 Design a user interface for a desk calculator. It must include at least one display to show the number currently being used. It must have buttons for the functions provided. These include a button for each of the digit buttons, and buttons for the common arithmetic operations. It should also have a clear button and an undo button. Use the guidelines and principles from the text during the design, construct a prototype, and carry out an evaluation of the design.

11.3 Design a user interface for a Web site that allows the user to browse a catalog of books and choose to buy selected books by entering a credit card number, a name, and address.

11.4 Perhaps the most notorious example of a poor HCI is the VCR. Design an HCI for programming a VCR to record one or more television programs using a remote control device. Assume that the television can be used as a display device during programming.

11.5 Design an HCI for a mobile phone. Design suitable buttons and assume that a small display is available as part of the phone. Make assumptions about the tasks that users of the phone want to carry out. Suggest criteria for evaluating your design and suggest how the design could be evaluated (and thereby improved).

11.6 Suggest features for a Web browser. Design an HCI for the browser. Suggest how the interface of the browser could be evaluated.

11.7 "HCI design is in its infancy." Discuss.

11.8 "HCI design methods are little more than a set of guidelines. There is no proper methodology for HCI design." Discuss.

11.9 Review and assess available tools that assist with the creation of user interfaces.

11.10 Devise a suitable toolkit to assist in the development of graphical user interfaces.

11.11 Assess the strengths and weaknesses of HCI methods.

11.12 Suggest a future for HCI devices and methods.

ANSWERS TO SELF TEST QUESTIONS

11.1 A principle is general, abstract; a guideline is specific, concrete and applicable.

11.2 Who is the user? How many users do you involve? How many times should you go round the loop?

11.3

FURTHER READING

This book gives good accounts of guidelines for HCI, by one of the HCI gurus: B. Shneiderman, *Designing the User Interface: Strategies for Effective Human–Computer Interaction*, Addison-Wesley, 3rd edition, 1998.

A widely used and liked textbook on the subject is: Alan Dix, Janet Findlay, Gregory Abowd and Russell Beale, *Human–Computer Interaction*, Prentice Hall, 2nd edition, 1998.

Another widely used and liked textbook is wide-ranging, readable, and comprehensive. It presents the views of a variety of people from different disciplines: Jenny Preece with others, *Human–Computer Interaction*, Addison-Wesley, 1994.

Some light reading, guidelines, and practical advice on designing GUI interfaces from the creator of Visual Basic: Alan Cooper, *About Face. The Essentials of User Interface Design*, IDG Books, 1995.

This book shows how to implement GUI's using statecharts: Ian Horrocks, *Constructing the User Interface with Statecharts*, Addison-Wesley, 1999.

Well worth a read is an oldie but a goodie: Donald Norman, *The Psychology of Everyday Things*, Perseus Books, 1988.

12
Formal development

This chapter:

- explains the stages of formal development
- explains the role for formal development within software engineering.

12.1 ● Introduction

Much of the documentation produced during software development is conventionally written in a natural language such as English. Because natural languages are inherently ambiguous and open to misinterpretation, one might argue that relying on natural language descriptions of tasks and deliverables (particularly program specifications) will inevitably lead to misunderstandings by both users and developers, thus increasing the likelihood of incorrect software. As we saw in Chapter 4, the alternative is to use a formal notation (i.e. one based on mathematics) to express specifications, thus opening up the possibility of producing *provably* correct software rather than software which has been shown to be correct for a small number of supplied test cases. It could be said that these claims are somewhat idealistic in an industry which works to strict standards and tight deadlines, and when CASE tools to support the approach are still in their infancy, but nevertheless there are convincing arguments that a formal approach does (at least) give increased confidence in the correctness of the software produced by such methods. Our intention here is not to suggest that formal methods provide some definitive answer to what has become known as the "software crisis." Rather, we view formal methods as a collection of techniques which *augment* existing informal approaches. By taking advantage of an armory of *all* appropriate methods and tools, the software developer minimizes potential problems and maximizes the effectiveness of the development process.

12.2 ● What is a formal method?

The first stage of software development is for the systems analyst to establish precisely what the users of the proposed system want. The output of this *requirements definition* stage is a *requirements specification* which contains both functional and nonfunctional requirements – that is, it details precisely what the software should do as well as any practical constraints which the developer should take into account (such as response times). The documentation produced is usually informal (i.e. written in a natural language), or at most semiformal (i.e. perhaps including data flow diagrams). Using formal methods, the task of constructing a piece of software based on the requirements specification can be split into the following three subsequent phases.

12.2.1 Specification

The requirements specification is for the use of the systems analyst and customer, not the software developer. Using the requirements specification, a *software specification* is now produced which formalizes the functional requirements for the benefit of the developer. Currently, the two most widely used formal specification notations are Z and VDM (Vienna Development Method). Both take a model-based approach; that is, they represent the data types and structures necessary to describe a problem using mathematical entities such as sets, functions, and sequences. In addition, they assume that at a particular moment the computer system being specified can be in any one of several discrete states, and operations required of the system are described by stating how they change the state for given inputs.

12.2.2 Design

The specification produced in 12.2.1 above is based on an abstract mathematical model; that is, the data types it uses probably bear no relation to the data types which will be used for an implementation in the target programming language. The abstract specification therefore has to be transformed into a "concrete design." A specification becomes a concrete design by substituting computable structures for abstract mathematical models. By "computable" we mean a structure which is closer to the actual data structures offered by the implementation language. The above procedure is known as *data refinement*. (The word *reification* is sometimes used instead of *refinement*, notably in the context of VDM.)

12.2.3 Implementation

The concrete design is expressed terms of data types and structures which correspond to those available in the target implementation language. The next problem is to turn the operation specifications into program code. This procedure is known as *operation refinement*.

Note that, using a formal approach, the distinction between specifications, designs, and implementations is blurred, in the sense that the deliverables from each phase can be expressed in the same notation. Each is a description which is derived from its predecessor by the process known as "refinement."

12.3 ● Formal development: a case study

We shall now illustrate the essence of the approach by taking a simple example of a specification for a library system, and showing how it could be refined into an implementation. But first, a word of warning to the reader. As we have said, formal methods are based on mathematics, and even though our intention is only to give a flavor of the approach, what follows necessarily uses some mathematical notation. Some people (including many working in the software industry) are frightened by mathematics, and there is no doubt that this fear can act as a barrier to the potential acceptance of formal methods. In the context of formal methods, think of mathematics as just another language for expressing ideas, more concise and less ambiguous than traditional languages such as English. (In what follows, we assume the reader has read and understood Chapter 4, on formal specification.)

12.3.1 Specification

In Chapter 4, we introduced the Z notation using the following specification of a library:

```
┌─Library──────────────────────────────────
│ shelved, loaned : ℙ CATNO
├──────────────────────────────────────────
│ shelved ∩ loaned = ∅
```

```
┌─Borrow───────────────────────────────────
│ Δ Library
│ book? : CATNO
├──────────────────────────────────────────
│ book? ∈ shelved
│ shelved' = shelved \ {book?}
│ loaned' = loaned ∪ {book?}
```

```
┌─Return───────────────────────────────────
│ Δ Library
│ book? : CATNO
├──────────────────────────────────────────
│ book? ∈ loaned
│ loaned' = loaned \ {book?}
│ shelved' = shelved ∪ {book?}
```

How do we know that the specification we have written is correct, that it contains no errors and is a true reflection of what the user wants? Just because it has been written in Z doesn't automatically *ensure* correctness – but the fact that it is mathematically based *does* mean that we have a better chance of systematically detecting errors. So the next task is to *validate* the specification.

Validating the specification

Does the specification correctly capture the sponsor's intentions? Are there mistakes in our use of Z? To try to answer these questions, we can *reason* about the specification (treating it as a piece of mathematics) with a view to validating it. For example, the precondition on the `Borrow` operation was

```
book? ∈ shelved
```

and the included ΔLibrary schema stated that

```
shelved ∩ loaned = ∅
```

Intuitively, we can see that the following is therefore also true:

```
book? ∉ loaned
```

Note that this predicate is not explicit in our definition of `Borrow`, but it can be derived from the predicates which are explicitly stated. This means that the `Borrow` operation will only be used in the case where the book being borrowed is both shelved *and* not on loan.

As a more formal example, consider the overall effect of borrowing a book on the total library stock. We would expect that at the conclusion of a borrow operation, the stock of the library would be unchanged. That is,

```
shelved' ∪ loaned' = shelved ∪ loaned
```

We can prove that this is indeed the case using the following argument:

```
shelved' ∪ loaned'
```

1. = `(shelved \ {book?}) ∪ (loaned ∪ {book?})`
  [from specification of `Borrow`]

2. = `(shelved \ {book?}) ∪ ({book?} ∪ loaned)`
  [union is commutative]

3. = `((shelved \ {book?}) ∪ {book?}) ∪ loaned`
  [union is associative]

4. = `(shelved ∪ {book?}) ∪ loaned`
  [law relating set difference to union]

5. = `shelved ∪ loaned`
  [from specification of `Borrow`, book? ∈ shelved]

Steps 2, 3, and 4 make use of some existing laws about set operations, namely that if A, B, and C are sets, then

```
A ∪ B = B ∪ A                        [Law of Commutativity]
A ∪ (B ∪ C) = (A ∪ B) ∪ C            [Law of Associativity]
((A \ B) ∪ B) ∪ C = (A ∪ B) ∪ C      [law relating set difference to union]
```

There are many such laws in set theory which can be used in the construction of proofs like this. For example, step 5 makes use of the fact that, because sets have no repeated elements, if $a \in A$, then $A \cup \{a\} = A$.

SELF TEST QUESTION

12.1 Outline a proof showing that when a book is borrowed, the size of the `loaned` set is increased by 1. (The cardinality operator # can be used to find the size of a set. For example, #{a, b} = 2.)

A specification is *consistent* if its *internal* structure is sound and free from logical defects. In effect, the validation process here seeks to establish that the specification describes something that could actually be built. For example, if the precondition of a given operation always evaluates to false, then that operation can never be used, which suggests an error in the operation definition. Such consistency checks are referred to as *proof obligations*.

However, there is a further *external* consideration – can we be sure that the specification describes software that the client actually wants? To try to establish that it does, we solicit questions from the client and formalize them (in Z) as conjectures about the specification. For example, in a real library system, a potential user might ask: "Books currently on loan which have been reserved by another reader cannot be renewed. Does your specification ensure this constraint?" Establishing an answer to this query by reasoning formally about the existing specification not only reassures the client, but also increases the specifier's confidence in the validity of the system model. Additionally, questions about the way the components of the specification fit together can be asked. For example, if the same book is borrowed and then immediately returned, the library stock as a whole should be unchanged. If we are unable to prove this, then clearly something in the specification is wrong. By systematically exploring the specification in this way, we can increase our confidence that it really is an appropriate model of the intended real system.

12.3.2 Design

We now have a validated specification expressed in terms of sets – a data type which (we shall assume) is not available in our target implementation language. The next step is to take the specification to a level which is expressed in terms of data types which have a direct counterpart in the target language (such as arrays). That is, we have to think about a concrete data structure to represent the components of our system state, `shelved` and `loaned`. Two arrays (which we'll call `Cshelved` and `Cloaned` – the c standing for "concrete") would seem to be a natural representation:

```
Cshelved, Cloaned : array [ 1 .. ] of CATNO
```

For example, suppose `shelved` was the set {c1, c2, c4} and `loaned` was {c3, c5}. Then `Cshelved` and `Cloaned` would look like this:

```
     Cshelved              Cloaned
   1 │ c1 │              1 │ c3 │
   2 │ c2 │              2 │ c5 │
   3 │ c4 │              3 │ xx │
   4 │ xx │              4 │ xx │
   5 │ :  │              5 │ :  │

    ns = 3                nl = 2
```

The purpose of the variables **ns** and **nl** is to mark the indices of the last entries in the arrays `Cshelved` and `Cloaned` respectively. For simplicity, we assume the arrays are infinite, but of course we shall only be using a finite part of them, defined by **ns** and **nl**. The rest of the arrays are filled with arbitrary default values of no interest to us, which we'll never access (we'll use **xx** for this default, representing *any* arbitrary value). These arrays are quite easy to model in Z. As usual, we record the concrete model in a schema:

```
┌─CLibrary──────────────────────────────────────────
│ Cshelved, Cloaned : ℕ₁ → CATNO
│ ns, nl : ℕ
├──────────────────────────────────────────────────
│ ∀ i,j : 1 .. ns • i ≠ j ⟹ Cshelved(i) ≠ Cshelved(j)
│ ∀ i,j : 1 .. nl • i ≠ j ⟹ Cloaned(i) ≠ Cloaned(j)
│ ∀ i : 1 .. ns ( ∀ j : 1 .. nl • Cshelved(i) ≠ Cloaned(j) )
└──────────────────────────────────────────────────
```

$ℕ_1$ is a another basic type provided by Z, standing for the set {1, 2, 3, ... }.

SELF TEST QUESTION

12.2 Why are `Cshelved` and `Cloaned` total rather than partial functions?

The arrays `Cshelved` and `Cloaned` are modeled as total functions, and **ns** and **nl** are natural numbers. So the example arrays above would be modeled by

```
Cshelved = {1 ↦ c1, 2 ↦ c2, 3 ↦ c4, 4 ↦ xx, ...}
Cloaned = {1 ↦ c3, 2 ↦ c5, 3 ↦ xx, ...}
ns = 3
nl = 2
```

Note that the programming language expression `Cshelved[2]`, which accesses the second element of the array called `Cshelved`, is equivalent to the function application `Cshelved(2)` in our concrete model.

What does the invariant in `CLibrary` say? All three lines use a "universal quantification" expression, which has the following general form:

∀ declarations • predicate

This can be read as "for all these declared variables, the following predicate holds." So the first line of the invariant says that if we choose any two different values of i and j in the range 1 to ns, then Cshelved(i) and Cshelved(j) will also be different. This is to ensure that there will be no repeated catalog numbers in Cshelved – a fact that can be taken for granted in our abstract model, because sets *can't* have repeated elements. The second line makes a similar assertion about Cloaned. The third line restates concretely the invariant from our original abstract version of the specification – that Cshelved and Cloaned cannot have any elements in common. Notice how this line already points towards an implementation as a nested for loop.

The abstract model recorded in Library and the concrete model recorded in CLibrary are clearly related. We describe this relationship formally by means of a "retrieve" schema, which states how the abstract model can be retrieved from the concrete model:

```
┌─Retrieve──────────────────────────────────────
│ Library
│ CLibrary
├───────────────────────────────────────────────
│ shelved = ran (1..ns ◁ Cshelved)
│ loaned = ran (1..nl ◁ Cloaned)
└───────────────────────────────────────────────
```

The construction of the retrieve schema constitutes a proof of *adequacy*.

The ◁ symbol is the *domain restriction* operator. The expression

```
s ◁ f
```

describes the function which results from restricting the domain of the function f to the set s. So for example, if

```
Cshelved = {1 ↦ c1, 2 ↦ c2, 3 ↦ c4, ...}
ns = 3
```

then

```
shelved   = ran (1..ns ◁ Cshelved)
          = ran (1..3 ◁ {1 ↦ c1, 2 ↦ c2, 3 ↦ c4, ...})
          = ran {1 ↦ c1, 2 ↦ c2, 3 ↦ c4}
          = {c1, c2, c4}
```

1..3 is the same as the set {1, 2, 3}.

SELF TEST QUESTION

12.3 From a programming point of view, how would the two arrays Cshelved and Cloaned be updated when a book was borrowed?

Now we are in a position to write the new concrete `Borrow` operation:

```
┌─CBorrow ──────────────────────────────────────
│ ΔCLibrary
│ book? : CATNO
├──────────────────────────────────────────────
│ ∃ i : 1 .. ns • book? = Cshelved(i)
│ Cshelved' = squash( Cshelved ▷ {book?} )
│ ns' = ns - 1
│ nl' = nl + 1
│ Cloaned' = Cloaned ⊕ {nl' ↦ book?}
└──────────────────────────────────────────────
```

ΔCLibrary gives us access to the before and after states of the concrete representation of the library and, as before, `book?` is the book we wish to borrow. The first line of the predicate establishes that there is indeed a book with that catalog number in the `Cshelved` array. It uses an "existential quantification" expression:

   ∃ declaration • predicate

which can be read as "there exists at least one value of the declared variable such that the predicate holds." Thus the predicate is true only if there is a value of `i` in the range `1` to `ns` such that `book?` is equal to `Cshelved(i)`. For example, if

```
Cshelved = {1 ↦ c1, 2 ↦ c2, 3 ↦ c4, ...}
ns = 3
```

and `book?` = `c2`, then the value of `i` which satisfies the predicate is `2`. Notice how the existential quantification points towards an implementation which uses an iterative loop to search for the book and its position in the array.

The ▷ symbol is the *range subtraction* operator. The expression `f ▷ s` describes the function that results from subtracting the set `s` from the range of the function `f`. So for example, if

```
Cshelved = {1 ↦ c1, 2 ↦ c2, 3 ↦ c4, ...}
book? = c2
```

then

```
Cshelved'  = squash(Cshelved ▷ {c2})
           = squash({1 ↦ c1, 2 ↦ c2, 3 ↦ c4, ...} ▷ {c2})
           = squash({1 ↦ c1, 3 ↦ c4, ...})
```

After the range subtraction, the resulting function models an array with a gap, or a missing value, in position 2. Fortunately, Z provides us with a `squash` operator, which resequences the indices:

```
squash({1 ↦ c1, 3 ↦ c4, ...}) = {1 ↦ c1, 2 ↦ c4, ...}
```

So `Cshelved'` describes the array which results from shuffling the elements in order to close the gap.

Finally, we have to add the borrowed book to `Cloaned`. Here, we make use of the *function override* operator, written ⊕. Suppose we have two functions `f` and `g`, where

```
f = {a ↦ 1, b ↦ 2, c ↦ 3}
g = {b ↦ 5, d ↦ 6}
```

Then

```
f ⊕ g = {a ↦ 1, b ↦ 5, c ↦ 3, d ↦ 6}
```

`f ⊕ g` is a bit like `f ∪ g`, except that maplets in `g` overwrite those in `f` that have the same left hand side.

Returning to `CBorrow`, suppose

```
Cloaned = {1 ↦ c3, 2 ↦ c5, ...}
nl = 2
book? = c2
```

Then

```
nl' = 3
Cloaned'  = Cloaned ⊕ {nl' ↦ book?}
          = {1 ↦ c3, 2 ↦ c5, 3 ↦ xx, ...} ⊕ {3 ↦ c2}
          = {1 ↦ c3, 2 ↦ c5, 3 ↦ c2, ...}
```

So now `Cloaned` contains the issued book in the first free position in the array.

Intuitively we can see that `CBorrow` is a correct refinement of `Borrow`. But this isn't enough – we must formally *prove* that this is the case. To do this, we must show that:

● The abstract precondition of `Borrow` is equivalent to the concrete precondition of `CBorrow` – or in other words, whenever `Borrow` can be legally invoked in some abstract state, `CBorrow` can be invoked in the corresponding concrete state. This constitutes a proof of *applicability*.

● The final states produced by `Borrow` and `CBorrow` are equivalent. In other words, any concrete state that can result from invoking `CBorrow` could also be produced (in its abstract form) by `Borrow`. This constitutes a proof of *correctness*.

(Mathematically, these proofs involve showing that, from the predicates in `CBorrow` and ΔRetrieve, we can prove the predicate in `Borrow`.)

We would have to show this "operation correctness" for all the specified operations, i.e. including our (as yet unwritten) refinement of the `Return` operation. Such proofs are outside the scope of this book. Suffice it to say that once these proofs are complete, we can have confidence that the concrete model is indeed equivalent to the original abstract model, and we can move towards an implementation based upon it.

The reader may be becoming uneasy about the lengthy (and difficult) design procedure we have described, and the obvious practical difficulties it would entail in the real world. Such uneasiness is well founded; we shall return to these concerns in Section 12.4.

12.3.3 Implementation

At the end of the design phase we should have a specification whose state is expressed in terms of data types which have a direct counterpart in the collection of data structures provided by the target programming language. The next task is to turn the operation specifications into program code, either by constructing algorithms by inspiration (much as programs are traditionally written from natural language specifications), and then formally verifying the equivalence of specification and code; or, better, by transforming the concrete specification gradually into code using transformation rules which are guaranteed to preserve the correctness of the original specification. This latter approach is known as *operation refinement*, and has the additional benefit of ensuring that the code is produced in small, manageable chunks rather than as a monolithic whole, thus minimizing the potential for error.

From a given concrete specification, an operation refinement system has to be able to introduce the usual programming constructs (such as blocks, procedures, local variables, assignment statements, and selection and iteration clauses) in order to implement the specified system. Most current refinement systems are based upon expressing algorithms in a so-called *guarded command language*, which is slightly different to the more familiar programming languages such as C++ and Java. The reader may find it difficult to see how the concrete specification CBorrow could be immediately *transformed* into code, although most practising programmers could very easily produce (by inspiration) code which implemented the functionality of the operation, based on an understanding of its meaning rather than its precise structure. However, the existential quantification in the CBorrow predicate certainly suggests an implementation which would use an iterative loop to find the position of the book to be issued in Cshelved. There is no such immediate iterative interpretation in the original Borrow operation. Refinement is actually an iterative process, in that there may be many concrete specifications produced *en route* to the least abstract one that is used to generate the implementation. Thus CBorrow would need further refinement to take it closer and closer to a version which mirrored typical iterative array accessing constructs.

12.4 ● The role of formal development

The use of the word "design" in the above is perhaps slightly different to its conventional use in a nonformal approach to software development. In formal methods, the design phase is that process which produces a concrete design from an abstract specification. Operation refinement is then used to produce an implementation from the concrete design.

To continue with the implementation in this way would require that the code produced from the concrete specification is itself proved to be correct. This can be done, but it is very labour intensive, and impractical in real industry-based situations. But there is an alternative. Refinement is about moving the specification towards the target programming language. Alternatively, we could move the target language closer to the specification, through the use of *abstract data types (ADTs)*. That is, we create, as ADTs in our target language, a library of the data types and functions used by Z. Each ADT consists of a set of values that a variable of that type can take, and a set of operations that can be applied to those values. We can then, in theory, rewrite our Z specification in the target language, using the defined ADTs, so as to produce an implementation.

The phases in formal development which involve mathematical proof, while offering obvious potential benefits, are currently not viable, in the sense that they require particular skills which only a minority in the software industry possess. However, there are other techniques for specification validation which are more accessible to the less mathematically inclined developer. For example, a specification can be *animated* by rewriting it in a suitable executable language (thereby producing a rapid prototype), and using this executable version to explore the specification's behavior, possibly with the sponsor's participation. Once everyone involved is happy that the specification (demonstrated by the animation) has captured the requirements, implementation can begin. Special-purpose tools are being developed to support this activity.

The *B-Method* (also developed by Abrial, the originator of Z) is a formal method for turning a formal specification (expressed in something called the *Abstract Machine Notation*, a model-based formal specification language resting on the same principles as Z) into program code. The method prescribes how to check specifications for consistency (i.e. that the invariant is preserved by the defined operations), and check designs and implementations for adequacy and operation correctness. An object-oriented approach (see Chapter 10) is taken in the construction of specifications and the design of implementations. B is supported by the *B-Tool*, a language interpreter and run-time environment, and the *B-Toolkit*, a collection of integrated tools. Among other things, the Toolkit provides tools for specification, design, and code configuration management; syntax and type checkers; a specification animator; verification tools for generating proof obligations and helping with proofs; coding tools such as translators and linkers; and a documentation support tool. The Toolkit's aim is to provide a development environment which ensures that all the files comprising a particular development are always in a consistent state.

Formal development can produce *provably* correct software – programs that we *know* will fulfill their sponsor's requirements because they have been systematically derived from validated formal specifications using correctness-preserving procedures. However, if formal methods are to fulfill their promise, the construction of integrated tools to support the approach (such as those provided by the B-Toolkit) is vital to the eventual acceptance of a formal software development scenario.

12.5 ● Summary

● Formal development is based on the premise that mathematics is a much more precise and unambiguous notation for describing program specifications than a natural language such as English; and that proving is better than testing, in that a program can be shown to be correct for all possible inputs rather than for a carefully chosen subset.

● A formal specification can be validated using mathematical reasoning.

● A formal method for software design uses a correctness-preserving procedure called refinement to transform a formal specification into an implementation.

● Formal development is particularly beneficial in sensitive domains in which program correctness is crucial, such as situations which are potentially life-threatening if software errors occur.

● CASE tools such as prototyping and animation systems, formal specification language editors, and proof support tools are in various stages of development in the computing industry and in academia.

EXERCISES

12.1 Write CReturn, the refinement of the Return operation.

12.2 Some readers of this book may still be doubters of the benefits of formal methods. A model for a proposed system to maintain a database of all readers is shown below:

[NAME]   (NAME is the set of unique people's names)

```
┌─Readers ──────────────────────────────────
│ allreaders, doubters : ℙ NAME
├───────────────────────────────────────────
│ doubters ⊆ allreaders
└───────────────────────────────────────────
```

Occasionally, doubters see the light:

```
┌─SeeTheLight ──────────────────────────────
│ ΔReaders
│ r? : NAME
├───────────────────────────────────────────
│ r? ∈ doubters
│ doubters' = doubters \ {r?}
└───────────────────────────────────────────
```

Devise a concrete design for the abstract model. Specify the concrete design and its invariant in Z, and show how a refinement of the SeeTheLight operation can be written in terms of this concrete design.

12.3 In Chapter 4, we considered an enhancement to the library model, specified as follows:

```
┌─Library1 ─────────────────────────────────
│ Library
│ members : ℙ MEMNO
│ loans : CATNO ↠ MEMNO
├───────────────────────────────────────────
│ loaned = dom loans
│ ran loans ⊆ members
└───────────────────────────────────────────
```

Devise a concrete model (documented in a schema called CLibrary1) which includes the new components, members and loans. Specify CBorrow2, the concrete version of Borrow2.

ANSWERS TO SELF TEST QUESTIONS

12.1 We have to show that `#loaned'` = `#loaned + 1`.

1. `#loaned'` = `#(loaned ∪ {book?})`

[from specification of `Borrow`]

2. = `#loaned + #{book?}`

[law relating set cardinality to union]

3. = `#loaned + 1`

Step 2 follows from step 1 because we know (from the argument given earlier) that `book? ∈ loaned`.

12.2 Because they can be applied to *any* member of $\mathbb{N}_1$, not just a subset, although such an application might return the default value `xx`.

12.3 The new book would have to be added into the next free position (i.e. `n1+1`) in `Cloaned`, and removed from `Cshelved`. This removal might involve some shuffling to fill the gap.

FURTHER READING

This book gives a thorough introduction to the Z notation, and also explains how Z specifications can be realized as programs in a guarded command language: J. B. Wordsworth, *Software Development with Z*, Addison-Wesley, 1992.

A thorough explanation of the refinement process is given in: J. Woodcock and J. Davies, *Using Z: Specification, Refinement and Proof*, Prentice Hall, 1996.

The B-Method is explained in: J. Wordsworth, *Software Engineering with B*, Addison-Wesley, 1996.

Programming paradigms

The programming language

This chapter discusses the ideal features of a programming language for software engineering.

13.1 ● Introduction

Everyone involved in programming has their favorite programming language, or language feature they would like to have available. There are many languages, each with their proponents. This chapter is not a survey of programming languages, nor is it an attempt to recommend one language over another. Rather, we wish to discuss the features that a good programming language should have from the viewpoint of the software engineer. We limit our discussion to "traditional" procedural languages such as Fortran, Cobol, Pascal, and Ada, and to the procedural features of languages such as C++ and Java. (An overview of the simpler Java features is given in the appendix.) Other approaches to programming languages are discussed in the chapters on object-oriented programming, functional programming, and logic programming. Other features of languages – exceptions and parallelism – are dealt with in other chapters.

The main thrust of this chapter will be a discussion of the features a language should provide to assist the software development process. That is, what features encourage the development of software which is reliable, maintainable, and efficient?

13.1.1 Classifying programming languages and features

It is important to realize that programming languages are very difficult animals to evaluate and compare. For example, although it is often claimed that language X is a general-purpose language, in practice languages tend to be used within particular communities. Thus traditionally Cobol is often the preferred language of the data processing community; Fortran, the language of the scientist and engineer; C, the language of the systems programmer; and Ada, the language for developing real-time or embedded computer systems. Cobol is not equipped for applications requiring complex numerical computation, just as the data description facilities in Fortran are poor and ill-suited to data processing applications.

Programming languages are classified in many ways. For example, "high-level" or "low-level." A high-level language such as Cobol, Fortran, or Ada, is said to be problem-oriented and to reduce software production and maintenance costs. A low-level language such as assembler, is said to be machine-oriented and to allow programmers complete control over the efficiency of their programs. Between high- and low-level languages, another class, the systems implementation language or high-level assembler, has emerged. Languages such as C attempt to bind into a single language the expressive power of a high-level language and the ultimate control which only a language that provides access at the register and primitive machine instruction level can provide. Languages may also be classified using other concepts such as whether they are block-structured or not, whether they are weakly or strongly typed, and whether they are compiled or interpreted. In the rest of this chapter we will examine how these concepts and others impact on the programmer.

It is useful to divide up the discussion into those features required to support *programming in the small* and those required to support *programming in the large*. By *programming in the small*, we mean those features of the language required to support the coding of individual program modules or small programs. In this category, we include the simplicity, clarity, and orthogonality of the language, the language syntax, and facilities for control and data abstraction. We will discuss these features one by one. By *programming in the large*, we mean those features of the language which support the development of large programs. Here, we define a "large" program as one whose size or complexity dictates that it be developed by a number of programmers and which consists of a collection of individually developed program modules. In this category we include facilities for the separate compilation of program modules, features for controlling the interaction between program modules, high-level functional and data abstraction tools, and programming environments or support tools associated with the language.

13.2 ● Design principles

13.2.1 Simplicity, clarity, and orthogonality

One school of thought argues that the only way to ensure that programmers will consistently produce reliable programs is to make the programming language simple. For programmers to become truly proficient in a language, the language must be small and simple enough that it can be understood in its entirety. The programmer can then use the language with confidence, probably without recourse to a language manual.

Cobol and PL/1 are examples of languages which are large and unwieldy. For example, Cobol currently contains about 300 reserved words. Not surprisingly, it is a common programming error to mistakenly choose a reserved word as a user-defined identifier. The ANSI standard for Cobol is 3 cm thick. By contrast, somewhat unfairly, the Pascal standard is 3 mm thick. What are the problems of large languages? Because they contain so many features, some are seldom used and, consequently, rarely fully understood. Also, since language features must not only be understood independently but also in terms of their interaction with each other, the larger the number of features, the more complex it will be to understand their interactions. Although smaller, simpler languages are clearly desirable, the software engineer of the near future will often have to wrestle with existing large, complex languages. For example, to meet the requirements laid down by its sponsors, the US Department of Defense, the programming language Ada is a large and complex language requiring a 300 page reference manual to describe it.

The clarity of a language is also an important factor. In recent years, there has been a marked and welcome trend to design languages for the programmers who program in them rather than for the machines the programs are to run on. Many older languages incorporate features that reflect the instruction sets of the computers they were originally designed to be executed on. As one example, consider the Fortran arithmetic if statement which has the following form:

```
if (expression) 11,12,13
```

This statement evaluates the expression and then branches to one of the statements labeled 11, 12, or 13 depending on whether the result is positive, zero, or negative. The reason for the existence of this peculiar statement is that early IBM machines had a machine instruction which compared the value of a register to a value in memory and branched to one of three locations. The language designers of the 1960s were motivated to prove that high-level languages could generate efficient code. Although we will be forever grateful to them for succeeding in proving this point, they introduced features into languages, such as Cobol and Fortran, which are clumsy and error-prone from the programmers' viewpoint. Moreover, even though the languages have subsequently been enhanced with features reflecting modern programming ideas, the original features still remain.

A programming language is the tool that programmers use to communicate their intentions. It should therefore be a language which accords with what people find natural, unambiguous, and meaningful – in other words, clear. Perhaps language designers are not the best judges of the clarity of a new language feature. A better approach to testing a language feature may be to set up controlled experiments in which subjects are asked to answer questions about fragments of program code. This experimental psychology approach is gaining some acceptance and some early results are discussed in the section on control abstractions.

A programmer can only write reliable programs if he or she understands precisely what every language construct does. The quality of the language definition and supporting documentation are critical. Ambiguity or vagueness in the language definition erodes a programmer's confidence in the language. It should not be necessary to have to write a program fragment to confirm the semantics of some language feature. As one example of the problems that may arise, consider the lack of type equivalence rules in Pascal.

The *Revised Pascal Report*, the document defining Pascal, did not define when two types were to be considered equivalent. Consider the following example:

```
type
    Vector = array [1 .. 10] of Integer;
var
        Vector1 : Vector;
        Vector2 : Vector;
        Vector3 : array [1 .. 10] of Integer;
        Vector4 : array [1 .. 10] of Integer;
```

Which of these variables `Vector1`, `Vector2`, `Vector3`, and `Vector4` are considered to be of the same type? Since the language definition does not help, we must determine what scheme the language implementor chose to follow. Two possible schemes are *structural equivalence* and *name equivalence*. Structural equivalence defines two types as being equivalent if they have the same structure. Thus, in our example, all the variables would be considered of the same type. Name equivalence, on the other hand, defines two objects to be of the same type only if the names of their types are the same. Using this scheme, only `Vector1` and `Vector2` are considered to be of the same type. The result of this definition problem is that, since different compilers have different notions of type equivalence, many programs do not immediately execute successfully when moved from one environment to another. This is a problem that is largely solved in an object-oriented language, where it is clear from the description of an object what the type of an object is.

Programming languages should also display a high degree of orthogonality. This means that it should be possible to combine language features freely; special cases and restrictions should not be prevalent. Although more orthogonal than many other languages, Pascal displays a lack of orthogonality in a number of areas. For example, it is entirely reasonable for a programmer to infer that values of all scalar types can be both read and written. In Pascal this is generally true, with the exception that booleans may be written but not read, and that enumerated types may not be read or written. Similarly, one would expect that functions would be able to return values of any type, rather than be restricted to returning values of only scalar types. A lack of orthogonality in a language has an unsettling effect on programmers; they no longer have the confidence to make generalizations and inferences about the language.

It is no easy matter to design a language that is simple, clear, and orthogonal. Indeed, in some cases these goals would seem to be incompatible with one another. A language designer could, for the sake of orthogonality, allow combinations of features that are not very useful. Simplicity would be sacrificed for increased orthogonality! While we await the simple, clear, orthogonal programming language of the future, these concepts remain good measures with which the software engineer can evaluate the programming languages of today.

13.3 ● Language syntax

The syntax of a programming language should be consistent, natural, and promote the readability of programs. Syntactic flaws in a language can have a serious effect on

program development. For example, Pascal uses the semicolon as a separator between statements rather than as a terminator of statements. In the example below, we must remember
that no semicolon is required after the `Writeln` statement as no statement follows it.

```
begin
    Read (IntegerValue);
    if IntegerValue > 0 then
        Write ('Value read was positive');
    Writeln
end.
```

If we now decide to add an `else` clause to the `if` statement, we must remember to
edit the previous line and remove the semicolon at the end of the `Write` statement. If we
do not, the semicolon will separate (terminate?) the `if` from the statement following and
the `else` will then cause a syntax error.

```
begin
    Read (IntegerValue);
    if IntegerValue > 0 then
        Write ('Value read was positive')
    else
        Write ('Value read was zero or negative');
    Writeln
end.
```

Studies have shown that syntax errors due to the misuse of semicolons are *ten* times more
likely to occur in a language using the semicolon as a separator than in a language using
it as a terminator.

Another syntactic flaw found in languages is the use of `begin` ... `end` pairs or brack-
eting conventions for grouping statements together. Omitting an `end` or closing bracket
is a very common programming error. The use of explicit keywords, such as `end if` and
`end while`, leads to fewer errors and more readily understandable programs. Such programs are also easier to maintain. For example, consider associating a second statement
with the Pascal `if` statement shown below.

```
if IntegerValue > 0 then
    NumberOfPositiveValues = NumberOfPositiveValues + 1
```

We now have to group the two statements together into a compound statement using
a `begin` ... `end` pair:

```
if IntegerValue > 0 then
    begin
        NumberOfPositiveValues := NumberOfPositiveValues + 1;
        NumberOfNonZeroValues := NumberOfNonZeroValues + 1
    end
```

Substantial editing is required here. Compare this with the explicit keyword approach
taken by Ada:

```
if IntegerValue > 0 then
    NumberOfPositiveValues := NumberOfPositiveValues + 1;
end if
```

in which the only editing required would be the insertion of the new statement.

In addition, explicit keywords eliminate the classic "dangling else" problem prevalent in many languages. Nested `if` structures of the form shown below raise the question of how `if`'s and `else`'s are to be matched. Is the "dangling" `else` associated with the outer or inner `if`? Remember that the indentation structure is of no consequence.

```
if boolean expression then
    if boolean expression then
        statement_1
else
    statement_2
```

Pascal resolves this dilemma by applying the rule that an `else` is associated with the most recent nonterminated `if` lacking an `else`. Thus, the `else` would be associated with the inner `if`. If, as the indentation suggests, we had intended the `else` to be associated with the outer `if`, there are two alternative suggestions. Either insert a null or empty `else` to match the inner `if` or surround the inner `if` with a `begin .. end` pair as follows.

```
if boolean expression then
    if boolean expression then
        statement_1
    else
else
    statement_2
if boolean expression then
    begin
        if boolean expression then
            statement_1
    end
    else
        statement_2
```

The clearest and cleanest solution is afforded by the use of explicit keywords.

```
if boolean expression then
    if boolean expression then
        statement_1
    end if
else
    statement_2
end if
```

The static, physical layout of a program should reflect as far as is possible the dynamic algorithm which the program describes. There are a number of syntactic concepts which can help achieve this goal. The ability to freely format a program allows the programmer the freedom to use techniques such as indentation and blank lines to highlight the structure and improve the readability of a program. For example, prudent indentation can help convey to the programmer that a loop is nested within another loop. Such indentation is strictly redundant, but assists considerably in promoting readability. Older languages such as Fortran and Cobol impose a fixed formatting style on the programmer. Components of statements are constrained to lie within certain columns on each input source line. For example, Fortran reserves columns 1 through 5 for statement labels and columns 7 through 72 for program statements. These constraints are not intuitive to the programmer; rather they date back to the time when programs were normally presented to the computer in the form of decks of 80-column punched cards. A program statement was normally expected to be contained on a single card.

The readability of a program can also be improved by the use of *meaningful identifiers* to name program objects. Limitations on the length of names, as found in early versions of Basic (2 characters) and Fortran (6 characters), force the programmer to use unnatural, cryptic, and error-prone abbreviations. These restrictions were dictated by the need for efficient programming language compilers. Arguably, programming languages should be designed to be convenient for the programmer rather than the compiler and the ability to use meaningful names, irrespective of their length, enhances the self-documenting properties of a program.

Another factor which affects the readability of a program is the consistency of the syntax of a language. For example, operators should not have different meanings in different contexts. The operator "=" should not double as both the assignment operator and the equality operator. Similarly, it should not be possible for the meaning of language keywords to change under programmer control. The keyword `if`, for example, should be used solely for expressing conditional statements. If the programmer is able to define an array with the identifier **if**, the time required to read and understand the program will be increased as we must now examine the context in which the identifier `if` is used to determine its meaning.

13.4 ● Control abstractions

A programming language for software engineering must provide a small but powerful set of control structures to describe the flow of execution within a program unit. In the late 1960s and 1970s there was considerable debate as to what control structures were required. The advocates of structured programming have largely won the day and there is now a reasonable consensus of opinion as to what kind of primitive control structures are essential. A language must provide primitives for the three basic structured programming constructs; sequence, selection, and repetition. There are, however, considerable variations both in the syntax and the semantics of the control structures found in modern programming languages.

Early programming languages, such as Fortran, did not provide a rich set of control structures. The programmer used a set of low-level control structures, such as the unconditional branch or `goto` statement and the logical `if` to express the control flow within a program. For example, the following Fortran program fragment illustrates the use of these low-level control structures to simulate a condition controlled loop.

```
      n = 10
10    if (n .eq. 0) goto 20
      write (6,*) n
      n = n - 1
      goto 10
20    continue
```

These low-level control structures provide the programmer with too much freedom to construct poorly structured programs. In particular, uncontrolled use of the `goto` statement for controlling program flow leads to programs which are, in general, hard to read and unreliable.

There is now general agreement that higher-level control abstractions must be provided and should consist of:

● *Sequence* – to group together a related set of program statements.

● *Selection* – to select whether a group of statements should be executed or not based on the value of some condition.

● *Repetition* – to repeatedly execute a group of statements.

This basic set of primitives fits in well with the top-down philosophy of program design; each primitive has a single entry point and a single exit point. These primitives are realized in similar ways in most programming languages. For brevity, we will look in detail only at representative examples from common programming languages. For further details on this subject refer to Chapter 5 on structured programming.

13.4.1 Selection

Ada, in common with most modern languages, provides two basic selection constructs; the first, the `if` statement, provides one or two-way selection and the second, the `case` statement provides a convenient multiway selection structure. Examples of `if` statements are shown below:

```
if ThisMonth = December then
    NextMonth := January;
endif

if ThisMonth = December then
    NextMonth := January;
else
    NextMonth := Month'Succ(ThisMonth);
endif
```

An example of a `case` statement is:

```
case ThisMonth is
    when January | March | May | July | August | October | December
                => NoOfDaysInMonth := 31;
    when April | June | September | November
                => NoOfDaysInMonth := 30;
    when February =>
        if LeapYear (ThisYear) then
            NoOfDaysInMonth := 29;
        else
            NoOfDaysInMonth := 28;
        endif;
    when others => null;
end case;
```

When evaluating the conditional statements in a programming language, the following factors need to be considered.

● Does the language use explicit closing symbols, such as `end if`, thus avoiding the "dangling else" problem?

● Nested conditional statements can quite easily become unreadable. Does the language provide any help? For example, the readability of "chained" `if` statements can be improved by the introduction of an `elsif` clause. In particular, this eliminates the need for multiple `endif`'s to close a series of nested `if`'s. Consider the following example, with and without the `elsif` form.

```
if condition_1 then                    if condition_1 then
    statement_1                            statement_1
else if condition_2 then               elsif condition_2 then
    statement_2                            statement_2
    else if condition_3 then           elsif condition_3 then
        statement_3                        statement_3
        else if condition_4 then       elsif condition_4 then
            statement_4                    statement_4
        else                           else
            statement_5                    statement_5
        endif                          endif
    endif
    endif
endif
```

● The expressiveness of the `case` statement is impaired if the type of the case selector is restricted. It should not have to be an integer.

● Similarly, it should be easy to specify multiple alternative case choices (e.g. `1 | 5 | 7` meaning 1 or 5 or 7) and a range of values as a case choice (e.g. `Monday ... Friday` or `1 .. 99`).

● The reliability of the `case` statement is enhanced if the case choices must specify actions for *all* the possible values of the case selector. If not, the semantics should, at least, clearly state what will happen if the case expression evaluates to an unspecified choice. The ability to specify an action for all unspecified choices through a `when others` or similar clause is optimal.

It would be natural to think that there would no longer be any controversy over language structures for selection. The `if...then...else` is apparently well established. However, the lack of symmetry in the `if` statement has been criticized. While it is clear that the `then` part is carried out if the condition is true, the `else` part is rather tagged on at the end to cater for all other situations. Experimental evidence suggests that significantly fewer bugs will result if the programmer is required to restate the condition (in its negative form) prior to the `else` as shown below:

```
if condition then
    statement_1
not condition else
    statement_2
endif
```

13.4.2 Repetition

Control structures for repetition traditionally fall into two classes; loop structures where the number of iterations is fixed, and those where the number of iterations is controlled by the evaluation of some condition. Fixed length iteration is often implemented using a form similar to that shown below:

```
for loop_control_variable := initial_expression to final_expression
                            step step_expression
do
    statement(s)
endfor
```

The usefulness and reliability of the `for` statement can be affected by a number of issues:

● The type of the loop control variable should not be limited to integers. Any ordinal type should be allowed. However, reals (floats) should not be allowed. For example, consider how many iterations are specified by the following:

```
for x := 0.0 to 1.0 step 0.33 do
```

It is not at all obvious exactly how many repetitions will be performed, and things are made worse by the fact that computers represent real values only approximately. (Note how disallowing the use of reals as loop control variables conflicts with the aim of orthogonality.)

● The semantics of the `for` is greatly affected by the answers to the following questions. When and how many times are the initial expression, final expression, and step expressions evaluated? Can any of these expressions be modified within the loop? What is of concern here is whether or not it is clear how many iterations of the loop will be performed. If the expressions can be modified and the expressions are re-computed on each iteration, then there is a distinct possibility of producing an infinite loop.

● Similar problems arise if the loop control variable can be modified within the loop. A conservative but safe approach similar to that taken by Pascal (which precludes assignment into the loop control variable) is preferred.

● The scope of the loop control variable is best limited to the `for` statement. If it is not, then what should its value be on exit from the loop or should it be undefined?

Condition controlled loops are far simpler in form. Almost all modern languages provide a leading decision repetition structure (`while` ... `do`) and some, for convenience, also provide a trailing decision form (`repeat` ... `until`).

```
while condition do                      repeat
    statement(s)                            statement(s)
endwhile                                until condition
```

The `while` form continues to iterate while a condition evaluates to true. Since the test appears at the head of the form, the `while` performs zero or many iterations of the loop body. The `repeat`, on the other hand, iterates until a condition is true. The test appears following the body of the loop, ensuring that the `repeat` performs at least one iteration. Thus the `while` statement is the more general looping mechanism of the two, so if a language provides only one looping mechanism it should therefore be the `while`. However the `repeat` is sometimes more appropriate in some programming situations.

SELF TEST QUESTION 13.1

13.1 Identify a situation where `repeat` is more appropriate than `while`.

Some languages provide the opposites of these two loops:

```
do
    statement(s)
while condition
```

and:

```
until condition do
    statement(s)
end until
```

C, C++, and Java all provide `while...do` and `do...while` structures. They also provide a type of `for` statement that combines together several commonly used ingredients. An example of this loop structure is:

```
for (i = 0; i < 10; i++) {
    statement(s)
}
```

in which:

● the first statement within the brackets is done once, before the loop is executed;
● the second item, a condition, determines whether the loop will continue;
● the third statement is executed at the end of each repetition.

The `while` and `repeat` structures are satisfactory for the vast majority of iterations we wish to specify. For the most part, loops which terminate at either their beginning or end are sufficient. However, there are situations, notably when encountering some exceptional condition, where it is appropriate to be able to branch out of a repetition structure at an arbitrary point within the loop. Often it is necessary to break out of a series of nested loops rather than a single loop. In many languages, the programmer is limited to two options. The terminating conditions of each loop can be enhanced to accommodate the "exceptional" exit, and `if` statements can be used within the loop to transfer control to the end of the loop should the exceptional condition occur. This solution is clumsy at best and considerably decreases the readability of the code. A second, and arguably better, solution is to use the much-maligned `goto` statement to branch directly out of the loops. Ideally however, since there is a recognized need for "N-and-a-half" times loops, the language should provide a controlled way of exiting from one or more loops. Java provides the following facility where an orderly `break` may be made but only to the statement following the loop(s).

```
while (condition) {
    statement(s)
    if (condition) break;
    statement(s)
}

here:
    while (while_condition) {
        for variable_name in discrete_range {
            statement(s)
            if (exit_condition) break here;
            statement(s)
        }
    }
```

In the first example above, control will be transferred to the statement following the loop when the condition is true. This may be the only way of exiting from this loop. In the second example, control will be transferred out of both the `for` and the `while` loops when `exit_condition` is true. Note how the `while` loop is labeled `here:` and how this label is used in the `if` statement to specify that control is to be transferred to the end of the `while` loop (not the beginning) when `exit_condition` is satisfied.

SELF TEST QUESTION

13.2 Sketch out the code for a method to search an array of integers to find some desired integer. Write two versions – one using the `break` mechanism and one without `break`.

The languages C, C++, Ada, and Java provide a mechanism such as the above for breaking out in the middle of loops.

Handling errors or exceptional situations is a common programming situation. In the past, such an eventuality was handled using the `goto` statement. Nowadays features are built in to programming languages to facilitate the more elegant handling of such situations. We discuss the handling of exceptions in Chapter 20.

13.5 ● Data types and strong typing

A significant part of the software engineer's task is concerned with how to model, within a program, objects from some problem domain. Programming, after all, is largely the manipulation of data. In the words of Niklaus Wirth, the designer of Pascal, "Algorithms + Data Structures = Programs" – which recognizes that both algorithms and data have structure and, sometimes, complexity. Moreover they have equal importance and are symbiotic. The data description and manipulation facilities of a programming language should therefore allow the programmer to represent "real-world" objects easily and faithfully. In recent years, increasing attention has been given to the problem of providing improved data abstraction facilities for programmers. Discussion has largely centered around the concept of a data type, the advantages of strongly typed languages, and language features to support *abstract data types*. The latter is an issue discussed later in this chapter.

A data type is a set of data objects and a set of operations applicable to all objects of that type. Almost all languages can be thought of as supporting this concept to some extent. Many languages require the programmer to explicitly define the type (for example, integer or character) of all objects to be used in a program and this information prescribes the operations that can be applied to the objects. Thus, we could state that Fortran, Cobol, C, C++, Ada, and Java are all typed languages. However, only Ada and Java would be considered strongly typed languages.

A language is said to be *strongly typed* if it can be determined whether or not each operation performed on an object is consistent with the type of that object. Operations inconsistent with the type of an object are considered illegal. A strongly typed language therefore forces the programmer to carefully consider how objects are to be defined and used within a program. In some languages, the type information provided by the programmer allows the compiler to perform automatic checking and discover type inconsistencies. Studies have shown that programs written in strongly typed languages are clearer, more reliable, and more portable. Strong typing necessarily places some restrictions on what a programmer may do with data objects. However, this apparent decrease in flexibility is more than compensated for by the increased security and reliability of the ensuing programs.

Languages such as Lisp (similar to Haskell, see Chapter 16 on functional programming), APL, and POP-2 allow a variable to change its type at run-time. This is known as *dynamic typing* as opposed to the *static typing* found in languages where the type of an object is permanently fixed. Where dynamic typing is employed, type checking must occur at run-time rather than compile-time. Dynamic typing provides additional freedom and flexibility but at a cost. More discipline is required on the part of the programmer so that the freedom provided by dynamic typing is not abused. That freedom is often very useful, even necessary, in some applications – for example, problem-solving programs which use sophisticated artificial intelligence techniques for searching complex data structures would be very difficult to write in languages without dynamic typing.

What issues need to be considered when evaluating the data type facilities provided by a programming language? We suggest the following list:

- Does the language provide an adequate set of primitive data types?
- Can these primitives be combined in useful ways to form aggregate or structured data types?
- Does the language allow the programmer to define new data types? How well do such new data types integrate with the rest of the language?
- To what extent does the language support the notion of strong typing?
- When are data types considered equivalent?
- Are type conversions handled in a safe and secure manner?
- Is it possible for the programmer to circumvent automatic type checking operations?

13.5.1 Primitive data types

Programmers are accustomed to having a rudimentary set of primitive data types available. We have come to expect that the primitive types, `Boolean`, `Character`, `Integer`, and `Real` (or `Float`), together with a supporting cast of operations (relational, arithmetic, etc.) will be provided. For each type, it should be possible to clearly define the form of the literals or constants which make up the type. For example, the constants `true` and `false` make up the set of constants for the type `Boolean`. Similarly, we should be able to define the operations for each type. For the type `Boolean`, these might include the operations =, <>, `not`, `and`, and `or`. For certain application domains, advanced computation facilities such as extended precision real numbers or long integers are essential.

The ability to specify the range of integers and reals and the precision to which reals are represented reduces the dependence on the physical characteristics, such as the word size, of a particular machine and thus increases the portability of programs. However, most languages (for example C and C++) leave the issue of the precision and range of numbers to the compiler writer for the particular target machine. Java gets around this sloppiness by precisely defining the representation of all its built-in data types. Whatever machine a program is executed on, the expectation is that data is represented in exactly the same manner. Thus the program will produce exactly the same behavior, whatever the machine.

Types should only be associated with objects through explicit declarations. Implicit declarations, such as those allowed in Fortran, where, by default, undeclared variables beginning with the letters "I" through "N" are considered to be of type integer, should be avoided. The use of such conventions encourages the use of cryptic names and mistakes.

13.5.2 User-defined data types

The readability, reliability, and data abstraction capabilities of a language are enhanced considerably if the programmer can extend the primitive data types provided as standard by the language. The ability to define user-defined types separates the languages Pascal, Java, and Ada from their predecessors. For example, consider the following definition of a Pascal enumerated type:

```
type
    Day = (Monday, Tuesday, Wednesday, Thursday, Friday, Saturday,
          Sunday);
var
    Today : Day;
```

The type Day is a new type, variables of which may *only* take literals of that type (that is Monday, Tuesday, ...) as values. Assignments such as the following will be flagged as type errors by the compiler because the type of the expression on the right-hand side of each assignment is incompatible with the type of the variable receiving the result.

```
Today := January;
Today := 7;
```

The equivalent in a weakly typed language such as Fortran might be:

```
integer Monday, Tuesdy, Wdnsdy, Thrsdy, Friday, Satrdy, Sunday,
          Today
DATA Monday /1/, Tuesdy /2/, Wdnsdy /3/, Thrsdy /4/
DATA Friday /5/, Satrdy /6/, Sunday /7/
```

The absence of user-defined types forces the programmer to map the values of a type Day onto a primitive type; the integers. While this increases the readability of assignments such as

```
Today = Sunday
```

it does not prevent the programmer from using the alternative,

```
Today = 7
```

or even the "illegal" assignment:

```
Today = 0
```

since `Today` is an integer variable and therefore may be assigned any integer value. In Fortran, even the assignment

```
Today = 2.3
```

would not be flagged as an error. The real value `2.3` would be coerced (or converted) into an integer value (`2`) which would then be assigned into the variable `Today`. The increased security for the programmer obtained from a language which is strongly typed can clearly be seen even from these simple examples. In addition to defining completely new types, it is also useful to be able to define types which are subranges of existing types. For example, we might define a new type `Weekday` whose literals are the subrange `Monday .. Friday` of the type `Day` or a type `PositiveInteger`, a subrange of the integers from `0 .. Maxint`.

```
type
    Weekday = Monday .. Friday;
    PositiveInteger = 0 .. Maxint;
```

The types `Weekday` and `PositiveInteger` inherit operations from their base types, the types `Day` and `Integer`. Any operation which is valid on an object of type `Day` is valid on an object of type `Weekday`. Of course, the programmer must be sure not to assign into a variable of type `Weekday`, a value of type `Day` which is not also a value of type `Weekend`. In a strongly typed language the compiler can automatically generate code to perform run-time checks to ensure that this will always be so. In a weakly typed language, the responsibility for adding such code falls on the programmer.

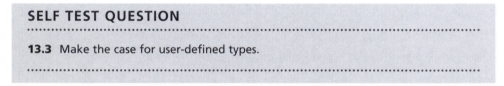

SELF TEST QUESTION

13.3 Make the case for user-defined types.

13.5.3 Structured data types – arrays

Composite data types allow the programmer to model structured data objects. The most common aggregate data abstraction provided by programming languages is the *array*; a collection of homogeneous elements (all elements of the same type) which may be referenced through their positions (usually an integer) within the collection. Arrays are characterized by the type of their elements and by the index or subscript range or ranges which specify the size, number of dimensions, and how individual elements of the array may be referenced. For example, the Pascal type definition shown below defines a type `Matrix`. Variables of type `Matrix` are two-dimensional arrays of integers with their first subscript varying from 1 through 5 and second subscript varying from 1 through 4.

```
type
    Matrix = array [1 .. 5, 1 .. 4] of Integer;
var
    ThisMatrix : Matrix;
```

Individual elements of the array can be referenced by specifying the array name and an expression for each subscript, for example, `ThisMatrix [2, 3]`. The implementation of arrays in programming languages raises the following considerations for the programmer.

● What restrictions are placed on the element type? For complete freedom of expression there should be no restrictions. Similarly the index type should be any valid subrange of any ordinal type.

● At what time must the size of an array be known? The utility of arrays in a programming language is governed by the time (compile-time or run-time) at which the size of the array must be known.

● What aggregate operations may be applied to arrays? For example, it is very convenient to be able to carry out array assignment or comparison between compatible arrays.

● Are convenient methods available for the initialization of arrays?

The time at which a size must be bound to an array has important implications on how the array may be used. In Pascal the size of an array must be defined statically – the size and subscript ranges are required to be known at compile-time. This has the advantage of allowing the compiler to generate code to automatically check for out-of-range subscripts. However, the disadvantage of this simple scheme is that, to allow the program to accommodate data sets of differing sizes, we often wish to delay determining the size of the array until run-time. Consider, for example, the problem of defining a general-purpose procedure to sort the contents of an array. In Pascal, we are forced either to change the declaration and recompile or, more probably, to make some reasonable estimate as to the maximum size array the procedure should handle. This is not an easy estimate for the programmer to make and clearly is often very inefficient in space. A further problem exists in Pascal in that formal array parameters to procedures must also specify their size statically. This makes it impossible to write a general routine to manipulate an arbitrary sized matrix. Rather, a specific routine must be defined for each particular size of matrix. This is very inconvenient and inefficient; many implementations of Pascal now include a feature (conformant arrays) to deal with this very problem.

Less restrictive approaches are to be found. Ada, for example, allows the specification of array types in which the subscript ranges are not fixed at compile-time. A general type definition for a two-dimensional matrix might be:

```
type
    Matrix = array (Integer range <>, Integer range <>) of
                    Integer;
```

A procedure with a formal parameter of type `Matrix` would now accept any actual parameter which is a two-dimensional array of integers with integer subscripts.

Moreover, the bounds of any array of type `Matrix` need only be available when the array declaration is encountered at run-time. The bounds themselves may be specified by expressions and thus the same array declaration may generate arrays of different sizes each time the declaration is encountered. For example, provided variables `M` and `N` have integer values the following declaration will generate an `M` × `N` matrix.

```
ThisMatrix : Matrix (1 .. M, 1 .. N);
```

In Java, the size of an array is determined at run time. However, subscripts always start at 0, betraying the C origins of the language as a language close to machine instructions.

SELF TEST QUESTION

13.4 Argue for and against the language making array subscripts start at 0.

13.5.4 Structured data types – records

Data objects in problem domains are not always simply collections of homogeneous objects (same types). Rather, they are often collections of heterogeneous objects (different types). Although such collections can be represented using arrays, many programming languages, but notably not Fortran, provide a record data aggregate. Records (or structures as they are termed in C and C++) are generalizations of arrays where the elements (or fields) may be of different types and where individual components are referenced by (field) name rather than by position. For example, the Pascal type definition shown below might describe information relating to a mortgage. Each object of type `Mortgage` has five components named `MortgageHolder`, `Principal`, etc.

```
type
    Mortgage =
        record
            MortgageHolder :        array [1 .. 30] of char;
            Principal :             PositiveInteger;
            AmortizationPeriod :    1 .. 35 {years};
            LengthOfMortgage :      1 .. 5 {years};
            InterestRate :          Real
        end;
```

Components of records are selected by name. The method used by Ada, PL/1, and C first specifies the record variable and then the component of that record. For example, given `ThisMortgage`, a record variable of type `Mortgage`, the following expression accesses the `InterestRate`:

```
ThisMortgage.InterestRate
```

Each component of a record may be of any type – including aggregate types such as arrays and records. Similarly, the element type of an array might be a record type. Programming languages which provide data abstractions such as arrays and records and allow them to be combined orthogonally in this fashion allow a wide range of real data objects to be modeled in a natural fashion. This is not true of all languages – for example Fortran.

Sometimes, records whose structure is not completely fixed can be useful. Such records normally contain a special field, known as the tag field, the value of which determines the structure of the record. Records with varying structures are known as *variant records* or, since the record type can be thought of as a union of several subtypes based on some discriminating tag field, as *discriminated unions*. For example, the type Mortgage might be extended as follows. Based on the value of the discriminant field MortgageType, no additional information will be stored in the case of an open mortgage, the prepayment penalty and the annual prepayment will be stored in the case of a closed mortgage, and the principal amount of the first mortgage in the case of a second mortgage.

```
type
    Mortgage =
        record
            MortgageHolder :            array [1 .. 30] of char;
            Principal:                  PositiveInteger;
            AmortizationPeriod:         1 .. 35 {years};
            LengthOfMortgage:           1 .. 5 {years};
            InterestRate:               Real;
            case MortgageType: (Open, Closed, Second) of
                Open:
                Closed:       (PrePaymentPenalty : PositiveInteger;
                               AnnualPrePayment : PositiveInteger);
                Second:       (FirstMortgagePrincipal : PositiveInteger)
        end;
```

We must guard against references to components of the variant part of the record which are incompatible with the value of the discriminant field MortgageType. So, for example, if for a particular record variable, the MortgageType were Open, then a reference to the PrePaymentPenalty component of the variable should be illegal. We would expect that the language should at least be able to generate code to check for such references at run-time. In Pascal, the implementation of variant records is very insecure and this is the cause of one of its famous insecurities. Pascal allows programmers to assign into the tag field of a variant record variable at any time. This logically indicates a dynamic change in the structure of the record. As a consequence no run-time checks are performed and the onus is on the programmer to write defensive code to ensure no illegal references to variant fields are made. Furthermore, Pascal allows the tag field to be omitted. Variant records are one reason why Pascal is not considered as strongly typed as Ada. Ada adopts a safer approach, restricting the programmer to specify the tag field when a record variable is created and disallowing subsequent changes to the value of the tag field.

The languages Cobol, PL/1, C, C++, and Ada support records. (In C and C++ a record is termed a `struct`.) The Java language does not provide records as described above because the facilities we have described can be implemented as objects, using the object-oriented features of the language (see Chapter 14).

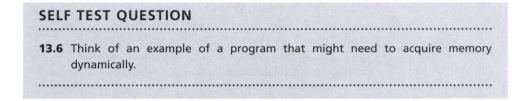

SELF TEST QUESTION

13.5 Make the case for arrays and records.

13.5.5 Dynamic data structures

Many programs need to acquire temporary memory to carry out their task. Examples are a graphics program that needs to acquire sufficient memory to hold an image in memory, and a word processor that needs memory to process the text of a document. In an OO language memory is required each time a new object is created (instantiated) to provide space for the data associated with the object. This space can be released when the object is no longer required. Similarly, if a non-OO language is used, a program will often need temporary workspace in which to build a data structure that grows and shrinks according to the demand. These are sometimes termed *dynamic data structures*, and clearly it requires dynamic memory management.

SELF TEST QUESTION

13.6 Think of an example of a program that might need to acquire memory dynamically.

In C or C++, the programmer can explicitly issue a request (using the function `malloc`) to the memory manager component of the operating system to obtain a region of memory. Subsequently a call to function `free` returns the space to the memory manager.

The *pointer* data type is provided by modern languages such as Pascal, Ada, and C++ but not by older languages such as Fortran and Cobol. More recently, the Java language does not provide pointers accessible to the programmer. Pointers provide the programmer with the ability to refer to a data object indirectly. We can manipulate the object "pointed" to or referenced by the pointer. Pointers are particularly useful in conjunction with dynamic data structures – situations where the size of a data aggregate cannot be predicted in advance or where the structures of the aggregates are dynamically varying. Pointers are often used to link one record to another in what is called a linked data structure.

In some languages, recursive data structures, such as lists and trees, are more easily described using pointers. Similarly, operations such as deleting an element from a linked list or inserting a new element into a balanced binary tree are more easily accomplished using pointers. Although such data types can be implemented using arrays, the mapping is less clear and certainly less flexible. Also performance is often faster when a dynamic structure is used.

SELF TEST QUESTION

13.7 Compare inserting a new item into a structure implemented as:

1. an array
2. a dynamic linked data structure.

The use of pointers brings considerable power and flexibility, but with the consequent responsibility. It is well recognized that the explicit use of pointers is extremely dangerous because it can lead to major errors (or subtle but dangerous errors). The use of pointers is not without pitfalls. The pointer is often mentioned in the same sentence as the infamous goto statement as a potential source for obtuse and error-prone code. A number of issues should be considered when evaluating a language's implementation of pointers.

● Since the same data object may be referenced through more than one pointer variable, care must be taken not to create a "dangling" pointer. That is, a pointer which references a location that is no longer in use. Does the language provide any assistance in reducing the opportunities for such errors?

● The security of pointers is enhanced in languages such as Ada, Java, and Pascal which require the programmer to bind a pointer variable to reference only objects of a particular type. Programs written in languages such as C and C++, which allow pointers to dynamically reference different types of object, are often awkward to debug.

● What provisions (for example, scoping mechanisms, explicit programmer action, or garbage collection procedures) does the language provide for the reclamation of space which is no longer referenced by any pointer variable? This issue is discussed below.

In Java, the program has no explicit access to memory addresses and it is therefore impossible for such a program to make the kind of mistake possible in C++. When a Java program needs memory, it creates a new object. For example, a program can instantiate an object of type Button by:

```
Button newButton = new Button("Press here");
```

This creates a pointer to the new object newButton. In Java this pointer is termed a *reference*, but there is no way in which the Java program can misuse this pointer. For example, arithmetic is not permitted on a reference, nor can the pointer be used to refer to some other object. (Both these operations are allowed in a C++ program.) Thus the Java program is prevented from causing a whole class of subtle and dangerous errors.

13.5.6 Garbage collection

A subtle source of errors can arise when memory is freed (or not) after being allocated to hold some dynamic data structure. In C++, the programmer explicitly issues a function call to free memory. The memory manager then adds the retrieved memory to its pool of available memory; this process is termed *garbage collection*. If used correctly, this causes no problems, but two sorts of errors can arise:

● *memory leaks* – memory is no longer in use, but has not been reclaimed by the memory manager.

● *memory corruption* (dangling pointer) – memory has been returned from use, but is still in use.

In a memory leak, a program acquires some memory, uses it, but then fails to return it for garbage collection. This memory is thereby rendered useless. In a program that only runs for a short time, the memory is reclaimed when the program terminates, so that there is no great problem. However, if the program is a component in a real-time system, it may have an effectively infinite lifetime, in which case memory loss is serious.

In memory corruption, a program acquires some memory, uses it, returns it for garbage collection, but then continues to use it. This is, of course, a programming error, but in large complex programs such a mistake is not unusual. The memory management system may now allocate this same memory area to some other program (or to the same program). The consequence is that two programs are now using the same area of memory, unknown to each other. This tends to result either in a program crash – if we are lucky or some subtle error, which manifests itself in some strange manner, some time after the crime has been committed. In such a situation, debugging becomes a nightmare.

In Java, the garbage collection system periodically and automatically checks for objects that are no longer in use. It then frees any available memory. Thus the programmer is freed from the task of keeping track of what memory is in use; many potential errors are therefore avoided. The disadvantage is that the programmer has limited control over when the garbage collector does its work. This might be done in a variety of ways, depending on the implementation:

● at periodic time intervals
● when available memory is exhausted
● never (planning that demand will not exceed supply)
● when a program explicitly requests it.

The garbage collector needs a stable situation in order to analyze and collect unused memory and therefore an implementation will normally freeze all running programs when the garbage collector goes into action. This means that programs may be suspended at unpredictable times. For some applications (for example Web page applets) this is probably acceptable. However, for real-time programs, sudden unpredictable stops are unacceptable and special attention to scheduling the garbage collection is required.

In summary, C++ supports explicit allocation and de-allocation of memory, with explicit access to memory pointers. This is power with considerable responsibility. In Java, allocation and de-allocation is implicit and automatic, with no access to memory pointers. This avoids a notorious class of programming bugs.

SELF TEST QUESTION

13.8 Draw up a table that compares the memory allocation scheme of C++ with that of Java according to the criteria: software reliability, development effort, and performance (run-time speed).

In Ada, pointers are explicitly accessible to the programmer, but a pointer may only point to an object of a particular type, specified when the pointer is declared and checked by the compiler. Responsibility for garbage collection is the responsibility of the run-time system and some implementations carry out automatic garbage collection. As an alternative a program can issue explicit requests to return (hopefully) unused space to the garbage collector.

13.5.7 Strong versus weak typing

The debate as to whether strongly typed languages are preferable to weakly typed languages closely mirrors the earlier debate among programming language aficionados about the virtues of the `goto` statement. The pro-`goto` group argued that the construct was required and its absence would restrict programmers. The anti-`goto` group contended that indiscriminate use of the construct encouraged the production of "spaghetti-like" code. The result has been a compromise; the use of the `goto` is restricted to cases where it is clearly the most convenient control structure to use. The anti-strongly typed languages group similarly argue that some classes of programs are very difficult, if not impossible, to write in strongly typed languages. The pro-strongly typed languages group argue that the increased reliability and security outweigh these disadvantages. We believe that a similar compromise will be struck; strong typing will be generally seen as most desirable but languages will provide well-defined escape mechanisms to circumvent type checking for those instances where it is truly required.

What programmer flexibility is lost in a strongly typed language? Weakly typed languages such as Fortran and C provide little compile-time type checking support. However, they do provide the ability to view the representation of an object as different types. For example, using the `equivalence` statement in Fortran, a programmer is able to subvert typing.

```
integer a
logical b
equivalence a, b
```

The `equivalence` declaration states that the variables a and b share the same storage. While economy of storage is the primary use of the `equivalence` statement, it also allows the same storage to be interpreted as representing an integer in one case and a logical (boolean) in the second. The programmer can now apply both arithmetic operations and logical operations on the same storage simply by choosing the appropriate alias (a or b) to reference it. This language feature is dangerous because programs using it will be unclear. Moreover such programs will not be portable because the representations used for integers and logicals are usually machine dependent. Variant records in Pascal can be used in a similar, underhand fashion to circumvent type-checking operations.

For a small number of systems programming applications, the ability to circumvent typing to gain access to the underlying physical representation of data is essential. How should this be provided in a language that is strongly typed? The best solution seems to be to force the programmer to state *explicitly* in the code that he or she wishes to violate the type checking operations of the language. This approach is taken by Ada where an object may be reinterpreted as being of a different type only by using the `unchecked_conversion` facility.

The question of conversion between types is inextricably linked with the strength of typing in a language. Fortran, being weakly typed, performs many conversions (or coercions) implicitly during the evaluation of arithmetic expressions. These implicit conversions may result in a loss of information and can be dangerous to the programmer. As we saw earlier, Fortran allows mixed mode arithmetic and freely converts reals to integers on assignment. Pascal and strongly typed languages perform implicit conversions *only* when there will be no accompanying loss of information. Thus, an assignment of an integer to a real variable will result in implicit conversion of the integer to a real. However, an attempt to assign a real value to an integer variable will result in a type incompatibility error. Such an assignment must be carried out using an explicit conversion function. That is, the programmer is forced by the language to explicitly consider the loss of information implied by the use of the conversion function. In Java, for example, a real can be converted to an integer, but only by using an explicit casting operator:

```
float f;
int i = (int) f;
```

13.6 ● Procedural abstraction

Procedural or algorithmic abstraction is one of the most powerful tools in the programmers' arsenal. When designing a program, we abstract *what* should be done before we specify *how* it should be done. Program designs evolve as layers of abstractions; each layer specifying more detail than the layer above. Procedural abstractions in programming languages, such as procedures and functions, allow the layered design of a program to be accurately reflected in the modular structure of the program text. Even in relatively small programs the ability to factor a program into small, functional modules is essential; factoring increases the readability and maintainability of programs. What does the software engineer require from a language in terms of support for procedural abstraction? We suggest the following list of requirements.

- an adequate set of primitives for defining procedural abstractions, including support for recursion
- safe and efficient mechanisms for controlling communication between program units
- simple, clearly defined mechanisms for controlling access to data objects defined within program units.

13.6.1 Procedures and functions

The basic procedural abstraction primitives provided in programming languages are *procedures* and *functions*. Procedures can be thought of as extending the statements of the language while functions can be thought of as extending the operators of the language. A procedure call looks like a distinct statement, whereas a function call appears as or within an expression. When a procedure is called, it achieves its effect by modifying the environment of the program unit which called it. Optimally, this effect is communicated to the calling program unit in a controlled fashion by the modification of the parameters passed to the procedure. Functions, like their mathematical counterparts, may return only a single value and must therefore be embedded within expressions. A typical syntax for procedures and functions is shown below:

```
procedureName(formalParameterList);
Declarations
begin
    Procedure Body
end procedure;

functionName(formalParameterList) :resultType;
Declarations
begin
    Function Body
end function;
```

The power of procedural abstraction is that it allows the programmer to consider the procedure or function as an independent entity performing a well-described task largely independent of the rest of the program. It is critical that the interface between program units be small and well defined if we are to achieve independence between units. Ideally procedures should only accept and return information through their parameters. Ideally functions should accept but not return information through their parameters. A single result should be returned as the result of invoking a function. Unfortunately, many programming languages do not enforce even these simple, logical rules. It is largely the responsibility of the programmer to ensure that procedures and functions do not have *side effects*. A side effect is any change to information outside a function or procedure caused by a call – other than the parameters to a procedure. Most programming languages do not prevent programmers from directly accessing and modifying data objects (global data) defined outside of the local environment of the procedure or function.

Along with pointers and the `goto` statement, global data has come to be regarded as a major source of programming problems. We shall see later how in programming structures called abstract data, access to global data is controlled.

Many abstractions, particularly those which manipulate recursive data structures such as lists, graphs, and trees, are more concisely described recursively. Amongst widely used languages, Cobol and Fortran, do not support recursion directly.

13.6.2 Parameter passing mechanisms

Programmers require three basic modes of interaction through parameters:

● *Input parameters* allow a procedure or function *read-only* access to an actual parameter. The actual parameter is purely an input parameter; the procedure or function should not be able to modify the value of the actual parameter.

● *Output parameters* allow a procedure *write-only* access to an actual parameter. The actual parameter is purely an output parameter; the procedure should not be able to read the value of the actual parameter.

● *Input–output parameters* allow a procedure *read-and-write* access to an actual parameter. The value of the actual parameter may be modified by the procedure.

Note that, by definition, output and input–output parameters should not be supplied to functions. Most programming languages, including Fortran and Pascal, do not automatically enforce this restriction. Again, the onus is on the programmer not to write functions with side-effects. These same languages also, unfortunately, restrict the type of result that may be returned from functions to scalar types only. Ada allows only input variables to functions but side-effects may still occur through modification of nonlocal variables.

A number of parameter-passing schemes are employed in programming languages but no language provides a completely safe and secure parameter passing mechanism. Fortran employs only a single parameter passing mode – *call by reference*. This mode equates to input–output parameters. Thus, undesirably, all actual parameters in Fortran may potentially be changed by any subroutine or function. The programmer is responsible for ensuring safe implementation. Using call by reference, the location of the actual parameter is bound to the formal parameter. The formal and actual parameter names are thus aliases; modification of the formal parameter automatically modifies the actual parameter. This method is particularly appropriate for passing large, aggregate data structures (such as arrays) as no time-consuming copying of the values of the parameters need be carried out.

Pascal uses both call by reference (annotated with the word `var`) and *call by value* (the default type of parameter). Call by reference is used for both input–output and output parameters while call by value provides a more secure implementation of input parameters. When parameters are passed by value, a copy of the value of the actual parameter is passed to the formal parameter which acts as a variable local to the procedure; modification of the formal parameter therefore does not modify the value of the actual parameter. This method is inefficient for passing large, aggregate data structures as copies must be made. In such situations, it is commonplace to pass the data structure by reference even if the parameter should not be modified by the procedure.

The parameter passing mechanisms used in Ada (`in`, `out` and `in out`) are similar to the input, output and input–output parameters described above and would therefore seem to be ideal. However, Ada does not specify whether they are to be implemented using sharing or copying. This is beneficial to the language implementor, since the space requirements of the parameter can be used to determine whether sharing or copying should be used. However, this ambiguity of implementation can be troublesome to the programmer seeking reliability and robustness.

In Java, two parameter-passing mechanisms are provided:

● call by value for the built-in data types, such as `int`

● call by reference for objects.

Thus, in general, the programmer can change the values of parameters passed to a procedure. However, the Java programming convention is to treat parameters as call by value, avoid changing their values, and return a single value from a method using the `return` statement. This convention accords with the purity of the mechanism used in functional languages.

13.6.3 Scoping mechanisms and information hiding within procedures and functions

It should not be necessary for the programmer to know the implementation details of a procedure or a function in order to use it. In particular, the programmer should not need to consider the names used within the procedure or function. Large programs use thousands of names; the names used within a procedure should not influence the choice of names outside it. Similarly, objects used within the procedure, other than output or input–output parameters, should have no effect outside the procedure. When programs are developed by more than one programmer these issues become critical. Programmers must be able to develop routines independently of each other. The software engineer requires that a language support the concept of *information hiding*; concealing information that is not required. Advanced language features for the support of information hiding will be discussed in the next section. We limit discussion here to the control of access to data objects through scoping.

Most programming languages use the concept of *scope* to control the visibility of names. The scope of a name in a program is the part of the program in which the name may be referenced. Support for scoping varies from language to language. The language Basic (in its original form) provides no scoping and all names may therefore be referenced anywhere in a program. That is, all variables are *global*. This severely limits the usefulness of the language for the development of large programs.

The unit of scope in Fortran is the subroutine or function. Since subroutines and functions may not be nested, the scope of a name is the subroutine or function in which it is implicitly or explicitly declared. That is, all names are *local* to the program unit in which they are declared. There are no global names although the same effect may be achieved through the use of shared `common` blocks.

Algol, Pascal, and Ada are known as *block-structured* languages. They use the more sophisticated concept of nested program blocks to control the scope of names. The following skeleton of a Pascal program illustrates scoping in block-structured languages:

```
program Main;
    var A, B : Integer;

    procedure Outer;
        var C, D : Char;

        procedure Inner;
          var A, E : Real;
        begin
          {statements for Inner}
        end {Inner};

    begin
        {statements for Outer}
    end {Outer};

begin
    {statements for Main}
end {Main}.
```

The scope of a name is the block (program, procedure, or function) in which it is declared. For example, consider the character variables c and D defined within Outer. They are said to be *local* to Outer and therefore may be referenced within the body of the procedure Outer. Also, since Inner is enclosed by Outer, they may also be referenced within the body of Inner. c and D are said to be global with respect to Inner. Similarly, the integer variable B declared in the main program is global (and therefore accessible) to both Inner and Outer. An identifier A is declared both in the main program and within the procedure Inner. The visibility rules here are that the integer variable A declared in the main body of the program may be referenced both in the main program and in the code for Outer since there is no A declared local to Outer and the integer A is global to it. However, since Inner does have an identifier A declared local to it, the scope or visible region of the integer A does not extend to the body of the procedure Inner.

SELF TEST QUESTION

13.9 Draw up a full list of the identifiers visible in each of Main, Outer, and Inner.

The multilevel scoping control offered by block-structured languages is of great assistance to the software engineer. Names may be re-used within the same program safely.

More importantly, some information hiding is now possible. For instance, the nesting of the procedure `Inner` within the procedure `Outer` in the example above is a statement by the programmer that `Inner` is only required by the procedure `Outer`. It is not required elsewhere in the program. The scoping rules of the language ensure that the programmers' declaration is enforced. In a situation where another programmer wishes to use Outer, they need only be given the specification of `Outer`. No reference to the procedure `Inner` need be made.

There is another point of view about block-structuring. Block structure implies nesting, as shown in the above example, where one procedure is nested inside another. Along with other nested structures – like `if`'s and loops – some studies have found that nested structures are more difficult to comprehend than linear structures. This has implications for constructing error-free programs and for accurate maintenance. Indeed it takes more than a cursory examination to identify the valid accesses in the above program fragment. Any nested structure can be transformed into a linear structure. This assumes that we need to improve an existing program; an alternative is to write a program from its inception as a linear structure. In the above program, the procedures have access to variables outside themselves. In other words, use of these procedures may cause side-effects. If the program was to be rewritten as a linear structure, the procedures could be restricted so as to access only their parameters – arguably a safer structure. The downside might be that some procedures might become more accessible than desired because, in a flat structure, all procedures are freely accessible. However, as we shall see, there are other programming language structures that can help fix this problem.

SELF TEST QUESTION

13.10 Argue for and against scope rules in block-structured languages.

Incidentally, Pascal is not a truly block-structured language. A genuine block-structured language permits the programmer to introduce a section of code – including data declarations – anywhere within the code. Pascal only supports this facility in the form of procedure declarations at the head of some other procedure.

13.7 ● Abstract data types

Functional abstraction is the traditional abstraction tool of the programmer. Programming methodologies such as top-down stepwise refinement rely totally on functional abstraction. In programming language terms, such abstractions can be thought of as extending the operations provided by the language and appear within programs in the form of procedures and functions. In recent years, increasing attention has been paid to the notion of data abstraction. Many program design decisions involve:

- selecting an internal representation for some set of data objects from the problem domain
- defining the operations to be performed on those objects.

In programming language terms, this can be thought of as extending the built-in primitive data types provided by a language with new *abstract data types*. The two abstraction mechanisms are complementary and are often used in concert with one another. Functional abstraction is often used to describe the implementation of the operations on abstract data types.

What do we require in terms of programming language support for data abstraction? An abstract data type consists of a set of objects and a set of operations which can be applied to those objects. The power of an abstraction mechanism is that it permits understanding of the essential ideas whilst suppressing irrelevant details. For example, when programming with integers in Pascal, we do not need to know whether two's complement or some other representation was selected by the implementor of the language. Thus, programming languages should support the concept of information hiding; that is, users should be provided with sufficient information to use the data type but nothing more. The most common way of achieving this is to separate out the specification of the data type from its implementation and to implement protection (scoping) mechanisms to ensure the privacy of information which should not be accessible to users. Users of a data type should be provided with a specification of the effect of each of the operations provided and a description of how to use each operation. They should not be required to know the representation of the data type nor be able to access it other than indirectly through an operation provided by the type. In summary, programming language support for abstraction should include:

- high-level encapsulation mechanisms for both functional and data abstraction
- a clear separation between the specification (the users' view) of an abstraction and its implementation (the implementors' view)
- protection mechanisms to prevent user access to private information
- support for re-usable program modules. That is, provision of library facilities and simple mechanisms for importing library modules into user programs. We discuss this aspect later, under the heading "Programming in the large."

13.7.1 Abstract data items in programming languages

Ada provides support for encapsulation in a mechanism called the package. A package can simply encapsulate a collection of related procedures or can be used to encapsulate an abstract data type. A package consists of two parts; a specification and a body (or implementation). Each of these parts may be separately compiled. The specification can be used by the programmer to describe to users how to use the package and to determine what components of the package are visible to the user. The package body contains the implementation of all procedures, functions, and data belonging to the package and is not normally seen by users of the package. Thus, Ada satisfies our requirements for a high-level encapsulation mechanism and for a clear separation between the specification of an abstraction and its implementation.

As an example of an abstract data item, consider the well-known example of a stack. (The stack is often used in these examples, because it is fairly short and demonstrates well the encapsulation of data and actions):

```
package body stack is

    size: constant := 1000;
    s: array(1..size) of integer;
    top: integer range 0..size;

    procedure push(item: integer) is
    begin
        top := top + 1;
        s(top) := item;
    end push;

    function pop return integer is
    begin
        top := top - 1;
        return s(top + 1);
    end pop;

begin
        top := 0;
end stack;
```

This piece of program (an Ada package) implements an abstract data item. It encapsulates and hides all the information about the stack and how it is to be used. The interior of the package is inaccessible from outside the package; this is enforced by the compiler. So no one can tamper – by mistake or malice – with the data that represents the stack. The only way that the stack can be accessed is via the procedure (`push`) and function (`pop`) that are provided. Thus access to the stack is carefully controlled. This constitutes the best form of modularity – access is via procedure (or function) calls, rather than by direct access to data. Good style means that only in rare cases will an abstract data item permit direct access to data within itself.

Examples of the use of this data structure are:

```
stack.push(42);
item = stack.pop();
```

In Ada, the declaration:

```
use stack;
```

imports into the scope of the user program, all the public resources of a package. This allows features of the package to be invoked without explicit qualification, for example:

```
push(42);
item = pop();
```

The Ada package mechanism allows the programmer to write a block of statements that initializes the data. In this case this is the single statement:

```
top := 0;
```

This initialization code is automatically called when the package data is created. An alternative is to provide a method that is called explicitly from outside the package when the stack needs to be initialized. This, again, contributes to the encapsulation of everything to do with the data structure.

SELF TEST QUESTION

13.11 Write a function as part of the stack package that returns true if the stack is empty and false otherwise.

It is common to see data items (variables) declared at the top of a package (as in the above example). These are global to the whole package and therefore accessible to all of the procedures and functions within it. Therefore in a real sense the procedures and functions access some global data and, as we have seen, this is generally regarded as poor style and poor modularity; it means using side-effects. However, the data that is accessible is limited and controlled by the scope of the package boundary to the procedures and functions within it. It is not data that is global to a whole program, or even a major section of a program. Moreover the procedures and functions cannot access data outside the package (unless it is explicitly flagged as accessible within some other package).

Often (though not in the stack example shown above) there will need to be additional procedures or functions that the package needs in order to carry out its tasks. These are procedures that need not and therefore should not be accessible from outside the package. The same is true of data items; while the norm is to exclude access to data, it is sometimes the case that selected data items need to be made accessible. The coding of a package therefore needs to distinguish between accessible and private items. Different programming languages have different ways of distinguishing these items:

● In Ada the programmer writes a separate description or specification that announces the public items. We shall see such descriptions very shortly.

● In Java, items are preceded either by the word `public` or the word `private` as appropriate.

Abstract data items represent a real fusion of data and actions. They are true data items, because they involve data. They extend the built-in data types provided by the language, so that the programmer can invent data suitable for the problem being solved. The programmer specifies how the data can be manipulated and thus creates truly abstract data.

By contrast with Ada, the language Pascal provides support for functional abstraction at the level of the procedure or function. But there are no standard mechanisms to encapsulate collections of procedures – although many non-standard extensions exist. Programming language support for abstract data types is variable; many programming languages, including Pascal, only provide support for what might be termed *transparent* data types; data types whose representation may be directly accessed by the programmer. That is, the representation is visible, not hidden.

SELF TEST QUESTION

13.12 Write a stack abstract data item in a language like Pascal, trying to encapsulate as much as possible the stack data together with its pop and push operations.

As can be seen from the stack example, there is no way of encapsulating a data type into a separate program module. Pascal provides little support for data abstraction. The data type and the application program are inextricably mixed. There is no clear mapping between the logical data type specified by the designer and the physical modules of the program. The lack of an encapsulation mechanism and the strict ordering (const, type, var) of declarations enforced by Pascal poses almost insurmountable organization problems in programs that require the use of multiple data types.

Pascal supports only transparent data types. The representation is visible; it is the programmers' responsibility to voluntarily refrain from directly accessing the representation. There is no protection provided by the language to the programmer who abuses the notion of a data type. For example, the programmer may directly reference the data within the stack. Such direct references to the representation would prove disastrous if the implementor of the data type were to decide to change the representation of the stack data.

The lack of an encapsulation mechanism for abstract data types can cause other problems not illustrated by the example above. For instance, the implementor of a data type often defines operations on the type simply to assist the implementation process. Such operations are private; they are not intended to be used by users of the type. Again, Pascal provides no general mechanism for hiding such private operations from the user.

13.7.2 Abstract data types in programming languages

The above example demonstrated a single abstract data item – a one-off. Very often a program needs a whole number of data items of the same type. For example, you might need several stacks in one program. Of course you could code each one of them as a distinct package. But a better way would be to declare an abstract data type (ADT). All the modern languages – C++, Ada, and Java – provide this facility. The way ADT's are coded in Ada is not particularly elegant, and therefore we will not present examples.

The facility to describe and use abstract data types is only a short step away from object-oriented programming (Chapter 14), in which an abstract data type is known as a class and particular instances of a class are known as objects.

13.7.3 Generics

The strong typing philosophy of programming languages such as Pascal and Ada can have a detrimental effect on programming efficiency. For example, suppose we defined a stack of integers as an abstract data type with the normal stack operations of push and pop, as posed in the self test question above. If we subsequently needed another stack type but one in which the elements were booleans rather than integers then clearly the specification and implementation would be identical apart from the different stack element types. In Pascal, our only recourse would be to duplicate the stack data type. Push and pop operations and a different representation would have to be provided for each of the two stack types. A more powerful stack abstraction is required which allows the stack element type to be parameterized.

The generic facility found in Ada and other languages provides a partial answer to this problem. Generics allow programmers to define templates (or patterns) for packages and procedures. These templates may then be used to instantiate actual packages and procedures with different parameters. For example, the specification below shows a generic stack package in which the type of each stack element is supplied as a parameter when a stack package is instantiated.

```
generic
    type StackElement is private;
    package Stack is
        procedure Push (Item: in StackElement);
        function Pop return StackElement;
        . . .
        . . .
    end Stack;
```

The following declarations instantiate two stack packages with stack element types of integers and boolean respectively.

```
package Stack_Of_Integers is new Stack (Integer);
package Stack_Of_Booleans is new Stack (Boolean);
```

Notwithstanding generics, statically typed programming languages restrict programmer flexibility in dealing with abstract data types. For example, in a statically typed language such as Ada all packages must be instantiated at compile-time. It is not possible, for example, to create stacks whose element types are determined dynamically or where the elements in the stack may not all be of the same type. For an alternative approach which offers a solution to these problems, the reader is referred to Chapter 14 on object-oriented programming.

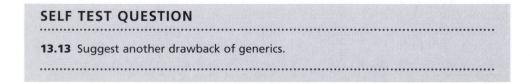

SELF TEST QUESTION

13.13 Suggest another drawback of generics.

Generics are provided in Ada and C++ but are not provided in C and Java.

13.8 ● Programming in the large

The programming of very large, complex software projects, or programming in the large, introduces many new problems for the software engineer. First, what are the characteristics of such software systems? The size of the code is an obvious factor. Large systems consist of tens of thousands of lines of source code; systems with hundreds of thousands of lines are not uncommon. Projects of this size must be developed by teams of programmers; for very large projects the programming team may consist of hundreds of programmers. Such systems are implemented over a long period of time and when completed are expected to undergo continual maintenance and enhancement over an extended lifetime.

Many of the problems associated with such large projects are logistical, caused by the sheer size of the task and the number of personnel involved. Methodologies for managing such projects have been developed and are discussed in other sections of this book. Clearly, many software tools, other than the programming language being used, are required to assist and control the development of such large systems. A recent trend has been to integrate these software tools with a particular programming language to form an integrated software development environment. These issues are discussed in Chapter 18. In this section we concentrate on support for programming in the large at the programming language level.

What support can we expect from a programming language? The programmers' chief tool in managing complexity is abstraction. Abstraction allows the programmer to keep a problem intellectually manageable. The programming language must therefore provide mechanisms which can be used to encapsulate the most common abstractions used by programmers; functional (or procedural) abstraction and data abstraction. The simplest mechanism, provided by nearly all programming languages, is the procedure; a program unit which allows the encapsulation of a functional abstraction. Programming in the large requires that higher-level abstraction primitives than the procedure be provided. We have already met one such structure – the abstract data type. This helps a lot, but we need still higher-level structuring mechanisms.

The use of abstractions promotes modularity which itself encourages the production of re-usable code, and promotes the notion of information hiding. Modularity and module independence are essential in an environment where individual modules will most often be developed by different programmers. The programming language can support development in multiprogrammer environments by providing mechanisms for hiding from a user irrelevant details concerning the implementation of a module. Additionally, the interface between modules must be carefully controlled. It is essential to eliminate the possibility that the implementation of one module may affect another module in some unanticipated manner. This is also important when a system is being maintained or enhanced in some way. It must be possible to localize the effect of some system enhancement or error fix to specific modules of the system; side-effects of changes should not propagate throughout the complete system. Clearly, many of these issues are as much system design issues as they are programming language issues. No programming language will solve the problems of a poor system design. On the other hand, the implementation of a good system design can be hampered if the implementation language is of limited expressive power.

If modules are to be developed independently, the programming language must also provide facilities for the independent compilation of program modules. In addition, the language should provide strong type checking across module boundaries to ensure the consistency of calls to externally defined modules. All the major modern programming languages for software engineering (C++, Ada, and Java) carry out such checks. Another acute problem in large programs concerns the handling of unexpected events during the execution of a program. Programming language features for exception handling are discussed in Chapter 20.

In summary we can identify several needs for programming in the large:

● to be able to see the overall structure of the system

● to separately compile program modules and link them together

● to be able to access software libraries – for example, graphics or mathematical procedures

● to be able to re-use software components that have been created for one system as part of a new system – in order to reduce development costs

● facilities to allow a large piece of software to be constructed by a team.

13.8.1 Packages

The idea of a package is to group together a set of procedures, functions, and data that are related in some way. This then constitutes a programming unit that is bigger than a single procedure, function, or data item. So instead of describing a large program as consisting of 50 procedures, 50 functions, and 10 data items, we can view it as a collection of, say, 10 packages. This is potentially easier to understand, design, code, debug, test, and maintain. (Even worse, we could think of a program in terms of 10,000 lines of coding.) Using packages also means that it should be easier to re-use software components in some other development project.

Packages represent the highest-level programming units which range as follows:

1. statements
2. blocks
3. procedures
4. packages.

We have already considered one useful facility for large-scale software – abstract data types. In many languages, including Ada, each ADT can be placed in its own package. Examples of related items that can be grouped into separate packages are:

● mathematical functions (examples – sine, cosine, logarithm)
● graphics procedures (examples – drawLine, drawCircle, setColor)
● file system procedures (examples – openFile, readRecord)
● Internet access procedures.

13.8.2 Module interconnection languages

The structure of a large program is often derived using some design method, as described in other chapters in this book. Typically the structure is described in a graphical notation, like a structure chart. However, some programming languages enable this large-scale, or architectural structure to be expressed within the programming language itself. In Ada, for example, the specification of each package is written in the programming language. The collection of specifications then constitutes a description of the architecture of the software. The language used to describe these components is sometimes termed a *module interconnection language*. Ada was one of the first major programming languages to incorporate such a notation as part of the language itself.

We will use the Ada notation to illustrate how packages can be described. First, here is the description of a stack package. (An implementation was presented earlier).

```
package stack is  -- this specification is visible to users
    procedure init;
        -- initializes the stack
    procedure push (item: in integer);
        -- pushes an integer item onto the stack top
    function pop return integer;
        -- removes an integer from the top of the stack
    function empty return boolean;
        -- returns true if the stack is empty
end stack;
```

A user of this stack package does not need to know how it works. The stack might be represented as an array, a linked list, or even (if it was large enough) as a file. This is abstraction at work. It frees the programmer from thinking about detail in order that they can concentrate on the bigger picture. The implementation of the stack could be changed (because of performance improvement or the elimination of bugs), but any packages that use it would not be affected. The stack package could easily be re-used in some other program because the interface to it is clean.

SELF TEST QUESTION

13.14 Suggest one drawback to this kind of specification.

Once the packages that comprise a new software project have been identified and specified, the packages can then either be written from scratch or retrieved from an existing library. Elements of this library are either supplied with the programming language (for example the Ada package `Text_Io`), bought from a supplier of library components, or written in-house.

Although Java supports encapsulation similar to packages (but called classes), there is no requirement within the language to specify the interface to modules, as there is in C++ and Ada. This is because (for other reasons) the compiler has access to the source code of the libraries and checks at compilation time that they are being used correctly (method names and parameters match). However, Java does provide a module interconnection language called interfaces. An interface declaration says what public methods and (rarely) data must be provided as a minimum by a class. In the case of methods the parameters are also specified. This notation can be used during design and also by the compiler in checking that a module complies with an interface specification. For a stack, the interface declaration looks like:

```
interface StackInterface {
    public void push(int item);
    public int pop();
}
```

Then a class that implements this interface (adheres to this description) declares in its heading:

```
class Stack implements StackInterface
```

Incidentally, in Java, an interface description specifies what a class must provide as a minimum; the class may also provide additional public methods.

In summary, the characteristics of a module description language are:

● It is textual (though we could think of tools to convert the text into graphics).

● It is an extension of the programming language (therefore consistent, easy to learn and checkable by the compiler).

● It allows specification of the external appearance of modules – their names, their visible procedures, the parameters required.

The advantages of being able to write descriptions like this are:

● During design, we can describe the grand structure of a piece of software in a fairly formal way. The description can be checked by a language processor.

● During coding, the description can be used as part of the module specification. The compiler can also check for consistency between the description and the module coding.

● During unit testing, the description can be used as a test harness or test bed.

● During maintenance, the description can be used as documentation in order to learn about the overall structure of the system. It can be used as input to a tool that creates various reports on the structure – for example, a structure chart. Finally, following update of the software, consistency checking can be re-applied using the compiler.

SELF TEST QUESTION

13.15 Write specifications for the modules of the following software system.

A patient-monitoring system monitors the vital signs of a single hospital patient and delivers messages to the nurses station. It consists of the following software modules, each followed by their procedure. Make assumptions about the parameters associated with the procedures.

Module `clock` provides procedures `init`, `waitSeconds`, and `getTime`.

Module `display` provides procedures `init`, `flashLight`, `unflashLight`, `soundKlaxon`, `unsoundKlaxon`, `displayMessage` and `clearScreen`.

Module `heart` provides procedures `readRate` and `readPressure`.

Module `lungs` provides procedures `readRate`.

Module `temp` provides procedure `readTemp`.

SELF TEST QUESTION

13.16 Specify the following abstract data structures:

1. A chess board. The package should provide procedures to do things like initialize, inspect a particular square, move a piece, and display the board.

2. A first-in first-out queue.

3. The score keeper module for a computer game.

4. A random number generator.

5. A serial file system.

13.8.3 Separate compilation

A programming language is ill suited for the development of large, complex programs if it does not provide facilities for the separate compilation of program modules. Large programs must necessarily be developed by teams of programmers; individual programmers must be able to work independently while at the same time be able to access programs written by other members of the team. Programming language support is required for the integration of routines that have been developed separately. Additional support in this area is often provided by environmental tools such as linkers, cross-reference generators, file librarians, and source code control systems. These tools and others which together make up a programming support environment are discussed in Chapter 18. What support should the programming language itself provide? We suggest the following:

- independent compilation of program modules
- easy access to libraries of pre-compiled software
- the ability to integrate together routines written in different languages
- strong type checking across module boundaries
- the ability to avoid the unnecessary recompilation of pre-compiled modules.

One of the foremost reasons for the continued popularity of Fortran is the tremendous resource of re-usable software available to scientists and engineers through the readily accessible libraries of scientific and engineering subroutines. Fortran provides independent compilation of modules at the subroutine level and easy access to library routines but performs no run-time checking of calls to external routines. It is the responsibility of the programmer to check that the correct number and type of parameters are used in the calling program.

Amongst the well-known languages, standard Pascal is the only one that provides no support for separate compilation. All modules must be integrated into a single, large program which is then compiled. In order to support the development of large programs, many implementations support language extensions which provide at least independent compilation, access to libraries, and the ability to integrate assembly language routines into Pascal programs. The major disadvantage of this approach is that programs using these nonstandard extensions are no longer immediately portable.

Ada provides far greater support for separate compilation than Pascal or Fortran. Both subprograms and packages may be compiled as separate modules with strong type checking across module boundaries to ensure that they are used in accordance with their specifications. The specification and implementation of a package may be compiled in two separate parts. This has a number of advantages for the software engineer. The strong type checking ensures that all specifications stay in line with their implementations. Also, it means that once the specification for a package has been compiled, modules which use that package may also be compiled (even before the implementation of the package has been completed).

C, C++, and Java are all (fairly) small languages and most of their functionality is provided by large and comprehensive libraries. These libraries are separately compiled. In Java, linking is performed at run-time.

13.8.4 Naming and scoping in large programs

We have discussed earlier the vexed question of scoping within programming-in-the-small. The same problem rears its head within programming-in-the-large. The issue is: what packages, procedures, functions and (rarely) variables are accessible to any given package?

In Ada, if a program needs to use a package, a `with` declaration is required at its head. For example:

```
with stack;
```

Thereafter, the program can use the publicly available items within the package. For example:

```
stack.push(22);
```

When it sees this declaration, the compiler accesses the description of the package `stack` and checks that it is being used correctly – that is, procedure, function, and variable names are correct and parameters match the declared types.

There is also a way of making references more concise by using a `use` declaration. For example:

```
use stack;
```

and thereafter, items within the package `stack` can be used like this:

```
push(22);
```

In C and C++, a program almost always begins with an `include` declaration. For a system package the declaration is typically:

```
#include <stdio.h>
```

or, for a programmers own package:

```
#include "myFile.h"
```

The `include` statement is a directive to the compiler to include within the current source file a copy of the named file. A file with the suffix `.h` is, by convention, a header file and it is files of this type that normally appear in the `include` statement. A header file is a source code file that contains the declaration of the functions to be found within a package. These declarations are, in C terminology, the prototypes of the available functions – their names and parameters. The C and C++ languages have a rule that a function has to be declared (textually) before it can be used. When a declaration like this is present, the program can refer to the functions within the package described and it will compile successfully. Subsequently the object code of the packages is linked.

In Java, programs usually begin with one or more `import` statements, which are similar in role to the `use` statement in Ada. The programmer can either use the long-winded:

```
java.awt.Button newButton = new java.awt.Button("Press here");
```

or precede the program with an `import` statement:

```
import java.awt.Button;
```

and then simply write the more concise statement:

```
Button newButton = new Button("Press here");
```

When there are many, large libraries, it is easy to get confused between packages or classes with identical names. To minimize possible confusion, Java dictates a much closer relationship between files and libraries than has been common in older programming languages. Usually, the source code of each class is placed in its own file, with a file name corresponding to the class name. Thus a class called `Whizz` goes in a file called `Whizz.java`. Further the compiled version of every class occupies its own file; the first part of the file name is the name of the class and the second part has the extension `.class`. So, for example, a class called `Whizz` goes in a file called `Whizz.class`. All the files for a particular Java package are held in the same directory (folder) and the directory name is the package name. Thus the structure of a library matches (and has the same names as) the structure of the files, held in a tree-structured filing system such as is provided by Unix and by Microsoft operating systems. Thus the compiled version of class `Whizz`, part of a package called `useful`, is stored within the directory `useful`. In turn, this might be within a directory called `secret`, which is in turn within a directory called `projects`. The name of the file containing the source code of the class `Whizz` is:

```
projects/secret/useful/Whizz.java
```

on a Unix system, or

```
c:\projects\secret\useful\Whizz.java
```

on a Microsoft system.

In order that the class `Whizz` can be referred to in a shorthand way, we would need the following `import` statement at the top of a class that uses the class `Whizz`:

```
import projects.secret.useful.Whizz;
```

This is the same on *any* operating system because the slashes have been replaced by periods to ensure that the `import` statement is independent of the convention for directory (folder) names. Incidentally, the period notation also makes for a uniformity of naming that is consistent with the period in a procedure call:

```
objectName.methodName;
```

The correspondence between the names in the program and names in the file system gives much less potential for confusion, given large libraries.

13.9 ● The role of programming languages

At the beginning of the 21st century, the major programming languages that are used for software engineering are Ada, C++ and Java. Ada was designed for use by the USA DoD (Department of Defense) for use primarily in real-time embedded systems. C++ evolved from the widely used C language, adding OO features to it. Java emerged as a secure and portable language that can be embedded in Web pages.

Any language for serious use in software engineering must have OO features. Ada, C++ and Java are OO languages and those aspects of languages are discussed in Chapter 14.

Historically programming language design goes in cycles: First a large and complex language (such as C++) is designed. This provokes the design of a small and concise language (such as Java). This has happened several times: Pascal was the small reaction to extravagant Algol68. Unix and its companion language C were a reaction to the sophisticated, but complex Multics operating system. Finally Java has been the reaction to complicated C++. Large languages are rich in facilities, but (because of complexity) can be hard to learn, master, and debug. By contrast, a small language can be elegant and concise, providing the fundamental building blocks needed for the construction of large systems.

Some people argue that the choice of programming language has only a small influence on the success of a software project. They argue that the coding phase of development is much less important than the design stage. They argue that desirable programming concepts can be implemented (with care) in any programming language – even, perhaps, assembler language. Other people argue that the features of an implementation language can have a profound effect on the success or failure of a project. They argue that the language must match the ideas used during design (for example, encapsulation). They argue that if the language embodies the required ideas, then the compiler can carry out checks that would be otherwise impossible. Further, when maintenance comes, the language is assisting in understanding the program.

We must not forget that there are other programming paradigms, with their own language features. Logic programming is discussed in Chapter 17. Functional programming is discussed in Chapter 16. Spreadsheet programming is widely used, by novices as well as skilled programmers. Visual Basic (a procedural language with some object-oriented features) is very widely used in application programming and is discussed in Chapter 18 on tools. Last, but not least, parallel programming (discussed in Chapter 15) adds a new dimension to procedural programming.

Fashion seems to play a huge role in determining which languages become widely used. Mandatory adoption by a powerful government agency (as in the case of Ada) also obviously affects adoption. The selection of a programming language for a particular project will be influenced by many factors not directly related to the programming language itself. For example, many organizations have a substantial investment in a particular programming language. Over a period of time, hundreds of thousands of lines of code may have been developed and the programming staff will have built up considerable expertise with the language. In such a situation, there is often considerable resistance to change even if a "superior" language is available.

There are other factors which can influence programming language selection. The software developer may be bound by a contract which actually specifies the implementation language. Decisions by the US government to support Cobol and, more recently, Ada, considerably influenced the acceptance of those languages. Support from suppliers of major software components, such as language compilers and database management systems, will influence language selection for many developers. If an apparent bug appears in a compiler, for example, they need to know that they can pick up the telephone and get the supplier to help them. Similarly, the availability of software tools such as language-sensitive editors, debugging systems, and project management tools may favor one programming language over another. The development of language-based programming environments which combine the programming language with an extensive set of development tools, such as Unix, will be an increasing influence on language selection.

There can be little doubt that news of the death of programming and programming languages has been greatly exaggerated. Software will continue to be written in languages like those we know for the foreseeable future. Old languages, like Fortran and Cobol, will not go away because of the huge amount of legacy software written in these languages which will continue to need maintenance. But new programming languages will continue to emerge and will become important.

13.10 ● Summary

In this chapter we have surveyed the characteristics that a programming language should have from the viewpoint of the software engineer. In summary, the following issues have been considered fundamentally important to the software engineer. A language should:

● be well matched to the application area of the project; do not use Cobol for implementing a symbolic differentiation package
● have clarity, simplicity, and orthogonality
● have a syntax that is consistent, natural, and promote the readability of programs
● have a small but powerful set of control abstractions
● have an adequate set of primitive data abstractions
● have strong typing
● have scoping mechanisms and information hiding
● have high-level support for abstract data types
● have clear separation of the specification and the implementation of program modules
● have separate compilation.

EXERCISES

13.1 What aims and what language features would you expect to find in a language designed for each of the following application domains?

(a) business data processing

(b) scientific programming

(c) systems programming

(d) real-time embedded systems.

How suitable is your favorite language for each of these application domains?

13.2 Suppose that you were asked to design a new programming language for software engineering.

(a) Select and justify a set of control structures.

(b) Select and justify a set of built-in data types.

(c) Select and justify a mechanism for extending the built-in data types.

(d) Select and justify a mechanism for encapsulation.

(e) Select and justify a mechanism for large-scale modularity.

13.3 Argue either for or against strong typing in a programming language.

13.4 The design goals of Ada were: readability, strong typing, programming in the large, exception handling, data abstraction, tasking, and generic units. Explain the meanings of these objectives and comment on their validity. Assess whether they are complementary or contradictory. If you are familiar with Ada, assess it against these aims.

13.5 The stated design aims for Java are that it should be simple, object-oriented, network-oriented, interpreted, robust, secure, architecture-neutral, portable, high-performance, multithreaded, and dynamic. Explain the meanings of these objectives. Assess whether they are complementary or contradictory. If you are familiar with Java, assess it against these aims.

13.6 Take a language of your choice. Search out the design aims and explain their meaning. Assess how well the language matches the design aims. Assess the language against the criteria developed in this chapter.

13.7 Explain what the term "modularity" means. Assess how well the following features of programming languages contribute to modularity:

(a) scoping

(b) procedures and functions

(c) information hiding

(d) abstract data types.

13.8 A data item in a program always has the following general characteristics:

● creation – who creates it and when

● destruction – who destroys it and when

● visibility (or scope) – who can access it and how.

Survey the following categories of data, analyzing them according to these characteristics:

(a) local data within a procedure or function

(b) data declared within a block-structured language

(c) parameters to a procedure or function

(d) data within an abstract data item

(e) dynamic data items.

13.9 Assess the difficulties of developing large-scale software and suggest programming language features to help solve the problems that you have identified.

13.10 The module interconnection language as seen in modern languages provides for the specification of the services provided by the package. Consider extending such a language so that it also describes:

● the packages that each package uses

● the packages that use each package.

What would be the advantages and disadvantages of this notation?

13.11 Compare and contrast Ada with C++.

13.12 Compare and contrast C++ and Java.

13.13 "In programming language design, small is beautiful." Discuss.

13.14 Cobol (or Fortran) is an outdated language. Discuss.

ANSWERS TO SELF TEST QUESTIONS

13.1 When some input from the users keyboard is required. It must be checked and, if necessary, new input solicited until the input is correct.

13.2
```
int[] table;

boolean search(int wanted) {
    boolean found = false;
    int i = 0;

    endSearch:
        while (i < table.length) {
            if (table[i] == wanted) {
                found = true;
                break endSearch;
            }
            i++;
        }
    return found;
}
```

Without using break:

```
int[] table;

boolean search(int wanted) {
    boolean found = false;
    int i = 0;
    while (i < table.length and found == false) {
            if (table[i] == wanted)
                found = true;
            else
                i++;
        }
    return found;
}
```

13.3 The benefits are program clarity, better modeling of the problem, compile-time checking, and run-time checking.

13.4 This is a case of expressive power and convenience versus fast performance.

13.5 Arrays and records allow the programmer to create and use data structures that match the problem to be solved in a convenient and natural fashion. This fosters fast development, reliability, and maintainability.

13.6 There are many possible answers. Here are just two:

● A file sort program, because you never know how long the file will be.

● A Web browser program, because you do not know in advance how big a Web page will be.

13.7 In an array, all items after the insertion point have to be moved down the array, a time-consuming process. In a dynamic structure, only the pointer in the immediately preceding item needs to be updated – a very fast operation.

13.8

Factor	C++	Java
Reliability	Poor	Good
Development effort	Greater	Smaller
Performance	Faster	Unpredictable

13.9 Main has access to:

    integer A
    integer B
    procedure Outer

procedure Outer has access to:

    integer A
    integer B
    procedure Outer
    character C
    character D
    procedure Inner

procedure Inner has access to

    integer B
    procedure Outer
    procedure Inner
    character C
    character D
    real A
    real E

13.10 For: control of visibility through block structuring.

Against: assisting free access to nonlocal data, constraining program structure to a tree structure.

13.11
```
function empty return boolean;
     return top = 0;
end empty;
```

13.12 The answer is that you cannot encapsulate an abstract data item in Pascal or any other block-structured language that does not explicitly support encapsulation. However hard you try, you end up having to describe the stack data at the top of the program, where it is accessible to all the program. In outline the structure is:

```
program stackDemo;

declaration of stack and any other variables;

procedure push(int item);
begin
     body of push
end;
function pop() : integer;
begin
     body of pop
end;
begin
     remainder of program that uses the stack
end.
```

13.13 Generics complicate the language.

13.14 A specification of this kind only specifies the procedure (and function) names and their parameters. It does not specify any more closely what a procedure (or function) does – other than via any comments.

13.15
```
package clock is
     procedure init;
     procedure waitSeconds(integer seconds);
     procedure getTime(integer hours, integer mins, integer
     seconds);
end clock;

package display is
     procedures init;
     procedure flashLight;
     procedure unflashLight;
     procedure soundKlaxon;
     procedure unsoundKlaxon;
     procedure displayMessage(string message);
```

```
          procedure clearScreen;
      end display;
      package heart is
          procedure readRate(integer rate);
          procedure readPressure(integer pressure);
      end heart;
      package lungs is
          procedure readRate(integer rate);
      end lungs;
      package temp is
          procedure readTemp(integer temp);
      end temp;
13.16 package board is
          procedure init;
          procedure getPiece(integer row, integer column);
          procedure movePiece(integer fromRow, integer toColumn,
                          integer toColumn, integer toRow);
             procedure display;
      end board;
      package queue is
             init;
          procedure add(integer item);
          procedure remove(integer item);
      end queue;
      package score is
          procedure init;
          procedure add(integer amount);
          procedure deduct(integer amount);
          procedure display;
      end score;
      package random is
          procedure init;
          procedure nextRandom return integer;
      end random;
      package fileSystem is
          procedure open(string file);
          procedure read(string file, string record );
          procedure write(string file, string record);
          procedure close(string file);
      end fileSystem;
```

FURTHER READING

A good collection of papers from the computer science literature which critically evaluate and compare three programming languages is: A. Feuer and N. Gehani, *Comparing and Assessing Programming Languages, Ada, Pascal and C*, Prentice Hall, 1984.

An excellent text for students wishing to explore further the fundamental principles underlying programming languages is: B. J. Maclennan, *Principles of Programming Languages: Design, Evaluation and Implementation*, Dryden Press, 1987.

A good guide to the use of sound software engineering practices with the programming languages, Ada and Modula-2 is: R. Wiener, and R. Sinovec, *Software Engineering with Modula-2 and Ada*, Wiley, 1984.

A fascinating read about Java and its rationale, written by one of the Java language team: Peter van der Linden, *Just Java*, Prentice Hall, 2nd edition, 1997.

An authoritative account of the ANSI standard version of the language in a classic book. Ritchie was the designer of C, a language originally closely associated with the UNIX operating system: Brian W. Kernighan and Dennis Ritchie, *The C Programming Language*, Prentice Hall, 2nd edition, 1988.

There are very many books on C++. This one we like particularly, for its clarity is: Frank L. Friedman and Elliot B. Koffman, *Problem Solving, Abstraction, and design Using C++*, Addison-Wesley, 1994.

The definitive source on C++, but not an easy read: Bjarne Stroustrup, *The C++ Programming Language*, Addison-Wesley, 2nd edition, 1991.

Two books that look at programming languages in general are: Carlo Ghezzi and Mehdi Jazayeri, *Programming Language Concepts*, John Wiley, 1997, and Michael L. Scott, *Programming Language Pragmatics*, Morgan Kaufman, 1998.

There are essentially two versions of Ada, the old Ada 83 (before object-orientation) and the new Ada 95 (with object-orientation). When looking at books, you need to be aware of which version you are interested in. A book that has appeared over a number of years in different editions, this edition describes the latest standard – Ada 95. It is readable and comprehensive. John Barnes, *Programming in Ada*, Addison-Wesley, 2nd edition, 1998.

This is about the old Ada 83. It gives examples of data flow diagrams translated into Ada programs: David A. Watt, Brian A. Wichmann and William Findley, *Ada: Language and Methodology*, Prentice Hall, 1987.

14

Object-oriented programming (OOP)

This chapter explains the principles of OOP, using Java as the main example language.

14.1 ● Introduction

There are three main principles of OOP:

- encapsulation
- inheritance
- polymorphism.

The best way to understand these ideas is probably one-by-one in the above order, because each concept is (arguably) more sophisticated than the preceding one.

Most OOP languages are built upon procedural programming languages – with additional concepts and facilities. Procedural programming (sometimes called imperative programming) is the most widely seen type of programming, in which the computer obeys one instruction after another in sequence.

In this chapter we use Java as the example language; the appendix gives an overview of the non-OO features of Java.

14.2 ● Encapsulation

The idea of encapsulation is simply to group together things that are closely related. This grouping is termed an *object*. Next define the interface to the object – the way that it is accessed or used. Finally we prevent access to the object in any way other than the prescribed interface. Thus the internal workings of the object are invisible from outside the object. The idea of modularity has been a constant theme of this book and is crucial to successful software development; encapsulation is one good way of creating modular structures. Here are several examples of objects.

● In a computer game, an object maintains the current score. Methods are provided to initialize the score, credit it, debit it, and display the current total. The score is not directly accessible to the remainder of the program, but can only be accessed using the methods provided.

● In a game, an object provides a random number when a method is called. A method is also provided to initialize the object. The algorithm for generating random numbers is completely invisible to the users of the object.

● In a software tool that allows the user to draw graphical images on the screen, an object maintains a list of the objects already drawn. It provides methods to add a shape to the list, delete a shape from the list and to display all the current shapes and to delete all the shapes from the list. Again, the way in which the list is represented is hidden from the users of the object.

SELF TEST QUESTION

14.1 Suggest the methods that might be provided by an object that provides serial access to a file.

All these examples display the following characteristics:

● methods that allow access to the object
● a hidden interior
● a grouping of strongly related methods and data.

So what is the purpose of this encapsulation? There are several. First, provided that the interfaces to the object are clearly specified, the author of the object can concentrate on the task of writing a software component that is highly modular. All the constituent parts of the object are strongly related and dedicated to one role which is distinct from those of any other object. Second, users of the object need not know how the object works. They can use the object using only the abstract view of the object presented by the methods that an object provides; the user is freed from concerns about the details of the object. Third, provided that the programming language supports encapsulation, mistakes can be automatically detected. Any reference to an object other than through the publicly available methods can be detected and flagged by the compiler. Fourth, an object can be created for use in one program but then later easily re-used in some other program. (We shall see more of this later.)

Many modern programming languages provide facilities for encapsulation, but they do not provide the full facilities of an OO language (which we shall identify later). Such restricted languages are sometimes referred to as *object-based languages* and examples are Modula 2 and Ada 83.

14.3 ● Classes

In Java, as in all OO languages, it is not possible to declare a single object directly. Instead the language makes the programmer describe the structure of any number of similar objects. This description is called a *class*. A class is a blueprint for any number of objects. A class describes the type of an object – how it is represented and what operations can be carried out on it. The programming language makes the programmer declare classes because of an optimism that a number of (similar) objects will be needed and created.

Let us now see how to write a class description in Java. Suppose we want to create one or more graphical objects to represent balls. Balls come in various sizes and occupy different positions in space. We will therefore describe the size (radius) and the position on the two-dimensional computer screen as integer x and y pixel coordinates.

```
class Ball {

    private int x, y;
    private int radius;

    public void setRadius(int newRadius) {
        radius = newRadius;
    }
}
```

Any methods that are to be available for access by users of objects derived from a class are labeled as `public` methods. (Thus the method `setRadius` is `public`.) Any method that is used purely within an object and is inaccessible from outside is labelled as `private`. (In this example class there are no private methods, because the class is so small and simple that it does not need to use any.) Variables are almost always declared as private and therefore inaccessible from outside objects. It is good programming practice to restrict all access to an object to method calls rather than direct access to data. Thus to change the x coordinate of a ball, we can provide a method named `setX`:

```
public void setX(int newX) {
    x = newX;
}
```

SELF TEST QUESTION

14.2 Write an additional method as part of the class `Ball` that sets the value of the *y* coordinate.

Preventing direct access to data items within an object like this prevents any interference with the internal workings of an object.

14.4 ● Creating objects

We can now at last create an object, called `football` using the class `Ball`. This is done as follows:

```
Ball football = new Ball();
```

This statement may seem strange at first, because the word `Ball` appears twice. What this statement accomplishes is:

1. It declares a variable named `football` which is capable of holding objects of type `Ball`.

2. It creates a new object from the class `Ball` using the language word `new` and assigns it to the variable called `football`.

Statements like this appear very commonly in Java programs, so much so that they are almost trademarks of the language. If the above statement looks strange, consider something that is similar, but is perhaps more familiar:

```
int i = 42;
```

which could be written in many programming languages (including Java). The left-hand side says that a variable named `i` is to be created, capable of holding data which is of type integer. The assignment statement then creates the value 42 and places it in the variable.

Here is a final part of the jargon of OOP: an individual object is called an *instance* of a class.

In Java there is a convention that the name of a class, like `Ball`, begins with a capital (upper-case) letter, while object names, like `football`, begin with a lower-case letter. This is an effective way of distinguishing them easily when reading programs.

Now that we have created an object, `Ball`, we can make some method calls on it. The instruction:

```
football.setRadius(10);
```

calls the method `setRadius` within the object `football`. This again is an example of a most important type of Java statement. The object name is always followed by a full-stop (period), which is then followed by the method name (and any parameters in brackets). This particular method call causes the value of the variable `x` within the object `football` to be set to the value `10`.

We have now seen how to describe classes, how to create objects, and how to make method calls on objects. Notice that the description of a class is static (just as the blueprint for a newly designed car does not actually do anything). But an object is created when the program runs, when a `new` is executed. An OOP behaves by creating the objects it needs and then using them (by making calls on their methods) to carry out its various tasks. Objects are also commonly passed as parameters in method calls. The programmer both:

- uses the many classes provided in the library, and
- defines classes which are of use in the particular program.

An example of a library class is the class Textfield. It allows a text field to be displayed on the screen. The user of the program can then enter text using the keyboard. To create a text field:

```
Textfield data = new Textfield();
```

which creates an object, named data, an instance of the library class Textfield. Having created the object, we can cause it to be displayed on the screen using the call:

```
add(data);
```

14.5 ● Constructor methods

There is one final element of creating objects that needs to be explained. When an object is created, the programmer can provide a method to be called to carry out any initialization. In the example of the class Ball, for example, we can include a new method written within the class:

```
Ball(int initialRadius) {
        radius = initialRadius;
}
```

Now we are able to create an instance of Ball like this:

```
Ball bigBall = new Ball(1000);
```

When the object bigBall is created, the method Ball within the object is called. This sets the variable radius to the value of the parameter. The method Ball is called a *constructor* method (because it is used when the object is constructed). It must have the same name as the class and usually has parameters.

An example of a library class with a constructor method is the class Button. It allows graphical buttons to be displayed on the screen. The user of the program can then click on the buttons to cause various things to happen. To create a button:

```
Button startButton = new Button("start now!");
```

which creates an object, named startButton, an instance of the library class Button. The button is displayed on the screen with the caption start now! upon its surface.

We now have the choice of how to create a new ball object – either with or without using a parameter:

```
Ball smallBall = new Ball(1);
Ball aBall = new Ball();
```

We now have two versions of the constructor method – one has no parameters, while the other has a single integer parameter.

SELF TEST QUESTION

14.3 Write an additional constructor method for `Ball` that allows the user to set the initial x and y coordinates of a ball.

Writing several versions of a method, all with the same name, but distinguishable by the number and/or the types of the parameters is termed method *overloading* (not to be confused with method overriding, which we shall meet later in this chapter). Although overloading is often used as described in conjunction with constructor methods, it is often considered bad style to do it in other circumstances, because of potential confusion and error.

14.6 ● Destructor methods

The complement of a constructor method is a destructor method, called just before an object is destroyed. The Java language does not provide for destructor methods, but some OO languages do – for example C++. So there is something of a debate about whether they are useful.

In Java, when an object is created, space in memory is allocated to hold all the variables within the object. (The code of an object is held just once in memory, because it is the same for all the instances of a particular class.) Once a Java object is no longer in use – more precisely, there is no longer any reference to it – the operating system automatically destroys it, along with any memory that it occupied. This approach is called *automatic garbage collection*. This system is convenient and tidy. It frees the programmer from having to worry about destructors.

In C++, the programmer must explicitly state that an object is to be destroyed. At this time, a destructor method can be called. This scheme has advantages: for example, the method can carry out any final housekeeping (last wishes) for the object. However, subtle programming errors can occur when objects are not properly disposed of. The programmer could inadvertently write code that destroys an object which is still in use somewhere else within the program. The opposite is if the programmer tries to use an object that has already been destroyed.

There is a further discussion of this topic in Chapter 13.

14.7 ● Class or static methods

Before we leave the topic of classes and objects, we need to examine a small topic called class methods. There are some methods in the Java library that do not logically belong to any object. Examples are mathematical methods and data conversion methods. For example, if we need to get the square root of a number, we can call the library method `sqrt` like this:

```
x = Math.sqrt(y);
```

`Math` is a library class, within which the method `sqrt` resides. It appears in this statement in the place that an object would normally appear. But there is no appropriate object in this case. There is no need to instantiate an object of class `Math` and we can simply use the method as shown. Such a method is called a *class method* – because it belongs not to an object but to a class.

Another example of a class method is one that converts an integer number into the equivalent string:

```
String s = Integer.toString(i);
```

where `i` is an integer. The class here is `Integer` and the class method is called `toString`. (Strings are objects supported by another comprehensive library in Java.)

As a last example, the library method `currentTimeMillis` returns the current time in milliseconds as a long. (A millisecond is one thousandth of a second.) This method is invoked like this:

```
long timeNow = System.currentTimeMillis();
```

In order to write a class method in Java, all that is necessary is to precede the heading of the method with the word `static`. (This word is used for historical reasons.)

14.8 ● Inheritance

It is a common desire to re-use existing pieces of software in new programs, and the potential advantages in saving development time can be huge. A class seems to be a convenient software component that can be re-used. If we are lucky, the class we need is already in the Java library or in a program we wrote last week. In practice, however, an existing class often does *some* of what is needed, but not quite everything. Sometimes an additional method is needed, or perhaps an existing method does not do exactly what is required. One approach to this scenario is to embark on modifying an old class to meet the changed requirements. This means studying, altering, and retesting the old class. This means meddling with a perfectly healthy class which, remember, has probably been beautifully encapsulated. At the end of the day we end up with two classes, which subsequently need separate maintenance.

The OO approach to this situation is different – it is to write only the parts of the class that need to be different, leaving the original class perfectly intact. The new class is said to *inherit* all the features of the old class, but with new additional features (or changed features). Let's see how this is coded.

Suppose we already have a class called `circle`:

```
class Circle{
    protected int x, y, radius;
    public void setRadius(int newRadius) {
        radius = newRadius;
    }
}
```

Suppose that in a new program (a program that allows someone to design a garden, with lawns, borders, and ponds) we need a class called RoundBed, which is similar to class Circle, except that it has a method to calculate the area of the circle (or bed). Here is the code for the new class:

```
class RoundBed extends Circle {
    public float getArea() {
        return (radius * radius * 3.142);
    }
}
```

The word extends means that the new class RoundBed inherits all the features of the old class Circle, including the method setRadius. The new class, however, contains an additional method getArea.

The relationship between the two classes is often described using a class diagram:

in which the direction of the arrow means that the class RoundBed inherits from or, in Java terminology, extends the class Circle. The class Circle in this example is called the superclass of the class Roundbed. A class diagram is one type of diagram within the repertoire of UML (Unified Modeling Language).

Note that the variables x, y, and radius, which might have been declared as private, have instead been prefixed by the word protected. If they were described as private, they would only be accessible within the class Circle. But the declaration protected gives the subclass (and any other subclass) the necessary access to these variables.

SELF TEST QUESTION

14.4 Write a new class called Pond that inherits from class Circle, and provides a method to calculate the perimeter (the distance around it) of a pond (as 3.142 * radius * 2). Draw the class diagram.

SELF TEST QUESTION

14.5 Write a new class `Balloon` that extends the class `Ball` used above, and provides a method that allows the radius of a balloon object to be obtained.

Another way in which a class might be different from an existing class is to change what an existing method does. To do this the inheriting class simply provides a new method to *override* what the method in the superclass does. In the example of the garden design program above, we already have a class `RoundBed` that represents a circular flower bed. One of its methods, `getArea`, calculates the area of the bed. Suppose we need a new class to represent a flower bed with a circular pond in the middle. We can use the existing classes, but override the method that calculates the area as follows:

```
class Ring extends RoundBed {

    private int innerRadius = 20;

    public void getArea() {

        return (radius*radius - innerRadius*innerRadius) * 3.142;

    }

}
```

In summary, a class that inherits from (extends) a superclass can do one or more of the following:

● provide additional methods (to extend what a class can do)

● override existing methods (to change what an existing method does)

● provide additional variables (for use as necessary in the additional or overriding methods).

Java, along with the other major OO languages, are small languages, with few built-in facilities. All the work is done by making use of an extensive and comprehensive library of classes. Any new classes that are required can often be created by inheriting from a class in the library. Thus OO *programming tends to be the act of extending the classes in the library* – it is extremely rare for a program not to use anything in the library. But in order to make full use of the library, the programmer needs to know what it provides. So development tools for OO languages usually provide a *browser* (not a Web browser) to enable the programmer to search out and inspect the available classes.

Faced with writing a new program, the programmer has the choice of doing one or several of the following:

● Use a class from the library unchanged. The Java library of classes is large and comprehensive. It can be browsed to find something useful.

● Extend a class from the library to create a new class. This, as we shall see, is how input and output are performed in Java.

- Write a completely new class. This is unusual in small programs.
- Use a class from an earlier program or extend such a class to create a new class.

14.9 ● Single versus multiple inheritance

As we have seen, Java supports single inheritance – a class can inherit from only one immediate superclass. Seen as a class diagram, the relationships between classes appear as a tree (a computer science tree, with the root at the top). Smalltalk and Ada 95 also provide single inheritance, but the widely used language C++ provides multiple inheritance. In such a language, the class chart becomes a directed graph. A directed graph is a diagram consisting of boxes and lines that join them. The lines have an implicit direction, so that some boxes are above others in the diagram. A box may be connected to several boxes (subclasses) below itself and several (superclasses) above itself.

14.10 ● Polymorphism

Polymorphism is not something that the OO programmer needs to consciously use very often, because it is a natural consequence of using objects and inheritance. Polymorphism works because of a rule of OOP:

- Once created, an object always preserves its identity, whatever happens to it. Therefore when a method call is made on an object, the method used is the method supplied in its class description. This means that an object always responds to its own appropriate method.

We will look at an example to see how this works and what it implies. Suppose we have a program that allows the user to draw shapes on a screen – a graphical authoring tool. The user can select various shapes – circle, rectangle, triangle, oval, etc. – from a menu and place them where desired on the screen. Each of these shapes is represented as an object in the program. These are instances of the matching classes (`circle`, `Rectangle`, `Triangle`, `Oval`, etc.). These are all subclasses of the class `Shape`:

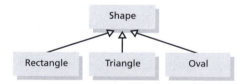

The program uses an array called `selection` to record what shapes have been selected. When the user selects a shape it is entered into the array, along with the existing selections. The array must be capable of holding all of the various types of object. This is allowed, provided that it is a type which is a superclass of any of the objects which can be assigned to it. Therefore it needs to be an array of `Shape`:

```
Shape[] selection = new Shape[20];
```

Now consider a method that needs to calculate the total area of the shapes already selected. This method will extract the entries in the array, one by one, placing them in a variable called `item`. Then for each shape we need to call the appropriate method to calculate its area. This method will differ from one shape to another, because, for example, the area of a rectangle is calculated differently from that of a circle. Naturally, we might write:

```
if(item instanceof Circle)
    area = item.getArea();
if(item instanceof Rectangle)
    area = item.getArea();
```

and so on, for all of the different shapes that the program handles.

(This code makes use of the Java word `instanceof` which, as its name suggests, allows us to test whether an object is an instance of a particular class.)

But this series of `if` statements is completely unnecessary. There is no need to test to see which shape is being used. Instead of this cumbersome sequence, all that is required is the single statement:

```
area = item.getArea();
```

because for each object (circle, rectangle, etc.) the appropriate version of method `getArea` is automatically called. This is polymorphism in action.

You can see that this program is shorter and neater than it otherwise might be. Another consequence is that certain changes to this program are made easy. Suppose, for example, that we incorporate a new kind of shape (perhaps a star object) into the program. Then the part of the program discussed above, to calculate the area, can remain unchanged. Better still, change is limited to a few specific objects. Thus there is a much greater significance to polymorphism than simply eliminating a series of `if` statements; polymorphism considerably enhances the information hiding feature of OOP.

There is a significant consequence of implementing polymorphism. You can see in the above example that it is not until the method call is actually made when the program is running that the computer knows which particular version of the method `getArea` needs to be used. So the linking to the method can only be done at the very last moment. This is termed *dynamic linking*. It contrasts with what is done in conventional programming languages, where the linking is carried out once, after compilation, but before the program is executed. Dynamic linking requires extra run-time support, and introduces a run-time performance overhead on the speed of OO programs.

14.11 ● Event-driven programming

OOP enables event-driven programs to be constructed very easily. We will illustrate this by presenting something of the input–output mechanism within Java. Consider window-based programs with icons, pull-down menus, buttons, scroll bars, and all the other widgets (window gadgets) of present-day GUIs (graphical user interfaces). When the mouse is clicked on a button or scroll bar an event is said to have occurred. The program must respond appropriately to all the different events which can occur. In OOP objects are created to respond to events and particular methods are provided to respond to events. For example suppose that the user moves a window or resizes it using mouse movements. In Java, these events cause the operating system to call a method called `paint`. The programmer must therefore provide this method to redraw everything on the screen. For example:

```
public void paint(Graphics g) {
    g.drawString(10, 20, "hello");
}
```

which displays on the screen the message `hello`, beginning at x coordinate 10 and y coordinate 20. A parameter, conventionally called `g`, is passed to `paint` when it is called. This is an object of the class `Graphics`, which maintains information about the screen display. Various calls can be made on the object `g`, as shown, to display text or graphical images.

The method `paint` is one of the methods provided within a library class belonging to the AWT (the abstract windowing toolkit, the library that supports graphical user interfaces). Any program that needs to do output to the screen (and that is most) needs to extend this class and supply a method `paint` which overrides the version provided as a part of the library class. This shows how even the simplest Java program makes use of inheritance.

We shall see further examples of an OO program as an event handler in the sample program that follows.

14.12 ● Case study – a complete Java program

We now present the complete text of a Java program to illustrate many of the ideas presented above. The program is a game in which the user tries to guess the combination for a digital lock for a safe or the door to a room. The program displays three buttons, one for each of the digits 1, 2, and 3 (Figure 14.1). The user presses three buttons, in

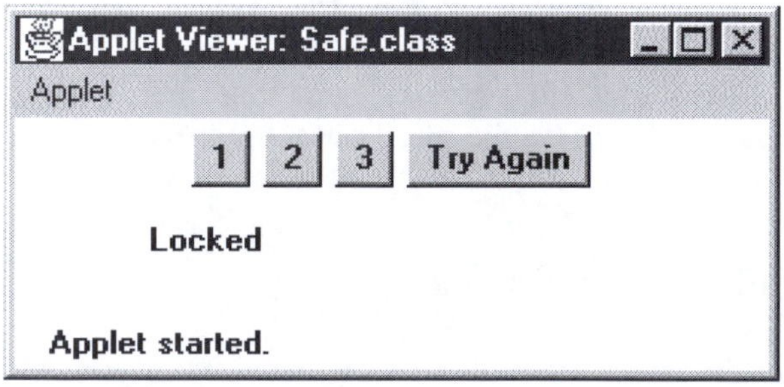

Figure 14.1 The Safe

attempting to enter the combination correctly. The user can also keep trying, by pressing a button labeled "try again."

This program is an applet – a program that runs as part of a Web page and viewed using an Internet browser such as Internet Explorer or Netscape Navigator.

The three `import` statements at the start of the program are required for nearly every applet program and specify which libraries the program is going to use.

The program consists of a single class, called `Safe`. Before the program is executed, the operating system creates an instance of this class, which then becomes an object ready for execution. Normally, of course, a program creates new objects as it executes, using the keyword `new`. But in this situation, it is the operating system that creates the object, just to get things started.

`Safe` extends the class `Applet`, which is in the Java library. This means that it inherits several useful methods from the superclass, `Applet`, and all its superclasses. It also means that it can override certain of the methods of the superclasses where necessary. One example is the method `init`, which overrides a method with the same name in class `Applet`. Method `init` is called by the operating system when the program starts to run. Its function is to initialize any variables within the program, create any objects, and create any widgets that the program needs. In this case four buttons are needed. Each is created (as we have seen earlier) and then added to the window using the method `add` within class `Applet`.

Method `paint` has to display whatever is needed on the screen. It overrides the method of the same name in class `Applet`. (The buttons are automatically redrawn and therefore do not need to be explicitly redrawn every time `paint` is called.)

Method `actionPerformed` is called when a button is pressed. It detects which button has been pressed and takes appropriate action to update the value of the complete number entered. Finally it calls method `repaint`, within `Applet`, to redraw the screen. This in turn causes `paint` to be automatically called to redraw the screen.

Like any other Java applet, the program consists of a single class with three methods, each of which is called by the operating system when some event occurs:

● `init` – when the program starts running
● `paint` – when the screen needs redrawing
● `actionPerformed` – when a button is pressed.

```
import java.applet.*;
import java.awt.*;
import java.awt.event.*;

public class Safe extends Applet implements ActionListener {
    private int guess = 0;
    private int combination = 321;
    private Button one, two, three, again;

    public void init() {
        one = new Button("1");
```

```
        add(one);
        one.addActionListener(this);
        two = new Button("2");
        add(two);
        two.addActionListener(this);
        three = new Button("3");
        add(three);
        three.addActionListener(this);
        again = new Button("Try Again");
        add(again);
        again.addActionListener(this);
    }

    public void paint(Graphics g) {
        if (guess == combination)
            g.drawString("Unlocked", 50, 50);
        else
            g.drawString("Locked", 50, 50);
    }

    public void actionPerformed(ActionEvent event) {
        if (event.getSource() == one)
            guess = guess*10 + 1;
        if (event.getSource() == two)
            guess = guess*10 + 2;
        if (event.getSource() == three)
            guess = guess*10 + 3;
        if (event.getSource() == again)
            guess = 0;
        repaint();
    }
}
```

SELF TEST QUESTION

14.6 Add to this program a text field which displays the number that the user has entered. The method that changes the value of a text field is called `setText`. In order to display a number, it must be converted to a text string, using the method `Integer.toString`.

The program as its stands illustrates several features of OOP:

● description of a class – the class `Safe`
● creating an object from a library class (for example, a `Button` object)

- inheritance from (extending) a library class, class `Applet`
- using methods within a library class, for example method `add`.

We will enhance the program so as to show how to describe a new, programmer-defined class, then create and use an object instantiated from the class. As shown above, the user interface to the game is closely intertwined with the calculations of the combination. In our modified version, we will create a new object which separates off and encapsulates everything about this code.

We will also enhance the program so that it chooses a random value for the combination. To do this, the program will make use of a library method named `random`, a class method within class `Math`. This supplies a new random number, a double in the range 0.0 up to but not including 1.0. What we need for our purpose is an integer in the range 1 to 3. So we need to convert the numbers that `random` produces into the ones that we want. During this process we need to convert the floating point number to an integer using the cast operator `(int)`, which truncates the floating point number, so that for example 2.7 becomes 2.

The formula to get a random digit is thus:

```
digit = (int) (Math.random() * 3) + 1;
```

Here is the code for the class that maintains the combination:

```
class Code {

    private int combination, guess;

    public void newCode() {
        combination = 0;
        for (int count = 0; count <= 2; count++) {
            combination = (combination * 10) +
                (int) (Math.random() * 3) + 1;
        }
    }

    public void newGuess() {
        guess = 0;
    }

    public void nextDigit(int next) {
        guess = next + (guess * 10);
    }

    public boolean isCorrectGuess() {
        return(guess == combination);
    }

}
```

and we can now use this class within the complete program, which creates an object `code` from the class `Code` and then uses it:

```java
import java.applet.*;
import java.awt.*;
import java.awt.event.*;

public class Safe extends Applet implements ActionListener {
    private Button one, two, three, again;
    public void init() {
        Code code = new Code();
        code.newGuess();
        one = new Button("1");
        add(one);
        one.addActionListener(this);
        two = new Button("2");
        add(two);
        two.addActionListener(this);
        three = new Button("3");
        add(three);
        three.addActionListener(this);
        again = new Button("Try Again");
        add(again);
        again.addActionListener(this);
    }
    public void paint(Graphics g) {
        if (code.isCorrectGuess)
            g.drawString("Unlocked", 50, 50);
        else
            g.drawString("Locked", 50, 50);
    }
    public void actionPerformed(ActionEvent event) {
        if (event.getSource() == one)
            code.nextDigit(1);
        if (event.getSource() == two)
            code.nextDigit(2);
        if (event.getSource() == three)
            code.nextDigit(3);
        if (event.getSource() == again)
            code.newGuess();
        repaint();
    }
}
```

14.13 ● The role of OOP

OOP is the current mainstream programming paradigm, and looks set to continue so for the foreseeable future. All new procedural languages are likely to be OO, and several languages have been retro-fitted with OO features – for example Ada (in Ada 95) and even Cobol.

The concept of the object offers high modularity through encapsulation of data (variables) and actions (methods). In addition, objects provide a higher-level (larger and more abstract) unit of program than methods. Inheritance offers clever re-usability by allowing features of an existing class to be used safely, but enhanced with additional features. Polymorphism further enhances information hiding and re-usability.

Historically the first OO language was Simula, a language mainly used (as its title suggests) for simulation. It was not widely used for wide-ranging applications in the way that OO languages are used today. Smalltalk was designed as a complete OO language; in Smalltalk, even the fundamentals of the language like integers and even control structures are object oriented. Smalltalk also pioneered the idea of a comprehensive library, which is employed either directly, or using inheritance. It has been very influential in computer science circles, though rarely used in anger for commercial purposes (except recently for prototyping the user interface for new systems). The design of Smalltalk displays a great beauty and elegance.

More recently, the most important OO language has been C++, which is widely used in industry and commerce. C++ has multiple inheritance, in contrast to both Java and Smalltalk. But C++ has been criticized as suffering from some of the drawbacks of its predecessor, C, such as permitting the programmer direct access to pointers, thereby allowing all sorts of subtle programming errors.

Real commercial use of OO languages bears out the claim that software re-use is the main benefit. Systems are reported to be from one tenth to one third of the size that they would be if programmed conventionally. The impact is reduced development effort and time, plus reduced maintenance.

Controversy rages about whether single (as in Java, Smalltalk, and Ada 95) or multiple inheritance (as in C++) is best. Another point of contention is whether destructors should be automatic (as in Java) or explicit (as in C++).

Another major issue in OOP is design; the essential problem in OOP is deciding what objects (classes) are needed for a new piece of software, what methods are needed, and how they use each other. This is the design issue which is addressed in Chapter 10.

There is no doubt that OOP is the most important programming paradigm of the present and of the foreseeable future. Complementing OO programming languages, a whole number of design and analysis methods are widely used; in addition, OO databases (outside the scope of this book) are starting to become important.

14.14 ● Summary

OOP is based on three principles:

- Encapsulation – grouping variables and procedures (termed methods) together in self-contained modules called objects. Objects are generalized into classes. An object is an instance of a class, created using the Java keyword `new`.

- Inheritance – enabling classes to be re-used, by inheriting the behavior (methods) of a class and then extending its behavior by providing new methods and variables.

● Polymorphism – an object always responds to the method calls that belong to that object.

The importance of OOP is in providing high modularity (through encapsulation of objects) plus software re-use (through inheritance).

EXERCISES

To do some of these exercises, you ideally need a Java development system so that you can compile and run programs.

14.1 Using a library class. The library class Date allows the programmer to create an object that represents information about the date and time (when it is created). Write a program that has a button you can press which displays the time in minutes and seconds. It has a second button which displays the day, month, and year.

The constructor method for Date has no parameters. The following methods are available:

getDate() returns the day of the month, from 1 to 31.
getHours() returns the hour, from 0 to 23.
getMinutes() returns the number of minutes past the hour, from 0 to 59.
getMonth() returns the month number, from 0 to 11.
getSeconds() returns the number of seconds past the minute, from 0 to 59.
getYear() returns the year minus 1900.

This class is within a group of utility classes and to use it you need the following declaration at the start of the program:

```
import java.util.Date;
```

14.2 Writing your own class. Enhance the safe program given in the text so that the user only has three guesses. The code for the lock is then changed to a new random value. Keep a record of how many times the user gets it right and how many times they fail to unlock the lock. Display the current score in the window. Create a class called Score and create an instance of called score that keeps count of correct and incorrect guesses. This object encapsulates the score and the operations on it.

14.3 Browsing. Browse the class libraries in your system, using the browser tool provided (or if necessary a text editor). You will see that the libraries are large and make extensive use of inheritance.

14.4 Complex Numbers. Write a class called Complex to represent complex numbers (together with their operations). A complex number consists of two parts – a real part (a float) and an imaginary part (a float). The constructor method should create a new complex number, using the float's provided as parameters, like this:

```
Complex c = new Complex(1.0f, 2.0f);
```

Write methods getReal and getImaginary to get the real part and the imaginary part of a complex number and used like this:

```
float f = c.getReal();
float r = c.getImaginary();
```

Write a method to add two complex numbers and return their sum. The real part is the sum of the two real parts. The imaginary part is the sum of the two imaginary parts. A call of the method looks like:

```
Complex c = c1.sum(c2);
```

Write a method to calculate the product of two complex numbers. If one number has components x_1 and y_1 and the second number has components x_2 and y_2:

the real part of the product is the product = $x_1 * x_2 - y_1 * y_2$

the imaginary part of the product = $x_1 * y_2 + x_2 * y_1$.

Write a test program that uses the class to create a number of complex numbers (a number of instances of `Complex`) and then use the complex numbers.

14.5 Extending a library class. The class `Date` described in question 14.1 has been criticized in the Java community, because some of its methods do not return convenient information. Write a class called `Clock` that improves the following methods:

`getMonth()` returns an integer 1 to 12.
`getYear()` returns the year itself.

Rather than completely rewrite these methods, which would be very time-consuming, it is best to use the existing versions. (Re-use is the whole point of inheritance anyway.) To call a method in the superclass, the Java word `super` is used, like this example:

```
int m = super.getMonth();
```

14.6 Using a library class. The Java library class `stack` provides storage for objects on a first-in, last-out basis. Methods are provided to:

- create a new stack using the constructor method `stack`
- add to the top of the stack using method `push`
- remove from the top of the stack using method `pop`
- test to see whether the stack is empty using method `empty` (returns `true` if the stack is empty).

Write a program that creates a stack and allows the user to enter text items (for example people's names) keyed into a text field when a button labeled "push" is pressed. A button labeled "pop" causes the top item to be popped and displayed in the text field.

14.7 Review the literature on the three languages Java, C++, and Smalltalk and write a critical comparison. Include the following headings in your discussion: multiple or single inheritance, garbage collection.

14.8 Explain how an OO language supports software re-use. Explain the benefits of software re-use throughout all stages of software development.

ANSWERS TO SELF TEST QUESTIONS

14.1 open a file
read a record
write a record
close the file
delete the file.

14.2
```
public void setY(int newY) {
    y = newY;
}
```

14.3
```
Ball(int initialX, int initialY) {
    x = initialX;
    y = initialY;
}
```

14.4

```
class Pond extends Circle (

    public float perimeter() {
        return (3.142 * radius * 2);
    }

}
```

14.5
```
class Balloon extends Ball {

    public int getRadius() {
        return (radius);
    }

}
```

14.6 To create the text field, add the following code to the method `init`:

```
Textfield display = new Textfield();
add(display);
```

Then add the following code to change the value of the text field within the method `actionPerformed`:

```
display.setText(Integer.toString(guess));
```

FURTHER READING

Java

Douglas Bell and Mike Parr, *Java for Students*, Prentice Hall International, 2nd edition, 1999. An excellent book that starts from scratch.

Ken Arnold and James Gosling, *The Java Programming Language*, Addison-Wesley, 1996. An authoritative and fascinating book by the designers of the language. Dense and full of concepts, for experts in programming; not novices.

David Flanagan, *Java in a Nutshell*, O'Reilly and Associates, 1997. Written as a reference book, this lists all the libraries, with easy referencing. It has a section on the Java language for those who know C++. Widely used and recommended, but not really suitable for novices. Later editions of this book have expanded to two volumes, to accommodate the description of all the Java libraries now available.

H. M. Deitel and P. J. Deitel, *Java: How To Program*, Prentice Hall, 1997. This is very comprehensive and readable. Some editions are accompanied by a CD with Microsoft's Visual J++ development system for Java.

Other OO languages

Java is the latest in a line of object-oriented languages. All share the concepts of encapsulation, inheritance, and polymorphism.

Graham Birtwistle, Ole-Johan Dahl, Bjorn Myrhaug and Kristen Nygaard, *Simula Begin*, Studentliteratur and Auerbach, 1973. Simula 67 was the first object-oriented language. It was called Simula because it was designed as a language to simulate events.

Adele Goldberg and David Robson, *Smalltalk-80, the Language*, Addison-Wesley, 1989. Smalltalk-80 is the Rolls-Royce of object-oriented languages. It is completely object-oriented so that even control structures like repetition and **if** statements are objects. Like Java it supports single inheritance. Like Java it provides a large and comprehensive library that the programmer uses and inherits from to provide facilities including windowing, graphics, and data structures. This is the definitive book on Smalltalk-80.

John English, *Ada 95. The Craft of OO Programming*, Prentice Hall, 1997. Looks at Ada in its OO version.

Frank L. Friedman and Elliot B. Koffman, *Problem Solving, Abstraction, and Design using C++*, Addison-Wesley, 1994. C++ has been the most widely used object-oriented language, but maybe Java will take over its role. It has a grammar similar to Java's, but is a much more complex language which supports multiple inheritance. If you want to know about C++, there are a large number of books, and many of them are very weighty and formidable! This is the simplest of many books.

Bertrand Meyer, *Object-Oriented Software Construction*, Prentice Hall, 2nd edition, 1997. This is a wonderfully clear exposition of the principles of OOP.

15

Concurrent programming

This chapter:

- reviews the main concepts of concurrent programming
- identifies the problems that arise when concurrent programs interact, including deadlock
- shows how software can be designed to accommodate interactions between concurrent programs.

15.1 ● Introduction

In this chapter we look at the distinctive topic of concurrent programming – the notion that two or more programs can be executing at one and the same time. The topic has important applications in:

- real time systems
- operating systems
- networking software.

If you use a personal computer you can usually ask it to do several things at once: print a file, edit a different file, display the time, and receive email. In reality of course, a single computer can only do one thing at a time, but because a computer works so quickly, it can share its time between a number of activities. It does this so fast that it gives the impression that it is doing them all at once.

In this chapter, we use the facilities of the language Java to illustrate the central principles of concurrent programming. (An introduction to Java is given in the appendix, and the object-oriented features of Java are explained in Chapter 14.) When a Java program does several things at once it is called *multithreading*. Such a program can, for example, simultaneously: display several animations, play sounds, and allow the user to interact. Any one of the activities that it is performing is called a *thread*.

A program is a series of instructions to the computer, which the computer normally obeys in sequence. The sequence is diverted by procedure calls, loops, and selection statements, but it is still a single path that moves through the program. We can use a pencil to simulate the execution of a program, following the path through the program. In multithreading, two or more paths are set in motion. To follow the paths of execution now needs several pencils. Remembering that a computer is only capable of doing one thing at once, we realize that it is dividing its available time between the different threads so as to give the impression that they are all executing at the same time.

Our first example of concurrency is a real, human one – a group of people shopping for a meal. Suppose that three students share a house. They decide to have a meal and to split up the work of shopping:

- one buys the meat
- one buys the vegetables
- one buys the lager

and these things they do concurrently. This way the whole shopping job gets done quicker. But notice that at some time they must synchronize their activities in order that the meal gets prepared and that they all sit down to eat it at the same time. This may just involve waiting until the last person has returned from the shops.

A group of musicians in an orchestra play different instruments simultaneously, reading their different parts from a musical score. The score tells each of them what to do and helps them synchronize their notes.

Next, the process of controlling a plant. In a biscuit factory controlled by a computer, which has ovens, weighing machines, valves, and pumps, the computer must ensure that each of a number of separate activities is carried out. There may be several different concurrent activities within the plant to be controlled.

The next example is a personal computer, which may have several things going on at once:

- displaying a clock
- printing a file
- carrying out editing of a file
- receiving electronic mail

and all of these are to be carried out as if the processor is devoting its time exclusively to one of the threads.

So concurrency is very common, both inside and outside computer systems. A concurrent activity inside a computer is called a *thread*, *task*, or sometimes a *process*. (We will use the first of these terms.) The code of each individual task looks like a normal sequential program. The operating system shares out the processor time amongst the tasks in such a way that it seems like they are all executing in parallel. This is sometimes called *apparent concurrency*. If two people are collaborating over a meal, or if a computer system consists of a number of processors, then there is *real concurrency*. Some computer scientists call apparent concurrency "parallelism" and real concurrency simply "concurrency." We shall adopt the single term "concurrency" in this chapter. Whatever the terminology we adopt, an essential characteristic of the situation is that the parallelism is explicitly in the hands of the programmer.

15.2 ● Independent threads

One graphic way to see threads in action is to look at a program that draws animations – a ball bouncing around a rectangle on the screen (Figure 15.1). This program uses two objects, each of which is run as a distinct thread:

● one thread to handle the user interface

● another thread to represent the ball object.

The user interface thread provides a button labeled start to start a ball bouncing. It also makes itself ready for any user events, which it will then handle. Most important, when the user clicks on the start button, it creates a second thread. Thereafter, the two threads run together in parallel, sharing the processor.

The second thread draws a bouncing ball. There is a delay in this thread so that the ball does not go too fast. To do this the thread calls a library procedure called sleep. The parameter passed to sleep is the time in milliseconds that the program wants to sleep. (To use this procedure it must be provided with an exception handler as shown. The explanation for the cause of an InterruptedException is given later in this chapter, and this particular exception can be safely ignored.)

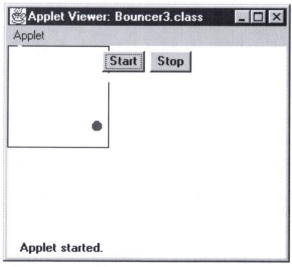

Figure 15.1 Bouncing balls screen

The user interface class (and thread) is, as usual in a Java applet, an extension of the library `Applet` class. The other class (thread) is an extension of the library class `Thread`. The only requirement of this class is that it must provide a procedure named `run`. It is this procedure that the Java system calls to set the thread running. The act of creating the thread is done by the user interface object. First it creates the new object, just as any other object is created, with:

```java
Ball ball = new Ball(g);
```

Then it asks the Java system to run the thread, by calling the library procedure **start**:

```java
ball.start();
```

So now here is the complete code for the program.

```java
import java.awt.*;
import java.applet.Applet;
import java.awt.event.*;

public class Bouncer2 extends Applet implements ActionListener {
    private Button start;
    public void init() {
        start = new Button("Start");
        add(start);
        start.addActionListener(this);
    }
    public void actionPerformed(ActionEvent event) {
        if (event.getSource() == start) {
            Graphics g = getGraphics();
            Ball ball = new Ball(g);
            ball.start();
        }
    }
}

class Ball extends Thread {
    private Graphics g;
    private int x = 7, xChange = 7;
    private int y = 0, yChange = 2;
    private int diameter = 10;
    private int leftX = 0, rightX = 100;
    private int topY = 0, bottomY = 100;
    public Ball(Graphics graphics) {
        g = graphics;
    }
    public void run() {
        g.drawRect(leftX, topY, rightX - leftX, bottomY - topY);
```

```
        for (int n = 1; n < 1000; n++) {
            eraseBall();
            moveBall();
            drawBall();

            try {
                Thread.sleep(50);
            }
            catch (InterruptedException e) {
                System.err.println("sleep exception");
            }
        }
    }
    void eraseBall() {
        g.setColor(Color.white);
        g.fillOval (x, y, diameter, diameter);
    }
    void moveBall() {
        if (x + xChange <= leftX)
            xChange = -xChange;
        if (x + xChange >= rightX)
            xChange = -xChange;
        if (y + yChange <= topY)
            yChange = -yChange;
        if (y + yChange >= bottomY)
            yChange = -yChange;

        x = x + xChange;
        y = y + yChange;
    }
    void drawBall() {
        g.setColor(Color.red);
        g.fillOval (x, y, diameter, diameter);
    }
}
```

When this program is running, clicking on the start button creates a thread that displays a ball that bounces around the rectangle. By clicking on the start button while a ball is already bouncing, an additional thread is created which displays another ball bouncing around along with the existing ball. The user can create new balls indefinitely. This is a graphic illustration of creating new threads.

This is all you need to write programs that do lots of things simultaneously. You can display a clock, display an animation, play a game, edit some text – all at the same time. You need to create a thread for each of these parallel activities as shown above.

SELF TEST QUESTION

15.1 Alter the program so that it creates two rectangles at different places on the screen, with a ball bouncing around in each. You need one thread for each ball. The user interface object is a third thread. Make maximum re-use of the existing classes.

We have seen how to create threads that run in parallel, sharing the processor. A key feature of these threads is that they do not interact or communicate with each other. Once created, they are independent threads. This is a common and very useful scenario in multi-threading. An alternative scenario is where the threads interact with each other as they are running. This introduces complications, as we shall see later in this chapter.

15.3 ● Dying and killing

The program as written makes the ball bounce for a limited time (1000 repetitions), controlled by the `for` loop. When the thread `ball` has finished looping, it exits the procedure `run` and dies. This is the normal way in which a thread dies.

Suppose we want to improve the bouncing ball program so that a ball keeps bouncing until we stop it, by pressing a button. In the user interface thread, we provide a new button, labeled `stop`:

```
Button stop = new Button("Stop");

add(stop);
```

A good way to terminate the bouncing ball thread is to set up a Boolean flag named `keepGoing`. This is initially made `true` when the object is created, but is set `false` when the user presses the `stop` button. The loop in the ball object is:

```
while (keepGoing) {
    // etc.
}
```

The part of the event handler now needed to handle the button labeled Stop is:

```
if (event.getSource == stop)
    ball.pleaseStop();
```

and the procedure in the class `Ball` is:

```
public void pleaseStop() {
    keepGoing = false;
}
```

This program now works very nicely. When you press the start button, a ball is created and bounces around the rectangle until you press the stop button. Pressing start again creates a new ball and so on.

Another thing you might want to do is to make a thread wait until another has died. This is done with the procedure join, as in:

```
ball.join()
```

which causes the thread that calls join to wait until thread ball has died.

SELF TEST QUESTION

15.2 Write a program that consists of two threads – the user interface thread and one other (which could be a thread that displays the time in minutes and seconds for a period of 2 minutes). The first thread initiates the second, using start. It then waits (using join) until the second has terminated. It should then display a message to say that it has terminated.

15.4 ● The state of a thread

It is useful to understand the idea of the states of a thread. A thread can be in any one of these states:

- **New** It has just been created with the **new** operator, just like any other object, but it has not yet been set runnable by means of the **start** procedure.
- **Running** It is actually running on the computer, executing instructions.
- **Runnable** It would like to run, is able to run, but some other thread is currently running.
- **Blocked** For some reason the thread cannot proceed until something happens. A typical example would be that the thread has called **sleep** and is suspended for a number of milliseconds.
- **Dead** The **run** procedure has exited normally.

One thread can find out the state of another thread by calling the library procedure **isAlive**. It returns **true** if the thread is runnable or blocked. It returns **false** if the thread is new or dead. For example:

```
if (ball.isAlive())
    g.drawString("The ball is alive", 20, 20);
```

15.5 ● Scheduling and thread priorities

Like any operating system, the Java system has the job of sharing the single (or sometimes multi-) processor among the threads in a program. It is often the case that there are several threads that are runnable – they are ready and able to run when the processor becomes available. The scheduler must choose between them. Different schedulers on different machines and Java systems may work differently. There is no guarantee that any particular scheduling is provided. The programmer must be careful not to make any assumptions about when a particular thread will be selected to run.

By default, the Java system gives all the threads that are created the same priority. Thereafter the Java system will share the processor equitably among the active threads. Even so, it is easy for a thread to hog the processor, shutting out other threads. Therefore any thread with a social conscience should call the procedure **yield** like this:

```
yield();
```

at such times as it may otherwise be too greedy. If no other threads are runnable, the thread continues.

15.6 ● Mutual exclusion

We now turn to the more complex situation where two or more threads interact as they are running. (Thus far we have considered only independent threads.) Suppose that two threads are each incrementing the value of a shared integer maintained within a separate object:

```java
import java.applet.Applet;
import java.awt.*;

public class TwoCounters extends Applet {
    public void init() {
        Graphics g = getGraphics();
        SharedNumber count=new SharedNumber(g);

        Counter1 counter1 = new Counter1(count);
        Counter2 counter2 = new Counter2(count);
        counter1.start();
        counter2.start();
    }
}
```

```
public class Counter1 extends Thread {
    private SharedNumber count;
    public Counter1(SharedNumber count) {
    this.count = count;
    }
    public void run() {
        for( int i = 1; i <= 10; i++)
            count.increment();
    }
}
public class Counter2 extends Thread {
    private SharedNumber count;
    public Counter2(SharedNumber count) {
        this.count = count;
    }
    public void run() {
        for( int i = 1; i <= 10; i++)
            count.increment();
    }
}
import java.awt.*;
public class SharedNumber {
    private int n = 0;
    private Graphics g;
    private int x = 0;
    public SharedNumber (Graphics g) {
        this.g = g;
    }
    public void increment() {
        n = n + 1;
        g.drawString(n + ", ", x*20, 30);
        x++;
    }
}
```

This is a simplified version of the sort of activity that occurs very often in multithreading. It could be that the threads are adding to the score in a computer game. It could be that the threads are keeping a log of the number of visits to a Web site.

What will happen if the above two threads are set running in parallel? Taking an obvious view, each will increment the shared variable, which will take on the values 1, 2, ... up to 20, as in Figure 15.2. You could run this program a thousand times and this is exactly what will happen. But although this will almost always happen, occasionally the

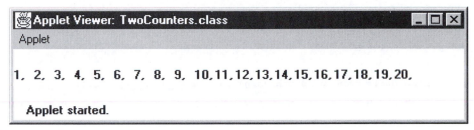

Figure 15.2 Screen output from the two counters program

outcome will be unpredictable, and sometimes very strange indeed. The outcome depends on when the scheduler chooses to suspend one thread and resume the execution of the other. The scheduler does not know what the intent of the two threads is, and might suspend either one of the two threads at any time. Indeed, the interval between successive suspensions may be random – hence the nondeterminacy. To see what might happen and therefore will happen eventually, consider the following sequence of events:

1. The thread `counter1` starts to increment the counter. It loads the value into a temporary storage area. Suppose the value happens to be `5`.

2. Thread `counter1` is suspended by the scheduler. The thread `counter2` resumes execution. It loads the value of the counter (still equal to `5`) into a temporary storage area.

3. Thread `counter2` is suspended. Thread `counter1` resumes. It increments the value, so that the value `5` becomes `6`. It stores the value back in the variable.

4. Thread `counter1` is suspended. `counter2` resumes. It increments the value that it is holding in temporary storage (which is `5`) to become `6`, and stores it back into the variable.

The outcome is that the value of the variable has become `6`, when it should have become `7`. Now you might argue that this is a rather bizarre sequence of events. You might argue that this particular sequence will happen once in a blue moon. The fact remains that it might happen and therefore we must avoid it happening.

To solve this problem, we need to ensure that the shared variable is accessed by one thread at once. We control the access so that one thread can carry out its business properly and to its conclusion. Only then do we allow any other thread access. The problem to be solved is to allow only one thread access to something (e.g. a shared data item) at a time. While one thread has access, the other should be excluded and vice versa. This requirement is known as *mutual exclusion*.

The way to ensure mutual exclusion is to specify any procedures which share variables as `synchronized` in their headers. These procedures must also be within the same class. The Java system ensures that within a particular object, only one of the synchronized procedures can be entered by a thread at a time. Any thread trying to enter any synchronized procedure in the object while any of them is in use is blocked until such time as the first has exited from the procedure. Thus:

```
public class SharedNumber {
    private int n = 0;
    private Graphics g;
    private int x = 0;
    public SharedNumber (Graphics g) {
        this.g = g;
    }
    public synchronized void increment() {
        n = n + 1;
        g.drawString(n + "," , x*20, 30);
        x++;
    }
}
```

SELF TEST QUESTION

15.4 Write procedures as a part of the class `SharedNumber` to:

1. decrement the value of the shared variable
2. `getValue` (obtain the value of the shared variable)
3. `display` (display the value of the shared variable).

Commonly, threads exhibit this general structure:

```
while (true) {
    doSomething();
    accessSomeSharedResource();
    doSomethingElse();
}
```

The thread is an infinite loop. In the body of the loop, the thread carries out some action. Then it needs access to some shared resource – a variable, a file, the screen, a communication link. Finally, the thread does something else. The part of the program where it accesses a shared resource is known as a *critical region*.

In summary, when a variable or a data structure is accessed by two or more threads, there is a need for mutual exclusion. This is achieved by placing the data in its own object and providing access via procedures. These procedures must be declared as `synchronized` so that only one thread can enter one procedure at a time, excluding any others.

15.7 ● Thread interaction

Our next problem also involves mutual exclusion, but rather than the shared resource of an integer counter, the resource will be the screen. Suppose that two threads want to display something on the screen. They are greedy – they both want the whole screen. Suppose they are poets and they each want to display a poem that they have written. Here is the code for the two threads:

```java
import java.applet.Applet;
import java.awt.*;
public class Poets extends Applet {
    public void init() {
        Graphics g = getGraphics();

        Nursery nursery = new Nursery(g);
        Revolutionary revolutionary = new Revolutionary(g);
        nursery.start();
        revolutionary.start();

    }
}
import java.awt.*;
class Nursery extends Thread {
    private Graphics g;

    public Nursery(Graphics g) {
        this.g = g;
    }

    public void run() {
        while (true) {
            g.drawString( "Mary had a little lamb", 10, 10);
            g.drawString( "Its fleece was white as snow", 10, 30);

            try {
                Thread.sleep(5000);
            }
            catch (InterruptedException e) {
                System.err.println("sleep exception");
            }
        }
    }
}
import java.awt.*;
class Revolutionary extends Thread {
    private Graphics g;

    public Revolutionary(Graphics g) {
        this.g = g;
    }

    public void run() {
        while (true) {
```

```
        g.drawString("Praise Marx", 10, 20);
        g.drawString("and pass the ammunition", 10, 40);
        try {
            Thread.sleep(5000);
        }
        catch (InterruptedException e) {
            System.err.println("sleep exception");
        }
    }
  }
}
```

What would we see on the computer screen when the two poet threads are running? You can see that they are both trying to display their message on the screen at the same time. Because their output is nearly in the same place, it looks like Figure 15.3, in which the poems are interleaved and therefore confused. We need to control the situation so that one thread has exclusive access to the screen for an appropriate length of time. But how do we control and coordinate the outputs from the poets? We *could* attempt to use `synchronized`, as in the previous counterexample, but this would be overkill – too restrictive. The structure of many threads is:

```
do some nonshared activities
access some shared resource
do some nonshared activities
etc.
```

We want a means of switching on a mutual exclusion around a critical region – a section of code which accesses a shared resource – just as traffic lights enclose the critical region at a road intersection.

Returning to the poets, we do not want to curb the poet's passion too much, but we will insist as part of the design of the program that each of them issues a request (calls a procedure) to use the screen before starting output. Then, after they have finished, they should issue a notification to say so. A poet thread now looks like this:

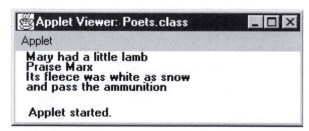

Figure 15.3 Output from the poets

```
import java.awt.*;
class Mowing extends Thread {
    private Graphics g;
    private ScreenController screen;

    public Mowing(Graphics g, ScreenController screen) {
        this.screen = screen;
        this.graphics = g;
    }

    public void run() {
        while (true) {
            screen.askFor();
            draw();
            screen.relinquish();
            try {
                Thread.sleep(5000);
            }
            catch (InterruptedException e) {
                System.err.println("sleep exception");
            }
        }
    }

    private void draw() {
        g.drawString( "one man went to mow", 10, 20);
        g.drawString( "went to mow a meadow", 10, 40);
    }
}
```

We create a guardian object or manager, called **screen**, for the screen. Its mission is to ensure that only one client is using the screen at once. It accepts requests to use the screen and notifications that users have finished using the screen. It maintains a Boolean variable called **inUse**, which is set **true** when some thread has been granted access to the screen, and **false** otherwise. (Initially the value is **false**.) The Boolean variable is accessed only by procedures that are **synchronized**. We saw earlier why any shared variable needs protection of this kind. The manager enforces the discipline that, once any thread has issued a request to use the screen, any other threads must wait until the first has completed its use. We are using synchronized access to a shared variable to control access to a shared resource – the screen.

To make a thread wait if the screen is already in use, it calls the **wait** procedure. This is a library procedure that causes the thread to wait until another thread calls a **notify** procedure. (When using **wait**, it must supply an exception handler to handle a possible **InterruptedException**. We shall see later how this might arise, but this particular exception can be safely ignored.) As soon as a waiting thread is released by a **notify**, it is free to run. If several threads are waiting, only the longest-waiting thread is released from its wait.

```
public class ScreenController {
    private boolean inUse = false;
    public void synchronized askFor() {
        while (inUse)
            try {
                wait();
            }
            catch (InterruptedException e) {
                System.err.println("Exception");
            }
        inUse = true;
    }
    public void synchronized relinquish() {
        inUse = false;
        notify();
    }
}
```

Now the poets can each display their poems for 5 seconds, free of interference. We have controlled access by competing threads to a shared resource (the screen). When a poet calls askFor, the value of the Boolean inUse is tested. If it is false, inUse is set to true, signifying that the resource is now in use. If the value of inUse is false, the thread that called askFor calls the wait procedure. This suspends the poet thread until a notify is called by some other thread. This happens when another poet finishes using the display, and calls relinquish. When procedure askFor is released from its wait, it sets the Boolean variable to true, signifying that the resource is in use.

The interaction between the threads is encapsulated within the object screen (an instance of ScreenController). Procedures within this object are protected using the description synchronized. Any use of wait and notify within this object, screen, refer to this object, and only this object. (There may be a number of threads within a particular program that call notify, but only an invocation of notify within the object screen can affect any thread waiting within this object.)

You might think that it is more appropriate to use an if statement rather than a while, as follows, omitting the try clause for clarity:

```
if (inUse)
    wait();
```

It is very tempting to write the program in this way, because it seems clear that the thread only has to wait if inUse is true. However, this is an unsafe way to write programs of this kind. It might work sometimes, but it is much better to write a while loop. The reason is as follows. Once it is released from waiting, a thread should and must go back to check again that the data has the desired value – in case some other thread has changed it. This is most neatly accomplished using a while loop as shown above.

Let us now summarize what wait and notify do:

`wait`: suspends the thread that calls it until such time as some other thread calls `notify` within this same object

`notify`: releases just one of any threads that are waiting within the object. If no thread is waiting, `notify` does nothing.

To complete this topic, and to illustrate that mutual exclusion is no minor problem, let us consider two real computer systems.

A bank maintains records of customer accounts on a computer with many terminals. One bank clerk at one terminal enters a transaction to credit a particular account by $1,000. Another clerk simultaneously enters a transaction to debit the same account by $1,000. What can go wrong?

An airline maintains records of bookings on a computer with many terminals. One travel agent interrogates the system to find out whether seats are available on a particular flight. On finding that two seats are available, he turns round to the client to ask whether she wants the seats. While they are conversing, someone at another terminal books the seats.

To summarize, sometimes two or more threads require intermittent access to some shared data. Uncontrolled access can cause strange things to happen. Mutual exclusion is the term used to describe controlling the access so that only one thread has access at once. It can be implemented by describing any procedures that access the shared resource (object) as `synchronized`. This handles short-term access to a shared variable.

For resources like the screen or a file, which are shared, a guardian object needs to be designed. It maintains a Boolean variable to control access. Waiting to use the resource is accomplished using the `wait` procedure. Another thread ends the waiting by executing `notify`. This handles long-term access to a shared resource.

One of the great strengths of objects is encapsulation of shared data. This is further exploited when different threads access shared variables. All that is needed is to add the one word `synchronized` to the procedure header.

15.8 ● The producer–consumer problem

In mutual exclusion and in the examples we have looked at so far, threads tend to compete with each other. Now, in contrast, we look at situations where two or more threads collaborate in carrying out some work. The scenario is this: one thread (a producer) will create some information which it passes on to a second thread (a consumer) which deals with the information.

15.8.1 The clock

This program acts as a digital clock, displaying hours, minutes, and seconds (Figure 15.4). Each of these is maintained by a distinct thread. The user interface thread serves only to create and start the threads:

Figure 15.4 The clock

```
import java.awt.*;
import java.applet.Applet;
public class Clock extends Applet {
    public void init() {
        Graphics g = getGraphics();
        TickTock minuteTick = new TickTock();
        Minute minute = new Minute(g, minuteTick);
        minute.start();
        Second second = new Second(g, minuteTick);
        second.start();
    }
}
```

The two other threads – minute and second – act like a production line. Figure 15.5 is the UML collaboration diagram for the program, showing the objects and their interactions. Thread second is the first in the chain. It goes to sleep for 1,000 milliseconds (1 second) by calling sleep(1000). When a second has elapsed it updates its count of the number of seconds. Meanwhile, thread minute is asleep, waiting to be woken up by thread second when 60 seconds have elapsed.

We have already seen the way that threads sleep and get woken up. To sleep, a thread executes procedure wait. This suspends the thread until an event occurs. The event

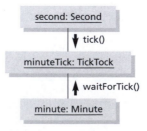

Figure 15.5 Structure of the clock program

happens when some other thread executes the procedure `notify`. Both these procedures must be used within `synchronized` procedures, which in turn are within an object.

Here is the code for class `Second`. It sleeps for a second. Then it updates its count of the number of seconds. If a minute has elapsed, it calls procedure `tick` in object `minuteTick` to wake up thread `minute`.

```java
import java.awt.*;

public class Second extends Thread {

    private int seconds = 0;

    private Graphics g;
    private TickTock minuteTick;

    public Second(Graphics g, TickTock minuteTick) {
        this.g = g;
        this.minuteTick = minuteTick;
    }

    public void run() {
        while(true) {
            try {
                Thread.sleep(1000);
            }
            catch (InterruptedException e) {
                System.err.println("Exception");
            }
            if(seconds == 59) {
                minuteTick.tick();
                seconds = 0;
            }
            else seconds++;
            g.clearRect(10, 0, 100, 20);
            g.drawString(seconds + " seconds", 10, 20);
        }
    }
}
```

The class for thread `minute` is given below. It calls procedure `waitForTick` in object `minuteTick` to suspend itself until a minute has elapsed. When it continues, it updates its count of the number of minutes.

```java
import java.awt.*;

public class Minute extends Thread {

    private int minutes = 0;
    private Graphics g;
    private TickTock minuteTick;
```

```
    public Minute(Graphics g, TickTock minuteTick) {
        this.g = g;
        this.minuteTick = minuteTick;
    }
    public void run() {
        while(true) {
            minuteTick.waitForTick();
            if (minutes == 59) {
                minutes = 0;
            }
            else
                minutes++;
            g.clearRect(10, 20, 100, 20);
            g.drawString(minutes + " minutes", 10, 40);
        }
    }
}
```

The object that handles the interaction between the threads second and minute contains two synchronized procedures. Procedure waitForTick causes its user to wait. Procedure tick signals that the other can continue by calling notify.

```
public class TickTock {
    private boolean tickHappens = false;
    public synchronized void waitForTick() {
        while (!tickHappens)
            try {
                wait();
            }
            catch (InterruptedException e) {
                System.err.println("Exception");
            }
        tickHappens = false;
    }
    public synchronized void tick() {
        tickHappens = true;
        notify();
    }
}
```

The above clock program is an example of two threads that co-operate with each other in a very simple way. From time to time the first thread needs to alert the other to the fact that something has happened. The second thread waits for this event and, when it happens, takes some action. This is an example of a very simple producer–consumer pair in which no information is passed from one thread to the other. We now look at a more complex example where information is passed from one thread to another.

15.8.2 The café

As the next example, consider a computer system for a café (Figure 15.6). This program could be used in a real café to keep track of orders. Alternatively it could act as a simulation of a café. In this program actual information is passed from one thread to another. An order is entered into the computer by pressing a button. The buttons available are burger, fries, and cola. An order is displayed on the screen and then entered into a queue. The queue is displayed on the screen. The chef takes orders from the queue on a first-come, first-served basis. The chef can only work on one order at a time, which is displayed on the screen. When the chef has completed the order, he or she presses a button labeled `complete` to remove the order from the screen.

There is a chain of objects involved in the café. We need three threads for this program:

1. the user interface
2. the waiter – to accept an order, display it and enter it into the queue
3. the chef – to remove an item from the queue, display it, and wait until it is cooked. If there is no order in the queue, the chef waits.

In addition to the three thread objects are two other objects (`order` and `complete`) which handle the interaction between the threads. These are all shown in Figure 15.7, the UML collaboration diagram describing the objects that make up the program.

First we will look at the code for the user interface, class `Cafe`. There is nothing new here. The two other threads (`waiter` and `chef`) are created and set running. These threads are passed the objects that they need to communicate and also the graphics context, `g`. The user interface thread also handles the events when the buttons are pressed. An order is passed to the `waiter` thread by calling procedure `notifyEvent` of the `order`

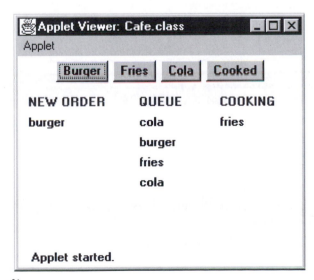

Figure 15.6 The café

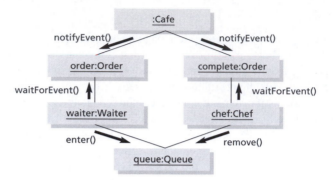

Figure 15.7

object. The information that cooking is complete is passed to the `chef` thread by calling
procedure `notifyEvent` of object `complete`.

```java
import java.awt.*;
import java.applet.Applet;

public class Cafe extends Applet implements ActionListener {
    private Button burger, fries, cola, cooked;
    private Order order, complete;

    public void init() {
    Graphics g = getGraphics();
    burger = new Button("Burger");
    add (burger);
    burger.addActionListener(this);
    fries = new Button("Fries");
    add (fries);
    fries.addActionListener(this);
    cola = new Button("Cola");
    add (cola);
    cola.addActionListener(this);
    cooked = new Button("Cooked");
    add (cooked);
    cooked.addActionListener(this);

    order = new Order();
    Queue queue = new Queue(g);
    complete = new Order();

    Waiter waiter = new Waiter(g, order, queue);
    waiter.start();

    Chef chef = new Chef(g, complete, queue);
    chef.start();
    }
```

```
    public void actionPerformed (ActionEvent event) {
        if (event.getSource() == burger)
            order.notifyEvent("burger");
        if (event.getSource() == fries)
            order.notifyEvent("fries");
        if (event.getSource() == cola)
            order.notifyEvent("cola");
        if (event.getSource() == cooked)
            complete.notifyEvent("cooked");
    }
}
```

The `waiter` thread loops forever and does the following:

1. waits for an order by calling procedure `waitForEvent` of object `order`
2. when an order is entered (by pressing a choice from one of the three buttons), the user interface thread notifies the `waiter` that there is an order
3. collects the order, displays it, waits for 5 seconds
4. enters the order into the queue
5. notifies the `chef` thread that something has been put in the queue.

Here is the code:

```
import java.awt.*;
public class Waiter extends Thread {
    private Order order;
    private Graphics g;
    private Queue queue;
    public Waiter(Graphics g, Order order, Queue queue) {
        this.order = order;
        this.g = g;
        this.queue = queue;
    }
    public void run() {
        g.drawString("NEW ORDER", 10, 50);
        while (true) {
            String newOrder = order.waitForEvent();
            g.clearRect(10, 50, 50, 25);
            g.drawString(newOrder, 10, 70);
            try {
                Thread.sleep(5000);
            }
            catch (InterruptedException e) {
                System.err.println("Exception");
            }
```

```
            g.clearRect(10, 50, 50, 25);
            queue.enter(newOrder);
        }
    }
}
```

The interaction between the user interface thread and the waiter takes place via an object named `order`. This object holds the order itself, together with the procedures that ensure that it is handled properly. Remember that any data that is accessed by two or more threads has to be enclosed in an object and that the procedures that access the data must be declared `synchronized`. When the waiter is collecting an order, it has first to `wait` for one to be entered via the buttons. When the user interface is placing an order, it must `notify` that it has done so. The code for an order is:

```
public class Order {

    private String order = "";

    public synchronized void notifyEvent(String newOrder) {
        order = newOrder;
        notify();
    }

    public synchronized String waitForEvent() {
        while (order.equals(""))
            try {
                wait();
            }
            catch (InterruptedException e) {
                System.err.println("Exception");
            }
        String newOrder = order;
        order = "";
        return newOrder;
    }
}
```

Now let us turn our attention to the queue. The queue allows us to decouple the waiter and the chef, allowing them – when possible – to work at their own pace. We will represent the queue as an array of strings:

```
String[] queue = new String[5];
```

Associated with the queue is a counter, named `count`, that describes how many orders are in the queue. Putting something in the queue involves:

```
queue[count] = item;
count++;
```

Taking something out of the queue is a little more difficult because we have to move everything up to fill the gap left when the first item is removed:

```
item = queue[0];
count--;
for (c=0; c < count; c++)
    queue[c] = queue[c+1];
```

Now we know that if two threads are to access the same data, then there has to be mutual exclusion. As before, we will create an object that looks after this shared data, the queue. It accepts requests to add an item to the queue:

```
queue.enter(item);
```

and requests to remove an item from the queue:

```
queue.remove(item);
```

and these procedures must be described as `synchronized`.

Finally, if there is nothing in the queue, the chef must `wait` until there is something to cook. And when the waiter puts something in the queue, it must `notify` the chef that there is an order to work on. If the waiter places, say, three items, in the queue, it will execute `notify` three times. The `enter` procedure counts up these three `notify`'s. The `remove` procedure waits for at least one `notify`, then extracts an item, and decrements the count. Thus `remove` can be called three times. The fourth time we call it (on an empty queue) its `wait` will be executed.

Here is the text of the `Queue` class:

```
import java.awt.*;]
public class Queue {
    private Graphics g;
    private String[] queue = new String[5];
    private int count = 0;

    public Queue(Graphics g) {
        this.g = g;
    }

    public synchronized void enter(String item) {
        queue[count] = item;
        count++;
        display();
        notify();
    }

    public synchronized String remove() {
        while (count == 0)
            try {
                wait();
            }
            catch (InterruptedException e) {
                System.err.println("Exception");
            }
```

```
        String item = queue[0];
        count--;
        for (int c = 0; c < count; c++)
            queue[c] = queue[c+1];
        display();
        return item;
    }
    private void display() {
        g.drawString("QUEUE", 120, 50);
        g.clearRect(120, 50, 50, 120);
        for (int c = 0; c < count; c++)
            g.drawString(queue[c], 120, 70 + c*20);
    }
}
```

Now this program is probably not the simplest you may ever have seen, and sometimes it helps to check that it is OK with the following sort of reasoning.

Let us first consider what happens to the variable `count`. The variable `count` simply counts how many items there are in the queue:

● Initially there are 0 items in the queue.

● Procedure `enter` increments `count`.

● Procedure `remove` decrements `count`.

Now let us turn our attention to the procedures. As far as procedure `remove` is concerned:

● If there is something in the queue, that is if `count` is greater than 0, it simply goes ahead and removes the item.

● If the queue is empty, that is if `count` is equal to 0, it must wait (using procedure `wait`) until such time as procedure `enter` releases it from the `wait` by doing a `notify`.

Note that `wait` and `notify` have no effect on the value of `count`. The relationship between `wait` and `notify` is that if one thread is waiting, `notify` wakes it up. If no thread is waiting, `notify` has no effect.

This completes our reasoning about the program, convincing ourselves that it works correctly. This helps because thread programs are notoriously difficult to debug and it is well worthwhile spending more time on checking.

As in an earlier program, you might think that it is more appropriate to use an `if` statement rather than a `while`, as follows (omitting the `try` clause for clarity):

```
if (count == 0)
    wait();
```

It is very tempting to write the program in this way, because the thread only has to wait if `count == 0`. However, this is an unsafe way to write programs of this kind. It might work sometimes, but it is much better to write a `while` loop. We will repeat the argument as follows. Suppose that there are a number of consumer threads rather than just one. In this case there are not, but it is better to write programs of this type on the assumption that there might be other threads around. Then at any time there might be several threads waiting for something to be placed in the empty array. They all have called wait and are suspended. Suppose that a thread is released from its wait and simply tries to remove a string from the array. It might just be that some other thread has intervened and removed the data. So it is better for a thread, once released, to check again that the data is available, using a while loop.

If using wait and notify seems difficult, you are right! Most people find it hard to get to grips with these procedures and everyone has to think very hard and very clearly to use them properly.

We have now completed most of the café program. One thing that remains is the object (called complete) that handles the interaction between the user interface thread and the chef. We re-use the class Order for this purpose. The class Order acts as an intermediary between two threads, one of which passes a string to the other. We re-use it instead simply to pass the information that the meal is complete.

The chef thread loops forever and does the following:

1. removes an order from the queue (or waits until there is an order in the queue)

2. displays the order

3. waits until the complete button is pressed

4. erases the display of the order.

The coding for the Chef class is:

```java
import java.awt.*;
public class Chef extends Thread{
    private Graphics g;
    private Order complete;
    private Queue queue;
    public Chef(Graphics g, Order complete, Queue queue) {
        this.g = g;
        this.complete = complete;
        this.queue = queue;
    }
    public void run() {
        g.drawString("COOKING", 200, 50);
        while (true) {
            String order = queue.remove();
            g.clearRect(200, 55, 50, 25);
            g.drawString(order, 200, 70);
            String cookedInfo = complete.waitForEvent();
            g.clearRect(200, 55, 50, 25);
        }
    }
}
```

We still have one matter to resolve. If there are a lot of orders the queue will become full. If the space available for the queue is very long, this will not happen very often, but we still have to cater for it. As the program is written, the procedure `enter` will simply try to place an order beyond the end of the queue array (which will result in an error). We can prevent this by providing a procedure as part of the `Queue` class that allows a user to ask whether the queue is full or not:

```
public synchronized boolean isFull(); {
    return count == queue.length;
}
```

and use this in the `waiter` thread:

```
if (!queue.isFull())
    queue.enter(newOrder);
```

Clearly, we will need to display a message to tell the user that this has happened. To sum up, the café consists of several threads that collaborate. Each thread produces some information, which it passes on to another thread. The interaction between threads is encapsulated within objects. Because these objects are accessing shared data items, the procedures are marked as `synchronized`. If a thread has to wait for an order it calls `wait`. If a thread needs to tell another that something has happened it calls `notify`.

This producer–consumer scenario is very common in computer systems. Another example is a computer that controls a jukebox in a pub. The computer controls the record player and inputs requests from consoles distributed about the pub. The computer queues up requests from the consoles in a first-come, first-served manner in a software queue. Information is passed from a producer thread (that receives and queues up requests) to a consumer thread (that plays the records).

Because the producer–consumer scenario is so widely used, and because it is complicated and error-prone to program it using `wait` and `notify`, it is likely that higher-level procedures for sending messages between threads will be available.

To summarize, a common situation in multithreading is where two or more threads collaborate to carry out some task. One thread creates some information to be passed on to a second. There is a need to communicate information and synchronize actions. This is entitled the producer–consumer situation. It can be programmed using an object that handles the communication between the threads. This object maintains the information that is passed from producer to consumer. It provides `synchronized` procedures for the producer and the consumer to access the data. It causes the consumer to `wait` when there is no information and it causes the consumer to `notify` when it provides new information.

15.9 ● Interruptions

Use of some of the procedures associated with threads, `sleep` and `wait`, must provide an exception handler to deal with a possible `InterruptedException`. This exception will not arise unless deliberately programmed and so it can safely be ignored. An interruption is the situation where one thread wants to interrupt what another thread is doing. This could arise in the café program when an order is canceled or it is the end of the day and time to shut the whole system down. A controlled closedown is desirable. To achieve this, one thread can interrupt another by calling the procedure `interrupt`, for example:

```
chef.interrupt();
```

This has no effect on the thread, unless it is in the process of a `wait` or a `sleep`. But a thread can check to see whether it has been interrupted using the procedure `interrupted`. For example, a typical style of usage would be:

```
while (!interrupted()) {
  // continue
}
```

If a thread is in the course of performing a `wait` or a `sleep` and some other thread causes an interrupt, then an exception is created, and this can be handled by providing an exception handler in the usual way.

15.10 ● Deadlock

In the early days of computers, some systems occasionally just seized up – they seemed in a way to be running normally, but no actual work was being done. The only remedy was to switch the machine off and boot up again – not a very satisfactory solution. The cause was a mystery. Only later was it realized that the cause was deadlock.

One way of seeing how deadlock arises is to consider the famous dining philosophers problem. Figure 15.8 shows five philosophers seated at a table eating. Between each pair of philosophers is a single fork. Each philosopher alternately eats and thinks (forever). In order to eat, a philosopher needs to use both of the forks on either side of the plate. Normally this will be OK, but occasionally someone will have to wait for a fork that is being used by their neighbor.

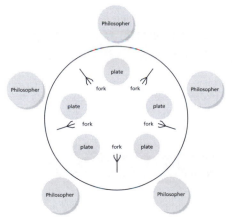

Figure 15.8 Dining philosophers

But what happens if it so happens that all the philosophers pick up their left fork? They all now have one fork and need the other. And they are all stuck. This is deadlock.

In a program, suppose that two threads each require intermittent access to the same two resources. The resources could be a file, the screen, or whatever. Suppose that the sequences are:

Thread 1	Thread 2
`acquireResourceA();`	`acquireResourceB();`
`acquireResourceB();`	`acquireResourceA();`
`etc.`	`etc.`

Then if it should so happen that thread 1 is suspended just after it acquires resource A, and thread 2 is suspended just after it acquires resource B, then each thread will then have something that the other needs in order to proceed. Each will be held up forever; we have deadlock. It may not happen very often, but if it does it is a catastrophe.

To sum up, we now have a new problem that may arise in multithreaded systems when threads interact or share resources.

We can't just ignore deadlock and hope it will never happen. The Java system does not help, unfortunately. It does not detect deadlock (and so it certainly does not solve the problem). The programmer has to ensure that it will not happen. There are several possible strategies. We will discuss only one – prevention.

In prevention, we design the system in such a way that we can guarantee that deadlock will never occur. One way to do this is to recognize that deadlock arises, not because of sharing but because of the *order* in which threads require resources. If all threads request the resources *in the same sequence*, deadlock cannot occur. So in the dining philosophers, if we number the forks from 1 to 5, and insist that philosophers only ever try to pick up forks according to that ordering, deadlock will never occur. We could put up a notice above the table, telling the philosophers to behave in this way. In a computer system, similarly, we could ensure during design that all threads access resources in the same sequence.

To summarize, deadlock is where two threads are stuck, each waiting for something that the other is holding.

15.11 ● Conclusions

The main motivation for multithreading is the need to do two or more things at once. So a software system is split up into parts that execute concurrently.

We can categorize various common cases in which threads interact as follows:

- threads ignore each other, e.g. the bouncing balls
- threads share data held in main memory, the critical region scenario, e.g. the counting threads
- threads compete for access to a resource, e.g. poets competing to use the screen
- threads collaborate in a task, the producer–consumer scenario, e.g. the café.

These cases can be handled as follows in Java:

1. If the threads do not interfere with each other, there is no problem.
2. If two or more threads access shared data (variables) in memory, place the data in an object. (You would probably do that anyway in an OO language.) Label the procedures within the object as `synchronized`. This ensures that the data is properly maintained.
3. If threads compete for a resource, like a screen or a communication line, create a resource manager object.
4. If threads need to coordinate their activities (as in the common producer–consumer scenario), use `wait` and `notify`, again within an object. These procedures must be called from within procedures that are `synchronized`. Calling `wait` causes the thread to be suspended until some other thread executes a `notify` within the same object.

`wait` and `notify` are almost always used in a standard pattern as follows. The thread that is waiting for some condition executes code that looks like this:

```
synchronized void waitThenDo() {
  while (!condition)
    wait();
  // carry out the required task
}
```

where `condition` is the condition that is awaited. The execution of `wait` causes this thread to be suspended. Another thread can then enter the same object, using one of the `synchronized` procedures. This is either another thread that has to wait, or a thread that releases a waiting thread. The thread that notifies this thread that something has happened simply executes:

```
synchronized void tellTheOther() {
    condition = true;
  notify();
}
```

If a number of threads are waiting within the same object, then only one thread is released from its wait. This is the thread that has been waiting longest.

Programming with threads requires care. In particular, it demands a great deal of skill and care to use `wait` and `notify` and any program that uses them has to checked very carefully for errors. These, however, are the low-level primitive operations as supplied with Java. Most software is designed to use higher-level procedures (available in a library) that are easier and safer to use. These are encapsulated inside an object that embodies a queue and provides procedures such as `addToQueue` and `removeFromQueue`.

To support multithreading, the programming language and/or the operating system must provide facilities to:

- create a new thread
- terminate a thread

● allow a thread to wait for a specified time period
● provide mutual exclusion when two threads need access to a shared data structure
● provide synchronization between threads.

Of these, the most discussion and variability between systems is about facilities for synchronization.

Most operating systems provide the programmer with facilities similar to those described above. An example is Unix, which provides two kinds of facility for multiprogramming. First, it allows the user to initiate processes using the command language. Second, it allows the programmer (typically using C) to make calls on library procedures that provide these facilities. Some programming languages allow these (or similar) facilities to be expressed within the programming language itself. Examples include Java, as we have seen, and Ada.

15.12 ● Summary

● It is common in software systems for two or more threads to run concurrently. Each thread looks like a normal sequential program. The scheduler shares the processor time among the threads that are ready to execute. In Java the `start` procedure is used to set a new thread running. A thread object must be declared as an extending class `Thread`, and must provide a procedure `run` that is executed when the thread is started.

● Strange, nondeterministic things can happen if two or more threads have uncontrolled access to some shared variables. There is therefore a need for mutual exclusion, the situation where only one thread is permitted access at any one time. Mutual exclusion can be enforced by creating an object to look after the resource. This object accepts requests from client threads as procedure calls that are labeled `synchronized`. Once a `synchronized` procedure is being used, no other thread can use it or any other `synchronized` procedure within the object. This ensures the correct behavior of the threads.

● A second major scenario in concurrent programming is where several threads collaborate in some goal, passing information from one to another, like an assembly line. Each pair of threads is called a producer–consumer pair. An intermediary object between each pair facilitates the communication, by providing the necessary storage for messages. The intermediary object provides `synchronized` procedures for entering information and for removing items. The client threads have to wait when necessary. In Java the library procedure `wait` causes a thread to wait until some other thread executes an invocation of procedure `notify`.

● If care is not exercised during design, deadlock can arise in concurrent programs. It can occur if two threads each acquire a resource which the other then requests.

EXERCISES

15.1 Two clocks. Write a program to show two clocks. One is an analog clock, with an hour hand, minute hand, and second hand. Draw the clock simply as a circle with simple lines for the hands. The other clock is a digital clock, showing hours, minutes, and seconds as digits. Create a thread for each of the clocks. Each clock should sleep for 100 milliseconds, which is 1/10 second. The program can get the time by calling library procedure currentTimeMillis, which returns the current time in milliseconds as a long. (A millisecond is one thousandth of a second.) The time is measured from 1 January 1970 (the so-called epoch). It is called UTC (Coordinated Universal Time) and is essentially the same as Greenwich Mean Time (GMT).

15.2 A stopwatch. Write a program that displays two buttons, labeled start and stop. When start is pressed, the program records the time. When stop is pressed, it displays the time that has elapsed since the start button was pressed. Display the time in seconds and tenths of a second. Use the library procedure currentTimeMillis (see Exercise 15.1) to get the time.

15.3 A reaction timer. A program displays two buttons, labeled start again and Now. When you press start again, the program waits for a random time in the range 5 to 20 seconds. When a message Press Now is displayed, you press Now as quickly as you can. The program displays how long you took, in seconds and tenths of a second. A reaction time of 1/10 second is about as fast as you can ever hope to be. Use the library procedure currentTimeMillis (see Exercise 15.1) to get the time.

15.4 The Breakout game. Breakout is a game shown in Figure 15.9. You can move the paddle left and right under the control of the mouse. A ball bounces off the paddle

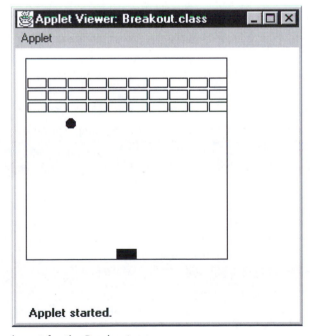

Figure 15.9 Screen layout for the Breakout game

towards a wall of bricks. When the ball hits a brick it bounces off the brick, but the brick is destroyed. When the ball breaks a hole in the wall, it can escape, or break out. In this case, you win. If you miss the ball with the paddle, it is lost. You get five balls. If you lose them all before breaking out, you lose.

A button labeled New Game allows you to start again.

One thread is the ball. Another thread is the paddle. The third thread is the user interface. Write a procedure mouseMove within the user interface object to handle the events that arise from moving the mouse, like this

```
public boolean mouseMove( Event event, int x, int y) {
    paddlePosition = x;
}
```

15.5 The car park. A car park has two entrances and two exits, each controlled by barriers. A transducer at the entrance detects the presence of a vehicle and tells the computer. If there is space in the car park it raises the barrier, issues a numbered ticket, and records the time of arrival. On exit an attendant keys in the ticket number, notifying the computer that the car is leaving. The computer calculates the cost, displays it, and raises the barrier. The computer also controls an illuminated sign on the entrance which displays FULL or SPACES.

Write a program that simulates the behavior of a car park. Create four buttons that correspond to cars entering and leaving at the two entrances and two exits. Start by assuming that the car park can accommodate any number of cars. Then alter it so that the car park can only deal with 10 cars.

15.6 The clock. Complete the coding of the clock program described in the text.

15.7 The café. Suppose that the café described in the text has not one but two cooks. How do the threads need to be modified in order to cope? (Do not write any new code. Just work out what changes are necessary and, of course, make maximum re-use of existing classes.)

15.8 Compare and contrast the features for multithreading provided in Java and Ada.

15.9 Investigate and review the facilities for multithreading provided in Unix.

ANSWERS TO SELF TEST QUESTIONS

15.1 Extend the class that represents the ball and create an additional constructor procedure so that the position and size of the rectangle can be specified as parameters. Here is the new additional class:

```
class FlexiBall extends Ball {
    public FlexiBall(Graphics g,
        int leftX, int rightX, int topY, int bottomY) {
        this.g = g;
```

```
            this.leftX = leftX;
            this.rightX = rightX;
            this.topY = topY;
            this.bottomY = bottomY;
        }
    }
```

Then rewrite the user interface class to create the two bouncing balls as follows:

```
import java.awt.*;

import java.applet.Applet;

public class TwoBouncers extends Applet {

    public void init() {

        Graphics g = getGraphics();

        Ball ball1 = new Ball(g);
        ball1.start();

        FlexiBall ball2 = new FlexiBall(g, 200, 300, 0, 100);
        ball2.start();

    }

}
```

15.2
```
import java.awt.*;

import java.applet.Applet;

public class Waiting extends Applet {

    public void init() {
        Graphics g = getGraphics();
        Clock clock = new Clock(g);
        clock.start();

        clock.join();
        g.drawString("All over", 40, 20);

    }

}

public class Clock extends Thread {

public void run() {

    for (int timeElasped = 0; timeElapsed < 120;
                        timeElapsed++) {

    try {

        Thread.sleep(1000);

    }

    catch (InterruptedException e) {

        System.err.println("sleep exception");

    }
```

```
        g.drawString(toString(timeElapsed), 20, 20);
      }
    }
  }
```

15.3 We will add an additional button called `status` to the user interface, which can be pressed to give a status report on the ball thread. When this button is clicked, the following code within procedure `actionPerformed` displays the appropriate message:

```
if (event.target == status) {
    Graphics g = getGraphics();
    if (ball.isAlive())
        g.drawString("The ball is alive", 300, 20);
    else
        g.drawString("The ball is dead", 300, 20);
}
```

15.4
```
public synchronized void decrement() {
    n = n - 1;
}

public synchronized int getValue() {
    return n;
}

public synchronized void display() {
    g.drawString(n + ", ", x*20, 30);
    x++;
}
```

FURTHER READING

This is a very good survey of concurrent programming and the different types of mechanisms for synchronization: M. Ben-Ari, *Principles of Concurrent and Distributed Programming*, Prentice Hall, 1990.

The concurrency patterns discussed in this chapter, along with others, are cataloged in: Mark Grand, *Patterns in Java*, vol. 1, John Wiley, 1998.

16

Functional programming

This chapter:

- identifies what is distinct about functional programming
- uses the language Haskell to illustrate the principles of functional programming
- briefly reviews other functional languages, including LISP
- explains the role of functional programming within software engineering.

16.1 ● Introduction

In the early days of computing, programming a computer consisted of constructing a sequence of very low-level instructions which directly manipulated the contents of physical memory addresses. Such programs were expressed in machine code – an instruction code built on the architecture of the machine. Since then, although programming languages have become progressively "higher" level, this cell-based view of the machine has colored not only the structure of new programming languages, but also the way in which we think about the nature of computation. Languages such as C++ and Java certainly act as a higher-level interface between programmer and machine, but the essentials of programming remain the same: to solve a problem, memory locations are assigned values, and the program systematically overwrites them with new values in order to achieve a configuration which represents a solution.

A different view of programming languages, and a different perspective on the nature of the programming task, has since evolved. Instead of asking the question "Given this machine architecture, what kind of language would run efficiently on it?", perhaps we should try to define programming languages that support the way in which humans prefer to think about problem solving, rather than letting the language structure be influenced by the architecture of the underlying machine. The question now is "This is the programming language I would like to use; what architecture would most efficiently support it?"

In this chapter, we shall consider a programming approach based on a mathematical formalism called the *lambda calculus*. A sound theoretical foundation for any programming style can be a great advantage, since the underlying theoretical results can be used to make assertions about programs in the language which rests upon it. In fact, conventional (procedural) languages have no such formal basis, which is one reason why proving the correctness of programs in such languages is so difficult.

The concept of function definition is familiar to most programmers. However, the definition and use of functions in functional languages is rather different from their purpose in conventional languages. Functional programming languages are usually described as *declarative* (as are logic programming languages – see Chapter 17). To illustrate the distinction between this and the traditional model, we shall begin by considering the meaning of the term *procedural* or *imperative*: the programming style exemplified by languages such as Pascal, Java, Ada, and many others.

16.2 ● Procedural languages

Procedural languages are *statement-oriented*: the programmer's task is to order statements so that when executed their combined effects achieve the desired result. In particular, procedural programming relies on the use of *variables*. Memory is composed of a large number of cells, some of which are given symbolic names by the programmer so that values can be placed in them and later retrieved. One might argue that from a human point of view this is unnatural: remembering facts (or values) does not, at least consciously, involve any indirect referencing of this kind. Humans think with *values*, not memory addresses where values are stored. Nevertheless, the idea of a variable, and its use as a higher-level reference to a physical memory address, and consequently to the value stored in that address, is probably the most important concept in procedural programming languages. This accounts for the fact that every procedural language has an assignment statement or its equivalent. This, together with the rather ambiguous use of a variable name to represent both a value and an address can lead to some unfortunate anomalies. For example, in the statement

```
a := a + 1
```

the use of a on the left refers to an address, while the one on the right refers to a value. One of the prerequisites of functional programming is that the use of an expression in one context means exactly the same as it does in another – and therefore has exactly the same value.

To summarize, the essence of procedural programming is the repeated execution of stored sequences of statements which assign values to, and retrieve values from, named memory cells, so as to achieve a result *by effect*. That is, although the purpose of a particular computation may be to produce a value, the conclusion of that computation is signalled by the value being left somewhere as a side-effect, rather than the value itself being handed back as a result.

This distinction may be easier to see if we consider some of the ways in which programming languages attempt to hide the low-level nature of the machine. The most obvious example is the arithmetic expression. For example, the expression 2+3 has a value which is not stored anywhere; the expression itself represents the value. Moreover, wherever the expression might appear in a program, we would expect it to have the same value. But consider what happens when we introduce variables into the expression. The value of the expression a+b depends on the values which have been assigned to a and b. That is, its value is a consequence of the previous history of the computation up to the place where the expression is used.

The point is, we can never assume that the value of an expression is the same wherever it occurs in a program because the values of variables in the expression may have changed since they were last used. The culprit for this is of course the assignment statement:

```
a := b + 1
```

for example computes the value of b+1 and, *as a side-effect*, assigns that value to a. We say that the expression 2+3 exhibits *referential transparency* because it has a consistent substitution property – its value is always the same. Of course, if we could assert that the values of a and b, once assigned, could never be changed, then a+b would exhibit the same property.

Why should referential transparency be a useful thing to achieve? There are two reasons: firstly, we would not need to consider the execution of a program in order to demonstrate its correctness (as is the case with procedural languages), since the result of evaluating an expression is independent of the computation which led to its use. We could therefore understand a program by considering only its static qualities. This is essentially what the term *declarative* means in the context of programming – a program can be read as a description of a solution to a problem rather than as a procedure for solving that problem. Secondly, since referential transparency ensures that expressions can be evaluated independently, irrespective of their context, there is (in theory) no reason why such expressions could not be evaluated in parallel. Potentially, this leads to a much more natural approach to the use of parallelism than that provided by parameter passing mechanisms used by concurrent languages built on, and constrained by, traditional computer architectures.

So expressions provide a way of hiding the cell-based nature of the machine by allowing the programmer to use values without storing them, except that the side-effects of assignment cause the benefits of referential transparency to be lost. Another way in which the behavior of variables can be constrained is by localizing their scope by declaring them within procedures. But here, too, the fact that procedures can use call-by-reference parameters, and also affect the values of global variables, effectively negates the benefits of an apparently high-level concept by enabling all memory locations to become addressable.

If all of the mechanisms described above serve to defeat the object of providing high-level constructs more suitable to human problem-solving needs, why do most languages incorporate them? The reason is simple, and brings us full circle: they are there because they achieve execution efficiency, and that efficiency relies on the characteristics of conventional computer architecture. Functional programming disregards this reliance, and seeks to view computation in a different way to that imposed upon it by implementational issues.

16.3 ● Characteristics of functional programming

In procedural languages, functions are defined procedurally, as a sequence of steps to be executed in order to compute a result. Moreover, a parameter to a function is a modifiable variable, as are other (global) variables known to the function and the calling program. By contrast, mathematical functions are defined by combining other existing functions using strict rules of composition, and a parameter simply represents some value which is fixed when the function is applied to its parameters, and never changes during the evaluation of the function body. The application simply results in another value. (A function application in the mathematical sense is analogous to the programming concept of a function call.) For this reason, mathematical functions can be combined hierarchically, like expressions; this tends not to be the case for programming language functions, due to the corrupting influence of side-effects.

In this section, we'll use the Haskell programming language for illustration. Haskell is named after Haskell Brooks Curry, whose work in mathematical logic contributed to the development of modern functional languages. A program (or *script*) in Haskell consists of a set of definitions of functions and other values. For example,

```
twice :: Int -> Int
twice x = 2*x
```

defines a function which, when applied to a numeric argument, returns a value equal to twice that argument. The first line declares the *type* of the function. It says that the new function `twice` can take as its argument any integer, and will return as its result another integer. `Int` is a built-in data type in Haskell. The second line associates the name of the function with the expression which will be evaluated when the function is invoked with a particular argument.

When the definition is loaded into the Haskell system, it can be tested like this:

```
Main> twice 2
4
```

`Main>` is the Haskell system prompt. Haskell outputs the value of the expression in the function definition, with the actual parameter `2` substituted for the formal parameter `x`.

A particular application of the function, the expression "`twice 2`" for example, *represents* a value, just as the expression "`2*2`" does. When a function is applied, the formal parameters are bound to the actual parameters for the duration of the application, and are not changed at any time during the evaluation. This is unlike the conventional representation of a parameter as a variable which is modifiable by statements which comprise the function body. (Such modifications may or may not be communicated back to the actual parameter; this depends on whether the parameter is defined to be call by value or call by reference.)

We can now define another function in terms of twice,

```
quadruple :: Int -> Int
quadruple x = twice (twice x)
```

such that quadruple 2 has value 8. The function nesting used here to construct quadruple effectively replaces what in procedural languages would be represented by a *sequence* of statements: apply twice to its argument (and perhaps store the result) and then apply twice to that result. If we relate this to the constructs required by structured programming, we still need an equivalent functional representation of selection – an if .. then .. else construct. Here is a complete program defining a function which computes the minimum of 3 numbers:

```
smallerOf :: Int -> Int -> Int
smallerOf x y = if x < y then x else y

minimumOf :: Int -> Int -> Int -> Int
minimumOf x y z = smallerOf (smallerOf x y) z
```

In the type declarations, the right-most Int is the type of the result, and the others are the types of the arguments. So smallerOf takes two integer arguments and returns one integer result. Notice that there is no implied ordering on these definitions: they are not definitions to be encountered in sequence, rather they are to be viewed as a collection which together define the required function.

In order to execute a functional program (or in other words, to evaluate an expression), a function application is rewritten according to the definitions of the program until it is reduced to a result. For example, the function application

```
minimumOf 3 2 5
```

would proceed as follows:

```
minimumOf 3 2 5      ⇒ smallerOf (smallerOf 3 2) 5
                     ⇒ smallerOf 2 5
                     ⇒ 2
```

For completeness, we also need a functional representation of the structured programming concept of repetition. Interestingly enough, we already have it, because we can define a function in terms of itself. For example, here is a definition of the factorial function (the operator == tests for equality):

```
factorial :: Int -> Int
factorial n = if n == 0 then 1 else n *  factorial (n-1)
```

A function definition which refers to itself is called *recursive*. An application of the factorial function when applied to an argument would proceed like this:

```
factorial 4      ⇒ 4 * factorial 3
                 ⇒ 4 * 3 * factorial 2
                 ⇒ 4 * 3 * 2 * factorial 1
                 ⇒ 4 * 3 * 2 * 1 * factorial 0
                 ⇒ 4 * 3 * 2 * 1 * 1
                 ⇒ 24
```

It can be shown that from a theoretical point of view, statement sequencing, selection, and recursion are the only control structures which are necessary in a programming language, which means that we now have a formalism which is in principle equal in power to a language which rests on the principles of structured programming.

A functional language naturally requires a formally defined set of data objects upon which computations can be performed. It is usual in such languages for this set to be limited in size, and for its members to have a primitive, regular structure. Thus, in addition to the atomic data objects used in the preceding examples (numeric values and the symbols standing for parameters), primitive functions are provided for constructing and accessing *lists* of data objects. A list is analogous to an array in procedural languages, with the essential difference that a list is a data structure whose elements can themselves be lists. For example,

```
[a,[b,c],d]
```

is a three-element list whose second element is the list `[b,c]`. Conventional arrays, trees, and graphs can all be represented using this simple and regular structure; it is typical of functional languages that their power arises from the provision of primitive facilities which can be combined in complex ways to achieve elegant and concise problem solutions.

Haskell provides a toolkit of functions and operators for manipulating lists. Here are some examples which should be self-explanatory.

```
Main> head [a,b,c]
a

Main> tail [a,b,c]
[b,c]

Main> concat [a,b,c] [d,e]
[a,b,c,d,e]

Main> reverse [a,b,c]
[c,b,a]
```

A particularly powerful feature of Haskell is the *list comprehension*. Here's an example:

```
Main> [2*x | x <- [3,4,5]]
[6,8,10]
```

This expression defines the elements of a list implicitly by a generating rule, rather than by explicitly enumerating the elements. It constructs the list consisting of all values of `2*x`, where the candidate values of `x` are taken from the list `[3,4,5]`.

`length` is a built-in Haskell function which returns the number of elements in a list:

```
Main> length [7,4,9]
3
```

How would `length` be defined if it wasn't built-in? Here's a possible recursive definition:

```
length :: [Int] -> Int
length l = if l == [] then 0 else 1 + length (tail l)
```

The declaration says that `length` takes a list of integers as argument and returns an integer as result.

SELF TEST QUESTION

16.1 Using this definition of `length`, show that the value of the expression `length([7,4,9])` is 3.

What if we wanted to find the length of a list of characters rather than integers? The definition above insists that *only* lists of integers are valid as argument. So if we were to try this definition with:

```
Main> length ['a','b','c']
```

a type mismatch error message would be generated. We could define a new, additional version of `length`:

```
length2 :: [Char] -> Int
length2 l = if l == [] then 0 else 1 + length2 (tail l)
```

and use `length2` whenever we need to find the length of a list of characters. But this would mean defining a whole family of length definitions, one for each specific type. Much better is to define a generic function which can take a list of anything as argument. Such a function is called *polymorphic*, and its type is declared like this:

```
length :: [any] -> Int
```

Here, `any` is a *type variable*, which stands for any arbitrary type. Any identifier beginning with a lower case letter can be used to name a type variable.

Haskell also supports *higher-order functions*, which provide a concise way of combining existing functions to create new ones. A higher-order function is a function which takes one or more function definitions as arguments and returns a new function definition as result. For example, given two functions `f` and `g`, the expression

```
f.g
```

represents a new function, which takes the same arguments as `g`, and computes its result by first applying `g` to its arguments and then applying `f` to the result. The ".'" is called the *forward composition* operator. For example, consider the definition

```
      twiceFact :: Int -> Int
      twiceFact = twice.factorial
  Main> twiceFact 3
  12
```

The result returned is twice the factorial of 3.

We could have used forward composition to construct `quadruple` like this:

```
  quadruple :: Int -> Int
  quadruple = twice.twice
```

We can think of `twice.twice` as *naming* a function (just as `quadruple` does), or as *representing* an unnamed function which computes the same result as `quadruple`. Whichever view we take, this means that, for example,

```
  Main> quadruple 2
  8
```

and

```
  Main> (twice.twice) 2
  8
```

SELF TEST QUESTION

16.2 If the function `f` is of type `b -> c`, and `g` is of type `a -> b`, what is the type of `f.g`?

This technique of defining a function without explicitly giving it a name is useful in the situation where a function is being used for no other purpose than as an argument to a higher-order function such as ".". There is then no necessity to give it a name, since the function is never referred to elsewhere.

Lambda expressions provide another way of representing unnamed functions. For example,

```
λx.2*x
```

is a lambda expression (as written in a branch of mathematics called the *lambda calculus*) defining a function which performs the same computation as `twice`. The period acts as a separator between the body of the lambda expression and its parameter. In Haskell, this lambda expression would be written like this:

```
\x -> 2*x
```

A lambda expression can be applied directly to an argument:

```
Main> (\x -> 2*x) 3
6
```

However, a lambda expression is more appropriate when used as an argument to a higher-order function in order to construct some other function:

```
squareTwice :: Int -> Int
squareTwice = (\x -> x*x).twice
```

defines a function which returns the square of twice its argument. So for example,

```
Main> squareTwice 3
36
```

Giving an explicit name to a function is actually only a matter of convenience rather than necessity.

This idea of functions as objects which can be passed around just as would any other data object is an important one, and can enable some very sophisticated programming techniques. Indeed, the definition of a function (such as that for `smallerOf` given above) is simply the binding of a name to a data object – the function definition. The subsequent application of the function is a request for a particular interpretation to be placed upon that data object. In a different context, the function definition might be treated as data to be manipulated or transformed in some way. This makes it possible to write program analyzers and generators – programs which can treat other programs as data, and output new, more powerful programs as result. It is this facility which has contributed to the adoption of LISP (which has a functional core) as one of the principal programming languages used by the artificial intelligence community.

Interestingly, any function of two or more arguments is actually a higher-order function. For example, consider the `smallerOf` function again:

```
smallerOf :: Int -> Int -> Int
smallerOf x y = if x < y then x else y
```

We would apply `smallerOf` like this:

```
Main> smallerOf 3 4
3
```

Haskell parses the application as

```
(smallerOf 3) 4
```

That is, apply `smallerOf` to the argument 3, thus returning a new function which is then applied to the argument 4. In effect, the expression "`smallerOf 3`" names the function that, given a single argument, compares it to the integer 3 and returns the smaller. This technique is known as *currying* – a function is applied to fewer than its defined number of arguments, and the result is another function. We could actually define an *uncurried* version of `smallerOf`:

```
smallerOf2 :: (Int,Int) -> Int
smallerOf2 (x,y) = if x < y then x else y
```

which we would have to use slightly differently:

```
Main> smallerOf2 (3,4)
3
```

The curried version is more flexible, in that it can be given just one argument in order to generate a new function. This is known as *partial application*.

SELF TEST QUESTION

16.3 Explain the reason for the difference in type of the two versions of `smallerOf`:

```
smallerOf :: Int -> Int -> Int
smallerOf2 :: (Int,Int) -> Int
```

It is important to emphasize one final feature of Haskell: *lazy evaluation*. Haskell will only evaluate an argument to a function if that argument is needed to compute a result. For example, consider this function:

```
test :: Bool -> Int -> Int -> Int
test x y z = if x then y else z
```

`Bool` is a built-in data type representing the values `True` and `False`. If `test` is applied like this:

```
Main> test True 3 (twice 4)
3
```

the expression `(twice 4)` is never evaluated because *it doesn't need to be*. This is particularly useful in a situation where evaluating the whole expression could lead to program errors. For example, suppose `test` is applied like this:

```
Main> test True 3 (div 6 0)
3
```

The result is the same, because `(div 6 0)`, which would produce a division by zero error, is never evaluated. However,

```
Main> test False 3 (div 6 0)
```

would produce the error.

Lazy evaluation is particularly useful in the manipulation of infinite data structures, because it is possible to generate and access only that portion of a data structure which is needed for a particular computation. This is all tied in to the idea of recursion; for example, a list is a naturally recursive structure – a list consists of a `head` and a `tail`, which is itself a list. This leads to a natural way of thinking about infinite lists (an infinite list has an immediately accessible first element attached to an infinite list, which has an immediately accessible first element attached to ...), which lazy evaluation exploits.

Haskell is characterized as a nonstrict (which means that arguments are passed unevaluated to function calls), purely functional programming language, providing polymorphic typing, lazy evaluation, and higher-order functions. In the next section we shall consider the approaches taken by some other languages in attempting to realize the benefits of functional programming.

16.4 ● Other functional languages

Haskell is an attempt to draw together the ideas and experience of a number of years' functional programming research and development into one unified language. A number of languages have contributed to this consolidation, and we discuss them briefly below.

Hope was developed by MacQueen, Burstall, and Sannella at the University of Edinburgh. Hope is a so-called *recursion equation* language – each function definition consists of a set of equations which constitute a case analysis of possible arguments and corresponding results. Hope is strongly-typed, which means that the type of all objects used in a program must be declared before use. However, the programmer can define polymorphic data types. Higher-order functions can also be defined. Pattern matching is central to the Hope philosophy, not only in its approach to list processing, but also in the way in which alternative recursion equations are chosen for matching against function invocations. Modularity can be achieved by constructing abstract data types – data structures and accessing operations packaged so that their implementation details are hidden from the user.

Standard ML is the result of a standardization and marriage of the languages Hope and ML (short for "Meta Language"). ML was developed by Gordon, Milner, and Wadsworth at Edinburgh University in the 1970s. Standard ML shares the features described for Hope above. It does not use lazy evaluation, and incorporates some procedural features for improving execution efficiency.

Miranda was designed by David Turner at the University of Kent in 1985. Miranda also uses pattern matching for case analysis, and provides polymorphic, user defined and abstract data types. Although strongly typed, there are no mandatory type declarations like those enforced in Hope. Miranda's aim is to provide a practical and useful functional language, supported by a reliable and robust programming environment. It has been used as a rapid prototyping tool, and as a vehicle for teaching functional programming.

Many programmers tend to think of *LISP* as the classic example of a functional language. However, this is only partly true. In its original form (developed by John McCarthy in the early 1960s) LISP was a pure functional language; since then many features have been incorporated which improve its execution efficiency (and its attractiveness as a sophisticated programming environment) at the expense of its theoretical basis. We shall take a brief look at that subset of LISP which characterizes it as a functional language.

The data objects used by pure LISP are called *atoms* and *s-expressions* (short for *symbolic expressions*). Atoms are essentially literals and *symbols* (such as 23 and smallerOf for example) and s-expressions are lists. LISP has a large toolkit of primitive functions to do arithmetic, create and manipulate lists, and perform various tests on data objects. Essentially, everything a programmer wishes to do is expressed as a function application. For example,

```
(* 2 3)
```

is an expression representing the application of the built-in multiplication function *, and has the value 6. The function application is itself an example of a list – LISP uses round rather than square parentheses to bracket lists, and uses spaces to separate list elements rather than commas. The context of the expression determines whether LISP is to interpret it as data or program. In fact, LISP uses the same storage scheme to internally represent both programs and data, and it views them as essentially the same thing. This accounts for the much maligned parenthesised syntax which LISP employs. LISP's view of functions as objects enables the programmer to construct higher-order functions – or, as mentioned earlier, to write programs which themselves construct other programs, or indeed modify themselves.

We use a *special form* called defun in order to define a new function:

```
(defun twice (x)
    (* 2 x))
```

This s-expression defines a new function called twice. Once this definition has been loaded into the LISP system, we can test it interactively like this (> is the LISP prompt):

```
> (twice 3)
6
```

Here's the smallerOf function in LISP:

```
(defun smallerOf (x y)
    (if (< x y)
        x
        y))
```

Incidentally, the indentation used here is a personal preference and has nothing to do with LISP syntax. LISP programs benefit from a clear layout just as do programs from any other language. LISP editors give the user a lot of help, often provide pretty-printers to automatically lay out code, and have an understanding of how brackets should match.

if takes three arguments; the first argument is an application of a predicate returning true or false. < is a built-in predicate which returns true if its first argument is less than its second, false otherwise. If the predicate application evaluates to true, the second argument (x) is returned as the value of the if expression. Otherwise, the third argument (y) is returned. So, for example:

```
> (smallerOf 3 4)
3
```

List processing is central to LISP, and many tools are provided for creating and accessing complex list structures. LISP also includes a collection of higher-order functions, such as `mapcar` which enables a function to be applied to every element of a list. For example,

```
(mapcar 'twice '(1 2 3 4))
```

has value (2 4 6 8). The single quote ' is used here to inhibit evaluation – without it, LISP would try to use the *value* of `twice` and the *value* of (1 2 3 4), rather than treating them as literals.

For completeness, here's the factorial function expressed in LISP:

```
(defun factorial (n)
    (if (= n 0)
        1
        (* n (factorial (- n 1)))))
```

Yes, there are a lot of parentheses. But before the reader falls into the common trap of condemning this syntax at face value, it's worth bearing in mind that LISP is not just another language, a variant of C++ or Java with brackets. Apart from taking a fundamentally different view of computation than that taken by conventional languages (and allowing for the program/data equivalence described earlier), LISP provides a theoretical basis for many profound computer science ideas. See Allen (1982) for an interesting and entertaining discussion on this theme.

LISP has also taken on board some nonfunctional features, in particular the special forms `setf` and `prog`. `setf` is the functional equivalent of an assignment statement, and therefore introduces the concept of variables. `prog` allows a list of s-expressions to be executed in sequence; this in effect allows function applications to be considered as statements. Additionally, explicit control structures have been incorporated within `prog` to handle iteration. Destructive list operations are also provided – that is, functions which change the internal structure of lists; this is against the spirit of a programming style in which nothing ever changes its value. There are many, many more features which have been added to LISP over the years, some faithful to the functional style, others not. The new commercial viability of artificial intelligence applications (such as expert systems and natural language processing) has caused a trend towards symbolic processing, and LISP is being used more and more widely as an implementation language. In addition, LISP has the advantage that it can be extended to accommodate other programming styles – for example, *CLOS* provides extensions for object-oriented programming (see Chapter 14). The power, elegance, and essential simplicity of the language's structure have led to the development of LISP systems which are among the most sophisticated interactive programming environments yet built.

16.5 ● The role of functional programming

What does functional programming have to offer the software engineer? What program design methods have resulted from users' experience of functional languages? LISP programmers tend to build programs "bottom-up" by essentially extending LISP until solving the given problem becomes a trivial task, or by first constructing those functions which will be the entry-points to the overall package which will form the solution – a conventional "top-down" design. LISP actually supports many alternative design methods; indeed, many programs written in LISP are so-called "throw-away" programs – written to support some theoretical proposal, where the overall structure of the program just isn't known in advance. Consequently, an *ad hoc*, try it and see approach is the only one possible. LISP specialists have coined the term "structured growth" to encompass this particular class of design methods.

In principle, the clean mathematical properties of *pure* functional languages (such as Haskell) support a program development methodology which is much more formally based and verifiable than conventional techniques used for procedural languages. There are difficulties in trying to meet the goals of clarity and efficiency simultaneously. The idea of program transformation (pioneered by Burstall and Darlington in 1977) seeks to separate these two concerns and approach them as independent tasks. The programmer first designs and writes a program with the sole aim of making it clear and understandable without any regard for its efficiency. There then follows a stage in which the program is successively transformed into more and more efficient versions of the original, without destroying its meaning. Ideally the transformations should be capable of mechanization, and therefore must conform to rigorous and verifiable manipulative procedures. Because of the side-effects of assignment, such a set of procedures is almost impossible to achieve in a procedural language. However the referential transparency properties of functional languages allow easily defined transformations to be applied which can be shown to be correctness preserving.

The fact that functional programs can be understood as static entities rather than by resorting to taking snapshots of their execution means that programs can be read as descriptions of their own purpose. Thus the program constructed as the first phase of program transformation can actually be thought of as a specification: it effectively provides a clear and precise description of the problem. The difference between this and a conventional specification is that this one can be executed, however inefficiently. Its correctness can therefore be demonstrated before any transformations take place. The attractiveness of this approach stems from the fact that specification and program are expressed in the same notation, thus showing a direct dependence of one upon the other, and that the correctness of the specification ensures the correctness of the resulting program. This seems much more natural, and less prone to error, than the specify–program–verify approach conventionally used for software development.

Much of the current interest in functional programming is a consequence of the Turing Award lecture given by John Backus (1978) in which he suggested that the "software crisis" can only be overcome by a revolutionary new approach to programming and language design. To this end, he developed a family of languages (known as *FP*) demonstrating a range of functional forms (i.e. strategies and tools for combining existing functions to create new ones). FP is to some extent a test-bed for features appropriate to the functional style.

Perhaps the most important benefits offered by functional languages are modularity and abstraction. Modularity has long been accepted as a goal of good software design (see Chapter 6), and the use of the function as the basic building block for programs imposes a discipline which contributes to achieving that goal. The potential for modularization is enhanced by lazy evaluation, because function applications can be suspended until a new value is needed rather than completing a function call on its first use. Moreover, viewing functions as objects enables problem solutions to be constructed by combining solutions to subproblems. That is, a pattern for a general-purpose solution to a class of problems can be abstracted from a solution to a specific case, and expressed in terms of the combining operations defined by one or more functional forms.

We have seen that one of the chief characteristics of functional programming is the lack of assignment (and therefore of side-effects). However, there may be problems for which the most efficient solution requires the updating of a shared data structure. While this could be accommodated by allowing transformations (from an initial "pure" functional program) which introduced assignments, this is against the spirit of the functional style, and the disadvantages might outweigh the benefits. Similarly, the absence of side-effects may be problematic in a situation which required the program to affect the outside world (such as in real-time applications).

Experimental machines exist which demonstrate the feasibility of executing functional programs with an efficiency comparable to that of procedural programs on conventional machines. Indeed, there are arguments to support Backus's view that the next revolution in programming will have its roots in today's functional languages.

16.6 ● Summary

- Functional languages are more oriented towards the needs of the human user rather than being constrained by machine efficiency considerations.
- Functional programming has a sound mathematical basis which lends support to formal reasoning about programs (such as proving correctness).
- Procedural programs are statement-oriented, and compute by effect; side-effects cause the benefits of referential transparency to be lost.
- Programs in a functional language consist of sets of equations defining new functions in terms of simpler ones.
- A functional language consists of a set of data objects, primitive functions, and functional forms.
- Haskell, Hope, Miranda, and the core of ML are pure functional languages.
- LISP is based on a functional notation; efficiency considerations have forced the inclusion of some nonfunctional features.
- Program transformation provides a natural approach to software development; specifications and programs can be expressed in the same functional notation.
- Functional programming could be the basis for a new revolution in language design.

EXERCISES

16.1 Do you think there are benefits to be gained from attempting to mimic the functional style of programming in a language such as Java? Can you see connections between the object-oriented programming model (Chapter 14) and the functional programming model?

16.2 Haskell has a built-in `sum` function which sums the numbers in a list:

```
Main> sum [2,3,4]
9
```

If `sum` didn't exist, how would you define it in Haskell?

16.3 In Haskell, `[1..5]` means the same as `[1,2,3,4,5]`. Define a Haskell function that, given an integer `n`, sums the numbers from 1 to `n` inclusive.

16.4 `succ` is a built-in Haskell function that returns the successor of a number:

```
Main> succ 3
4
```

Suppose the higher-order function `rep` is defined like this:

```
rep :: (a -> a) -> (a -> a)
rep f = (f.f)
```

So `rep` takes a function as argument and returns a function of the same type as result. How would Haskell respond to the following?

```
Main> (rep succ) 3
```

16.5 A higher-order function takes another function as argument, or returns a function as result, or both. What other higher-order functions would be useful to complement the forward composition operator "`.`"? For example, the LISP `mapcar` function might suggest a family of higher-order functions that manipulate lists. (Try to find out about FP to gain an appreciation of the many possibilities which exist for new functional forms.)

16.6 Give LISP definitions of `minimumof` and `sum` (see Question 16.2).

16.7 Chapter 4 pointed out that a Z specification can be *animated* by rewriting it in a suitable executable language (thereby producing a rapid prototype), and using this executable version to explore the specification's behavior. Why would Haskell be a good specification animation language?

16.8 Functional programs are an order of magnitude shorter than procedural programs. Does "concise" mean "better"?

ANSWERS TO SELF TEST QUESTIONS

16.1 `length([7,4,9])`   ⇒ `1 + length([4,9])`
            ⇒ `1 + 1 + length([9])`
            ⇒ `1 + 1 + 1 + length([])`
            ⇒ `1 + 1 + 1 + 0`
            ⇒ `3`

16.2 `a -> c`

16.3 `smallerOf` takes an integer as argument and returns as result a function which takes an integer as argument and returns an integer as result. `smallerOf2` takes a pair of integers as argument and returns an integer as result.

FURTHER READING

The Turing Award lecture by John Backus which prompted much of the current interest in functional programming has been published as: J. Backus, Can Programming be Liberated from the Von Neumann Style?, *Communications of the ACM*, 21 (8), (1978), pp. 613–41.

A good introductory text on functional programming, which also includes an introduction to standard ML is: G. Michaelson, *An Introduction to Functional Programming through the Lambda Calculus*, Addison-Wesley, 1988.

A more general discussion of functional languages and related topics, together with an introduction to Hope, is contained in: S. Eisenbach, (ed.), *Functional Programming: Languages, Tools and Architectures*, Ellis Horwood, 1987.

A good introduction to Haskell is: R. Bird, *Introduction to Functional Programming using Haskell*, Prentice Hall, 1998.

Miranda is comprehensively covered in: S. Thompson, *Miranda: The Craft of Functional Programming*, Addison-Wesley, 1995.

For an entertaining and thought-provoking article on the philosophy of LISP, see: J. Allen, Computing, LISP and You, *Microcomputing* (February 1982), pp. 28–42.

An excellent textbook which serves both as an introduction to LISP and as a study of advanced programming techniques and applications is: P. Winston and B. Horn, *LISP*, Addison-Wesley, 3rd edition, 1989.

The CLOS extensions to LISP are described in: S. E. Keene, *Object-Oriented Programming in Common LISP*, Addison-Wesley, 1989.

This paper has a self-explanatory title: J. Hughes, Why Functional Programming Matters, *Computer Journal*, 32 (2), (1989), pp. 98–107.

17

Logic programming

This chapter:

- identifies what is distinct about logic programming
- uses the language Prolog to illustrate the principles of logic programming.

17.1 ● Introduction

Programming languages such as C++ and Java are conventional in the sense that they all impose an algorithmic approach on program construction. The programmer is forced to present to the machine a precise, unambiguous sequence of instructions which, if the underlying algorithm is correct, will result in a solution. In other words, a program is a description of *how* to solve a problem, not *what* that problem is. Nevertheless, a problem that a human being is trying to solve is usually posed as a relationship between input and output: "I know these facts, and I want to know some other facts as a consequence" – "I have an integer and I want to know the factorial of it." A problem description presented as a program to solve that problem wouldn't be very helpful – consider for example the task of learning how to choose an appropriate move in a chess game by minutely inspecting a listing of a chess playing program!

Programming languages which use this algorithmic approach are called *procedural*, or *imperative* – a program is an imperative sequence of instructions which is to be obeyed in a prescribed order. (We discussed the nature of procedural languages in more detail in Chapters 10 and 13.) However, it is possible even in these conventional languages to see an ambiguity in how some sequences are to be obeyed. For example, consider the following iterative definition of the factorial function:

```
function factorial(N)
fact = 1
while N > 0 do
    fact = fact * N
    N = N - 1
endwhile
factorial = fact
endfunction
```

This definition is unambiguous in the sense described. There is only one way it could possibly be executed.

Here is a recursive definition of a function performing exactly the same computation:

```
function factorial(N)
if N = 0 then factorial = 1
else factorial = N * factorial(N-1)
endif
endfunction
```

We can define (at least) two interpretations as to how this should be executed for a particular call. Those familiar with the way in which recursion is conventionally handled would impose the following sequence:

To find `factorial(4)`:

```
factorial(4) is 4*factorial(3)
        which is 4*3*factorial(2)
        which is 4*3*2*factorial(1)
        which is 4*3*2*1*factorial(0)
        which is 4*3*2*1*1 = 24.
```

This constitutes a *top-down* execution: working from the problem posed to a solution expressed in terms of primitives whose solutions are known. However, the same function definition could be executed in a bottom-up manner:

To find `factorial(4)`:

```
            factorial(0) is 1.
Hence   factorial(1) is 1*factorial(0) = 1,
        factorial(2) is 2*factorial(1) = 2,
        factorial(3) is 3*factorial(2) = 6,
        factorial(4) is 4*factorial(3) = 24.
```

Notice that this particular execution sequence has been *imposed* on the function definition – it is not actually explicit in the program text. Programming languages usually execute recursive definitions top-down, although in fact this isn't necessarily the most efficient execution mechanism – bottom-up, or even a 'middle-out' approach might be better in particular cases. For example, here is a recursive definition of a function to compute the Nth Fibonacci number:

```
function fibonacci(N)
if N = 1 or N = 2 then fibonacci = 1
else fibonacci = fibonacci(N-2) + fibonacci(N-1)
endif
endfunction
```

Try calculating `fibonacci(5)` by executing the function in both directions. You should find that a bottom-up execution is much more efficient. Nevertheless, if presented with this definition, Java for example would treat it as it treats all recursive definitions, and execute it top-down.

The idea behind logic programming is to make this division between program text and execution mechanism more explicit. The above recursive definition of factorial can be thought of as the *logic* of the problem, and each of the various ways of executing the function as the *control* to be imposed upon that logic. In effect, the logic component is a description (or specification) of the problem to be solved – what is to be done rather than how to do it. A logic program consists *only* of a problem description – a relationship between known and required facts. The control is provided by the language interpreter, not explicitly by the programmer. A conventional program has logic and control inextricably entwined; by separating the two the purpose of the program becomes more transparent, since in a sense the program is its own description. Program verification is also easier because only the logic has to be shown to be correct – the control imposed on the logic affects only the efficiency of its execution, not its correctness.

Since Prolog is the best-known and most widely available programming language embodying these ideas, we shall use it for illustration. In the next section we shall consider how Prolog programs are constructed and executed.

17.2 ● Facts and rules

Prolog is a simple but powerful programming language based on symbolic logic, developed by Roussel at the University of Marseille in 1975. Since then, many implementations have been produced which differ only in details of syntax: the underlying concepts and conversational approach to programming are identical. We'll use a simplified syntax, intended to illustrate the flavor of the language, rather than worrying about the precise details of any particular implementation.

Let's return to the recursive definition of factorial and look at it more closely. As is usual with recursive definitions, it is made up of two parts: a primitive or trivial case (the "stopper" on the recursion), and a recursive call of the defined function, whose purpose is to reduce the problem to some other problem which is easier to solve (or closer to the trivial case). The trivial case asserts a *fact*:

"The factorial of 0 is 1."

The recursive call represents a *rule* for finding factorials from known facts:

"In order to find factorial(N), first find factorial(N–1) and then multiply the result by N."

This is the conventional, *procedural* view of the recursive call. It states how to go about calculating factorial(*N*).

However, there is another interpretation – as a definition rather than a procedure:

"Factorial(N) is F
   if factorial(N–1) is G
   and F *is* N*G"*
where F *and* G *are arbitrary variables.*

This is the so-called *declarative* interpretation – it states what factorial means without explicitly saying how to go about calculating it. Extracting this declarative interpretation from the function definition is admittedly rather contrived; however, this is exactly how the function would be expressed in Prolog:

```
factorial(0,1).
factorial(N,F)  :-  M is N-1,
                    factorial(M,G),
                    F is N*G.
```

The above is a definition of a procedure, made up of two clauses, each terminated by a period. These clauses serve to define a *relation* (or *predicate*) called `factorial`.

Prolog uses the convention that any name beginning with a lower-case letter is a *constant*, which may be user-defined (as in "factorial") or system defined (as in "is"). Any name which begins with an upper-case letter (such as N, F, M, and G) is a *variable*. The first clause represents a fact, asserting that the factorial of 0 is 1. The second is a rule, having two possible interpretations:

(a)

   the factorial of *N* is *F*

   if *M* is *N*–1

   and the factorial of *M* is *G*

   and *F* is *N*G*

   (the declarative reading)

or

(b)

   in order to show that the factorial of *N* is *F*,

   first find an *M* such that *M* is *N*–1,

   then find a *G* such that the factorial of *M* is *G*,

   and then show that *F* is *N*G*

   (the procedural reading).

Note the general form of rules and their corresponding procedural interpretation: the left-hand side (or *head*) of the clause constitutes a *goal*. The sequence of terms in the right-hand side (or *body*) is a sequence of subgoals which must be satisfied in order to satisfy the head. A fact is simply a special case of this – there is no body, and therefore no subgoals to be satisfied in order to prove it.

17.3 ● Execution mechanisms

How are Prolog programs executed? A Prolog program like the one above is in effect a database of facts and rules. Executing a procedure call involves searching the database in some order to deduce new facts from facts which are already known, or to confirm the truth of some assertion. To illustrate this, let's leave our factorial procedure for the moment and construct a Prolog program which represents the relationships between employees in a small, imaginary company.

We can represent the hierarchy of responsibilities pictorially as a tree, Figure 17.1.

A collection of facts using a relation `manages` will serve to define the tree:

```
manages(smith, jones).
manages(smith, brown).
manages(jones, green).
manages(jones, evans).
etc.
```

If we wished to specify the gender of each employee we could add a few more facts using a relation `male`:

```
male(jones).
male(evans).
male(williams).
etc.
```

Now we can define some rules which describe other relationships which exist between employees. Two people who are managed by the same person are colleagues:

```
colleagues(X,Y) :- manages(Z,X),
                   manages(Z,Y).
```

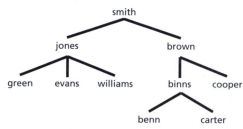

Figure 17.1 Hierarchy of responsibilities

Remember that **x**, **y**, and **z** are variables, and can therefore stand for any constant (or in other words any employee). Hence the above rule states that **x** and **y** are colleagues if there is some other person **z** who manages both **x** and **y**.

A person is a superior of someone else if they manage that person, or they are a superior of someone who manages that person:

```
superior(X,Y)  :- manages(X,Y).
superior(X,Y)  :- manages(Z,Y),
                   superior(X,Z).
```

Notice that superior is a recursively defined procedure, and the two alternative definitions of superiority are written as separate clauses.

Though what we have here is a program, it is not a program in the traditional sense; rather than constructing an algorithm, we have merely been expressing various aspects of what it means to be an employee as a database of facts and rules. As such, the database can be queried. Prolog is an interactive language – each of the clauses can be typed in one by one exactly as they appear above. If we were now to type

```
?-manages(jones,williams).
```

Prolog would interpret it as the question 'Is it true that **jones** manages **williams**?' To try to satisfy the query, Prolog searches the database sequentially from the top in an attempt to find a clause which matches this goal. In this case Prolog replies

```
yes
```

since a matching clause does indeed exist. The reply would be

```
no
```

if there was no matching clause.

Here are some other queries and their corresponding output:

English : Who manages Binns?
Prolog : `?-manages(X,binns).`
Output : `X=brown`

English : Who is managed by Binns?
Prolog : `?-manages(binns,X)`
Output : `X=benn`

binns actually manages two people – Prolog tells us only the name of the first it finds in its search. We can prompt Prolog to continue the search by typing a ';' in response to its last output. We should then receive the output

```
X=carter
```

The examples above show the pattern-matching nature of the search. The pattern

```
manages(X,binns)
```

can be matched with an existing clause by *instantiating* the variable **x** to **brown**. (The process of matching a goal with a clause by instantiating variables to particular values is known as *unification*. This is an important concept in logic programming, since it is the only way in which bindings of variables to values can take place – there is no concept of assignment in the traditional sense.)

The pattern to be matched can be more general:

English : Tell me a manager/managed pair.
Prolog : `?-manages(X,Y).`
Output : `X=smith`
         `Y=jones.`

Once again this is the first match which was found.

English : Are Jones and Brown colleagues?
Prolog : `?-colleagues(jones,brown).`
Output : `yes.`

Let's watch how Prolog satisfies this query.
The initial goal is

```
colleagues(jones,brown).
```

Using the colleagues rule, Prolog sets up two subsidiary goals to be satisfied in sequence:

```
manages(Z,jones),manages(Z,brown).
```

That is find someone who manages `jones`, then see if that same person manages `brown`. The search through the `manages` clauses instantiates `z` to `smith`, so Prolog continues to search from the point where this match occurred to see if `smith` manages `brown`. This succeeds and the reply `yes` is output.

Strictly speaking, `williams` and `binns` might be considered to be colleagues since they are at the same level in the hierarchy. As an exercise, try modifying the colleagues relation to accommodate this.

By now the reader may be becoming a little suspicious: if the programmer has to be aware of goals, subgoals, and the order of evaluation, isn't this going against the spirit of declarative programming? Such suspicions are well founded: we'll address this apparent anomaly again a little later in the chapter.

We can pose queries which are a *conjunction* of goals to be satisfied in sequence:

English : Who is a colleague of Carter's manager?
Prolog : `?-manages(X,carter),colleagues(X,Y).`
Output : `X=binns`
         `Y=cooper.`

`x` is first instantiated to `binns` by a simple pattern match with the clause

```
manages(binns,carter).
```

Prolog then proceeds to attempt to satisfy

```
colleagues(binns,Y)
```

by setting up the subsidiary goals

```
manages(Z,binns),manages(Z,Y).
```

The first of these goals is satisfied by instantiating z to brown. The value of z is passed on to the second goal, which becomes

```
manages(brown,Y).
```

This succeeds by instantiating Y to cooper.

Note that since there are two variables in the query, Prolog gives two results, despite the fact that we're only really interested in one of them. These values are output by the interactive read-evaluate-display strategy which is built in to the Prolog interpreter. It is of course possible to write Prolog programs which converse with a user much more naturally, but such details are outside the scope of this chapter.

Suppose we now wish to find a male employee who is managed by jones. The following query should suffice:

```
?-manages(jones,X),male(X).
```

The search here is rather different. The first goal matches

```
manages(jones,green)
```

which instantiates x to green. This value is passed on to the next goal, so Prolog now attempts to satisfy

```
male(green).
```

This goal fails. Prolog therefore backtracks to the previous goal and attempts to resatisfy it. This results in a match with

```
manages(jones,evans)
```

which instantiates x to evans. Once again, this value is passed on to the next goal, so Prolog now attempts to satisfy

```
male(evans).
```

This succeeds, resulting in the output

```
X=evans.
```

This is the essence of Prolog's execution mechanism: it is in effect a backtracking theorem prover. Prolog will always search every possible path, backtracking where necessary, in its attempt to satisfy a conjunction of goals. Only when there is no way of satisfying all of the goals will its search result in failure.

Prolog attempts to satisfy the goals in a conjunction from left to right. Changing the order can often have a dramatic effect on the efficiency of execution. For example, if the previous query were posed as

```
?-male(X),manages(jones,X)
```

Prolog would attempt to satisfy it by testing each male to see if he is managed by `jones`, whereas previously each person managed by `jones` was tested for maleness. In a company where the number of males far exceeds the number of people managed by `jones`, the latter ordering would be very inefficient in its execution. Earlier we saw a query for finding a colleague of `carter`'s manager. If this query has its ordering reversed thus:

```
?-colleagues(X,Y),manages(X,carter)
```

the search is much more involved. Try it and see.

Finally, let's look at a query using the `superior` relation:

> English : Is Brown a superior of Benn?
> Prolog : `?-superior(brown,benn).`
> Output : `yes.`

Prolog attempts a pattern match using the first of the two clauses which make up the `superior` procedure. Thus we have

```
superior(brown,benn) :- manages(brown,benn).
```

The subgoal in the body of this clause fails, so Prolog tries to resatisfy the head using the second `superior` clause:

```
superior(brown,benn) :- manages(Z,benn),
                        superior(brown,Z).
```

The subgoal

```
manages(Z,benn)
```

succeeds by instantiating `Z` to `binns`. This value is passed on to the second subgoal in the body:

```
superior(brown,binns).
```

Prolog now attempts to satisfy this goal using the first superior clause:

```
superior(brown,binns) :- manages(brown,binns).
```

This succeeds by a simple pattern match, and the original goal specified in the query is therefore achieved.

Note that the superior relation is multipurpose. For example, it can be used to find someone who is a superior of `binns`:

```
?-superior(X,binns).
```

Or to find someone `binns` is superior to:

```
?-superior(binns,X).
```

Or indeed to find anyone who is superior to anyone else:

```
?-superior(X,Y).
```

This latter query can be used to generate all possible instantiations of x and y (for which the superior relation holds) by replying with a ; after each pair of values is displayed. This provides useful support for program testing, since it enables a relation to be used to effectively generate its own test data. This isn't always the case, however, because not all relations are multipurpose. We'll see why this is so a little later.

As in the colleagues relation, there is something missing in our definition of superiority, as jones, for example, might be considered to be a superior of binns. The superior relation as it stands doesn't include this possibility. As an exercise, modify the clauses of superior so that it does include it.

Now let's return to the factorial procedure:

```
factorial(0,1).
factorial(N,F) :- M is N-1,
                  factorial(M,G),
                  F is N*G.
```

One thing to notice is that its recursive structure is very similar to that of superior. Its execution is very similar too. The simplest query we could pose would be:

English : Is 1 the factorial of 0?
Prolog : ?-factorial(0,1).
Output : yes.

More usefully, we might want to find the factorial of a particular integer:

English : What is the factorial of 3?
Prolog : ?-factorial(3,X).
Output : x=6.

Let's trace the execution of this query. The goal

```
factorial(3,X)
```

fails to match the first of the factorial clauses, so Prolog tries the second. This causes three subgoals to be invoked:

```
factorial(3,X) :- M is 2,
                  factorial(M,G),
                  X is 3*G.
```

The first of these subgoals is immediately satisfied ("is" is a built-in relation which succeeds by making its arguments equal; thus M is instantiated to 2). Passing this value of M on reduces the problem to finding an instantiation of x which satisfies

```
factorial(3,X) :- factorial(2,G),
                  X is 3*G.
```

Prolog therefore attempts to satisfy the subgoal

```
factorial(2,G),
```

again using the second factorial clause:

```
factorial(2,G)  :-  factorial(1,G'),
                    G is 2*G'.
```

(G' represents a new activation record for the variable G at one level deeper in the recursion). To solve this subgoal, Prolog must similarly satisfy

```
factorial(1,G')  :-  factorial(0,G"),
                     G' is 1*G".
```

The subgoal

```
factorial(0,G")
```

immediately matches with the first factorial clause, instantiating G" to 1. This value is passed on to the second subgoal, which is solved by giving G' the value 1*G" (=1). The recursion can now begin to unwind: G becomes 2*G' (=2), and finally X becomes 3*G (=6). The original goal is thus achieved and the instantiation of X which caused it is output as result.

It is important to emphasize again that the execution of a query (even if, as in this case, the query represents a mathematical computation) constitutes a *search* for a solution. Prolog systematically looks for values of the variables which will cause the goal to be satisfied. Following on from our earlier comments about the multipurpose nature of some Prolog relations, it might therefore seem logical that factorial could be used like this:

English : What integer has 24 as its factorial?
Prolog : ?-factorial(X,24).

This is asking too much of Prolog. The first subgoal invoked by the query above is

```
M is X-1
```

that is an equality involving two unknowns. Because there are an infinite number of ways this goal could be satisfied, Prolog takes the view that there is no point in embarking upon a search for its solution. Such a query is possible, however, if the factorial procedure is redefined so that it systematically generates the candidate possible values of X in fixed order. We leave it to the reader to discover how this might be done by consulting the Prolog texts referenced at the end of this chapter.

There is much more to Prolog than the above, necessarily superficial, description might imply. We have concentrated on giving a flavor of the programming style, rather than on details of the particular facilities the language provides. In the next section we shall give a brief overview of some other important Prolog features.

17.4 ● Prolog in use

The purpose of any programming language is to make available a set of facilities which encourage and assist its users in the construction of working programs. Prolog is no exception to this, although the particular features provided are heavily influenced by the unconventional structure of the language, and naturally enough by the application areas for which it is intended. Above all, Prolog is consistent in its declarative approach: everything a programmer wishes to do is expressed as a goal or conjunction of goals to be satisfied. For example, the arithmetic operator + is simply a built-in relation defined by a set of implicit facts listing the results of adding arbitrary pairs of numbers together. Thus the computation of the expression 2+3, say, is once again a search (or table-lookup effectively) for the answer to this particular sum. Naturally it isn't implemented in this way, but the user's view is just as if it was.

Goals either succeed or fail; in addition, the success of some goals is accompanied by a *side-effect*. The built-in relation

```
write(X)
```

for example always succeeds, and as a side-effect prints the value of its argument. (For the mathematically inclined, this is one aspect of Prolog which conflicts with formal symbolic logic.)

Prolog has a comprehensive set of arithmetic and input–output facilities in addition to those mentioned above, and also includes list processing facilities, based on a pattern-matching accessing strategy. Record structures with any number of fields can also be created. Moreover, program and data have an identity of form which allows Prolog clauses to be manipulated as data structures. The idea of a Prolog program being synonymous with a database can be capitalized upon – programs can add or delete clauses from the database at run-time, thus giving the facility for a program to edit itself textually as it runs. It is this facility which lends itself to the construction of programs which can acquire new knowledge (such as expert systems). A Prolog program has in fact many similarities with something called a production system, the knowledge representation scheme used by many expert systems.

We have already seen that the programmer can exert some control over the way in which a search satisfying a conjunction is effected by ordering the subgoals which comprise it. Prolog also provides two "extra-logical" features which allow the user to further control the backtracking execution mechanism. Without going into unnecessary detail, it is possible to place a marker (known as a "cut") in a conjunction of goals which acts as a one-way door – Prolog can pass the marker in one direction as it satisfies a sequence of goals, but should it become necessary to backtrack, it will abandon the parent goal if it backs into the marker. This, together with a built-in relation called FAIL which always fails wherever it is invoked (and therefore forces back-tracking) gives the programmer the ability to improve the efficiency of execution, and also to use knowledge about the problem in order to apply control constraints which guide the search in a specific way. For example, a strategically placed cut might ensure that an expert system, having received a reply to a particular question, would never backtrack far enough to ask the same question again.

Given a problem specification, how should a programmer go about designing a program for its solution? One view of a logic program is as a "runnable specification." There has been much interest recently in formal methods of program specification (see Chapter

4), and one use of Prolog is as a specification language. That is, the objectives of a program are first expressed as a set of relationships in Prolog, and the programmer then constructs the program, in whatever language they choose, from that specification. Since Prolog has none of the ambiguities which beset English, the conventional specification language, the correctness of the resulting program should be easier to achieve. But better still, a Prolog program is runnable, so we seem to be in the happy position of being able merely to run the specification (through a Prolog interpreter) rather than actually constructing a program based on it. It has been argued that a Prolog program can be viewed as either a program without a specification, or as a specification which executes efficiently enough not to need a program. Although this is perhaps an oversimplification (because Prolog is actually a rather corrupt form of formal logic), the implications for software engineering would seem to be far reaching. (A functional notation provides an alternative basis for program specification. Chapter 16 describes this approach.)

Experienced Prolog programmers are in a minority. Consequently few guidelines exist as to how the task of program design should be approached. It seems clear that building programs in a top-down manner is appropriate, starting with the problem to be solved as the initial goal, and breaking each goal down into subgoals (much as one would using step-wise refinement). However, although algorithm design is not part of this process, the programmer has to be constantly aware of the control which Prolog will impose on their program. Special attention must therefore be paid to

1. the ordering of clauses within a procedure
2. the ordering of subgoals within a clause
3. the effect that the cut and FAIL may have on the way the program executes.

Debugging a Prolog program is not the same as debugging a procedural program, because a logic program's execution path can be much more complex. It is therefore essential to have debugging aids which allow a backtracking search to be traced and interrupted. The point of logic programming is that one should be able to divorce one-self from any consideration of control and be able to think purely in declarative terms. Unfortunately this objective is not easy to realize in Prolog. The programmer must have a fairly deep understanding of Prolog's execution mechanism in order to use the language to best effect. We shall conclude this chapter by discussing to what extent Prolog does achieve the aim of "programming in logic."

17.5 ● Conclusions

We began this chapter by establishing a formal distinction between the *logic* and *control* components of a program, and outlined the benefits of doing so. Following Prolog's relationship with symbolic logic, we can think of Prolog programs as hypotheses about the problem, and queries are theorems we would like to have proved. Programming in Prolog consists (rather simplistically) of stating that certain things are true, and asking Prolog to draw conclusions. However, our procedural interpretation of clauses imposes something which is just not present in formal logic: control information about how the proof is to be carried out. A programmer can enforce control in many ways, and has to, to get the best out of Prolog. In addition, there are built-in relations (such as `write`) which don't have any interesting logical properties, but merely act as a communication device between program and user. Also, adding and deleting clauses at run-time violates the self-contained nature of symbolic logic; attempting a proof of a theorem when the set of axioms is constantly changing is a tricky business!

So some Prolog programs can only be understood by being aware of how the program executes; yet this is exactly what logic programming is supposed to avoid. It conflicts with the objective of expressing what is to be done without worrying about how it is to be carried out. However, there are well-established programming techniques which can at least get the maximum advantage out of Prolog's relation to logic, even if the ultimate aim is still unrealized.

As to the future, improvements to Prolog are being researched, with particular reference to the development of a practical system which can do without the cut, and in which the goals in a conjunction can be investigated using some parallel execution mechanism. In fact, the reason traditional languages do have logic and control entwined together derives from the sequential nature of the execution of conventional computers. It should be of no consequence to the Prolog programmer whether a conjunction of goals is executed left to right, right to left, in parallel, or using some other mechanism. Similarly the nature of the underlying machine should be immaterial to the expected result of a program execution.

Given the current interest in logic programming, it seems likely that many of logic programming's aims will ultimately be realized. In particular, the exploitation of parallelism is seen as central to the success of practical logic programming environments, and much research is being carried out in this area.

Above all, the existence of Prolog reminds us that there are alternatives to the usual procedural style of programming, and who knows what types of language may be used in the future.

17.6 ● Summary

- Algorithms can be considered to have a logic component and a control component.
- In procedural languages these two components are inextricably entwined.
- A logic program consists only of the logic component – the control is imposed by the interpreter.
- The logic component governs a program's correctness, and the control component its efficiency.
- A Prolog program is a database of facts and rules which have a procedural and a declarative interpretation.
- In order to satisfy a query, Prolog uses a pattern-matching search of the database; a back-tracking theorem prover guides the search.

- There are ways in which a programmer can influence the control imposed on a program.
- One view of a Prolog program is as a "runnable specification."

EXERCISES

17.1 Is the execution of the factorial procedure expressed in Prolog top-down or bottom-up? What would be the effect of reversing the order of the two clauses which make up the procedure?

17.2 Define a Prolog procedure which computes the *N*th Fibonacci number.

17.3 Redefine the superior relation to express the fact that a person is a superior of someone else if they manage that person, or they manage someone who is a superior of that person. What are the consequences for answering queries about superiority?

17.4 Construct a Prolog database representing family relationships such as father, mother, grandparent, ancestor, etc.

17.5 What program development and debugging aids would you expect to find in a Prolog system?

FURTHER READING

Prolog owes a great deal to the work of Robert Kowalski, who originated the idea of predicate logic being viewed as a programming language. A seminal paper is: R. A. Kowalski, Predicate Logic as a Programming Language, *Proceedings of the IFIP-74 Congress*, North-Holland, 1974, pp. 569–74.

A very readable introductory article on Prolog is: R. Ferguson, PROLOG – A Step Towards the Ultimate Computer Language, *BYTE* (November 1981), pp. 384–99.

For an introductory text on Prolog see: W. F. Clocksin and C. S. Mellish, *Programming in Prolog*, Springer-Verlag, 3rd edition, 1987.

The use of Prolog for expert systems implementation is described in: K. A. Bowen, *Prolog and Expert Systems*, McGraw-Hill, 1991.

For a collection of papers on various aspects of logic programming, see: K. L. Clark and S.-A. Tarnlund (eds.), *Logic Programming*, Academic Press, 1982.

Implementation

18

Software tools

This chapter:

- reviews the facilities provided by software tools
- discusses the type of office accommodation suitable for software developers.

18.1 ● Introduction

Software tools can be defined as any pieces of software that aid or automate the process of software development. The general aims of such tools is

- to decrease the human effort required to develop software (increase productivity and lessen software costs)
- to improve the quality of software (for example, reliability and re-usability).

There is a whole range of software tools. Some, like a compiler, are associated with the specific programming language that is being used. Some tools, like a word processor are general-purpose computing tools. Other tools are associated with a specific method. For example, tools are available to support the drawing of class diagrams in object-oriented design. Indeed no current methodology is complete without a set of tools that support it.

There is an enormous proliferation of tools at present. As an illustration, a software engineer who changes jobs may well continue to use the same programming language, but will almost certainly have to learn a new program development system.

Both the variety of current tools and the throwaway outlook have led to pressure for the standardization of tools throughout the software industry. This has not yet been achieved.

Tools have grown in scope and variety so that collections of tools are available for CASE (Computer Aided Software Engineering).

Most tools run under the mainstream operating systems (Unix, Windows, Mac OS) and present a GUI (graphical user interface) with windows, drop-down menus, and mouse selection for user-friendly operation.

In this chapter we review the kinds of tools that are currently available. We also look at suggestions that have been made about the physical environment that is best for the software development task.

18.2 ● Tools for programming

Imagine you could have any software tools that you wanted. What would they be? We will draw up a wish list and then in the next section we will look at examples of actual tools.

We will start our list with those tools associated with the programming phase of software development:

- a compiler
- a text editor
- a linker
- a loader.

Some other tools relate to the particular programming language in use. A *prettifier* formats the program text into a standard, readable layout (for example, with uniform indentation of `if...then...else` statements). A *cross-referencer* displays data, function, and procedure names used in a program, along with information about where each is declared and used.

A *debugger* allows the programmer to place breakpoints in the program, single-shot the execution of the program, and display the values of variables as the program executes.

We need a *library* of useful procedures so that we can make the best re-use of software that has already been written. This library is split into the major sections – mathematical routines, file handling software, graphics procedures, communications software, etc.

Tools can display the structure of a program graphically, for example as a collaboration chart or as a flowchart. These alternative representations can help the programmer to visualize the program in a different way from the way that it was created. This can help in debugging, testing or in improving the structure of a program.

Conditional compilation is sometimes useful so that debug code can be readily inserted or removed, or so that code can be generated for different hardware and software configurations.

We will also need a *file system* or *database* to store (at the very least) program source code. The file system should provide the usual facilities to create new files, display and print the contents of files, copy a file, delete a file, display all file names and group files together into folders (directories).

Sometimes performance is an issue. A *timing/performance analyzer* monitors program execution to identify which parts of a program are consuming most processor time. It is common experience that small fragments of program make the overwhelming demands. Once identified, these particular elements of the program can be studied and made to run faster.

A *file compare tool* can be used to check for any difference between actual and expected test results, or identify what has (deliberately or erroneously) been changed in a program.

For real-time and embedded systems, a software package that *simulates the environment* may be necessary. Such a simulator emulates interrupts, timing constraints, and data codes associated with peripherals like a robot arm, a communications line, or a power plant.

The tools we have identified look rather disparate – they seem like a rag-bag of separate tools having only a tenuous relationship with each other. There is a growing tendency to demand that tools are *integrated* – that they relate well to one another. We will explore the meaning of this idea later in this chapter.

18.3 ● Not programming tools

Thus far we have looked at tools that the programmer uses to assist with coding and debugging. But programming is only a part of software development. We now briefly explore these wider aspects.

Remembering that much information associated with a project, like specifications, user guides, test schedules, and fault reports, will be in the form of natural language, a *word processor* is essential.

Many design methods use diagrams to describe designs. Tools can assist in editing and maintaining these diagrams. The simplest tools merely act like editors, allowing creation editing and filing. A more advanced tool carries out simple checks on a diagram – such as checks that the diagram is self-consistent. Better still, some tools automatically create code from a diagram. In this book, we have chosen to discuss tools alongside the explanation of individual methods.

When a large piece of software is constructed from many component modules, it is a difficult clerical task to keep records that describe exactly which versions of the individual modules have been incorporated into a particular version of the complete package. A *configuration management* package keeps records of which versions of which procedures make up particular systems.

In a large project, tools can assist in keeping track of who does what, schedules, and deadlines. A spreadsheet program can have a role here.

18.4 ● Examples of tools

In this section we review three major examples of sets of tools. Unix has become well known because programmers have become enthusiastic about its command language, filing system, and the simplicity of its concepts. Smalltalk is a programming environment that surrounds the Smalltalk 80 programming language. Similarly, Interlisp surrounds a Lisp system, and reflects many of the novel features of LISP.

18.4.1 Unix

Unix is a general-purpose operating system available widely on personal computers, servers, and mainframe computers. It was reputedly developed in an attic by two workers at Bell telephones. This pedigree explains its conceptual simplicity and beauty. From such small beginnings Unix has become widely popular and has spawned derivatives such as Linux. For reasons that we shall shortly see, it has been realized that Unix can act as an excellent basis for software tools.

Unix provides:

● a filing system, with tree-structured directories (folders)
● a textual command language, based on command verbs followed by parameters
● the facility to write *programs* in the command language
● multithreading (see Chapter 15)
● a useful set of utility programs, called filters, e.g. a file copy tool
● a facility, called pipes, for joining filters together.

These facilities are now commonly found in many operating systems, but Unix was the first system to provide them.

Unix consists of a small kernel, augmented by a rich set of small utility programs, the filters. An example of a filter is a program to display a list of the files within a particular directory. Perhaps because it was designed by only two people, Unix is built around a few, simple concepts. One of the fundamental ideas of Unix is the notion that software (including Unix itself) should be built from small general-purpose components that are developed individually. These components can be used individually but also combined as necessary in order to satisfy a new requirement. In Unix, an individual software component is called a filter. A filter is a program that inputs a serial stream of information, processes it, and outputs a second serial stream. Other examples of Unix-provided filters are:

● count the number of lines or characters in a file
● copy a file
● print a file with specified formatting
● spool a file to the printer
● print all lines in a file that contain a specified textual pattern
● lexically analyze a file.

Filters are combined by taking the output from one and feeding it as input to another. The stream of data that flows from one filter to another is known as a pipe. This combination of filters and pipes is carried out by Unix under the control of the command language.

As an example of combining filters, consider the command:

```
ls
```

When you type a Unix command such as this, you invoke the filter with the same name. The filter named `ls` displays on the screen the names of all the files in the current directory, one per line. Another tool, named `wc`, inputs a file and gives a line, word and character count for that file. The output of `wc` can be controlled by providing parameters, and the parameter `-l` specifies that lines should be counted, so that the command:

```
wc -l file
```

tells us how many lines the file `file` contains. (The majority of Unix commands offer a choice of parameters to modify their output.) Putting these two tools together, the Unix command:

```
ls | wc -l
```

pipes the output from the filter `ls` into the input for the filter `wc`. The final output is therefore the number of files in the current directory.

SELF TEST QUESTION

18.1 The command:

```
grep "Alice" < file
```
outputs those lines in the file `file` that contain the string `Alice`. Write a pipelined command to count how many lines in the file contain the string `Alice`.

The vertical bar symbol in a Unix command signifies that the output stream from one filter is to be directed not to its default file, but to the input of another filter. It also directs that the two filters are to be executed in parallel. On a single processor, this is done by sharing the available processor between the two filters. The Unix system takes care of the necessary synchronization and buffering. This parallel execution reduces both response time and the size of intermediate buffering files.

We have seen that Unix provides a useful, but limited number of facilities as filters. It also provides a facility to combine filters. Thus when some new software is required, there are three options:

1. Use an existing filter.
2. Combine the existing filters using pipes.
3. Write a new filter and combine it with existing filters using pipes.

Combining filters is rather like writing programs, but at a higher level – the Unix filters are the language primitives, and pipes provide the control structures for combining them to produce more powerful facilities.

Filters tend to be short and simple – 90 of the standard Unix filters (other than compilers) are less than 1200 lines (about 20 pages) of high-level programming language statements. An individual filter is usually written in the programming language C, which is the core language of Unix. A filter reads from an input pipe and outputs to an output pipe. It opens an input pipe, just as if it was opening a file. Then it reads data serially from the pipe (or file) until the end of data (file) is encountered. The filter sends its output to an output stream by writing data as if to a serial file.

All the Unix tools are designed to do a specific single task well, rather than supporting many, optional features. However, any options are specified using parameters.

In addition to the general-purpose Unix filters, there are three tools that are particularly relevant in assisting software development. These are named `lint`, `make` and `sccs`. `lint` attempts to detect features of programs written in C (the Unix system programming language) which are likely to be bugs, or non-portable, or wasteful. It also detects such things as unreachable statements, loops not entered at the top, variables declared but not used, and illegal function definition and usage. `make` is used for controlling multiprogrammer projects. It enables the programmer to keep track of which files need to be recompiled after a change is made in some part of the source, and maintains up-to-date versions of programs composed of many such files. `sccs` (source code control system) is used for similar purposes – it acts as a custodian of files, retrieving particular versions, administering changes, and recording when, where and why a change was made, and who made that change.

In summary, the main virtues of Unix as a basis for software tools are:

● A number of small, highly modular, general-purpose components called filters are provided.

● Software is constructed by combining filters with other filters using pipes.

The Unix approach is based on the fundamental assumption that connecting programs via serial streams is modular and flexible. Chapter 6 looks at the general issue of modularity and discusses several approaches to achieving good modularity.

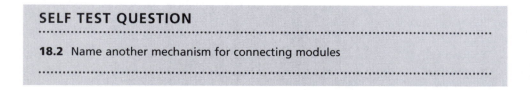

SELF TEST QUESTION

18.2 Name another mechanism for connecting modules

18.4.2 Interlisp

Interlisp is a programming environment based on the LISP programming language. The aims of Interlisp were that it should be co-operative and helpful to the user community for which it was intended – those programmers actively engaged in implementing artificial intelligence applications such as theorem provers, problem solvers, language understanding, and vision systems. Programs like these are experimental because the problems they are trying to solve are ill defined – it is difficult to specify in advance what the precise problem is, to say nothing of its solution. Interlisp was designed specifically to support this experimental style of software development – or "structured growth" as it has become known. Another major influence on Interlisp's development was to make the machine do the work wherever possible, on the grounds that computer resources were cheaper than human resources, and that computer costs could be expected to continue to fall. This has led to a collection of tools which are both sophisticated and general. Consequently, mastery of all the facilities is not easy – an acknowledgment that Interlisp is primarily for expert programmers.

Nearly the whole of the Interlisp system is written in LISP. The development of sophisticated software tools is helped by the fact that it is very easy to treat other LISP programs as data structures which can be manipulated and transformed. Also, since LISP is both the systems language and the applications language, it allows the user to easily understand (and modify) the source code of the provided tools, as well as writing their own. Furthermore, the maximum *integration* of tools can be assured.

During an interactive session, the user talks exclusively to Interlisp. The user's program is held as a data structure, and it is this data structure which is changed during editing. (This is a characteristic of a so-called *residential* system.) LISP editors tend to be language sensitive – that is, they are aware of the structure of the language they are editing. The editor EMACS, for example, will perform automatic bracket matching, and will allow the programmer to walk through the data structure representation of the user's program, making whatever changes are necessary. Interlisp uses a collection of tools called the "file package" to automate the book-keeping necessary for the organization of a large system consisting of many source files and their compiled equivalents. The file package began as a facility which was explicitly invoked by the user to perform specific tasks. More capabilities were added (prompted by user suggestions), and eventually the tool was integrated into the system in such a way that it would be invoked automatically in certain circumstances. Nevertheless, the source code of the tools was still accessible to the general user, so that if some unforeseen situation arose, he or she could extend the package to accommodate it in a straightforward manner.

"Masterscope" is an interactive tool for analyzing and cross-referencing user programs – to determine which functions are called, where variables are referenced and given values, and so on. It maintains a database of the results of its analyses which the user can query explicitly, or ask the editor to use in order to guide the editing session in a specific way.

The DWIM ("Do What I Mean") facility is invoked when the system detects an error: it attempts to guess what the user might have intended. It incorporates a spelling corrector which is automatically called from many parts of the Interlisp system. The correction of a particular misspelled name may of course have repercussions elsewhere. DWIM will notify the file package of the change so that the same correction is made wherever necessary in other dependent files. Since the intention is that the user should feel that he or she is conversing with the system in as natural a way as possible, DWIM often makes changes without seeking user approval. Not all of these changes are spelling corrections. For example, the omission of various parameters to a particular function might not lead to a fatal error, since DWIM will cause them to default to "obvious" values – such as the last thing this function operated upon. The above, necessarily brief, description has really only touched the surface – DWIM is generally considered to be one of the most note-worthy facilities in Interlisp.

The "programmer's assistant" extends the usefulness of all the tools discussed above. It maintains a history of the interactive session so far which can be referred to explicitly or implicitly by the programmer. The programmer's assistant can be called upon to redo a sequence of operations, perhaps with some modifications. Similarly, the effects of a sequence of operations can be undone: this is obviously useful to recover information lost through typing errors, but in addition the "undo" command can be used to experiment with a program's execution – make some changes, run the program, undo the changes, run the program again, undo the undo, and so on. The system also remembers what the user has typed so that the latter can be re-used if necessary.

Interlisp has been described as "friendly, co-operative, and forgiving". Its particular strengths compared with other environments are its *extensibility* (achieved by writing the source code of the tools in LISP and making it available to all), and its *integration*.

Interlisp is integrated in the sense that one tool can be invoked from within another without in any sense losing the context of the original call. Every tool can use every other tool to any depth while preserving the right (and need) to climb back through the levels of invocation to the original context.

Interlisp is an example of an early but prophetic system – it displays many features that are now common in many modern program development environments, but it was years before its time. It is worthy of study because of its integration of facilities and its extensibility, which remain second-to-none.

Interlisp is now being used more and more in applications outside of the AI field, particularly on dedicated work stations (or LISP machines) which incorporate high-resolution window displays, each of which corresponds to a different task or context. In the future, environments building on Interlisp may well incorporate the facility to manipulate graphical displays which represent programs or data structures directly by cursor control or pointing. Software construction and development then becomes the task of drawing or editing pictorial rather than textual representations of the underlying program. Such systems would provide a powerful, friendly, and versatile user interface.

18.4.3 Smalltalk

Individual programmer tools

The Smalltalk programming environment was designed largely as an exploratory object-oriented programming system for individual programmers and can be used as an exemplar for tools of this type. Programming environments for C++, Java, and other object-oriented languages have largely been modeled after the Smalltalk system.

Smalltalk provides an integrated set of tools for developing Smalltalk programs. It is similar to the Interlisp environment in many respects. Smalltalk itself supports many of the tools we would normally associate with an operating system. For example, a compiler, file system, debugger, text editor, spelling checker, and print utility are all provided within the Smalltalk system. An integrated programming environment such as Smalltalk allows a user to carry out multiple tasks within the development environment. The programmer can move quickly and easily from one development task to another without loss of context or information. Any interrupted task may be resumed at any time from its last point of interruption. The Smalltalk environment is characterized by a near absence of modes.

The Smalltalk tools are themselves written in Smalltalk and the extensive library of system classes is available to the programmer in source form. Thus programmers have the facility to browse through the code and modify the tools, if necessary, to suit their personal requirements. Smalltalk pioneered this incredible openness. It would be a brave person, however, who attempted to edit any of the Smalltalk tools. A more feasible way of modifying what they do is to create new classes that inherit from the Smalltalk classes. Like other object-oriented languages, Smalltalk supports "programming by extension" rather than "programming by reinvention"; programmers create application systems by extending the existing Smalltalk environment. What support tools and operations are required?

Some of the major tools that assist the Smalltalk programmer are browsers. Browsers are navigational tools which enable a programmer to rapidly browse through the source code present in the class library. To speed access, classes and methods are organized into categories. Using one of the browsers to view a particular method, the programmer selects the appropriate class category, class, method category and finally, method name within the appropriate panes of the browser. The source for the method is then displayed in another pane. A class hierarchy browser allows the library to be viewed along the class hierarchy (inheritance tree) dimension rather than class categories. This provides a more convenient view of the methods and variables inherited by classes. It is typical for Smalltalk programmers to have a number of browsers open simultaneously.

Browsers are not simply used as navigational tools – new classes and methods are added to the system in the context of a browser. The normal mode of development is to incrementally compile an addition (typically a new method) into the system and then immediately test it by interactively evaluating some suitable expression.

Within a large program it is invaluable to be able to extract cross-referencing information of various types. A few examples follow:

- *Implementations of a method*: when adding a new method, it is useful to be able to view the implementation of methods that perform the same task in other similar classes. This often gives the programmer some insight into how the new method should be implemented.

- *Users of a method*: when modifying a method, it is useful to be able to view those methods that use it. This may give some insight into the repercussions of any change.

- *References to a variable*: when modifying the representation of a class, perhaps by renaming a variable, all references to the old name must be replaced by the new name. It is useful to have a tool to collect all the methods which must be modified. For similar reasons, it is useful to view all references to class variables and class names.

A Smalltalk inspector tool allows programmers to look inside an object and examine and modify its component parts (and their component parts, etc.). Specialized inspectors are useful for presenting different views of an object (or collection of related objects) to the programmer. For example, a normal inspector opened on a dictionary would reveal that the implementation uses a hash table. But this is the wrong level of information for most viewers of dictionaries. Instead a specialized inspector for dictionaries would provide a view where key-value pairs can be viewed, modified, added, or deleted.

The importance of a source code debugger for a language like Smalltalk cannot be underestimated. It allows programmers to view the methods involved in the current computation, insert breakpoints, inspect the values of variables, and interactively modify a method to correct an error. Because of the distributed nature of object-oriented code and (because of dynamic linking) the fact that code cannot be statically analyzed, it is even more important than in traditional languages to be able to single-step through a computation. As well as discovering the cause of bugs, this facility is very often used as a tracing tool to discover how code in the existing system works.

Smalltalk also provides change management tools. Smalltalk automatically tracks all changes made to the system in a changes log. This log can be used to recover from a system crash or to revert to an earlier version of a method or class. It is possible to view the change log in a filtered way, e.g. to view only the changes made to a particular class or method.

Tools for teams of programmers

In this area, Smalltalk, like many other object-oriented languages, is noticeably weak. Smalltalk has evolved from being used for prototypes of projects which could be implemented by two or three programmers to a mainstream development language. An initial tendency has been to rely on the tools provided by Unix or some other underlying operating system. However these tools were designed to support traditional application development. What is the best approach to the problems of multiprogrammer development in an object-oriented setting? For large teams of programmers, a distributed programming environment based around the use of a shared class library accessed over a network may be the best approach. Tools are required to manage both source and object code sharing, to provide control over the visibility of code, to provide code access rights (e.g. view and/or modify), to provide version control, and to allow for the packaging of application releases. Although these tools run counter to the spirit of Smalltalk as an exploratory programming environment for small groups, they will be needed by Smalltalk and other object-oriented systems when they are used for large software engineering projects.

18.4.4 An archetypal program development system

We have chosen not to describe one of the latest integrated program development systems available from one of the major software houses; instead we take a more generic and academic survey of a typical programming toolkit.

A modern program development system provides the user with a graphical user interface (GUI), displaying a number of windows. The main window displays the code of the procedure under development. It automatically formats the code with indentation and other white space. It may use color to distinguish reserved words and comments. It may prompt the programmer with context-sensitive suggestions as the programmer keys in text – for example, the available parameters associated with a library procedure.

A second window displays a graphical representation of the program, showing the role of the current procedure within the context of the bigger picture.

Yet another window displays selected information about the available libraries. This may be in textual or graphical form.

When the debugger is invoked, breakpoints are highlighted within the program text, and a pointer signals the instruction currently under execution.

There is a strong sense of integration of the tools within the programming environment.

18.5 ● Discussion

Several principles emerge from efforts to provide software tools.

A set of tools should be *integrated* and not merely a number of distinct tools. Smalltalk 80 and Interlisp both clearly demonstrate an integration, but Unix rather less. So for example, while you are using one Smalltalk tool you can invoke another tool (and another) without leaving off what you were doing in the first place. In contrast, Unix tools can only be used one at a time, in isolation (though they can be combined, using pipes).

Tools should cover *all stages* of software development – not just program development. Thus we see tools to document requirements, assist design, and to monitor project progress.

Tools need to be *standardized*, just as programming languages are, so that users do not have to retrain each time they use a different machine or operating system.

A set of tools should *support the particular method* being used. Thus, for example, tools are available that support particular object-oriented design methods.

Tools can incorporate varying degrees of support:

● a simple editor provides for the creation, saving and editing of diagrams such as class diagrams
● a more sophisticated tool checks for consistency between parts of a diagram and between different representations of the same software; for example a tool can check that a class diagram is consistent with a collaboration diagram
● a tool creates code from a diagram – for example the creation of a Java code skeleton from a class diagram.

18.6 ● Application development tools

The idea of application development tools is to construct software without the need to write down conventional programming language statements. Instead, the developer designs the system interactively at the computer, specifying screen layouts and the processing of information. The area of application of these tools is usually information systems, typically on free-standing or networked PCs. Examples of packages of this type are Microsoft Access (a database management system), Visual Basic, and spreadsheets.

To illustrate how a database management package might be used, suppose that we want to develop a personal telephone directory. One consideration is the input of the information – people's names and telephone numbers. The designer first designs a screen layout to be used for the input. This design is carried out interactively using menus provided for this purpose. In this case we might want to specify that a name is entered in one text box and the number in another. The design completed, the package stores the screen layout for subsequent use. It also records information about the way that the name and number information is to be stored on the disk. We have now constructed a data-entry program that allows the user to key in the names and telephone numbers.

Since the purpose of the system is to look up a telephone number, the designer constructs a second screen layout. This allows the user to enter a name, which implicitly instructs the package to search the database for the corresponding information and display it. The designer can similarly design screens so that the user can also use the package to alter (edit or update) existing information (when someone changes their telephone number), to add new records, and to delete existing records.

Most packages will allow selective searches to be made on the information – for example, in a personnel information system, to look for all records describing people who are male and over 60 years old. Again, using the package, layouts for reports can be designed. Such reports typically use selected information from the database and, if necessary, draw on information entered using several different screen layouts. Calculations on data items can also be specified – for example that a particular field on a report is to be the product of two specified fields in the database.

Packages of this type exploit the essential similarities of information systems. All such applications require access to files of data; therefore the file access software is common and built in to the package. All that is special for an application is the particular layout and content of the database, the input screen layouts, and the output screen layouts.

Now to Visual Basic (VB). Visual Basic allows the developer to create programs (applications) that display the widely used Microsoft Windows interface very quickly. The package does the hard work of creating windows, message boxes, menus, detecting mouse clicks. As an example of the use of Visual Basic, let us consider the construction of a desktop calculator. The first step is to design the user interface – Figure 18.1 – using the toolkit.

Visual Basic provides a toolkit to support the design of this interface interactively using menus and the mouse. The programmer selects widgets (such as a button) from a menu and places them in their appropriate place within the window. Once an interface has been constructed, it need not provide any functionality but can act simply as a prototype for demonstration to potential users.

If functionality is required, it is accomplished by writing code to act in response to clicking on each of the buttons. In Visual Basic, a procedure is automatically called for each possible event in the user interface.

Figure 18.1 The user interface for the calculator program

For the calculator program, we need some global variables. In Visual Basic, the word
Dim introduces variable declarations:

```
Dim newNumber As Boolean
Dim first As Boolean
Dim ans As Integer
Dim op As String
```

and these need initializing when the program starts running. A procedure called
Form_Load (if provided by the programmer) is called when the form (window) is loaded.
In Visual Basic, a procedure is introduced using the word Sub:

```
Sub Form_Load()
newNumber = True
first = True
op = "="
ans = 0
End Sub
```

We now write a procedure that is called when each digit button is clicked on:

```
Sub zero_button_Click
setDigit(0)
End Sub

Sub one_button_Click
setDigit(1)
End Sub

Sub two_button_Click
setDigit(2)
End Sub
```

and so on, for each of the digit buttons. These call a procedure:

```
Sub setDigit(digit As Integer)
If newNumber Then
    display = digit
Else
    display = display & digit
End If
newNumber = False
first = False
End Sub
```

Now the code that is called when the operator buttons are clicked on:

```
Sub add_Click()
calculate
op = "+"
End Sub

Sub subtract_Click()
If first Then
    display = "-"
    first = False
Else
    calculate
    op = "-"
End If
End Sub

Sub equals_Click()
calculate
op = "="
End Sub
```

And finally the procedure that carries out a calculation:

```
Sub calculate()
If op = "+" Then ans = ans + display
If op = "-" Then ans = ans - display
If op = "=" Then ans = display
display = ans
newNumber = True
End Sub
```

This completes the coding for the calculator. The reader can imagine that only simple enhancements are necessary to implement the clear button and add additional buttons to make the calculator do multiplication, divide, and any other operation.

The point to note from this example is that no coding is required to create a user interface and very little coding is required to handle events from the user interface.

Visual Basic is a full-strength programming language, with arrays, strings, procedures with parameters, file handling, graphics, and facilities for modularity. In addition object-oriented features are gradually being introduced as new versions emerge. So it is easily possible to implement any software feature that is desired. The strength of Visual Basic is that the user interface can be constructed very easily as compared with the hundreds of lines of code that would be needed in, say, C++. All the familiar Windows-type facilities can be presented to the user – scroll bars, option buttons, check boxes, menus, etc. This makes it very appealing for prototyping. The other attraction of the system at a conceptual level is that it supports event-driven programming – the software is written so as to respond to events initiated by the user, such as clicking a mouse button.

The drawback of Visual Basic is that it supports a particular type of interface (the Microsoft Windows style of interface) and runs only under Microsoft operating systems – and this might not be what users require.

Another tool is spreadsheet programming which provides another way of short-cutting the traditional approach to software development in applications where the information to be processed can be visualized as being in tabular form.

18.7 ● The physical environment

Many other factors besides tools influence the job of software development. One of these is office layout, which we now look at. It is common to treat software developers just like any other office workers, and many such people work in open plan offices. But arguably software development requires periods of intense concentration, which is threatened by noise or other disturbance.

Some years ago, IBM was faced with the task of designing purpose-built accommo-dation for 2,000 people involved in software development. In preparation, IBM commissioned a study into the office requirements for these people. Of interest in itself is the result of a study into how programmers spend their time at work:

working alone	30%
working with others	50%
travel, etc.	20%

The design study made the following recommendations about the needs of software developers:

- private, personal work area that permits intense concentration, screens distractions, and discourages interruptions
- space to lay out and store paper
- proximity to meeting rooms
- ready access to a library and to a food service area
- special furniture.

The designers went on to specify "programming pavilions", consisting of clusters of individual offices, each 10 feet by 10 feet, with nearby meeting rooms. The furniture in each room was tailor-made to suit a computer and computer stationery.

In another study, DeMarco and Lister investigated the effects of various factors on software quality. One of the factors that they studied was noise. They found that those developers who reported that their workplace was acceptably quiet produced software that had markedly fewer defects. These effects were not just a few percent, but had a major effect on performance. DeMarco and Lister suggest a number of measures for controlling noise and enhancing concentration:

- adequate space for each worker
- private space (an individual office or effective partitions)
- muting the telephone (if necessary with paper tissue) or alternatively diverting calls
- using electronic mail in preference to the telephone to eliminate uncontrolled interruptions.

At their headquarters in Washington, Microsoft provide software developers with a pleasant working environment, modeled on a college campus. Each developer has their own office, often with views of the landscaped gardens outside. Meeting rooms and cafeterias are on hand.

18.8 ● Summary

There is tremendous interest in automating some or all of the software development task. There is currently a proliferation of tools, encompassing all aspects of software development. Several famous and successful sets of tools – Unix, Smalltalk 80, Interlisp – act as signposts for the future. We have also reviewed the facilities of an archetypal program development system.

Current thinking is that tools should:

- support the methods actually used
- provide facilities in an integrated fashion
- cover all stages of software development
- be standardized.

These aims are the basis for CASE tools, which aim to provide assistance in all phases of software development – specification, design, testing, and maintenance – as well as enabling a disciplined and controlled approach to project management.

An alternative to using a conventional program development tool is to use an application development tool, such as Visual Basic, a database management system, or a spreadsheet package, to create those software systems that are essentially similar – systems such as PC-based information systems.

Arguably the physical layout of office space has an influence on the software developers' performance.

EXERCISES

18.1 Investigate and assess the software development facilities provided on the computer(s) available to you and assess how good the facilities are.

18.2 Devise a toolkit that would provide good support for the development of programs written in a language of your choice.

18.3 Review and assess the toolkits provided by:

(a) Interlisp

(b) Smalltalk

(c) Unix.

18.4 Choose a program design method, for example, object-oriented design. Devise a tool or tools that assist in the use of the method.

18.5 Compare and contrast the Unix with the Smalltalk approaches to providing software tools.

18.6 Suggest a methodology (series of steps) for the complete process of developing software. Draw up a specification for an integrated set of software tools to support this process.

18.7 Suggest facilities for a good physical working environment for the software developer.

ANSWERS TO SELF TEST QUESTIONS

18.1 `grep "Alice" < file | wc -l`
18.2 Procedure calls

FURTHER READING

There are lots of good books on Unix. But if you want to read the original classic paper, it is: B. W. Kernighan and J. R. Mashey, The Unix Programming Environment, *IEEE Computer* (April 1981), pp. 12–24.

A beautifully written exposition of the radically different Smalltalk approach to interacting with a program development system is: L. Tesler, The Smalltalk Environment, *BYTE* (August 1981).

Interlisp is described in: W. Teitelman and L. Masinter, The Interlisp Programming Environment, *IEEE Computer*, 14 (4), (1981).

Some of the above articles are collected together in: D. R. Barstow, H. E. Shrobe and E. Sandewall (eds.), *Interactive Programming Environments*, McGraw-Hill, 1984.

The authors of the following book argue strongly for paying good attention to the physical layout of office space. Some of their work and suggestions are reported above. Tom DeMarco and Timothy Lister, *Peopleware, Productive Projects and Teams*, Dorset House Publishing Co., 1987.

You can read about the design of IBM's programming pavilions in: G. M. McCue, IBM's Santa Teresa Laboratory – Architectural Design for Program Development, *IBM Systems Journal*, 17 (1), (1978).

The following book stands back from the details of tools and assesses why tools are not more widely used: Peter Degrace and Leslie Hulet Stahl, *The Olduvai Imperative: CASE and the State of Software Engineering Practice*, Prentice Hall International, 1993.

19

Verification

This chapter:

- explores the limits of testing
- explains how to carry out black box (functional) and white box (structural) testing
- explains how to carry out inspections and walkthroughs
- explains how to carry out system (integration) testing.

19.1 ● Introduction

In Chapter 2, we distinguished between two important activities that must go on during software development:

- validation – making sure that the software meets its users' needs
- verification – producing fault-free software.

Validation was discussed in Chapters 2 and 3. This chapter explains several approaches to verification.

Software is complex and it is difficult to make it work correctly. Currently the dominant technique used for verification is testing. And testing typically consumes an enormous proportion (sometimes as much as 50%) of the effort of developing a system. At Microsoft there are as many people involved in testing as there are in programming.

Arguably, verification is a major problem and we need good techniques to tackle it. Often, towards the end of a project, the difficult decision has to be made between continuing the testing or delivering the software to its customers or clients.

We begin this chapter by discussing the general problem of testing, and discover that there is a significant problem. We consider approaches called black box and white box testing and go on to suggest a practical test strategy.

Formal verification, using the power and rigor of mathematics to establish correctness, is being used, particularly in safety-critical systems. We outline this approach.

Studies have shown that it is helpful for people other than the developer themself to test the software; we describe some team approaches to testing – structured walkthroughs and inspections. Microsoft employ teams of programmers (who write programs) and completely separate teams of testers (who test them).

The problems of testing large pieces of software that consist of many modules are severe – particularly if all the modules are combined together at one and the same time. An alternative is incremental testing and one version of this is top-down development and testing. Top-down development also provides a way of showing users an early version of a system. It is therefore useful for validation.

19.2 ● The nature of errors

It would be convenient to know how errors arise, because then we could try to avoid them during all the stages of development. Similarly, it would be useful to know the most commonly occurring faults, because then we could look for them during verification. Regrettably, the data is inconclusive and it is only possible to make vague statements about these things.

Specifications are a common source of faults. A software system has an overall specification, derived from requirements analysis. In addition, each component of the software ideally has an individual specification that is derived from architectural design. The specification for a component can be:

● ambiguous (unclear)

● incomplete

● faulty.

Any such problems should, of course, be detected and remedied by verification of the specification, prior to development of the component. But, of course, this verification cannot and will not be totally effective. So there are often problems with a component specification.

This is not all – there are other problems with specifications. During programming, the developer of a component may misunderstand the component specification.

The next type of error is where a component contain faults so that it does not meet its specification. This may be due to two kinds of problem:

● errors in the logic of the code – an error of commission

● code that fails to meet all aspects of the specification – an error of omission.

This second type of fault is where the programmer has failed to appreciate and correctly understand all the detail of the specification and has therefore omitted some necessary code.

Finally, the kinds of faults that can arise in the coding of a component are:

● data not initialized
● loops repeated an incorrect number of times
● boundary value errors.

Boundary values are values of the data at or near critical values. For example, suppose a component has to decide whether a person can vote or not, depending on their age. The voting age is 18. Then boundary values, near the critical value, are 17, 18, and 19.

As we have seen, there are many things that can go wrong and perhaps therefore it is no surprise that verification is such a time-consuming activity.

19.3 ● The problem of testing

We now explore the limitations of testing. Consider as illustration a procedure to calculate the product of its two integer parameters. First, we might think of devising a *selection* of test data values and comparing the actual with the expected outcome. So we might choose the values 21 and 568 as sample values. Remembering negative numbers, we might also choose –456 and –78. If we now look at possible coding for the procedure, we can immediately see the drawback with this approach:

```
public int product(int x, int y) {
    int p;
    p = x * y;
    if (p == 42) then p = 0;
    return p;
}
```

The problem is that, for some reason – error or malice – the programmer has chosen to include an `if` statement which leads to an incorrect value in certain cases. The test data that was chosen above would not reveal this error. Nor, almost certainly, would any other selection of test data. Thus use of selective test data cannot guarantee exposure of bugs. Now it could be argued that the bug is obvious in this example – simply by looking at the program. But looking at a program is not testing – it is a technique called inspection that is discussed later in this chapter.

A second method of testing, called exhaustive testing, would be to use all possible data values, in each case checking the correctness of the outcome. But even for the procedure to multiply two 32 bit integers this would take 100 years (assuming a 1 millisecond integer multiply instruction is provided by the hardware of the computer). So exhaustive testing is almost always impracticable.

These considerations lead us to the unpalatable conclusion that it is impossible to exhaustively test any program. Thus any program of significant size is likely to contain bugs.

19.4 ● Black box (functional) testing

Knowing that exhaustive testing is infeasible, the "black box" approach to testing is to devise sample data that is representative of all possible data. Then we run the program, input the data, and see what happens.

Black box testing is so-called because no knowledge of the workings of the program is used as part of the testing – we only consider inputs and outputs. The program is thought of as being invisible within a black box. Black box testing is also known as functional testing because it uses only a knowledge of the function of the program.

As an example, we will consider testing a procedure that carries out multiplication, using black box testing. The specification of the procedure is that it accepts two 16 bit integers and returns the product of the two numbers.

We need some representative data. Being bold, we might argue that any integer is typical of any other integer. So all we need to do is to choose any two integers as representatives of all the possible integers. Thus we choose one set of test data:

Test number	Data	Expected result
1	8, 12	96

and the testing is complete.

Cautious, we might worry that this is too limited. Recognizing that negative numbers are different somehow to positive numbers, we choose representatives of the negative numbers, and use all combinations:

Test number	Data	Expected result
1	8, 12	96
2	–7, 8	–56
3	12, –20	–240

Still slightly concerned that this testing is inadequate, we might argue that the number zero is special and that therefore we should also test the program with:

Test number	Data	Expected result
1	8, 12	96
2	–7, 8	–56
3	12, –20	–240
4	0, –7	0
5	–7, 0	0
6	0, 8	0
7	8, 0	0
8	0, 0	0

which completes the testing of this program according to the black box approach.

We reasoned that we needed eight sets of test data. These eight sets, together with a statement of the expected outcomes from the testing, constitute a *test specification*.

This approach to devising test data for black box testing is to use *equivalence partitioning*. This means looking at the nature of the input data to identify common features. Such a common feature is called a partition. In the program to multiply integer numbers, all the integers are similar in the sense of being equally valid as data for this program. To emphasize the idea of partitions, a good idea is to sketch the nature of the data and the partitions within it. The permissible data for our program is integers in the range −32768 to 32767 which we can diagram like this:

−32768	32767

in which all the integers are visualized as being in a single partition, with the limits of the numbers at each end. We then take the step of asserting that every number within this partition is equivalent to any other, for the purpose of this program. Hence the term equivalence partitioning. So any number chosen from within the partition is representative of (or equivalent to) any other. Thus the pair of numbers, 8 and 12, chosen above, are representative of all the others.

We then refined our vision of the range of numbers, to recognize that negative numbers and the number zero constitute different partitions:

−32768	−1	0	1	32767

Note that throughout the complete discussion, we have not considered how the procedure works. This is absolutely appropriate for a black box approach.

As another example, consider the case of a program that inputs someone's age and decides whether or not they can vote. Suppose that the voting age is 18. We draw the diagram of the partitions:

0	17	18	32767

There are two partitions, one including the age range 0–17 and the other partition with numbers 18–32767. A number like 12 is equivalent to any other in the first partition and the number 21 is equivalent to any number in the second. So we devise two tests:

Test number	Data	Outcome
1	12	Cannot vote
2	21	Can vote

Unfortunately we can see that these tests have not investigated the important distinction between someone aged 17 and someone aged 18. Anyone who has ever written a program knows that carrying out comparisons using `if` statements is error-prone. Studies indicate that programmers tend to make mistakes when they write the conditions within `if` statements and loops. Other studies suggest that in testing, unusual values are ignored at the expense of typical values. Both these results suggest that test data should explore values at the extremes of data values and around the boundaries of tests. So it is advisable to investigate this particular region of the data. This is termed *boundary value* testing. This is the same as recognizing that data values at the edges of the partitions are worthy of inclusion into the testing. Therefore we create two additional tests:

Test number	Data	Outcome
3	17	cannot vote
4	18	can vote

In summary, the rules for selecting test data for black box testing using equivalence partitioning is:

1. Partition all possible input data values
2. Select representative data from each partition (equivalent data)
3. Select data at the boundaries of partitions.

SELF TEST QUESTION

19.1 A program's function is to input three integer numbers and find the largest. Devise black box test data for this program.

SELF TEST QUESTION

19.2 In a program to play the game of chess, the player specifies the destination for a move as a pair of subscripts, the row and column number. The program checks that the destination square is valid, that is not outside the board. Devise black box test data to check that this part of the program is working correctly.

19.5 ● White box (structural) testing

White box testing makes use of a knowledge of how a procedure works – it uses the listing of the program code. The knowledge of how the procedure works – its structure – is used as the basis of devising test data. Ideally, the tester writes down the expected outcome of the test, a test specification. Then the procedure is run, the data is input, and the output compared with the expected output.

If we tried to test by executing every path through a procedure, we would quickly meet the same problem that we faced in trying to exhaustively black-box test a program – there are just too many possibilities. As soon as a procedure contains a loop, the number of possible paths explodes.

An alternative, to reduce the number of test cases, is to use *statement* testing. Here is the procedure we considered earlier, to test whether someone can vote:

```
public String vote(int age) {
    if (age > 18) return ("can vote");
    else return ("cannot vote");
}
```

The principle of white box statement testing is that every statement in the program should be executed at some time during the testing. In this procedure, the `if` statement is always executed, whatever the data. But two different data values are needed to execute the two possible outcomes of the comparison. Thus suitable test data is:

Test number	Data	Outcome
1	12	Cannot vote
2	21	Can vote

Note that black box testing needed exactly the same kind of data to test this procedure, but this is not generally the case.

In white box testing, the same argument is used as in black box testing – special cases need special investigation. Thus white box testing should also select test data that:

● explores the decisions that control the choice of path

● takes care to test actions that are taken in special cases.

As in black box testing, this is called boundary value testing.

Notice that statement testing will find the error in the product procedure, introduced earlier as an example in discussing the general problems of testing.

SELF TEST QUESTION

19.3 A program's function is to find the largest of three numbers. Devise white box test data for this section of program.

The code is:

```
int a, b, c;
int largest;

if (a > b)
    if (a > c)
        largest = a;
    else
        largest = c;
else
    if (b > c)
        largest = b;
    else
        largest = c;
```

SELF TEST QUESTION

19.4 In a program to play the game of chess, the player specifies the destination for a move as a pair of integer subscripts, the row and column number. The program checks that the destination square is valid, that is, not outside the board. Devise white box test data to check that this part of the program is working correctly.

The code for this part of the program is:

```
if ((row > 8) || (row < 1))
    g.drawString ("error", 10, 10);
if ((col > 8) || (col < 1))
    g.drawString ("error", 10, 10);
```

19.6 ● Walkthroughs and inspections

An approach that doesn't make use of a computer at all in trying to eradicate faults in a program is called inspection or a walkthrough.

19.6.1 The individual and the error

Programmers are often seen as loners. Given a clear specification, a programmer often carries out the complete process of program design, coding and testing entirely on their own. Programmers are seen as low-profile techies in contrast to the articulate extrovert systems analysts. Thus a program is sometimes seen as a personal work of art; the creation of an individual programmer. These attitudes denied that "two heads are better than one," that through discussion with others we can produce better work.

The common experience that someone else can spot errors better than the author led to the invention of the *structured walkthrough*. Credit for its invention belongs to Weinberg, in his book *The Psychology of Computer Programming*. Weinberg suggested that programmers see their programs as an extension of themselves. He suggested that we get very involved with our own creations and tend to regard them as manifestations of our own thoughts. We are unable to see errors in our own programs, since to do so would be to find a fault in ourselves, and this, apparently, is unacceptable to us. The term for this is *cognitive dissonance*. The solution is to seek help with fault finding. In doing this we relinquish our private relationship with our work. Programming becomes *ego-less programming*. This is a completely informal technique, carried out by colleagues in a friendly manner. It is not a formalized method carried out at fixed times and made into a rigid procedure of the organization. Indeed, to formalize ego-less programming would be to destroy its ethos and therefore its effectiveness. In a walkthrough or inspection, someone simply studies the program listing (along with the specification) in order to try to see bugs. It works better if the person doing the inspecting is not the person who wrote the program. This is because people tend to be blind to their own errors. So if you get a friend or a colleague to inspect your program, it is extraordinary to witness how quickly someone else sees an error that has been defeating you for hours. Studies also show that different people tend to uncover different errors. This further suggests the use of team techniques.

19.6.2 Structured walkthroughs

A structured walkthrough is simply the term for an organized meeting at which a program (or some other product) is examined by a group of colleagues. The major aim of the meeting is to try to find bugs which might otherwise go undetected for some time. (There are other goals, which are explained later.) The word "structured" simply means "well organized." The term "walkthrough" means the activity of the programmer explaining step-by-step the working of his/her program. The reasoning behind structured walkthroughs is just this: that by letting other people look at your program, errors will be found much more quickly.

To walkthrough a program you need only:

● the specification
● the text of the program on paper.

In carrying out a walkthrough, a good approach is to study it one procedure at a time. Some of the checks are fairly straightforward:

● variables initialized
● loops correctly initialized and terminated
● procedure calls have the correct parameters.

Another check depends on the logic of the procedure. Pretend to execute the procedure as if you were a computer, avoiding following any calls into other procedures. Check that the logic of the method achieves its desired purpose.

During inspection you can also check that:

● variable and procedure names are meaningful
● indentation is clear and consistent.

The prime goal of a walkthrough is to find bugs, but checking for a weakness in style may point to a bug.

The evidence from controlled experiments suggests that walkthroughs are a very effective way of finding errors. In fact walkthroughs are at least as good a way of identifying bugs as actually running the program (doing testing).

Although structured walkthroughs were initially used to find bugs in program code, the technique is valuable for reviewing the products at every stage of development – the requirements specification, a formal software specification, architectural design, program design, the code, the test data, the results of testing, the documentation.

There are several key points in organizing walkthroughs successfully:

● Gauge the size and membership of the group carefully so that there are plenty of ideas, but so that everyone is fully involved.

● Expect participants to study the material *prior* to the meeting.

● Concentrate attention on the *product* rather than the person, to avoid criticizing the author.

● Limit the length of the meeting, so that everyone knows that it is business-like.

● Control the meeting with the aid of agreed rules and an assertive chair.

● Restrict the activity to *identifying* problems, not solving them.

● Briefly document the faults (not the cures) for later reference.

The benefits of structured walkthroughs can be:

1. **Software quality is improved** because
   ● more bugs are eliminated
   ● the software is easier to maintain, because it is clearer.

2. **Programmer effort is reduced** because
   ● specifications are clarified before implementation
   ● errors are detected early, and so costly rework is avoided
   ● the time spent at the meeting (and in preparation for it) is more than repaid in time saved.

3. **Meeting deadlines is improved** because
   ● visibility of the project is better (so potential catastrophes are prevented)
   ● major errors are avoided early.

4. **Programmer expertise is enhanced** because
   ● everyone learns from everyone else.

5. **Programmer morale is improved** because
   ● people gain satisfaction from better work
   ● people get to find out what is going on
   ● people enjoy the discussions with colleagues.

Of course walkthroughs do mean that the individual has to be relaxed about presenting their work to colleagues.

19.6.3 Inspections

Inspections are similar to structured walkthroughs – a group of people meet to review a piece of work. But they are different from walkthroughs in several respects. Checklists are used to ensure that no relevant considerations are ignored. Errors that are discovered are classified according to type and carefully recorded on forms. Statistics on errors are computed, for example in terms of errors per 1000 lines of code. Thus inspections are not just well organized, they are completely formal. In addition management is informed of the results of inspections, though usually they do not attend the meeting. Thus inspections are potentially more threatening to the programmer than walkthroughs.

There are other, minor, differences between inspections and walkthroughs. Normally there are only four members in an inspection team:

- the moderator, who coordinates activities
- the designer who designed the program component being inspected
- the programmer
- the tester – a person who acts as someone who will be responsible for testing the component.

The essence of inspections is that the study of products is carried out under close management supervision. Thus inspections are overtly a mechanism for increased control over programmers' work, in a similar fashion to the way that quality control is carried out on a factory floor. Many programmers would feel threatened in this situation and become defensive, perhaps trying to hide their mistakes. Perhaps this worsens the discovery of errors, and makes programming a less enjoyable activity.

From an organizational point of view, keeping records of faults discovered during inspections provides information to predict the quality of the software being written. Also, by highlighting common mistakes it can be used to improve programmers' self awareness and thereby improve their skills.

19.7 ● Other testing strategies

19.7.1 Stepping through code

Some debuggers allow the user to step through a program, executing just one instruction at a time. This is sometimes called single-shotting. Each time you execute one instruction you can see which path of execution has been taken. You can also see (or watch) the values of variables. It is rather like an automated structured walkthrough.

In this form of testing, you concentrate on the variables and closely check their values as they are changed by the program to verify that they have been changed correctly.

A debugger is usually used for debugging (locating a bug); here it is used for testing (establishing the existence of a bug).

19.7.2 Testing the test data

In a large system or program it can be difficult to ensure that the test data is adequate. One way to try to test whether it does indeed cause all statements to be executed is to use a *profiler*. A profiler is a software package that monitors the testing by inserting probes into the software under test. When testing takes place the profiler can expose which pieces of the code are not executed and therefore reveal the weakness in the data.

Another approach to investigating the test data is called *mutation testing*. In this technique, artificial bugs are inserted into the program. An example would be to change a

"+" into a "–". The test is run and if the bugs are not revealed, then the test data is obviously inadequate. The test data is modified until the artificial bugs are exposed.

19.7.3 Team techniques

Many organizations set up separate teams to carry out testing and such a team is sometimes called a *quality assurance* (QA) team. There are, of course, fruitful grounds for possible conflict between the development group and the QA team.

One way of actually exploiting conflict is to set up an *adversary* team to carry out testing. Such a team is made up of what we might normally think of as being antisocial people – hackers, misfits, psychotics. Their malice can be harnessed to the effective discovery of bugs.

Another approach is to set up *bounty hunters*, whose motivation for finding errors is based on financial reward.

19.7.4 Beta testing

In beta testing, a preliminary version of a software product is released to the customer or client, knowing that its has bugs. Users are asked to report on faults so that the product can be improved for its proper release date. Beta testing gets its name from the second letter of the Greek alphabet. Its name therefore conveys the idea that it is the second major act of testing, following on after testing within the developing organization.

19.8 ● Discussion

We have seen that exhaustive testing is infeasible. Therefore complete testing is impossible and whatever testing methods are used, they can never ensure that the software is free from bugs. Thus testing is a poor technique but until formal verification becomes widely applicable it is a vital technique.

However much we test our programs, using all our skill and intuition, we can never be sure that we have eradicated all the faults. The situation is well summed up by Dijkstra's famous remark: "Testing can only show the presence of bugs, never their absence." This has been (anonymously) re-phrased as: "Just because you have never seen a mermaid doesn't mean that they don't exist." It can be reassuring to adopt the view that a test that reveals no bugs is a successful test. But rather we should look upon such a test as unsuccessful!

It is difficult to get accurate data on the number of bugs present in production software because, unsurprisingly, organizations do not want to reveal this kind of information. But the indications are that there are typically between 2 and 50 bugs per 1,000 lines of source code in commercial production software. A figure like this is more properly called a *fault density*. It measures the number of known faults per 1,000 lines of code (LOC). A figure of 2 is considered to be most creditable. Ways of measuring this quantity are explained in Chapter 21.

The trouble is, of course, that bugs always surface at the worst possible time – for example when you are demonstrating the completed software to the client. This phenomenon has long been known to students of reliability, who quote Murphy's laws:

1. "If a system can fail, it will" ...

2. "and at the worst possible moment."

Another, more objective, observation is that some bugs create serious faults, while others lie dormant and do not give any trouble.

A number of experiments have been carried out in order to assess the effectiveness of testing. For example, in an early carefully controlled experiment, 59 people were asked to test a 63-line PL/1 program. The people were workers in the computer industry, most of whom were programmers, with an average of 11 years experience in computing. They were told of a suspicion that the program was not perfect and asked to test the program until they felt that they had found all the errors (if any). An error meant a discrepancy between the program and the specification. The people were provided with the program specification, the program listing, a computer to run the program on, and as much time as they wanted.

Thus the people were experienced and the program was quite small. However their performance was surprisingly bad. The mean number of bugs found was 5.7. The most errors any individual found was nine. The least any person found was three. The actual number of bugs was 15. There were four bugs that no-one found. The overwhelming conclusion must be that people are not very effective at carrying out verification – whichever technique they use.

Additional findings were that the people were not careful enough in comparing the actual output from the program with the expected outcome. Bugs that were actually revealed were missed in this way. Also the people spent too long on testing the normal conditions that the program had to encounter, rather than on testing special cases and invalid input situations.

The effectiveness of a verification method is judged either:

● by measuring how many bugs are discovered, given unlimited time spent on testing, or

● by measuring the number of bugs found per hour of developer time.

The evidence from experiments suggests that inspections are a very effective way of finding errors. In fact inspections are at least as good a way of identifying bugs as actually running the program (doing testing). So, if you had to choose one method for verification, it would have to be inspection. Studies show that black box testing and white box testing are roughly equally effective.

However, the evidence suggests that the different verification techniques tend to discover different errors. Therefore the more techniques that are employed the better, provided that there is adequate time and money. So black box testing, white box testing, and inspection all have a role to play. If there is sufficient time and effort available, the best strategy is to use all three methods.

Formal verification is very appealing because of its potential for rigorously verifying a program's correctness beyond all possible doubt. This approach is discussed in Chapter 12. However, it must be remembered that these methods are carried out by fallible human beings who make mistakes. So they are not a cure-all.

The worrying conclusion to any discussion of verification is that all software (of any significant size) contains faults.

19.9 ● System (integration) testing

Thus far we have only considered unit verification – the verification of an individual software component, a method, or an object. We have implicitly assumed that such a component is fairly small. This is the first step in the verification of software systems – which typically consist of tens or hundreds of individual components. The task of testing complete systems is called system or integration testing.

Following requirements engineering, software development proceeds by carrying out architectural design – specifying the constituent programs, procedures and objects. The method of achieving this design could be, for example, object-oriented design, data flow design, or functional decomposition. Having drawn up detailed specifications of all the components, a project proceeds by designing and coding the individual components. But a problem now arises: "How can we test these components and how can we test the complete system?"

Consider three different approaches to system testing:

● big bang – bring all the components together, without prior testing, and test the complete system

● improved big bang – test each component individually, bring them all together and test the complete system

● incremental – build the system piece-by-piece, testing the partial system at each stage.

The first approach – big bang or *monolithic* testing – is a recipe for disaster. There is no easy way of knowing which module is the cause of a fault, and there is an enormous debugging task. The second approach is slightly better because when the components are brought together, we have some confidence in them individually. Now any faults are likely to be caused by the interactions between the components. Here again, there is a major problem of locating faults.

An alternative is to use some form of *incremental* testing. In this approach, first just one component of the system is tested. Then a second module is linked with the first and the system tested. Any fault is likely to be localized either in the newly incorporated module or in the interface between the two. We continue like this, adding just one module at a time. At each stage, any fault that presents itself is likely to be caused by the new module, or by its interface to the system. Thus fault finding is made considerably easier.

There are two main approaches to incremental testing – bottom-up and top-down. They are discussed below.

19.10 ● Bottom-up testing

The bottom-up testing technique is to start with the lowest-level components of the system. These are the components that everything else uses, but that don't use anything themselves. The first task is to construct a *test harness* or *test bed* for each component. This is a specially constructed program whose sole function is to invoke the component under test in a way that is consistent with its eventual role in the complete system. Almost certainly, special test data is also required. Figure 19.1 shows two components at the lowest level of a system and their test harnesses.

One matter of immediate note is that a test harness may itself be a sizable complex program, requiring considerable development and testing time itself. Preparation of the test data may also involve considerable effort. These both constitute a big overhead on the project – and they are not even part of the completed system.

When the lowest-level components have been tested in this manner, modules are combined into subsystems that are tested in a similar manner, again using a test harness (Figure 19.2). The procedure continues until the complete system is finally assembled and tested as a whole.

This, then, is the bottom-up method of testing. It suffers from the following drawbacks:

(a) Considerable time can be spent on the construction of test harnesses and test data. Worse still, they are sometimes thrown away when testing is complete. This has been likened to the act of a carpenter, who, having made him or herself a new set of tools specially to build a new house, destroys the tools when the house is complete. (The analogy is intended to demonstrate the waste of effort that is involved.) Alternatively test beds and test data are retained so that when enhancements or corrections are carried out it can be ensured that the components that worked previously still work. In this case the test material has itself to be stored and maintained, consuming more valuable effort.

(b) Errors that are found at the integration stages of subsystem testing require repetition of the whole process of designing, coding, and unit testing. Subsystems or components may have to be repeatedly reworked as more and more of the system is integrated. No wonder that it is common experience that system testing

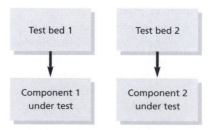

Figure 19.1 Bottom-up testing of the lowest-level components

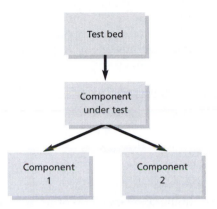

Figure 19.2. Bottom-up testing at an intermediate stage

can account for the major proportion (roughly between a third and a half) of a project timescale.

Why is it that system testing is so time-consuming? After all, if all the individual modules work correctly, why don't they all work when they are combined? The answer is, of course, that it is precisely in their interaction that errors will be exposed. For example, there may be a discrepancy in understanding the exact task of a procedure or the nature of the parameters to be supplied. A more complex situation is where modules access shared data or data structures.

(c) Because testing of the complete system is carried out towards the end of the project, it is often the case that major flaws in the system design are not discovered until near the planned completion time. This discovery could lead to the reconstruction of large parts of the system at a very embarrassing time.

(d) There is no visible, working system until the very last stage, system testing, is complete. True there are tested components and subsystems, but there is normally nothing that can be demonstrated to the client as even providing a limited vision of what the system will eventually do.

All these problems can compound the problems of a team already struggling to meet a deadline. No wonder that long hours of work result and, in turn, mistakes occur as circumstances appear to conspire against the project.

Top-down development helps to avoid some of these problems, as we now explain.

19.11 ● Top-down development

Top-down development is one valuable approach to the development of software. It proceeds as follows. Design commences with the highest-level components of the system or program. However, before lower levels are designed, the highest level is coded. In an on-line system that presents a hierarchy of screens to the user, this highest level is probably the piece of program that presents the initial main screen to the user. Program "stubs" are used to stand in for invoked but as yet unwritten lower-level components. These stubs are rudimentary replacements for missing programs or procedures. A stub does one of the following:

1. carries out an easily-written simulation of the mission of the component
2. outputs a message indicating that the component has been executed.
3. does nothing.

Test data is constructed as necessary and the system is assembled and tested. An immediate outcome is that we can very quickly have something that works. Not only that but it is the most crucial part of the system. We can also have something that can be demonstrated to the client as performing some imitation of the total system.

Implementation proceeds by selecting lower-level components (formerly stubs) for design and coding and incorporation into the system. In general, at any stage in the development there are (see Figure 19.3):

● higher-level components which have already been tested
● the single component which is under test
● stubs.

Clearly, development will not, and should not always proceed according to the above textbook prescription. Some variations of the method and some difficulties that may arise are as follows.

First, development will not always proceed on a rigid level-by-level basis. In practice some low-level components need to be designed, coded, and tested at an early stage. An example might be the development of those parts of a program that interact with the user. The screen formats could be shown to the eventual user of the program who will often request modifications. The sooner these requirements are clarified, the better. A system that is developed using Visual Basic (Chapter 18) demonstrates this perfectly.

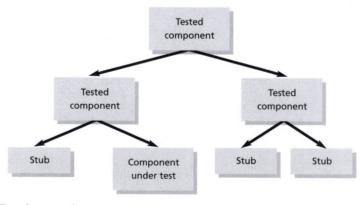

Figure 19.3 Top-down testing

Using Visual Basic, the screen layouts for the application are designed first. The screens can be shown to a potential user for validation of their requirements. The application runs, but all the screen widgets do nothing. Next, one of the widgets – a button, for example – is selected and the code that responds to it keyed in for execution. This can continue in a top-down fashion until the application is complete.

Second, some programmers favor a variation of the approach we have described. They fear that having translated some of their design into code and tested it, they will later find that, as a result of developing lower-level components, there is a mistake in the higher-level components. This would necessitate annoying redesign, recoding, and retesting. An alternative approach, which retains many of the benefits of the method, is to complete the design of the entire program or system before embarking on top-down coding and testing.

Finally another objection to strict use of the method is that it is often much easier for the programmer to test a component in isolation, rather than as a part of the higher-level system. Indeed sometimes it is difficult in top-down testing to generate enough test data for a module. In cases where this is true, it may be best that the new component is incorporated in good time to test its interfaces in its true environment.

Some of the claims made for top-down implementation are as follows:

(a) *Early detection of major flaws* One of the main problems with bottom-up development is that faults with the highest level of design are not discovered until the complete system is tested – at the very end of the project. Such major design problems can require the reconstruction of large parts of the system. On the other hand, top-down development ensures that the major components and interfaces are tested first, when any errors can be corrected without rewriting a lot of program. Thus the method can reduce the effort spent in developing a system and help with meeting the completion deadline.

 The argument assumes that the higher-level parts of a program are in some sense the most important. On the contrary, however, it may well be that some low-level aspect of the problem, in the data perhaps, has been neglected and is crucial. If top-down development is being employed this could lead to major redesign effort at a late stage.

(b) *Reliability* Once incorporated into top-down testing, software components are thereafter tested again and again, acting as test beds for lower-level parts of the program. With so much repeated testing of the final code (rather than temporary test beds), there is a greater chance of detecting faults. Note also that it will be the higher-level program components that will tend to be most reliable.

(c) *Debugging* Finding out exactly where a fault is located is easier in top-down implementation. This is because stubs are replaced one at a time by the fully implemented component. Thus there is a high probability that any fault lies in the single new component or in its interface with the higher-level modules. In contrast, in a bottom-up environment, usually a number of components are combined together for the first time in a single step. So in this case any errors which arise are due to faults in any of the new components or any of the newly tried interfaces. This poses a much more formidable problem of pin-pointing.

Note, however, that this advantage is not peculiar to top-down implementation – it is shared by any scheme in which just one new component is incorporated at a time. (This is sometimes known as *incremental testing*.) What top-down testing does is to systematically create situations where incremental testing is straightforward. But the same can be done in a bottom-up fashion.

(d) *Morale* A feature of top-down implementation can be the appearance of a tangible, working system at a very early stage in the development of the software. Although the system does not have the full capabilities of the final system, its presence can reassure managers, clients, and the members of the team that something has actually been produced and that the full system is not too far away.

(e) *Prototyping* Top-down implementation means that an early version of a system can be demonstrated as a prototype to its users. The users can therefore comment on the system and suggest changes before any significant work has been carried out. They can continue to be involved as the software is developed making suggestions so that eventually the system matches their needs exactly.

(f) *Programmer time* Overall top-down implementation may involve significantly less programmer time. Two reasons have already been mentioned – the early detection of major flaws (reducing rework) and the fast location of bugs. But perhaps the greatest saving is in constructing test beds and test data. In top-down implementation and testing, test beds do not need to be constructed, as the already-tested higher-level part of the program acts in this role. Although program stubs do need to be constructed, they tend to be significantly simpler. Similarly the data that is prepared to test the whole system can often be used from the start in the top-down method, avoiding the time spent in devising data especially for each unit test.

Top-down development is a technique that is well-suited to projects that are undertaken by a team of programmers. Some of the difficulties of working in teams are discussed in Chapter 22, but there is one issue that relates particularly to this method. Top-down development begins with the complete implementation of the highest levels of the program or system. In most organizations this would be carried out by a single senior software engineer. At this stage, therefore, there is nothing for the other, possibly more junior, members of the team to do. There can be a strong temptation to assign to the other members of the team the development of some low-level modules that are expected to be required. This is a tendency that should be firmly resisted, since it brings with it all the problems inherent in bottom-up development. One solution to this problem is to delay the assignment of programmers to the project until the high-level parts of the system are complete. This, of course, requires careful planning, but no more so than any other development scheme.

19.12 ● Summary

● Verification is about software correctness; validation is about meeting the users' needs.
● Exhaustive testing is a practical impossibility.

● In black box (or functional) testing, sample data based on the specification is used.
● In white box (or structural) testing, the internal structure of the software is used to select test data.
● People tend to be blind to their own errors, so a variety of team verification techniques such as walkthroughs and inspections allow others to attack the problem.
● Formal methods of verification provide a definitive technique for demonstrating program correctness, but it requires special skills and is extremely labor intensive.
● Particularly with a large piece of software, monolithic testing can be very time-consuming and so incremental techniques can be very valuable. Bottom-up testing requires the time-consuming construction of test beds, and it often tests new modules in groups rather than individually, but it has a role in certain circumstances. Generally, top-down development probably requires less programmer time, gives better awareness of project progress, and leads to more reliable software. Most important, perhaps, users of the system can see early, working versions of the software – prototypes – in order to check that it meets their requirements. This is a powerful aid to validation.

EXERCISES

19.1 Consider a program that has 16 `if...then` statements in it. Then there are 2^{16} possible paths through it. If each test takes 50 microseconds and each action takes 50 microseconds (a gross underestimate), how much computer time is needed to test all program paths?

19.2 Devise black box and white box test data to test the following program. The program specification is:

The program inputs a series of integers from the keyboard using a text field. The program finds the largest of the numbers. The numbers are terminated when a button labeled `Start Again` is pressed.

Try not to look at the text of the program, given below, until you have completed the design of the black box data.

The program involves the following class:

```
class Biggest {
    private int largest;

    public Biggest() {
        largest = 0;
    }

    public void nextNumber(int n) {
        if (n > largest)
            largest = n;
    }
```

```
        public void display(Graphics g) {
            g.drawString(" largest so far is" + largest, 50, 50);
        }
        public void startAgain() {
            largest = 0;

        }
    }
```

19.3 Devise black box and white box test data to test the following program. The program specification is:

The program is to determine insurance premiums for a holiday, based upon the age and gender (male or female) of the client.

For a female of age ≥18 and ≤30 the premium is $5. A female aged ≥31 pays $3.50. A male of age ≥18 and ≤35 pays $6. A male aged ≥36 pays $5.50. People aged 50 or more pay half premium. Any other ages or genders are an error, which is signaled as a premium of zero.

The code for this program is:

```
public float calcPremium(float age, String gender) {
    float premium;
    if (gender.equals("female"))
        if ((age >= 18) && (age <= 30))
            premium = 5.0f;
        else
            if (age >= 31)
                premium = 3.50f;
            else
                premium = 0.0f;
    else
        if (gender.equals("male"))
            if ((age >= 18) && (age <= 35))
                premium = 6.0f;
            else
                if (age >= 36)
                    premium = 5.5f;
                else
                    premium = 0.0f;
        else
            premium = 0.0f;
    if (age >= 50)
        premium = premium * 0.5f;
    return premium;
}
```

19.4 Suggest features for software tools that could assist in using each of the following techniques:

(a) black box testing
(b) white box testing
(c) inspection.

19.5 Substantial testing of a system uncovers not a single error. What conclusions would you draw?

19.6 Is there any difference in the work involved during testing whether it is carried out top-down or bottom-up?

19.7 Suggest examples of situations in which top-down implementation and testing would/would not be advantageous.

19.8 Compare and contrast walkthroughs with inspections.

19.9 Suggest how walkthroughs could be introduced into an organization.

ANSWERS TO SELF TEST QUESTIONS

19.1 The specification does not stipulate any limits on the size of the integers, so we assume the maximum range possible.

Each of the data values can take values from minus a large number to plus a large number. We partition the range of each data value into negative, zero, and positive. We then choose a representative value from each:

First number:	−9	0	+34
Second number:	−56	0	+4
Third number:	−2	0	123

So the black box test data is all combinations of these values:

Test No			
1	−9	−56	−2
2	−9	−56	0
3	−9	−56	123
4	−9	0	−2
5	−9	0	0

etc.

Any one of the three data values could be the largest, so we check that we have tested for all three cases (we have).

Finally we realize that the specification does not stipulate what happens if two or more of the inputs are equal. So we either query the specification with the client, or we make a reasonable assumption. Suppose we assume that if two or more values are equal, the program should display the largest value. Test data for this is:

Test No			
1	4	4	2
2	2	5	5
3	6	4	6
4	3	3	3

19.2 A row number is in three partitions:

- within the range 1 to 8 (say 3)
- less than 1 (say –3)
- greater than 8 (say 11).

If we choose one representative value in each partition and a similar value for the column numbers (5, –2, and 34), the test data will be:

Test No		
1	3	5
2	–3	5
3	11	5
4	3	–2
5	–3	–2
6	11	–2
7	3	34
8	–3	34
9	11	34

We might consider that data near the boundary of the partitions is important and therefore add to the test data for each partition so that it becomes:

- within the range 1 to 8 (say 3)
- less than 1 (say –3)
- greater than 8 (say 11)
- 1
- 8
- 0
- 9

which now gives many more combinations to use as test data.

19.3 There are four paths through the program which can be exercised by the following test data:

Test No			
1	3	2	1
2	3	2	5
3	2	3	1
4	2	3	5

19.4 There are three paths through the program extract, including the path where neither of the conditions in the `if` statements are true. But each of the error messages can be triggered by two conditions. Suitable test data is therefore:

Test no	row	col
1	5	6
2	0	4
3	9	4
4	5	9
5	5	0

FURTHER READING

This book surveys studies of the types of fault that occur and explains the different testing methods, in a very readable way: Marc Roper, *Software Testing*, McGraw-Hill, 1994.

The following book describes lessons in debugging and testing learned at Microsoft. The author, Steve Maguire, is a strong advocate of stepping through code using the debugger as a good way of finding bugs. The examples given are in C. Steve Maguire, *Writing Solid Code*, Microsoft Press, 1993.

The classic book which introduced the idea of ego-less programming, the precursor to walkthroughs and inspections: G. Weinberg, *The Psychology of Computer Programming*, Van Nostrand Reinhold, 1971.

The original reference describing the technique of inspections: M. E. Fagan, Design and Code Inspections to Reduce Errors in Program Development, *IBM Systems Journal*, 15 (3), (July 1976), pp. 182–211.

Full of practical advice and case studies, jointly authored by one of the industry gurus, all you ever wanted to know about inspections is explained in: Tom Gilb and Dorothy Graham, *Software Inspection*, Addison-Wesley, 1993.

A collection of useful papers on how to do inspections and what the benefits are: David A Wheeler, Bill Brykczynski and Reginald N. Meeson, *Software Inspection. An Industry Best Practice*. IEEE Computer Society Press, 1996.

An example of an experiment, mentioned in the text, comparing the effectiveness of various verification methods: G. J. Myers, A Controlled Experiment in Program Testing and Code Walkthroughs/Inspections, *Communications of the ACM*, 21 (9), (September 1978).

The Open Source movement suggest that the best way to reduce errors in software is to publish the source code on the Internet and allow anyone in the world to debug it. This approach is discussed in: Chris DiBona, Sam Ockman and Mark Stone, *Open Sources: Voices from the Open Source Revolution*, O'Reilly Publishing, 1999.

20

Software fault tolerance and exceptions

This chapter explains:

- how to categorize faults
- how faults can be detected
- how recovery can be made from faults
- exception handling
- recovery blocks
- *n*-version programming.

20.1 ● Introduction

Computer faults are often classified according to who causes them:

- user errors
- software faults (bugs)
- hardware faults.

An example of a user error is entering alphabetic data when numeric data is expected. An example of a software fault is any of the many bugs that inhabit any software system. An example of a hardware fault is a disk failure or a telecommunication line that fails to respond.

In fault tolerance, the hardware and software collaborate in a kind of symbiosis. Sometimes the hardware detects a software fault; sometimes the software detects a hardware fault. Normally it is the software that takes remedial action. In some designs, when a hardware fault occurs, the hardware copes with the situation. But often it is the role of the software to deal with the problem. When a software fault occurs it is usually the job of the software to deal with the problem. In some systems, when a user error arises, again it is the role of the software to cope. In many situations, of course, when a fault arises nothing is done to cope with it and the system crashes. This chapter explores measures that can be taken to detect and deal with all types of computer fault, with emphasis on remedial measures that are implemented by software.

We have seen in Chapter 19 that eradicating every bug from a program is almost impossible. Even though using formal mathematical methods for program development helps to improve the reliability of software, human error creeps in. In striving to make a piece of software as reliable as possible we have to use a whole range of techniques. The algorithm for developing reliable software looks something like this:

```
use a good method to design the software
use a structured walkthrough to check the design and coding
employ a compiler with good compile-time checking
if compilation errors then correct errors manually endif
test the software systematically
if errors then correct errors manually endif
provide run-time checking
if there is a failure
then
        halt the system
        correct errors manually
else
        carry out fault tolerance
endif
```

Software fault tolerance is concerned with trying to keep a system going in the face of faults. The term *intolerance* is sometimes used to describe software that is written with the assumption that the system will always work correctly. By contrast, fault *tolerance* recognizes that faults are inevitable and that therefore it is necessary to cope with them. Moreover, in a well-designed system, we strive to cope with faults in an organized, systematic manner.

We will distinguish between two types of faults – *anticipated* and *unanticipated*. Anticipated faults are unusual situations, but we can fairly easily foresee that they will occasionally arise. Examples are

● division by zero
● floating point overflow
● numeric data that contains letters
● attempting to open a file that does not exist.

What are *unanticipated faults*? The name suggests that we cannot even identify, predict or give a name to any of them. (Logically, if we can identify them, they are anticipated faults.) In reality this category is used to describe very unusual situations. Examples are:

- hardware faults (e.g. an input–output device error or a memory parity fault)
- a software design fault (i.e. a bug)
- an array subscript that is outside its allowed range
- the detection of a violation by the computer's memory protection mechanism.

Take the last example of a memory protection fault. Languages like C++ allow the programmer to use memory addresses to refer to parameters and to data structures. Access to pointers is very free and the programmer can (for example) actually carry out arithmetic on pointers. This sort of freedom is a common source of errors in C++ programs. Worse still, errors of this type can be very difficult to eradicate (debug) and may persist unseen until the software has been in use for some time. Of course this type of error is a mistake made by a programmer, designer, or tester – a type of error sometimes known as a logic error. The hardware memory protection system can help with the detection of errors of this type because often the erroneous use of a pointer will eventually lead to an attempt to use an illegal address.

Clearly the difference between anticipated and unanticipated faults is a rather arbitrary distinction. A better terminology might be the words "exceptional circumstances" and "catastrophic failures." Whatever jargon we use, we shall see that the two categories of failure are best dealt with by two different mechanisms.

Having identified the different types of faults, let us now look at what has to be done when a fault occurs. In general, we have to do some or all of the following:

1. detect that a fault has occurred
2. assess the extent of the damage that has been caused
3. repair the damage
4. treat the cause of the fault.

As we shall see, different mechanisms deal with these requirements in different ways.

SELF TEST QUESTION

20.1 Categorize the following eventualities:

1. The system stack (used to hold temporary variables and procedure return addresses) overflows.
2. The system heap (used to store dynamic objects and data structures) overflows.
3. A program tries to refer to an object using the null pointer (a pointer that points to no object).
4. The computer power fails.
5. The user types a URL that does not obey the rules for valid URLs.

How serious a problem may become depends on the type of the computer application. For example power failure may not be serious (though annoying) to the user of a personal computer. But a power failure in a safety-critical system is serious.

20.2 ● Fault detection by software

We have seen that faults can be prevented and detected during software development using the following techniques:

- good design
- using structured walkthroughs
- employing a compiler with good compile-time checking
- testing systematically
- run-time checking.

Techniques for software design, structured walkthroughs, and testing are discussed elsewhere in this book. So now we consider the other two techniques from this list – compile-time checking and run-time checking. Later we go on to discuss the details of automatic mechanisms for run-time checking.

20.2.1 Compile-time checking

The types of errors that can be detected by a compiler are:

- a type inconsistency, e.g. an attempt to perform an addition on data that has been declared with the type `character`.
- a misspelled name for a variable or procedure
- an attempt by an instruction to access a variable outside its legal scope.

These checks may seem routine and trivial. But remember the enormous cost of the NASA probe sent to Venus, which veered off course because of the erroneous Fortran repetition statement:

```
DO 3 I = 1.3
```

This was interpreted by the compiler as an assignment statement, giving the value `1.3` to the variable `DO 3 I`. In the Fortran language, variables do not have to be declared before they are used and if Fortran was more vigilant, the compiler would have signaled that a variable `DO 3 I` was undeclared.

20.2.2 Run-time checking

Errors that can be automatically detected at run-time include:

- division by zero
- an array subscript outside the range of the array.

In some systems these are carried by the software and in others by hardware.

There is something of a controversy about the relative merits of compile-time and run-time checking. The compile-time people scoff at the run-time people. They compare the situation to that of an aircraft with its "black box" flight recorder. The black box is completely impotent in the sense that it is unable to prevent the aircraft from crashing. Its only ability is in helping diagnose what happened, after the event. In terms of software, compile-time checking can *prevent* a program from crashing, but run-time checking can only detect faults. Compile-time checking is very cheap and it needs only to be done once. Unfortunately, it imposes constraints on the language – like strong typing – which limits the freedom of the programmer (see Chapter 13 for a discussion of this issue). On the other hand run-time checking is a continual overhead. It has to be done whenever the program is running and it is therefore expensive. Usually, in order to preserve performance, it is done by hardware rather than software.

In general, it seems that compile-time checking is better than run-time checking. However, run-time checking has the last word. It is vital, because not everything can be checked at compile time.

SELF TEST QUESTION

20.2 Add to the list above checks that can only be done at run-time and therefore, by implication, cannot be done at compile-time.

Incidentally, it is common practice to switch on all sorts of automatic checking for the duration of program testing, but then to switch off the checking when development is complete – because of concern about performance overheads. For example, some C++ compilers allow the programmer to switch on array subscript checking (during debugging and testing), but also allow the checking to be removed (when the program is put into productive use). C. A. R. Hoare, the eminent computer scientist, has compared this approach to that of testing a ship with the lifeboats on board but then discarding them when the ship starts to carry passengers.

We have looked at automatic checking for general types of fault. Another way of detecting faults is to write additional software to carry out checks at strategic times during the execution of a program. Such software is sometimes called an *audit module*, because of the analogy with accounting practices. In an organization that handles money, auditing is carried out at different times in order to detect any fraud. An example of a simple audit module is a procedure to check that a square root has been correctly calculated. Because all it has to do is to multiply the answer by itself, such a module is very fast. This example illustrates that the process of checking for faults by software need not be costly – either in programming effort or in run-time performance.

SELF TEST QUESTION

20.3 Devise an audit module that checks whether an array has been sorted correctly.

Another term used to describe software that attempts to detect faults is *defensive programming*. It is normal to check (validate) data when it enters a computer system – for example, numbers are commonly scrupulously checked to see that they only contain digits. But within software it is unusual to carry out checks on data because it is normally assumed that the software works correctly. In defensive programming the programmer inserts checks at strategic places throughout the program to provide detection of design errors. A natural place to do this is to check the parameters are valid at the entry to a procedure and then again when a procedure has completed its work.

Using *assertions* is a similar technique. Assertions are statements written into software that say what should be true of the data. Assertions have been used since the early days of programming as an aid to verifying the correctness of programs. An assertion states what should always be true at a particular point in a program. Assertions and invariants are also discussed in Chapter 4. Assertions are usually placed:

● at the entry to a procedure – called a precondition, it states what the relationship between the parameters should be

● at the end of a procedure – called a post-condition, it states what the relationship between the parameters should be

● within a loop – called a loop invariant, it states what is always true, before and after each loop iteration, however many iterations the loop has performed

● at the head of a class (in an object-oriented software component) – called a class invariant, it states what is always true before and after a call on any of the class's public procedures. This is a relationship between the variables of an instance of the class.

An example should help see how assertions can be used. Take the example of a class (in an object-oriented program) that provides a data structure called a stack. Items can be placed in the data structure by calling the public procedure `push` and removed by calling `pop`. Let us assume that the stack has a fixed length, described by a variable called `capacity`. Suppose the class uses a variable called `count` to record how many items are currently in the stack. Then we can make the following assertions at the level of the class. These class invariants are:

```
assert(count >= 0);
assert(capacity >= count);
```

These are statements which must always be true for the entire class, before or after any use is made of the class. We can also make assertions for the individual procedures. Thus for procedure `push`, we can say as a post-condition:

```
assert(count' = count + 1);
```

where the ' annotation means the new value of `count`, on exit from the procedure. For
the procedure `push`, we can also make the following pre-condition:

```
assert(count < capacity);
```

SELF TEST QUESTION

20.4 Write pre- and post-conditions for procedure `pop`.

Note that truth of assertions does not guarantee that the software is working correctly.
However, if the value of an assertion is false, then there certainly is a fault in the software. Note also that violation of a pre-condition means that there is a fault in the user
of the procedure; a violation of a post-condition means a fault in the procedure itself.

There are two main ways to make use of assertions. One way is to write assertions as
comments in a program, to assist in manual verification. On the other hand, as indicated
by the notation used above, certain programming languages allow assertions to be written as part of the language – and their correctness is checked at run-time. If an assertion
is found to be false, a fault has been detected. The choice is to allow the software to crash
or to take some action to tolerate the fault (as we shall see later).

20.3 ● Fault detection by hardware

We have already seen how software checks can reveal faults. Hardware can also be vital
in detecting consequences of software errors such as:

● division by zero, more generally arithmetic overflow
● an array subscript outside the range of the array
● a program which tries to access a region of memory that it is denied access to, e.g. the
operating system.

Of course hardware also detects hardware faults, which the hardware often passes on to
the software for action. These include:

● memory parity checks
● device time-outs
● communication line faults.

20.3.1 Memory protection systems

One major technique for detecting faults in software is to use hardware protection mechanisms that separate one software component from another. (Protection mechanisms

have a different and important role in connection with data security and privacy, which we are not considering here.) A good protection mechanism can make an important contribution to the detection and localization of bugs. A violation detected by the memory protection mechanism means that a program has gone berserk – usually because of a design flaw.

To introduce the topic we will use the analogy of a large office block where many people work. Along with many other provisions for safety, there will usually be a number of fire walls and fire doors. What exactly is their purpose? In the olden days, people were allowed to smoke in offices and public buildings. If someone in one office dropped a cigarette into a waste paper basket and caused a fire, the fire walls helped to save those in other offices. In other words, the walls limited the spread of damage. In computing terms, does it matter how much the software is damaged by a fault? After all it is merely code in a memory that can easily be reloaded. The answer is "yes," for two reasons. First, the damage caused by a software fault might damage vital information held in files, damage other programs running in the system, or crash the complete system. Second, the better that the spread of damage is limited, the easier it will be to attempt some repair and recovery. Later, when the cause of the fire is being investigated, the walls help to pinpoint its source (and identify the culprit). In software terminology, the walls help find the cause of the fault – the bug.

One of the problems in designing buildings is the question of where to place the firewalls. How many of them should there be, and where should they be placed? In software language, this is called the issue of *granularity*. The greater the number of walls, the better any damage will be limited and the easier it will be to find the cause. But walls are expensive and they also constrain normal movement within the building.

SELF TEST QUESTION

20.5 Sum up the pros and cons of fine granularity.

Let us analyze what sort of protection we need within programs. At a minimum we do not want a fault in one program to affect other programs or the operating system. We therefore want protection against programs accessing each other's main memory space. Next it would help if a program could not change its own instructions, although this would not necessarily be true in functional or logic programming. This idea prompts us to consider whether we should have firewalls *within* programs to protect programs against themselves. Many computer systems provide no such facility – when a program goes berserk, it can overwrite anything within the memory available to it. But if we examine a typical program, it consists of fixed code (instructions), data items that do not change (constants), and data items that are updated. So at a minimum, we should expect these to be protected in different ways. But of course, there is more structure to a program than this. If we look at any program, it consists of procedures, each with its own data. Procedures share data. One procedure updates a piece of data, while another merely references it. The ways in which procedures access variables can be complex.

In many programs, the pattern of access to data is not hierarchical, nor does it fit into any other regular framework. We need a matrix in order to describe the situation. Each row of the matrix corresponds to a procedure. Each column corresponds to a data item. Looking at a particular place in the table gives the allowed access of a procedure to a piece of data.

To summarize the requirements we might expect of a protection mechanism, we need the access rights of a program to *change* as it enters and leaves procedures. An individual procedure may need:

- execute access to its code
- read access to parameters
- read access to local data
- write access to local data
- read access to constants
- read or write access to a file or i/o device
- read or write access to some data shared with another program
- execute access to other procedures.

SELF TEST QUESTION

20.6 Investigate a piece of program that you have lying around and analyze what the access rights of a particular procedure need to be.

Different computer architectures provide a range of mechanisms ranging from the absence of any protection in most early microcomputers, to sophisticated segmentation systems in the modern machines. They include the following systems:

- base and limit registers
- lock and key
- mode switch
- segmentation
- capabilities.

A discussion of these topics is outside the scope of this book, but is to be found in books on computer architecture and on operating systems.

This completes a brief overview of the mechanisms that can be provided by the hardware of the computer to assist in fault tolerance. The beauty of hardware mechanisms is that they can be mass-produced and therefore can be made cheaply, whereas software checks are tailor-made and may be expensive to develop. Additionally, checks carried out by hardware may not affect performance as badly as checks carried out by software.

20.4 ● Dealing with damage

Dealing with the damage caused by a fault encompasses two activities:

1. assessing the extent of the damage
2. repairing the damage.

In most systems, both of these ends are achieved by the same mechanism. There are two alternative strategies for dealing with the situation:

1. forward error recovery
2. backward error recovery.

In *forward error recovery*, the attempt is made to continue processing, repairing any damaged data and resuming normal processing. This is perhaps more easily understood when placed in contrast with the second technique. In *backward error recovery*, periodic dumps (or snapshots) of the state of the system are taken at appropriate *recovery points*. These dumps must include information about any data (in main memory or in files) that is being changed by the system. When a fault occurs, the system is "rolled back" to the most recent recovery point. The state of the system is then restored from the dump, and processing is resumed. This type of error recovery is common practice in information systems because of the importance of protecting valuable data.

If you are cooking a meal and you burn the pan, you can do one of two things. You can scrape off the burnt food and serve the unblemished food (pretending to your family or friends that nothing happened). This is forward error recovery. Alternatively you can start the preparation of the damaged dish again. This is backward error recovery.

SELF TEST QUESTION

20.7 You are driving your car, when you get a flat tire. You change the tire and continue. What strategy are you adopting – forward or backward error recovery?

Now that we have identified two strategies for error recovery, we return to our analysis of the two main types of error. Anticipated faults can be analyzed and predicted. Their effects are known and treatment can be planned in detail. Therefore forward error recovery is not only possible but most appropriate. On the other hand, the effects of unanticipated faults are largely unpredictable and therefore backward error recovery is probably the only possible technique. But we shall also see how a forward error recovery scheme can be used to cope with design faults.

20.5 ● Exceptions and exception handlers

We have already seen that we can define a class of faults that arise only occasionally, but are easily predicted. The trouble with occasional error situations is that, once detected, it is sometimes difficult to cope with them in an organized way. Suppose, for example, we want a user to enter a number, an integer, into a text field, see Figure 20.1.

The number represents an age, which the program uses to see whether the person can vote or note. First we look at a fragment of this Java program without exception handling. When a number has been entered into the text field, the event causes a procedure called `actionPerformed` to be called. This procedure extracts the text from the text field called `ageField` by calling the library procedure `getText`. It then calls the library function `parseInt` to convert the text into an integer and places it in the integer variable `age`. Finally the value of age is tested and the appropriate message displayed:

```java
public void actionPerformed(ActionEvent event) {
        String string = ageField.getText();
        age = Integer.parseInt(string);
        if (age > 18)
            response.setText("you can vote");
        else
            response.setText("you cannot vote");
    }
```

This piece of program, as written, provides no exception handling. It assumes that nothing will go wrong. So if the user enters something that is not a valid integer, procedure `parseInt` will fail. In this eventuality, the program needs to display an error message and solicit new data, see Figure 20.2.

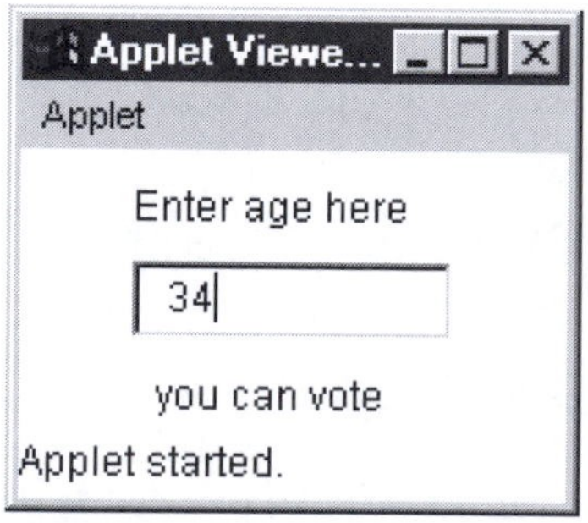

Figure 20.1 Program showing normal behavior

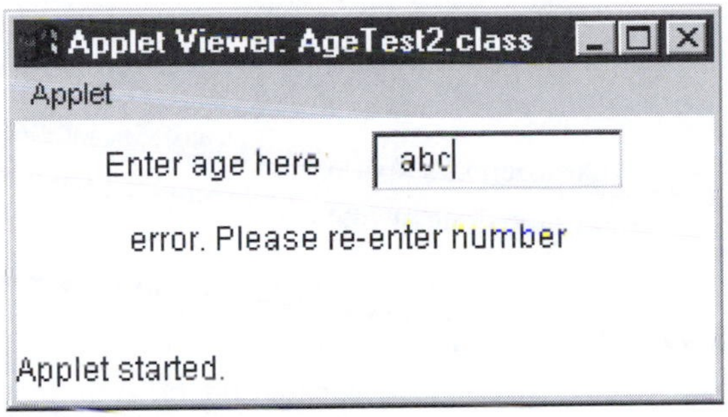

Figure 20.2 Program showing exceptional behavior

To the programmer, checking for erroneous data is additional work, a nuisance, that detracts from the central purpose of the program. For the user of the program, however, it is important that the program carries out vigilant checking of the data and when appropriate displays an informative error message and clear instructions as to how to proceed. What exception handling allows the programmer to do is to show clearly what is normal processing and what is exceptional processing.

Here is the same piece of program, but now written using exception handling. In the terminology of exception handling, the program first makes a *try* to carry out some action. If something goes wrong, an exception is *thrown* by a piece of program that detects an error. Next the program *catches* the exception and deals with it.

```
public void actionPerformed(ActionEvent event) {
    String string = ageField.getText();
    try {
        age = Integer.parseInt(string);
    }
    catch (NumberFormatException e){
        response.setText("error. Please re-enter number");
        return;
    }
    if (age > 18)
        response.setText("you can vote");
    else
        response.setText("you cannot vote");
}
```

In the example, the program carries out a `try` operation, enclosing the section of program that is being attempted. Should the procedure `parseInt` detect an error, it throws a `NumberFormatException` exception. When this happens, the section of program enclosed by the `catch` keyword is executed. As shown, this displays an error message to the user of the program.

The addition of the exception-handling code does not cause a great disturbance to this program, but it does highlight what checking is being carried out and what action will be taken in the event of an exception. The possibility of the procedure `parseInt` throwing an exception must be regarded as part of the specification of `parseInt`. The contract for using `parseInt` is:

1. It is provided with one parameter (a string).
2. It returns an integer (the equivalent of the string).
3. It throws a `NumberFormatException` if the string contains illegal characters.

There are, of course, other ways of dealing with exceptions, but arguably they are less elegant. For example, the `parseInt` procedure could be written so that it returns a special value for the integer (say –999) if something has gone wrong. The call on `parseInt` would look like this:

```
age = Integer.parseInt(string);
if (age == -999)
    response.setText("error. Please re-enter number");
else
    if (age > 18)
        response.setText("you can vote");
    else
        response.setText("you cannot vote");
```

You can see that this is inferior to the `try-catch` program. It is more complex and intermixes the normal case with the exceptional case. Another serious problem with this approach is that we have had to identify a special case of the data value – a value that might be needed at some time.

Yet another strategy is to include in every call an additional parameter to convey error information. The problem with this solution is, again, that the program becomes encumbered with the additional parameter and additional testing associated with every procedure call, like this:

```
age = Integer.parseInt(string, error);
if (error) etc
```

Let us turn to examining how an exception is thrown, using the same example. In Java, the method `parseInt` can be written as follows:

```
public int parseInt(String string) throws NumberFormatException {
    int number = 0;
    for (int i = 0; i < string.length(); i++) {
        char c = string.charAt(i);
        if (c < '0' || c > '9') throw new NumberFormatException();
        number = number 1 10 + (c - '0');
    }
    return number;
}
```

You can see that in the heading of the procedure the exception that may be thrown is declared, along with the specification of any parameters and return value. If this procedure detects that any of the characters within the string are illegal, it executes a `throw` instruction. This immediately terminates the method and transfers control to a `catch` block designed to handle the exception. In our example, the `catch` block is within the method that calls `parseInt`. Alternatively the `try-catch` combination can be written within the same procedure as the `throw` statement. Or it can be written within any of the procedures in the calling chain that led to calling `parseInt`. Thus the designer can choose an appropriate place in the software structure at which to carry out exception handling. The position in which the exception handler is written helps both to determine the action to be taken and what happens after it has dealt with the situation.

SELF TEST QUESTION

20.8 The procedure `parseInt` does not throw an exception if the string is of zero length. Amend it so that it throws the same exception in this situation.

What happens after an exception has been handled? In the above example, the `catch` block ends with a `return` statement, which exits from the current procedure, `actionPerformed`, and returns control to its caller. This is the appropriate action in this case – the program is able to recover and continue in a useful way. In general the options are either to recover from the exception and continue or to allow the program to gracefully degrade. The Java language mechanism supports various actions:

● Handle the exception: control flow then either continues on down the program or the procedure can be left using a `return` statement.
● Ignore the exception: this is highly dangerous and always leads to tears, probably after the software has been put into use.
● Throw another exception: this passes the buck to another exception handler further up the call chain, which the designer considers to be a more appropriate place to handle the exception.

SELF TEST QUESTION

20.9 What happens if the `return` statement is omitted in the above example of the exception handler?

In the above example, the application program itself detected the exception. Sometimes, however, it is the operating system or the hardware that detects an exception. An example is an attempt to divide by zero, which would typically be detected by the hardware. The hardware would alert the run-time system or operating system, which in turn would enter any exception handler associated with this exception.

The mechanism described above is the exception handling facility provided in Java. Similar mechanisms are provided in Ada and C++.

In old software systems the simplest solution to handling exceptions was to resort to the use of a `goto` statement to transfer control out of the immediate locality and into a piece of coding designed to handle the situation. The use of a `goto` was particularly appealing when the unusual situation occurred deep within a set of procedure calls. The `throw` statement has been criticized as being a `goto` statement in disguise. The response is that `throw` is indeed a "structured `goto`," but that its use is restricted to dealing with errors and therefore it cannot be used in an undisciplined way.

In summary, exception handlers allow software to cope with unusual, but anticipated, events. The software can take appropriate remedial action and continue with its tasks. Exception handlers therefore provide a mechanism for forward error recovery. In Java, the mechanism consists of three ingredients:

1. a `try` block, in which the program attempts to behave normally
2. the program `throws` an exception
3. a `catch` block handles the exceptional situation.

20.6 ● Recovery blocks

Recovery blocks are a way of structuring backward error recovery to cope with unanticipated faults. In backward error recovery, periodic dumps of the state of the system are made at recovery points. When a fault is detected, the system is restored to its state at the most recent recovery point. (The hope is that this is a correct state of the system.) The system now continues on from the recovery point, using some alternative course of action, so as to avoid the original problem.

An analogy: if you trip on a banana skin and spill your coffee, you can make a fresh cup (restore the state of the system) and carry on (carefully avoiding the banana skin).

As shown in Figure 20.3, backward error recovery needs:

1. the primary software component that is normally expected to work
2. a check that it has worked correctly
3. an alternative piece of software that can be used in the event of the failure of the primary module.

We also need, of course, a mechanism for taking dumps of the system state and for restoring the system state. The recovery block notation embodies all of these components. Taking as an example a program that uses a procedure to sort some information, a fault-tolerant fragment of program looks like this:

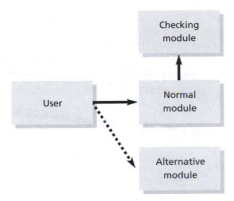

Figure 20.3 Components in a recovery block scheme

```
ensure dataStillValid
by
    superSort
else by
    quickSort
else by
    slowButSureSort
else error
```

Here superSort is the primary module. When it has tried to sort the information, the procedure dataStillValid, tests to see whether a failure occurred. If there was a fault, the state of the program is restored to what it was before the sort procedure was executed. The alternative procedure quickSort is then executed. Should this now fail, a third alternative is provided. If this fails, there is no other alternative available, and the whole module has failed. This does not necessarily mean that the whole program will fail, as there may be other recovery blocks programmed by the user of this sort module.

What kinds of fault is this scheme designed to cope with? The recovery block mechanism is designed primarily to deal with unanticipated faults that arise from bugs (design faults) in the software. When a piece of software is complete, it is to be expected that there will be residual faults in it. But what cannot be anticipated is the whereabouts of the bugs.

Recovery blocks will, however, also cope with hardware faults. For example suppose that a fault develops in the region of main memory containing the primary sort procedure. Then the recovery block mechanism can recover by switching over to an alternative procedure. There are stories that the developers of the recovery block mechanism at Newcastle University, England used to invite visitors to remove memory boards from a live computer, and observe that the computer continued apparently unaffected.

We now examine some of the other aspects of recovery blocks.

20.6.1 The acceptance test

You might think that acceptance tests would be cumbersome procedures, incurring high overheads. But this need not be so. Consider for example a procedure to calculate a square root. A procedure to check the outcome, simply by multiplying the answer by itself, is short and fast. Often, however, an acceptance test cannot be completely fool-proof – because of the performance overhead. Take the example of the sort procedure. The acceptance test could check that the information had been sorted, i.e. is in sequence. However, this does not guarantee that items have not been lost or created. An accept-ance test, therefore, does not normally attempt to ensure the correctness of the software, but instead carries out a check to see whether the results are acceptably good.

Note that if a fault like division by zero, a protection violation, or an array subscript out of range occurs while one of the sort procedures is being executed, then these also constitute the result of checks on the behavior of the software. (These are checks carried out by the hardware or the run-time system.) Thus either software acceptance tests or hardware checks can trigger fault tolerance.

20.6.2 The alternatives

The software components provided as backups must accomplish the same end as the pri-mary module. But they should achieve this by means of a different algorithm so that the same problem doesn't arise. Ideally the alternatives should be developed by different programmers, so that they are not unwittingly sharing assumptions. The alternatives should also be less complex than the primary, so that they will be less likely to fail. For this reason they will probably be poorer in their performance (speed).

Another approach is to create alternatives that provide an increasingly degraded serv-ice. This allows the system to exhibit what is termed *graceful degradation*. As an example of graceful degradation, consider a steel rolling mill in which a computer controls a machine that chops off the required lengths of steel. Normally the computer employs a sophisticated algorithm to make optimum use of the steel, while satisfying customers orders. Should this algorithm fail, a simpler algorithm can be used that processes the orders strictly sequentially. This means that the system will keep going, albeit less efficiently.

20.6.3 Implementation

The language constructs of the recovery block mechanism hide the preservation of vari-ables. The programmer does not need to explicitly declare which variables should be stored and when. The system must save values before any of the alternatives is executed, and restore them should any of the alternatives fail. Although this may seem a formid-able task, only the values of variables that are changed need to be preserved, and the notation highlights which ones these are. Variables local to the alternatives need not be stored, nor need parameters passed by value. Only global variables that are changed need to be preserved. Nonetheless, storing data in this manner probably incurs too high an overhead if it is carried out solely by software. Studies indicate that, suitably implemented with hardware assistance, the speed overhead might be no more than about 15%.

No programming language has yet incorporated the recovery block notation. Even so, the idea provides a framework which can be used, in conjunction with any programming language, to structure fault-tolerant software.

20.7 ● *N*-version programming

N-version programming means developing *n* versions of the same software component. For example, suppose a fly-by-wire airplane has a software component that decides how much the rudder should be moved in response to information about speed, pitch, throttle setting, etc. Three or more versions of the component are implemented and run concurrently. The outputs are compared by a voting module, the majority vote wins and is used to control the rudder (see Figure 20.4).

It is important that the different versions of the component are developed by different teams, using different methods and (preferably) at different locations, so that a minimum of assumptions are shared by the developers. By this means, the modules will use different algorithms, have different mistakes and produce different outputs (if they do) under different circumstances. Thus the chances are that when one of the components fails and produces an incorrect result, the others will perform correctly and the faulty component will be out-voted by the majority.

Clearly the success of an *n*-programming scheme depends on the degree of independence of the different components. If the majority embody a similar design fault, they will fail together and the wrong decision will be the outcome. This is a bold assumption, and some studies have shown a tendency for different developers to commit the same mistakes, probably because of shared misunderstandings of the (same) specification.

The expense of *n*-programming is in the effort to develop *n* versions, plus the processing overhead of running the multiple versions. If hardware reliability is also an issue, as in fly-by-wire airplanes, each version runs on a separate (but identical) processor. The voting module is small and simple, consuming minimal developer and processor time.

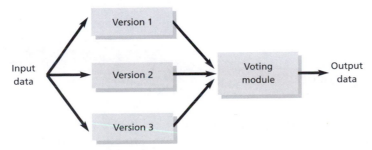

Figure 20.4 Triple modular redundancy

For obvious reasons, an even number of versions is not appropriate.

The main difference between the recovery block and the n-version schemes is that in the former the different versions are executed sequentially (if need be).

Is n-programming forward error recovery or is it backward error recovery? The answer is that, once an error is revealed, the correct behavior is immediately available and the system can continue forwards. So it is forward error recovery.

20.8 ● The role of fault tolerance

Fault tolerance in hardware has long been recognized and accommodated. Electronic engineers have frequently incorporated redundancy, such as triple modular redundancy, within the design of circuits to provide for hardware failure. Fault tolerance in software has become more widely addressed in the design of computer systems as it has become recognized that it is almost impossible to produce correct software. Exception handling is now supported by all the mainstream software engineering languages – Ada, C++, and Java. This means that designers can provide for failure in an organized manner, rather than in an *ad hoc* fashion. Particularly in safety-critical systems, either recovery blocks or n-programming is used to cope with design faults and enhance reliability.

Fault tolerance does, of course, cost money. It requires extra design and programming effort, extra memory and extra processing time to check for and handle exceptions. Some applications need greater attention to fault tolerance than others, and safety-critical systems are more likely to merit the extra attention of fault tolerance. However, even software packages that have no safety requirements often need fault tolerance of some kind. For example, we now expect a word processor to perform periodic and automatic saving of the current document, so that recovery can be performed in the event of power failure or software crash. End-users are increasingly demanding that the software cleans up properly after failures, rather than leave them with a mess that they cannot salvage. Thus it is likely that ever-increasing attention will be paid to improving the fault tolerance of software.

20.9 ● Summary

Faults in computer systems are caused by hardware failure, software bugs, and user error. Software fault tolerance is concerned with:

- detecting faults
- assessing damage
- repairing the damage
- continuing.

Of these, faults can be detected by both hardware and software.

One hardware mechanism for fault detection is protection mechanisms, which have two roles:

1. They limit the spread of damage, thus easing the job of fault tolerance.

2. They help find the cause of faults.

Faults can be classified into two categories – anticipated and unanticipated. Recovery mechanisms are of two types:

● backward – the system returns to an earlier, safe state

● forward – the system continues onwards from the error.

Anticipated faults can be dealt with by means of forward error recovery. Exception handlers are a convenient programming language facility for coping with these faults. Unanticipated faults – such as software design faults - can be handled using either of:

● recovery blocks, a backward error recovery mechanism

● n-programming, a forward error recovery mechanism.

EXERCISES

20.1 For each of the following computer systems suggest typical faults that could arise, categorizing them into user errors, hardware faults, and software faults. Decide whether each of the faults is anticipated or unanticipated. Suggest, in outline, how the faults might be dealt with:

● the control system for a fly-by-wire aircraft

● a network of PCs (personal computers) within an organization, which are used for word processing and e-mail.

20.2 Explain the following terms, giving an example of each to illustrate your answer: fault tolerance, software fault tolerance, reliability, robustness, graceful degradation.

20.3 Consider a programming language with which you are familiar. In what ways can you deliberately (or inadvertently) write a program that will:

(a) crash

(b) access main memory in an undisciplined way

(c) access a file protected from you.

What damage is caused by these actions? How much damage is possible? Assuming you didn't already know it, is it easy to diagnose the cause of the problem? Contemplate that if it is possible to *deliberately* penetrate a system, then it is certainly possible to do it by accident, thus jeopardizing the reliability and security of the system.

20.4 Compile-time checking is better than run-time checking. Discuss.

20.5 The Java system throws an `IndexOutOfBoundsException` exception if a program attempts to access elements of an array that lie outside the valid range of subscripts. Write a procedure that calculates the total weekly rainfall, given an array of floating point numbers (values of the rainfall for each of seven days of the week) as its single parameter. The procedure should throw an exception of the same type if an array is too short. Write code to catch the exception.

20.6 Outline the structure of recovery block software to cope with the following situation. A fly-by-wire aircraft is controlled by software. A normal algorithm calculates the optimal speed and the appropriate control surface and engine settings. A safety module checks that the calculated values are within safe limits. If they are not, it invokes an alternative module that calculates some safe values for the settings. If, again, this module fails to suggest safe values, the pilots are alerted and the aircraft reverts to manual control.

20.7 Compare and contrast the recovery block scheme with the *n*-programming scheme for fault tolerance. Include in your review an assessment of the development times and performance overheads associated with each scheme.

20.8 Searching a table for a desired object is a simple example of a situation in which it can be tempting to use a goto to escape from an unusual situation. Write a piece of program to search a table three ways:

(a) using goto

(b) using exceptions

(c) avoiding both of these.

Compare and contrast the three solutions.

20.9 Consider a program to make a copy of a disk file. Devise a structure for the program that uses exception handlers so that it copes with the following error situations:

(a) the file does not exist (there is no file with the stated name)

(b) there is a hardware fault when reading information from the old file

(c) there is a hardware fault when writing to the new file.

Include in your considerations actions that the filing system (or operating system) needs to take.

20.10 Explain the difference between using a goto statement and using a throw statement. Discuss their relative advantages for dealing with exceptions.

20.11 There is no such thing as an exceptional situation. The software should explicitly deal with all possible situations. Discuss.

20.12 Some word processors provide an undo command. Suppose we interpret a user wanting to undo what they have done as a fault. What form of error recovery does the software provide and how is it implemented?

20.13 Consider a computer system that is controlling a critical activity, like a power station or a life-support system. Make reasonable assumptions about what might go wrong in this situation, and structure the system in a fashion suitable for handling the problems. Use exception handling and recovery blocks as appropriate.

20.14 Study the architecture and operating system of a computer for which you have documentation. Investigate what facilities are provided for detecting software and hardware faults.

20.15 Compare and contrast approaches to fault tolerance in software with approaches for hardware.

ANSWERS TO SELF TEST QUESTIONS

20.1 **1.** unanticipated

2. unanticipated

3. unanticipated

4. anticipated

5. anticipated.

20.2 stack overflow

use of a null pointer.

20.3 The module could check that all the items in the new array are in order. (This is not foolproof, because the new array could contain different data to the old.)

20.4 The precondition is `assert(count > 0);`

The post-condition is `assert(count' = count - 1);`

20.5 Pros: prevent the spread of damage, assist in diagnosing the cause.

Cons: expensive hardware and software, reduction in performance (speed).

20.6 The answer depends on the particular software.

20.7 Forward, because you continued your journey. It was an anticipated fault.

However, as far as the tire is concerned, it is backward error recovery, because it is replaced by some other component.

20.8 Add the line:

`if (string.length() == 0) throw new NumberFormatException();`

at the start of the procedure.

20.9 Control continues down the program, which dangerously tests the value of the information returned by `parseInt`.

FURTHER READING

The programming language Pascal has a strong reputation for being a secure language, with extensive compile-time checking to prevent software faults. But these three authors set out to show how vulnerable it actually is. Ambiguities and Insecurities in Pascal, J. Welsh, W. J. Sneeringer and C. A. R. Hoare, *Software – Practice and Experience*, 7 (1977), pp. 685–96.

For a more detailed treatment of the topics described in this chapter, see: Hoang Pham (ed.), *Fault-Tolerant Software Systems; Techniques and Applications*, IEEE Computer Society Press, 1992.

The following book has a chapter that explains how software errors can be quantified: M. L. Shooman, *Software Engineering*, McGraw-Hill, 1983.

21

Software metrics and quality assurance

This chapter:

- explains the nature of metrics
- explains the concept of a complexity metric
- reviews reliability metrics
- explains the meaning of the terms "quality" and "quality assurance"
- explains how to prepare a quality assurance plan for a project.

21.1 ● Introduction

The issue of quality and quality assurance has become generally important throughout the industrialized world. It has become particularly important for software because of the increasing reliance of business on software and because of the notorious reputation that software enjoys. As a minimum, software is of good *quality* if it:

- meets its users' needs
- is reliable (that is, it does not fail)
- is easy to maintain (that is, to correct or change).

There are, of course, other factors involved in quality which we will review shortly.

Quality assurance means the measures that are taken to ensure that software is of good quality.

A vital aspect of quality is measurement. In software engineering, measures are termed *metrics*. A metric is a measure, such as cost or size that can be applied to software. Metrics can be obtained and applied throughout the software development process. Metrics address issues like:

- How big will the software be?
- How complex is this module?
- How reliable is this software?
- How much will this software cost?
- How much effort will be needed to alter this software to meet changed needs?

In this chapter we review various ways of applying metrics to software. The purposes of metrics in software engineering include:

- predicting qualities of software that is about to be developed
- making judgments on the quality of a piece of software that has been developed
- monitoring and improving the software development process
- comparing and assessing different development approaches.

In this chapter we first review metrics, then look at the application of quality assurance.

The simplest measure of software is its size. Two possible metrics are the size in bytes and the size in number of statements. The size in statements is often termed LOC (lines of code). The size in bytes obviously affects the RAM and disk space requirements and affects performance. The size measured in statements relates to development effort and maintenance costs. But a longer program does not necessarily take longer to develop than a shorter program, because the complexity of the software also has an effect. A metric such as LOC takes no account of complexity. (We shall see shortly how complexity can be measured.) There are different ways of interpreting even a simple metric like LOC, since it is possible to exclude, or include, comments, data declaration statements, and so on.

The second major metric is person-months, a measure of developer effort. Since people's time is the major factor in software development, person-months usually determine cost.

21.2 ● Complexity metrics

In the early days of programming, main memory was small and processors were slow. It was considered normal to try hard to make programs efficient. One effect of this was that programmers often used tricks. Nowadays the situation is rather different – the pressure is on to reduce the development time of programs and ease the burden of maintenance. So the emphasis is on writing programs that are clear and simple, and therefore easy to check, understand, and modify.

What are the arguments for simplicity?

- It is quicker to debug simple software.
- It is quicker to test simple software.
- Simple software is more likely to be reliable.
- It is quicker to modify simple software.

If we look at the world of design engineering, a good engineer insists on maintaining a complete understanding and control over every aspect of the project. The more difficult the project the more firmly the insistence on simplicity – without it no-one can understand what is going on. Software designers and programmers have frequently been accused of exhibiting the exact opposite characteristic; they deliberately avoid simple solutions and gain satisfaction from the complexities of their designs. Perhaps programmers should try to emulate the approach of traditional engineers.

Many software designers and programmers today strive to make their software as clear and simple as possible. A programmer finishes a program and is satisfied both that it works correctly and that it is clearly written. But how do we know that it is clear? Is a shorter program necessarily simpler than a longer one (that achieves the same end), or is a heavily nested program simpler than an equivalent program without nesting? People tend to hold strong opinions on questions like these; hard evidence and objective argument are rare.

Arguably what we perceive as clarity or complexity is an issue for psychology. It is concerned with how the brain works. We cannot establish a measure of complexity – for example, the number of statements in a program – without investigating how such a measure corresponds with programmers' perceptions and experiences. We now describe one attempt to establish a meaningful measure of complexity. An aim of such work is to guide programmers in selecting clear program structures and rejecting unclear structures, either during design or afterwards.

The approach taken is to hypothesize about what factors affect program complexity. For example, we might conjecture that program length, the number of alternative paths through the program, and the number of references to data might all affect complexity. We could perhaps invent a formula that allows us to calculate the overall complexity of a program from these constituent factors. The next step is to verify the hypothesis. How well does the formula match up with reality? What correlation is there between the complexity as computed from the formula and, for example, the time it takes to write or to understand the program?

Amongst several attempts to measure complexity is McCabe's cyclomatic complexity. McCabe suggests that complexity does not depend on the number of statements in a module. Instead it depends only on the decision structure of the program – the number of `if`, `while`, and similar statements. To calculate the cyclomatic complexity of a program, count the number of conditions and add one. For example, the program fragment:

```
x := y
if a = b
then
    c := d
else
    e := f
endif
p := q
```

has a complexity of 2. This corresponds to the number of independent paths through the program. Similarly a `while` and a `repeat` each count one towards the complexity count. Compound conditions like:

```
if a > b and c > d then
```

count 2 because this `if` statement could be rewritten as two nested `if` statements. Note that a program that consists only of a sequence of statements has a cyclomatic complexity of 1 – however long it is. Thus the smallest value of this metric is 1. Also this metric is independent of the program length.

There are two ways of using McCabe's measure. Firstly, if we had two algorithms that solve the same problem we could use this measure to select the simpler. Secondly, McCabe suggests that if the cyclomatic complexity of a module is greater than 10, then it is too complex. In such a case, it should either be rewritten or else broken down into several, smaller modules.

Cyclomatic complexity is a useful attempt to quantify complexity, and it is claimed that it has been successfully applied. It is, however, open to several criticisms as follows.

Firstly, why is the value of 10 adopted as the limit? This figure for the maximum allowed complexity is somewhat arbitrary and unscientific.

Second, the measure makes no allowance for the sheer length of a module, so that a one page module (with no decisions) is rated as equally complex as a thousand page module (with no decisions).

Third, the measure depends only on control flow, ignoring, for example, references to data. One program might only act upon a few items of data, while another might involve operations on a variety of complex objects. (Indirect references to data, say via pointers, are an extreme case.)

Finally, there is no evidence to fully correlate McCabe's measure with the complexity of a module as perceived by human beings.

So McCabe's measure is a crude attempt to quantify the complexity of a software module. But it suffers from obvious flaws and there are various suggestions for devising an improved measure. However, McCabe's complexity measure has become famous and influential as a starting point for work on metrics.

SELF TEST QUESTION

21.1 Suggest one formula for calculating the complexity of a piece of program.

A valid complexity measure can potentially help software developers in the following ways:

● in estimating the effort needed in maintaining a component
● in selecting the simplest design from amongst several candidates
● in signaling when a component is too complex and therefore is in need of restructuring or subdivision.

21.3 ● Faults and reliability – estimating bugs

The terminology adopted in this book is that a human error in developing software causes a fault (a bug) which may then cause a failure of the system (or several different failures). We have seen in Chapter 19 that every significant piece of software contains faults. Therefore if we are buying a piece of software it makes sense to ask the supplier to tell us how many faults there are. If they respond by saying that there are none, then they are either lying or incompetent. Similarly if we have developed a piece of software, it would be professional (if we are honest) to be able to tell users how many (estimated) faults there are and thus to give the users some idea of the expected reliability.

A commonly used metric for faults is *fault density*, which is the estimated number of faults per 1,000 lines of code. Faults are detected both during verification and during normal use after the software is put into productive use. Some faults are, of course, corrected and therefore do not count towards the fault density. We must not forget that, in addition to known faults, there are faults that are present, but undetected. In commercially written software, there is an enormous variation in fault densities – figures observed are between 2 and 50 faults per KLOC. A figure of 2 is rated highly creditable. The fault density metric is useful in assessing the effectiveness of verification methods and as a measure of correctness (see below) in quality assurance.

Experimental studies suggest that most faults cause only rare failures, whereas a small number of faults cause most of the failures. Thus it is more cost-effective to fix the small number of faults which cause most of the trouble – if they can be found.

It would seem to be impossible to gauge how many faults remain in a thoroughly tested system. After all if we knew what faults there are, we could correct them. One technique arises from the earth sciences. How do you find out how many fish there are in a lake? It would be costly (and kill many fish) to drain the lake. An alternative is to insert additional, specially marked fish into the lake. These could be fish of a different breed or slightly radioactive fish. After waiting a sufficient time for the fish to mix thoroughly, we catch a number of fish. We measure the proportion of specially marked fish, and, knowing the original number of special fish, scale up to find the total number of fish. We can do the same thing in software by deliberately putting in artificial faults into the software some time before testing is complete. By measuring the ratio of artificial to real faults detected, we can calculate the number of remaining real faults. Clearly this technique depends on the ability to create faults that are of a similar type to the actual faults.

One major problem with utilizing the fault density metric is that, as we have just seen, some bugs are more significant than others. Thus a more useful metric for users of a system is *Mean Time To Failure* (MTTF). This is the average time for a system to perform without failing. This can be measured simply by logging the times at which failures occur and simply calculating the average time between successive failures. This then gives a prediction for the future failure rate of the system.

21.4 ● Software quality

How do you know when you have produced good-quality software? There are two ways of going about it:

● measuring the attributes of software that has been developed
● monitoring and controlling the process of development of the software.

Let us compare developing software with preparing a meal, so that we can visualize these options more clearly. If we prepare a meal (somehow) and then serve it up, we will get ample comments on its quality. The consumers will assess a number of factors such as the taste, color, and temperature. But by then it is too late to do anything about the quality. Just about the only action that could be taken is to prepare further meals, rejecting them until the consumers are satisfied. We can now appreciate a commonly used definition of quality:

> *A product which fulfills and continues to meet the purpose for which it was produced is a quality product.*

There is an alternative course of action: it is to ensure that at each stage of preparation and cooking everything is in order. So we:

1. Buy the ingredients and make sure that they are all fresh.
2. Wash the ingredients and check that they are clean.
3. Chop the ingredients and check that they are chopped to the correct size.
4. Check the cooking time.

At each stage we can correct a fault if something has been done incorrectly. For example, we buy new ingredients if, on inspection, they turn out not to be fresh. We wash the ingredients again if they are not clean enough. Thus the quality of the final meal can be ensured by carrying out checks and remedial action if necessary throughout the preparation. Putting this into the jargon of software development, the quality can be assured provided that the process is assured.

For preparing the meal we also need a good recipe – one that can be carried out accurately and delivers well-defined products at every stage. This corresponds to using good tools and methods during software development.

Here is a commonly used list of desirable software qualities. It corresponds to factors like taste, color, texture, and nutritional value in food preparation. The list is designed to encompass the complete range of attributes associated with software, except the cost of construction.

● Correctness – the extent to which the software meets its specification and meets its users' requirements.
● Reliability – the degree to which the software continues to work without failing.
● Efficiency – the amount of RAM and processor time that the software uses.
● Integrity – the degree to which the software enforces control over access to information by users.

- Usability – the ease of use of the software.
- Maintainability – the effort required to find and fix a fault.
- Flexibility – the effort required to change the software to meet changed requirements.
- Testability – the effort required to test the software effectively.
- Portability – the effort required to transfer the software to a different hardware and/or software platform.
- Re-usability – the extent to which the software (or a component within it) can be re-used within some other software.
- Interoperability – the effort required to make the software work in conjunction with some other software.

These attributes are related to the set of goals discussed in Chapter 1. As we saw, some of these qualities can be mutually contradictory – for example, if high efficiency is required, portability will probably suffer. Also, not every attribute is desired in every piece of software. So for each project it is important to identify the salient factors before development starts.

SELF TEST QUESTION

21.2 Software is to be developed to control a fly-by-wire airplane. What are likely to be the important factors?

This list of quality factors can be used in one or more of the following situations:

1. at the outset of a software development, to clarify the goals
2. during development, to guide the development process towards the goals
3. on completion, to assess the completed piece of software.

The above quality attributes are, of course, only qualitative (rather than quantitative) measures. And as we have seen earlier in this chapter, the purpose of metrics is to quantify desirable or interesting qualities. Thus a complexity measure, such as McCabe's, can be used to measure maintainability. Reliability can be measured as MTTF. However, for many of these attributes, it is extremely difficult to make an accurate judgment and a subjective guess must suffice – with all its uncertainties.

SELF TEST QUESTION

21.3 List some other quality factors that can be quantified

21.5 ● Quality assurance

Quality assurance means ensuring that a software system meets its quality goals. The goals differ from one project to another. They must be clear and can be selected from the list of quality factors we saw earlier. To achieve its goals, a project must use effective tools and methods. Also checks must be carried out during the development process at every available opportunity to see that the process is being carried out correctly.

To ensure that effective tools and methods are being used, an organization distills its best practices and documents them in a *quality manual*. This is like a library of all the effective tools, methods, and notations. It is like a recipe book in cooking, except that it contains only the very best recipes. This manual describes all the standards and procedures that are available to be used.

A *standard* defines a range, limit, tolerance, or norm of some measurable attribute against which compliance can be judged. For example: during white box testing, every source code statement must be executed at least once. In the kitchen, all peeled potatoes must have no skin remaining on them.

A *procedure* prescribes a way of doing something (rules, steps, guidelines, plans). For example: black box testing, white box testing, and a walkthrough must be used to verify each component of software. In the kitchen, all green vegetables will be steamed, rather than boiled.

To be effective, quality assurance must be planned in advance – along with the planning of all other aspects of a software project. The project manager:

1. decides which quality factors are important for the particular project (e.g. high reliability and maintainability); in preparing a family meal, perhaps flavor and nutritional value are the paramount goals

2. selects standards and procedures from the quality manual that are appropriate to meeting the quality goals (e.g. the use of complexity metrics to check maintainability); if the meal does not involve potatoes, then those parts of the quality manual that deal with potatoes can be omitted

3. assembles these into a *quality assurance plan* for the project; this describes what the procedures and standards are, when they will be done, and who does them.

More and more the organizations that produce software are having to convince their customers that they are using effective methods. More and more commonly they must specify what methods they are using. Moreover, the organization must demonstrate that they are using the methods. Thus an organization must not only use sound methods but must be seen to be using them. Therefore a quality plan describes a number of *quality controls*. A quality control is an activity that checks that the project's quality factors are being achieved and produces some documentary evidence. In the kitchen, an example is an inspection carried out after potatoes have been peeled. The documentary evidence is the signature of the chief cook on a checklist. These documents are then available to anyone – such as the customer – with an interest in checking that the quality of the product is assured. Depending on the quality factors for the project, quality controls might include:

Action	Document	Factor being checked
Collect a complexity metric for each component in the system	Data on complexity	Maintainability
Module test	Test result	Correctness
Walkthrough to examine module for re-usability	Minutes of walkthrough	Re-usability

SELF TEST QUESTION

21.4 What quality factors would the measurement of fault density help achieve?

21.6 ● Process improvement

We have seen how quality can be measured, attained, and ensured. A more ambitious goal is to improve quality. One perspective on improving quality is suggested by Deming, an influential management guru who suggests that processes can be *continuously* improved. In his approach, the work processes are subject to continuous examination by the workers themselves as well as the organization in order to see how things can be done better.

So, for example, suppose that the number of faults discovered during testing is measured. But simply measuring does not achieve anything; measurements may help to ensure repeatability, but this is not the same as improvement. To improve the process, someone looks at how and why the faults were caused and what can be done to improve the processes. So, for example, it might be that a significant number of faults arise because of lack of clarity in module specifications. Therefore to improve the process it might be decided that module specifications should be subject to walkthroughs before they are used. Alternatively it might be suggested that a more formal notation is to be used for documenting module specifications. After any changes have been made, measurements are continued, and the search goes on for further improvements. Deming suggests that improvements can always continue to be made – indefinitely.

Deming argues that quality improvements of this type benefit everyone:

● workers, because they can take control and pride in their work
● organizations, because they can make increased profits
● customers, because they get better quality.

21.7 ● The capability maturity model (CMM)

The capability maturity model is a grading system that measures how good an organization is at software development. This scheme specifies five levels, ranging from level 1 (bad) to level 5 (good). An organization's ranking is determined by questionnaires administered by the Software Engineering Institute (SEI) of Carnegie Mellon University (CMU), USA. The levels are:

Level 1, Initial. The development process is *ad hoc* and even, occasionally, chaotic. Few processes are defined and the success of any project depends on effort by individuals. Thus the organization survives through the actions of individual heroes and heroines who help ensure some success in spite of the way that the organization is run.

Level 2, Repeatable. Basic project management processes are established within the organization to track cost, schedule, and functionality. The processes enable the organization to repeat its success with earlier, similar applications.

Level 3, Defined. The development process for both management and software engineering activities is documented, standardized, and integrated into an organization-wide development process. All projects use an approved and documented version of the standard process. This level includes all the characteristics defined for level 2.

Level 4, Managed. Detailed measures of the development process and of the software product are collected. Both are quantitative and measured in a controlled fashion. This level includes all the characteristics defined for level 3.

Level 5, Optimizing. Measurements are continuously used to improve the process. New techniques and tools are used and tested. This level includes all the characteristics defined for level 4.

Any particular development organization will typically use a mix of good and bad practice and so the level achieved is the average for the organization. An organization with a good rating can clearly advertise the fact to get increased business. If an organization, or individual, is buying or commissioning software, it is clearly better to buy from a CMM level 5 software development organization, who will probably supply better software and not necessarily at a more expensive price. Indeed, the evidence is that an organization that uses better methods achieves higher-quality software at a lower cost.

21.8 ● Summary

Metrics support software engineering in several ways:

1. They help us decide what to do during the act of design, guiding us to software that is clear, simple, and flexible.
2. They provide us with criteria for assessing the quality of software.
3. They can help in predicting development effort.
4. They help choose between methods.
5. They help improve working practices.

Software complexity can be measured using McCabe's cyclomatic complexity measure, which is based upon the number of decisions within the software.

Coupling and cohesion are qualitative terms that describe the character of the interaction between modules and within modules, respectively. These are described in Chapter 16.

Correctness can be measured using fault density as a metric. Reliability can be measured using MTTF as a metric.

The quality goals for a project can be clarified using a list of factors.

Quality assurance is the application of a plan, involving procedures, standards, and quality factors to ensure software quality.

The CMM (capability maturity model) is a classification scheme to assess an organization's ability to develop quality software.

EXERCISES

21.1 Write down two different programs to search a table for a desired element. Calculate the cyclomatic complexity of each and hence compare them from the point of view of clarity.

21.2 What factors do you think affect program complexity? What is wrong with McCabe's approach to calculating complexity? Devise a scheme for calculating a satisfactory complexity measure.

21.3 Devise a plan to measure faults and failures revealed during the course of a software development project. How could this data be used?

21.4 Compare the list of software quality factors identified above in the text with the list of software engineering goals given in Chapter 1.

21.5 Suggest appropriate quality factors for each of the following software systems:

(a) a microcomputer-controlled washing machine

(b) a system to control a power station

(c) software to calculate and print an organization's payroll

(d) a general-purpose operating system or database management system

(e) a system to monitor and control medical equipment

(f) a general-purpose mathematical routine

(g) a computer game.

21.6 It is common practice for software development organizations to lay down standards for coding. Suggest a number of coding standards for a programming language of your choice. Suggest quality factors that are enhanced by adherence to the standards.

21.7 Suggest a quality assurance plan for each of the software development projects listed in question 21.5 above. Assume that each project will use the waterfall model as its process model.

ANSWERS TO SELF TEST QUESTIONS

21.1 There are many possible suggestions. One formula that builds on McCabe, but takes some account of references to data is:

complexity = number of decisions + (number of data references – number of statements)

This has the characteristic that if each statement refers to one data item only, the second term is zero.

21.2 Correctness and reliability.

21.3 Cost, size.

21.4 Correctness, reliability.

FURTHER READING

A most comprehensive and readable book is: N. E. Fenton and S. Lawrence Pfleeger, *Software Metrics: A Rigorous and Practical Approach*, International Thomson Computer Press, 1996.

McCabe's famous original cyclomatic complexity is described in this paper: T. J. McCabe, A Complexity Measure, *IEEE Trans. on Software Engineering*, SE-2 (4), (December 1976).

A well-known book that presents a whole number of ways of measuring software: M. H. Halstead, *Elements of Software Science*, Elsevier, 1977.

A most readable book on software quality. It explains what measures can be used during each stage of software development: Darrel Ince, *Software Quality Assurance: A Student Introduction*, McGraw-Hill, 1995.

The seminal book on continuous process improvement: W. Edwards Deming, *Out of the Crisis: Quality, Productivity and Competitive Position*, Cambridge University Press, 1986.

22

Project management

This chapter:

- analyzes the challenges of project management
- identifies the tasks of project management
- explains how to estimate the cost of a software project
- explains different ways to organize a team to carry out a development
- explains how to select suitable tools and methods
- explains how to plan a development
- briefly describes the informal processes that go on in teams and the ideas of "peopleware."

22.1 Introduction

Project management is the means by which an orderly control process can be imposed on the software development process in order to ensure software quality. Project management is difficult and software projects commonly run late, are over-budget, and fail to meet the users requirements.

Why is a large-scale software project such a complex task?

- It comprises a number of individually complex and interacting activities, commonly identified as analysis, specification, design, implementation, and maintenance.
- It is carried out by possibly large numbers of people working over lengthy time-spans.
- It aims to develop a complex product which should conform to prescribed, sometimes stringent, requirements and standards.

Clearly, if software projects are to have any chance of successfully delivering quality products on time within budget, they must be thoroughly planned in advance and effectively managed as they are executed.

22.2 ● The challenges of project management

A project manager has a legacy of bad publicity to overcome – the widespread perception that projects nearly always run over-budget and beyond deadline. There is no doubt that this is due to the near-impossibility of predicting in advance how much effort is required to develop software. Estimates are commonly too low; the result is embarrassing.

The problems are compounded by knowledge of the immense differences between individual developers – it is common to see a 20-fold difference in productivity between individual developers in the same organization. If you estimate the development time for a software component and then assign the job of designing and coding it to an individual, you have no real idea of how long it should take or will take. This is a nightmare situation for any project manager.

The problems are not helped by the available software engineering methodologies. What a manager wants is a well-defined method, with clear products delivered at short intervals. With such a weapon, the manager can closely monitor progress and, if necessary, do something about it. Regrettably, no such methodology exists. Instead it is common to experience the well-known "90% complete" paralysis. The manager asks the engineer about progress. The engineer replies "Fine – it is 90% complete." Reassured the manager does nothing. A week later they ask the same question and receive exactly the same reply. And so on. Given the nature of software development there is no good way in which the manger can verify whether the report is accurate or misleading. The schedule slips, out of control.

22.3 ● The ingredients of project management

Project management involves the following ingredients:

1. Estimation – estimating effort, time, and cost.

2. Planning – scheduling deliverables, review points, allocation of staff to the project.

3. Replanning – re-estimating and rescheduling to adjust previous estimates as more accurate information emerges as the project proceeds. At the outset of a project, the requirements for the system are usually vague and ill-defined. In consequence, any planning is at best tentative. As the requirements become clearer, more meaningful and accurate plans can be made.

4. Organization – establishing an organizational structure within which all staff involved in the project can effectively communicate and carry out the different parts of the development work.

5. Configuration management and maintenance – information is needed to record the state of the product, both as it is developed and during its operational lifetime. Software tools can be particularly useful here.

6. Quality assurance – a plan is needed to ensure that the software product demonstrates its required quality factors (Chapter 21).

A process model is a model for the framework or plan for a project. Individual tools and techniques fit within the overall skeleton. Chapter 2 reviews a number of process models for software development.

Project management involves monitoring and control – monitoring what is happening and taking control to remedy things that are going wrong. In order to monitor a project, what is happening must be visible. Reliable information concerning the state of the development process must be available at all times – without it, monitoring and control are impossible. This issue is discussed in Chapter 21 on metrics and quality assurance.

There are other important tasks associated with project management – such as motivating the people involved. Such management topics are largely outside the scope of this book. However, at the end of this chapter, we look at one set of ideas – peopleware – for influencing the behavior of a development team.

What is certain is that difficulties and crises will arise during a project. We have mentioned these in Chapter 2. They include people leaving the project and the client making significant changes to the requirements.

22.4 ● Cost estimation

The classic way of estimating software costs is to guess a figure, double it, and hope for the best. A better way, often used, is to check out whether the organization has carried out a similar project and use the actual figures from that project as a basis for the estimate.

Early methods for cost estimation rely on being able to guess the eventual size of the software (measured in lines of code). From this figure the effort is then derived. This simply shifts the difficulty from one intractable problem to another.

The most recent methods recognize that a number of factors affect the required effort:

● size of the product
● difficulty of the project
● expertise of the developers
● effectiveness of tools
● how much software can be reused from elsewhere.

At the outset of a project it is impossible to estimate the development effort. If someone says "We want to develop a new word processor," the requirement is so vague that any estimate of effort is meaningless. It is not until requirements analysis is complete that some estimate can be made. Thus in a word processor, for example, it is relatively easy to assess the effort required to write the software for one small function – such as to save text in a file. Even then, there are too many uncertainties to make an accurate estimate. It is only as the project continues that the situation becomes clearer and more accurate estimates can be achieved.

Nonetheless it is often necessary to make an initial estimate of software cost so that a decision can be made about the feasibility of the project. This is sometimes called *investment appraisal* or a *feasibility study*. The estimate of the software development cost is compared with the value of the benefits that will accrue. If the benefits are greater than the costs, the project goes ahead; otherwise it is canceled. Thus a crucial decision depends upon an estimate that is almost impossible to make.

The best-known approach to cost estimation is the COCOMO (Constructive Cost Model) approach, developed by Barry Bohm and explained in his well-known book *Software Engineering Economics*. This suffers from the drawback mentioned above – the cost estimate is based on a size estimate. However, the most recent version of this approach, COCOMO 2.0, adopts an approach similar to the method we will describe.

The effort required to develop some software depends on what the software does – the number of functions it implements. This is called *function point analysis*. Let us consider firstly one common type of system – information systems. An information system typically allows the user to browse information or update information held in a database. Consider an information system that holds information about the employees in an organization. A screen is to be implemented that allows information about a single employee to be displayed. This is a straightforward function and, supposing that a high-level tool such as Visual Basic is available, we estimate one person-month for the effort. This includes clarifying the requirements, creating the specification, verification, and validation. Obviously there will be other screens available to users – for example a screen to change the details of an employee. The number of functions is measured by the number of screens available to the user and the development effort is proportionate. Thus for six screens, we estimate six person-months.

But where does the figure of one person-month per function point come from? The answer is that this figure is likely to differ from one organization to another, depending perhaps on the general level of expertise within the organization. To obtain the appropriate factor, a calibration needs to be carried out within the particular organization. This means measuring the development effort on an initial series of projects to obtain an average figure. This might be 0.75 person-months per function point. Whatever the factor, the assumption of this prediction model is that the effort is proportional to the number of function points, and the number of function points is determined by the number of screens.

There are, however, other considerations – we have neglected to consider the effort to design and access the database. For each table in the relational database we add 1 to the count of function points and therefore an additional person-month to the total effort. As part of the information system, reports are probably required – on-screen and on hard copy. Again for each report we add 1 to the count of function points.

In summary, the count of function points is the sum of:

● the number of data input screens
● the number of data display screens
● the number of database tables
● the number of reports
● the number of interfaces with other software systems.

Perhaps the information system is implemented across a network of PCs, linked to a server that maintains the database. This involves extra complexity and therefore effort. A complexity multiplier of, say, 1.6 could be applied to the effort figure to take account of implementation complexity.

Finally, the new software may be able to re-use software either from a library or from earlier projects, thus reducing the development effort. This can be estimated by deducting the proportion of the software that is being implemented by re-use.

Thus the function point approach caters for factors including the size of a project, the expertise of the developers, the power of the software tools, the complexity of the implementation and the degree of re-use. Most of the factors need to be calibrated within the context of a particular organization, with its own staff expertise, tools, and methods.

The function point estimate method uses as its foundation a knowledge of the number of functions that the software needs to provide and this is based on the number of input and output activities. These are not known at the outset of a project, but become clearer during requirements analysis.

Although software cost estimation models such as this attempt to take account of all relevant factors, they are notoriously inaccurate in their predictions. There are a number of reasons – including widely different productivity rates amongst developers.

22.5 ● Team organization

How are teams organized? There are two common methods of organizing teams involved in software development – functional teams and project teams.

In the *functional team* organization, all the members of the team carry out the same type of work, so that there is a team of programmers, a team of analysts, a team of testers, a team who run the computer facility, and a team of technical writers. Each team handles a number of different projects at the same time. Equally, the work of a single project is carried out by people from different teams.

One problem of the functional team is that the person responsible for a project is not the manager or leader of the people working on his or her project. Thus he or she may not have as much control over them (and the project) as they would like.

In a *project team*, all the team members contribute towards one single project. The team members deploy all the necessary skills of requirements analysis, design, coding, verification, and documentation. The choice is whether everyone carries out all the tasks of development, or whether each team member practices their specialism. People are recruited to (and leave) the project team as and when their skills and efforts are needed as the project progresses.

Two major features of team activity are:

1. the communication between the people in the team
2. deciding who does what work.

These issues are now discussed in turn.

22.5.1 The communication problem

When two or more people are working on a piece of software they obviously have to liaise with each other. At the very least they have to communicate module specifications – module names, module functions, parameter types, and so on. Often such interfaces are complex, perhaps involving detailed file layouts. Always there are queries, because of the difficulty of precisely specifying interfaces. During the lifetime of a project someone always leaves or is ill or goes on holiday. Someone has to sort out the work in their absence. New people join the team and have to be helped to understand what the software is for, what has been done, and why the structure is as it is. They may need to learn about the standards and procedures being used on the project, or even learn a new programming language. This induction of a new person takes up the time of those who remain.

All this adds up to a great deal of time spent in communication that would not be necessary if only a single person were developing the software. Adding two people to a team of four does not increase the communication overhead by half – it more than doubles it. Clearly as more and more people are added to a team the time taken in liaising can completely swamp a project.

Compare the activity of picking potatoes. Imagine a large field with a relatively small number of people. They can each get on with the job without getting in each other's way. If we increase the number of people, the work will get done proportionately quickly, at least until there are so many people that they are tripping each other up. The graph showing how the number of potatoes picked depends on the number of people employed is shown in Figure 22.1.

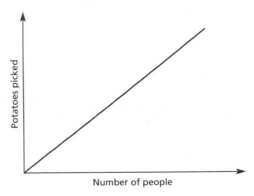

Figure 22.1 Picking potatoes

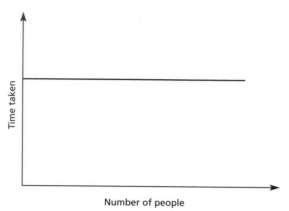

Figure 22.2 Having a baby

If we now consider the task of having a baby, increasing the number of people will do nothing to the timescale – it always remains 9 months. The graph is shown in Figure 22.2.

Software development comes somewhere between these two extremes. Initially, if we increase the number of people, the job will get done faster (like the potato picking). But, eventually, the communication overheads will become overwhelming, and the project will actually slow down. The graph is as shown in Figure 22.3.

One of the gurus of computing, Brooks, has described this problem as follows: if a project is late, then adding further people will only make it even later.

To make matters worse, human beings are not well known for precise communication with each other. Thus it is likely that there will be faults in a system constructed by a team.

This argument has assumed that each and every team member communicates with every other. We shall see that this is what some forms of organization attempt to avoid.

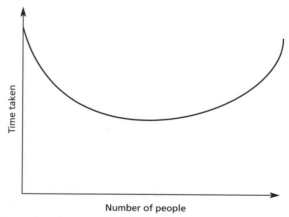

Figure 22.3 Developing software

22.5.2 The division of labor

The second major question in team organization is deciding how to break down the complete task of constructing a large piece of software into smaller tasks so that several people can carry them out. This is not purely the technical issue of how to decompose a system into suitable modules; there are other ways of splitting up the work. Any programmer knows that he or she spends only about 10% of his or her time actually programming (by which we mean coding). The rest of the time is spent in activities like program design, testing, and writing documentation. Programmers carry out a whole variety of tasks, some of which, like design, are challenging and others, like writing documentation or filing listings may be less demanding. One way of dividing the work of software development amongst a set of people is to create specialists so that one person does all the design, one person does all the coding, and another all the testing.

This principle of the division of labor has long been recognized. A major feature of this type of organization is that instead of paying several highly skilled people uniformly high wages, the organization can pay people who have different skills different salaries. Overall the wages of the people with unequal skills will be lower than those of the skilled people. Thus the wages bill is reduced. To give a crude example, it would be cheaper to employ a programmer at $40,000 and an analyst at $80,000, rather than employ two analyst/programmers each at $70,000.

It is no coincidence that Charles Babbage, one of the founding fathers of computing, was well aware of this effect. As long ago as 1832, in his book *On the Economy of Machine and Manufacturers*, Babbage wrote:

> *The master manufacturer, by dividing the work to be executed into different processes, each requiring different degrees of skill or of force, can purchase exactly that precise quality of both which is necessary for each process; whereas, if the whole work were executed by one workman, that person must possess sufficient skill to perform the most difficult, and sufficient strength to execute the most laborious, of the operations into which the art is divided.*

Figure 22.4 illustrates a (possibly controversial) conjecture about the differing skills involved during the development of software.

As we shall see, some techniques exploit this principle of the division of labor.

22.5.3 The chief programmer team

The chief programmer team is a project team organization in which the division of labor is implemented in an extreme form. The principles behind the chief programmer team organization are:

● to divide the work amongst skilled specialists

● to minimize communication.

A chief programmer team is like a surgical team in which the chief surgeon is assisted by an assistant surgeon, an anesthetist, and one or two nurses. Each is a highly trained

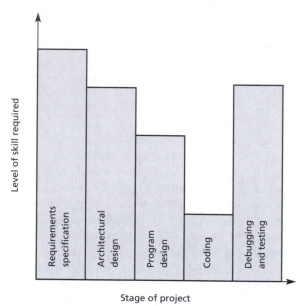

Figure 22.4 Skill requirements at each stage of a project

specialist. In the chief programmer team the job titles are chief programmer, back-up programmer, librarian, and other specialist programmers as and when necessary.

The roles of the team members are:

Chief programmer This is a highly skilled software engineer who produces the high-level parts of the system. This is usually the architectural design of the software – determining and specifying the constituent programs and modules of the software. If there is some crucial controlling part to the system, like the nucleus of the operating system, he or she does this as well.

The chief programmer specifies all the other components in the system and oversees the integration or system testing of the complete system.

The chief programmer's role is intended to be almost entirely a technical one. To this end administrative affairs like reporting to management and monitoring budgets and timescales are dealt with by a project manager. The project manager is not really part of the team and usually will deal with the administrative aspects of several teams.

Back-up programmer This is a programmer whose skill is comparable to that of the chief programmer. The job is to help the chief programmer with his or her tasks and act as the chief programmer when the latter is absent for any reason. Should the chief programmer leave the organization, the back-up programmer can immediately take over.

Librarian The librarian maintains the documentation associated with the project. He or she may be a secretary with some training in using a computer system.

Other specialist programmers When needed, other programmers are brought into the team to develop subsystems specified by the chief programmer. Each of these programmers is probably expert in a particular software area like databases or graphical user interfaces.

The structure of the team is hierarchical, with the chief programmer at the top. In contrast to a network of people, each of whom communicates with everyone else, the hierarchy restricts information so that it flows along far fewer paths – only up and down the hierarchy. The use of top-down design, implementation, and testing (which are also hierarchical) complement this scheme very neatly.

There can be no doubt that the technique of the chief programmer team represents a creative application of scientific management to team programming. From the organization's point of view the division of labor offers:

1. greater control over the work process by management

2. greater productivity, since the team member does just one type of work; he or she therefore becomes very good at it

3. the possibility of automating some aspects of the work; an example of this is the job of the librarian, which is increasingly being carried out by software tools

4. the opportunity to pay the different team members according to the separate skills involved in their work, rather than pay everyone at the same rate for the most highly skilled work.

The benefits of the chief programmer team to the organization are thus:

(a) **improved programmer productivity** because
   – less time is spent in communication
   – each programmer is carrying out specialized work at which they are highly skilled.

(b) **improved software quality** because
   – the team is organized around a highly skilled programmer
   – the interfaces between software components are clearer
   – fewer bugs arise from communication problems because there are fewer programmers.

(c) **meeting deadlines more reliably** because
   – there is greater visibility of the project through the high technical involvement of the chief programmer.

22.5.4 Team organization in an object-oriented environment

Different programming paradigms often require special approaches to team programming. Object-oriented (OO) development tries to achieve two objectives:

● re-use of existing components from either the standard library or the in-house library

● the creation of new re-useable components for the in-house library.

Thus organizations using the OO paradigm have found it desirable to divide their personnel into teams of application programmers on the one hand, and teams of class or component programmers on the other. The motivation here is that the benefits of the

OO paradigm will only be realized if a concerted effort is made to identify re-usable software components and to organize such components within an accessible library. A domain-specific class library becomes viewed as one of the major assets of the organization. Indeed, some large companies have reported that they have been able to reduce the amount of new code written on large projects by a factor of 50% through the use of such libraries.

In such a scenario, application programmers become thought of as *consumers*; they implement application-specific classes, but are always seeking to re-use existing library components whenever possible. They seek better re-usable components from the class programmers and also have a responsibility to identify useful abstractions that can be migrated from the application to the library.

Class programmers (or component developers) are thought of as *producers*; they produce re-usable components of general use to the organization. Their job is to polish, generalize, reorganize, and augment library classes. Their task should not be underestimated – producing re-usable components is difficult.

In a moderate size project the project personnel are divided up along class versus application lines. The architecture team contains the key designers and programmers; their responsibility is to oversee the project as a whole and also take responsibility for critical modules of the system. They are supported by teams of subsystem developers who are responsible for the development of "large grain" subsystems. The class developers are responsible for the development of a re-usable component library. This kind of approach has given rise to a plethora of new job titles and functions; for example application directors, class managers, re-use evaluators.

The key to the success of such an approach is communication between team members, particularly between the architecture/subsystem teams and the component developers. It is highly desirable to develop a culture in which team members are rewarded for producing components that have a broad applicability or design frameworks that can be re-used.

22.5.5 Discussion

The chief programmer team is hierarchical and tree-structured. Its very shape tends to produce software that has a matching structure. This may be completely appropriate for certain types of software. Indeed, much software is hierarchical in structure. Generalizing, it can be hypothesized that teams tend to produce software whose structure matches their own structure. Suppose, for example, that some software is designed by a committee, acting democratically. What would the structure of the software look like? Perhaps it would be complex, with many interactions (reflecting the many interactions between its designers) or perhaps it would display haphazard structure, without the single clear vision provided by a charismatic leader. But for certain types of software – for example expert systems – these structures might be completely appropriate. Thus it may be that different forms of organization are appropriate for different types of software project.

22.6 ● Selecting tools and methods

Suppose you are the manager of a software development project. What tools and methods would you select for use? How can you go about deciding whether a particular tool or method is worth using?

Some development methods are inapplicable to particular domains and can therefore be disregarded. For example prototyping is not usually of any use in developing scientific or mathematical software. Again, the Michael Jackson method is only really applicable for serial file processing and it would be difficult or impossible to apply it to scientific programming or to process control.

The customer may demand the use of particular methods. For example a military client may require the use of Ada in conjunction with a formal specification.

The next step is to establish a checklist of requirements and criteria. These must reflect the nature of the software to be developed, the customer, and the organization developing the software. When evaluating a new technique, a generic checklist of criteria that can be used might include:

● special features and strengths

● weaknesses

● philosophy/perspective?

● systematic?

● appropriate application areas

● inappropriate application areas

● good for small-scale design?

● good for large-scale design?

● extent of tool support

● training time for the people who will use the method

● level of skill required by the people using the method

● whether the software produced is easy to maintain

● whether the software will meet performance targets

● whether documentation is automatically produced

● whether the method is enjoyable to use

● whether the method can be used in the required area of application

● productivity

● reliability of the software.

Any software development organization has expertise in particular tools and methods. It also has its own standards and procedures. These are huge investments. A project manager within an organization must usually adhere to local methods and standards. The introduction of any new method requires effort and time to be devoted to training. Training costs typically include buying training and the time that developers spend away from productive work. But that is not all. While a new technique is being adopted, the organization is still learning and therefore productivity slumps, at least temporarily (see below).

While the technical merits of development methods are important, it is often practical considerations that determine which development approach is used. Examples are:

● the computer facility only supports specific tools and languages
● the cost of software tools associated with a specific method.

22.7 ● Introducing new methods

Suppose that it has been decided that a new method should be introduced into an organization or into a particular project. The first alarming thing to be prepared for is that there will inevitably be a temporary drop in productivity while people spend time becoming familiar with the method. So the initial experiences with any method will be negative; courage and patience are needed before any benefits kick in.

Perhaps the most important aspect of any new method is its effect on the people in the organization. In most organizations there is a hierarchy, with the senior and more-skilled, perhaps older people in senior positions. A new method can pose a threat to such people. First they may fear that they will find it impossible to learn or adapt to a new method. Second they may see a new method as a criticism of the methods they have used successfully in the past. Third, a new method will mean that everyone is a novice again, so that their status will be eroded.

It is generally agreed that new methods should be introduced one at a time. If too many new approaches are adopted at once (big-bang), it is difficult to see which of them are being effective. In addition, too many of the existing skills are destroyed, threatening morale.

22.8 ● The project plan

A project manager must create a plan for a project which specifies:

● the deadline
● intermediate milestones
● the deliverables at each stage
● who is involved and when
● when walkthroughs and inspections are scheduled
● the dependencies between the stages of the project.

This plan must take account of the process model, the total predicted effort, the tools and methods, the team organization, and the expected final deadline.

There are a number of notations, diagrams, and tools that can assist in documenting a project plan:

- Pert chart – shows activities and their interrelationships
- Gantt chart – shows resources (people) and what they are doing
- Microsoft Project – a software package designed to assist in project planning and monitoring
- a spreadsheet package such as Excel – can be used to model a project.

Suppose, for example, that the waterfall model of development is to be used. A Pert (Project Evaluation and Review Technique) chart shows the stages of development, their interdependencies, and the milestones. Each activity is shown as a line, with time proceeding left-to-right. An individual activity, for example, the requirements engineering stage, can be shown as:

1. needing an effort of four person-months
2. starting 1 April
3. ending 31 July.

A Pert chart shows dependencies – for example that architectural design must be completed before detailed design. Parallel activities, such as designing the two components at the same time, can be shown. A Pert chart like this allows the critical path to be identified easily. This is the path through the chart that determines the overall duration of the project.

During the course of the development, progress of the project is monitored and compared with the Pert diagram. Should any stage take longer or shorter than planned, the diagram is updated to reflect the new situation. If it seems that any major milestone will not be achieved on time, extra effort can be applied to rectify the situation. But, as we saw in the discussion of teams, applying extra people will not necessarily solve the problem.

22.9 ● Peopleware

There have been many attempts to analyze the problems of software projects and suggest informal ways of developing a successful project team. In their well-known book *Peopleware*, Tom DeMarco and Timothy Lister discuss many of the informal aspects of software development – individually and in teams. They attach great importance to the informal processes that take place in organizations. In their treatment of teams, they identify a number of ways of killing a project team and a number of ways of promoting successful teams.

First, some ways of weakening a team are:

- distrust of the team by its management
- over-emphasis on the paperwork associated with the project, rather than on thinking

- scattering the team members in different locations
- asking team members to work on a number of different projects (functional team), rather than focusing on the particular project (project team)
- pressing for earlier delivery at the expense of reducing the quality of the software
- setting unrealistic or phony deadlines
- breaking up an effective team.

Some of the approaches suggested for enhancing team activity are:

- emphasizing the desirability of the quality of the software product
- planning for a number of successful completed stages (milestones) during the lifetime of the project
- emphasizing how good the team is
- preserving a successful team for a subsequent project
- eliminating hierarchy in the team, promoting egalitarianism, placing the manager outside the team
- celebrating diversity in the team members.

22.10 ● Summary

- Software project management is difficult.
- Project management involves selecting a process model, a team organization, tools, and methods.
- Team organization is either functional or project-based.
- One approach to estimating the cost of a software system involves counting function points.
- Tools and methods are selected according to their appropriateness for the project.
- Introducing new methods must be done with care.
- Planning involves deciding on milestones and scheduling tasks amongst people.
- The informal aspects of team working during software development can be as important as the technical aspects.

EXERCISES

22.1 Suggest facilities for a software tool that supports the planning of software project activities.

22.2 Draw up a plan for the following software development project. Document the plan as a Pert chart, in which each activity is shown as an arc, with a bubble at its starting point (the event which triggers the activity) and a bubble at its completion (the event which concludes the activity). The plan is to adopt the waterfall model. The development must be completed in 2 years. The following activities are envisaged:

1. requirements analysis – four person-months

2. architectural design – three person-months

3. detailed design – four components each at six person-months per component

4. coding – two person-months for each component

5. unit testing – six person-months for each component

6. system testing – six person-months.

How many people will be required at each stage of the project to ensure that the deadline is met?

22.3 Suggest features for a software tool to support software cost estimation.

22.4 You are the manager of a software development project. One of the team members fails to meet the deadline for the coding and testing of a component. What do you do?

22.5 You are the project leader for a large and complex software development. Three months before the software is due to be delivered, the customer requests a change that will require massive effort. What do you do?

22.6 Investigate the importance of the time taken in communicating within a team. Assume initially that there are four people in a team. Each is capable of developing 3,000 lines of code per year left to themselves. However, 250 lines per year are sacrificed for each communication path to or from an individual. Assume that the team is organized so that everyone needs to discuss problems with everyone else.

22.7 Calculate the productivity (lines of code per year) of each member of the team and investigate how it changes as the team expands to six and then to eight members.

22.8 Carry out the same calculations assuming that a chief programmer team is in operation. (In this case each member of the team communicates only with the chief programmer.)

22.9 Compare and contrast the functional team with the project team organization.

FURTHER READING

A good collection of articles on project management is presented in: Richard H. Thayer, Winston W. Royce and Edward Yourdon (eds.), *Software Engineering Project Management*, IEEE Computer Society, 1997.

This book is a readable and practical discussion of dealing with software costs: T. Capers Jones, *Estimating Software Costs*, McGraw-Hill, 1998.

The seminal book on software cost estimation is still the classic: B. W. Boehm, *Software Engineering Economics*, Prentice Hall, 1981.

This view is updated in: B. Boehm, C. Clark, E. Horowitz, C. Westland, R. Madachy and R. Selby, Cost Models for Future Life Cycle Processes: COCOMO 2.0, *Annals of Software Engineering*, 1(1), (November 1995), pp. 57–94.

This account of the development of Windows NT reads like a thriller and has significant lessons for software developers. It charts the trials, tribulations and the joys of developing software: Pascal Zachary, *Showstopper*, Warner Books, 1994.

This book has the subtitle "Practical Strategies for Staying Focused, Hitting Ship Dates and Building Solid Teams". Life within Microsoft and the lessons that can be learned are well-presented in this readable book. Steve Maguire, *Debugging the Development Process*, Microsoft Press, 1994.

Accounts of failed projects are given in: Stephen Flowers, *Software Failure: Management Failure: Amazing Stories and Cautionary Tales*, John Wiley, 1996 and in Robert Glass, *Software Runaways*, Prentice Hall, 1998.

The classic book which deals at length and in a most interesting way with the informal, social aspects of working in a team. It is a most enjoyable read. G. Weinberg, *The Psychology of Computer Programming*, Van Nostrand Reinhold, 1971.

This is the classic book on the problems of running a large-scale software project. Worth reading by anyone who is contemplating leading a project. There is a section on chief programmer teams. This is a definitive book, revisited in a celebratory second edition with additional essays. Frederick P. Brooks, *The Mythical Man-Month*, Addison-Wesley, 2nd edition, 1995.

A most readable book about the informal processes that are at work in software development and how teams can best be organized: Tom DeMarco and Timothy Lister, *Peopleware, Productive Projects and Teams*, Dorset House Publishing Co., 1987.

This book dramatically describes a number of problem team predicaments – and how to try to fix them. It is written as a catalog of situations, mirroring the catalogs of (successful) re-usable design patterns: William J. Brown *et al.*, *Anti-Patterns*, John Wiley, 1998.

There is a whole host of management books – serious and popular – about how to run teams and projects. Many of the ideas are applicable to software projects. This is one example, actually about software development, with lessons learned at IBM. It covers recruitment, motivation, power struggles, and much more. Watts S. Humphrey, *Managing Technical People*, Addison-Wesley, 1997.

Review

23

Review

This chapter:

- discusses the problem of assessing tools and methods
- assesses the role of software tools
- assesses the role of software re-use
- reviews current techniques
- suggests that there is no single best method
- examines the evidence of how software engineers really work
- briefly reviews the issue of skill in software engineering
- assesses the future of software engineering.

23.1 ● Introduction

We saw in Chapter 1 that there are usually a number of objectives to be met in the construction of a piece of software. A major goal used to be high performance (speed and size), but with improved hardware cost and performance, this issue has declined in importance. Nowadays factors like software costs, reliability and ease of maintenance are increasingly important. For any particular project, it is, of course, vital to carefully assess what the specific aims are. Having done this, we will usually find that some of them are mutually contradictory, so that we have to decide upon a blend or compromise of objectives.

This book has described a variety of techniques for software construction. All of the techniques attempt in some way to improve the process of software development and to meet the various goals of software development projects. The purpose of this chapter is to survey this spectrum, see how they fit together, and try to look into the future.

23.2 ● Assessing and comparing development methods

Is it possible to identify a collection of tools and methods that are ideal in all circumstances? The answer is no. Software engineering is at an exciting time. There are a dozen schools of thought competing to demonstrate their supremacy and no single package of tools and methods seems set to succeed. Some methods seem particularly successful in specific areas, for example the Michael Jackson method in data processing. Other methods, like structured walkthroughs, seem generally useful. In the field of programming languages, declarative languages have become important in expert systems, while highly modular imperative languages are widely used in real-time and command and control systems.

Ideally, metrics (Chapter 21) would enable us to determine the best method or combination of software development methods. Regrettably, this is virtually impossible. The first problem is identifying the criteria for a best method. As we saw in Chapter 1 on problems and prospects, there are usually a number of goals for any software development project. In order to choose between methods it is necessary to establish what blend of criteria is appropriate for the particular project. For example, the set of goals for a particular project might be to optimize:

● development effort
● reliability
● maintainability

and these are in conflict with each other. In general, the most significant conflict is probably between development effort and reliability of the product. For example a safety-critical system needs to be highly reliable. However, for a one-off program for a user to extract information from a database, the prime goal may be quick delivery. There can be no set of factors that allow universal comparison between methods. Equally, it is unlikely that there will ever be a single best method.

Suppose that we had narrowed down the choice to two applicable methods, called A and B. What we would like to have is hard evidence like this:

"Method A gives 25% better productivity than method B."

Regrettably there is no such data available today, because of the enormous difficulty of creating it. Let us examine some of those difficulties. Because of cost, it is virtually impossible to conduct any realistic experiments in which two or more methods are compared. (The cost of developing the same piece of software twice is usually prohibitive.) Usually the only experimental evidence is based on scaled-down experiments. Suppose, for example, that we wanted to compare two design methods, A and B. We could give 10 people the specification of a small system and ask them to use method A, and similarly we could ask a second group to use method B. We could measure the average time taken to complete the designs and hence hope to compare the productivities of the methods. We could go on to assign additional problems and employ more people to increase our confidence in the results. Ultimately we might gain some confidence about the relative productivity of the two methods.

But many criticisms can be aimed at experiments like these. Are the backgrounds of the participants equal? Is the experience of the participants typical? (Often students are used in experiments, because they are cheap and plentifully available. But are students typical of professional software developers?) Have a sufficient number of people taken part so that the results are statistically significant? Is the problem that has been chosen typical, or is it a small "toy" problem from which it is unreasonable to extrapolate? Is there any difference between the motivation of the participants in the experiment and that of practitioners in a real situation? These questions are serious challenges to the validity of experiments and the significance of the results. The design of experiments must be examined carefully and the results used with caution.

While the problem of measuring and comparing productivity is fearsome, the story gets worse when we consider software quality. Again, what we desire is a statement like:

"Method A gives rise to software that is 50% more reliable than method B."

Whereas with productivity we have a ready-made measure – person-months – how do we measure reliability? If we use the number of bugs as a measure, how can we actually count them? Again, do we count all the bugs equally or are some worse than others? Such questions illustrate the difficulties. Similarly, if we want to quantify how well a method creates software that is easy to maintain, then ideally we need an objective measure or metric.

There are, of course, additional criteria for assessing and comparing methods (see Chapter 22 on project management). We might choose from amongst the following checklist:

- training time for the people who will use the method
- level of skill required by the people using the method
- whether the software produced is easy to maintain
- whether the software will meet performance targets
- whether documentation is automatically produced
- whether the method is enjoyable to use
- whether the method can be used in the required area of application.

The outcomes of experiments that assess methods are not encouraging. For example, though it is widely accepted in the computer industry that structured programming is the best approach, one review of the evidence concluded that it was inconclusive (because of problems with the design of experiments). Similarly, there seems to be very limited evidence that OO methods or that formal methods are better than traditional methods.

Clearly there are many problems to be solved in assessing methods, but equally clearly developers need hard evidence to use in choosing between methods. We can expect that much attention will be given to the evaluation of tools and methods and it is, in fact, an active area of current research. This research centers on the design of experiments and on the invention of useful metrics.

23.3 ● Software tools

Earlier in this book we devoted a chapter to the topic of software tools. Treating tools as a separate subject is misleading because they permeate the whole of software development. Software tools are relevant to every method and every chapter included in this book. Just as in production engineering, architecture, electronic design, and in design generally, computer aids are being used throughout software development. There is an explosion in the demand for software products that aid or automate parts, or the whole of software development. The whole process of development is now commonly carried out entirely on a computer-based system, without any resort to paper. Not only the development itself, but the planning, allocation of people, monitoring of progress, the documentation are all maintained on computers.

23.4 ● Software re-usability

Software re-use is an important approach to constructing software that has been repeatedly addressed in this book. The argument goes like this: software developers are continually re-inventing the wheel. Instead of writing software from scratch over and over again, they should emulate people like computer hardware designers. Hardware designers make heavy use of reference manuals that describe hundreds of off-the-shelf components. All that the designer has to do is to select components and collect them together to carry out the required purpose.

The proponents of re-use, therefore, envisage comprehensive libraries of reliable and well-documented software from which developers can select. The controversy starts with the choice of mechanism for representing the components in the library. Three main contenders are on offer:

● libraries of filters like those in Unix
● libraries like those offered by conventional procedural languages such as Ada 83 or C
● libraries like the classes provided in object-oriented systems such as Smalltalk, Ada 95, C++, or Java.

One of the main issues here is modularity, which has been mentioned often throughout this book.

23.5 ● The current state of methods

A number of methods and approaches discussed in this book are well established and widely used:

● requirements analysis
● structured programming
● object-oriented design

- object-oriented programming
- functional decomposition
- data structure design (Jackson structured programming)
- data flow design
- parallel programming
- structured walkthroughs
- prototyping.

Some methods are beginning to be used and are about to become popular:

- formal specification (particularly for safety-critical systems)
- logic programming (for example, in expert systems)
- re-usable design patterns.

Some methods are more speculative; they may or may not be amongst the mainstream methods of the future:

- formal verification
- functional programming.

Do not forget, however, that there are many legacy systems, written some time ago that were developed and documented using what are now antiquated methods. These systems need maintaining and so the methods that were used in their development live on.

23.6 ● A single development method?

Given the proliferation of methods, how can they be combined, or used together? Let us use, for the present, the framework of the traditional software development lifecycle:

1. requirements specification
2. architectural design
3. detailed design
4. implementation
5. verification
6. maintenance.

This sequential life-cycle approach to development is being overtaken by the use of prototyping in order to continually check that the system meets the users' needs. Increasingly the approach is to use:

1. analysis of requirements as described in Chapter 3
2. prototyping
3. object-oriented design for architectural design

4. C++ or Java for coding

5. a combination of testing methods

6. top-down implementation.

All of these steps are supported by software tools and all of them can be accompanied by structured walkthroughs. Another possibility would be to use formal specification after requirements analysis to clarify the specification of important aspects of the software.

At the present time all these approaches – and every other combination of methods – are considered feasible. Indeed, it is perhaps strange that, as with designing an auto-mobile, we do not consider using different approaches for different parts of the system. Most software systems consist of qualitatively different parts:

● the human–computer interface

● the database management system

● the network software

● real-time or parallel processing

and it is reasonable that these different ingredients are developed using different approaches.

23.7 ● The real world of software engineering

In an academic book like this, it is expected that a number of systematic methods are presented. But are they really used in practice? Real-world practices often differ from the theory. For example, Microsoft generally use the following methods:

● training on the job, rather than formal study

● minimal documentation other than source code

● C rather than object-oriented C++.

In spite of these surprising methods, they are (at least in one sense) highly successful.

If you talk to a professional software developer, the likelihood is that they will say that they use one of the respectable methods described in this book. Nowadays there is tremendous pressure to use a "proper" design method. The truth is, however, different. Let us hypothesize that design is a crucial part of software development (or at least design is a representative part of software development). A number of studies have been carried out to discover how professional engineers really carry out design. This work really started back in the 1960s when people like Peter Naur tried to observe their own thought processes as they carried out a program design. Later studies usually proceed by observing developers as they carry out the task, or else by getting them to speak aloud what they are thinking as they go about development. In this section we review the results of such studies. (It should be pointed out that the observational methods used to obtain these results are not without problems and so some caution must be used in interpreting the results.)

The first revelation is that there is an enormous diversity amongst programmers as to the strategies they adopt. There is also an enormous diversity amongst the designs that developers will produce to solve the same problem. Different developers use different methods and construct different designs. Some designs are good and some are bad. Moreover the evidence is that there are enormous productivity differences between individual software developers.

The second revelation is perhaps even more surprising – *programmers do not use the approved methods*. This evidence must be qualified – it seems that professional developers do use a method, but only when they understand all aspects of the situation very thoroughly. If the developer has a mastery of the language and if the problem seems to be very simple (to them), then the developer may use an approved method. In other words, programmers use top-down only very rarely.

If, as it seems, software engineers do not use a proper method, what do they do? It appears that what they commonly do is to break the problem down into smaller problems – but not in an approved way. They select fragments of the problem for consideration. They do this by using a whole range of personal strategies. At the end of the day, when they have completed their design, they then legitimize it by documenting it according to one of the credible design notations. So they pretend that it was done properly.

It seems that there are other ways that competent developers carry out design. They re-use parts of old programs, like parts of scrap cars. They remember a program that they may have written some time ago that is in some way similar to the new program. They retrieve the listing and copy those parts that are useful. Another similar approach is to use memories of old programs. Experienced developers build up Aladdin's caves of memories of the designs that they have created. The establishment of catalogs of re-usable design patterns explicitly recognizes this approach.

No survey of design approaches would be complete without a mention of *hacking*. This term has two distinct meanings. One meaning describes the act of getting admittance to a secure computer system in order to steal money or secrets or to cause mayhem. The other meaning describes a style of programming. Hacking is plunging into a solution to a problem without any design whatsoever. A hacker takes the program specification and immediately starts to write down programming language instructions. Probably the hacker will not even pause to write them down – they will immediately start to key-in instructions to the computer. Hacking makes use of intuition, creativity, and individuality. It dates from the early days of programming, when programming was regarded as an individual creative act and when there were no well-established design methods. Nowadays hacking is often frowned upon as being unsystematic. So hacking is either famous or notorious, depending on your point of view.

LISP programmers have long championed a program design strategy which lies somewhere between hacking and the disciplined approaches described in this book. Perhaps this is because the application areas in which LISP is used (such as artificial intelligence) demand an exploratory approach in which programs may be written in order to try to demonstrate a theoretical premise. Thus AI tries to solve "ill-formed problems" – it is difficult to determine when (or if) we have solved such problems, because they are only partially understood. Moreover, LISP programmers regularly embark on the design and construction of programs they don't know how to write. This kind of "exploratory programming" clearly requires a great deal of help from the language and its programming environment, and a flexibility in the way in which ideas can be expressed which is not found in languages like Java and C.

For example, in LISP you can use variables without declaring their type, or define functions which can take arbitrary numbers of arguments. You can define and use functions which call other functions that haven't been written yet. You can edit, test, and debug a program incrementally even while the program is running. And very importantly, LISP blurs the distinction between program and data – which is the reason for LISP's much maligned bracketed syntax. It is this dynamic, rather than static, approach to program construction which enables and supports exploratory programming. Erik Sandewall has described this method of program development as *structured growth*: "... an initial program with a pure and simple structure is written, tested, and then allowed to grow by increasing the ambition of its modules. The growth can occur both horizontally, through the addition of more facilities, and vertically through a deepening of existing facilities ... ." Sandewall argues against the moralistic view that this could be considered as hacking under another name, on the grounds that "... even if some kinds of program changes are dangerous and/or bad, that does not prove that all of them are." He also makes the point that stepwise refinement and structured growth are variants of top-down design, in that both refine a program's component parts from an initial high-level view of its overall structure.

Finally, there is evidence that men and women carry out design differently. Men, it seems, tend to regard the computer as a slave that has to be controlled, dominated, and brought under the will of the programmer. In this approach, the computer may have to be wrestled with or struggled with in order that it does the programmer's bidding. In contrast, women approach the computer as a machine that has to be accommodated to, something that has quirks to come to terms with. The female designer proceeds by trying something and, if it is not successful, trying something else. The design emerges from the process of negotiation.

Assuming that most professional software engineers are required by the organization that employs them to use a systematic design method, what do they do? We speculate that a professional programmer first creates a design using their own personal method. They then legitimize it by casting it into the shape of one of the approved methods. This involves producing the charts as the documentation that accompanies proper use of the method.

In summary there is evidence to suggest that:

- software engineers do not use the approved methods
- the productivity and quality of work differs significantly from one individual software engineer to another.

If we believe this analysis, the best strategy for a software producer is to hire individuals who are good at it and let them get on with it. (This, in fact, appears to be the Microsoft solution.)

23.8 ● The question of skill

As we have seen, software is hugely expensive, difficult to construct, often late and over-budget. Current software engineering tools and techniques are helpful, but not totally effective. Thus software development currently requires enormous skill. However, research into software engineering methods strives to devise new and more effective methods. This research tries to analyze the processes involved in software development and thereby suggest more systematic methods. In software development, the Jackson method (Chapter 8) serves as the most dramatic example of the regimentation of the process of design. Scrutiny of the software development process also means that certain tasks can be identified as requiring minimal skill and these can be automated. An example is the use of a program generator that automatically creates source code from descriptions of screen and file layouts.

Thus the tendencies in software engineering are:

● more systematic methods
● automation and tool support.

The fear is that more systematic methods will reduce the scope for individual creative design. In addition, automation tends to mean that fewer people are needed than would otherwise be required. The introduction of new methods has always been linked with the erosion of skills. In England, the Luddites revolted against employers who replaced their labor by machinery, then reduced wages, and the number of jobs. Thus more effective methods often imply:

● less skill (de-skilling)
● reduced wages
● fewer jobs

and at the same time a small, highly-skilled elite to carry out the difficult tasks.

The argument for using systematic approaches is that simple tasks should be made simple – there is no point in struggling to design a software component when there is an easy way. So a method can be empowering, creating time to spend on intrinsically difficult tasks.

In conclusion, there is a tension between, on the one hand, the desire of an individual software engineer to exercise their individual creativity and, on the other hand, the wish of organizations to systematize methods and exercise quality control.

23.9 ● The future of software engineering

The demise of applications programming has been regularly predicted for a number of years, and yet the demand for programmers is ever-increasing. What methods are likely to be used in the future? What is likely to happen to the jobs of those involved in software development?

Let us first look at some of the history of software development methods. In the early days of computing, the hardware was the challenge; programming was considered to be easy – an undemanding activity very similar to clerical work. The first programmers were exclusively women because it was considered work unsuitable for men. Fairly soon it was realized that programming demanded a logical approach and abstract thinking. (The women were replaced by men.)

As the problems of software production began to restrict the application of computers, the principle of the division of labor was applied to software development. First, the job of the analyst was separated from that of the programmer. Later, with the invention of high-level languages, operating systems and packages, the work of applications programmers was distinguished from that of systems programmers.

Today, the cost of software generally overwhelms the cost of the hardware it runs on. Software production is labor intensive and programmers are in short supply. A major remedy offered is to provide programmers with more powerful tools – usually computer based. Examples are program generators, high-level languages, and software development environments.

In the short-term future, it seems likely that we can expect to see enormous effort spent in developing tools and in ensuring that a set of tools fits together in an integrated manner. At the same time we can expect that end-users will carry out their own system development using software packages that require them to know little about the computer. Coupled with the availability of inexpensive applications packages, the applications programmer seems (as ever) doomed.

In the long term, the nature of programming itself could be transformed by a declarative style of programming, in which the programmer describes a solution to a problem rather than having to specify explicitly how that solution is to be obtained. This revolution in programming, together with the blossoming commercial interest in knowledge-based systems, seems likely to spawn a new breed of software engineer – with the emphasis on *knowledge* engineering, rather than software in the traditional sense.

While the applications programmer may vanish, the role of the systems programmers may be enhanced. Their mission will be to develop products of high quality – reliable, powerful, and easy to use. The skills involved in their development may be considerable – not least in the requirement to create demonstrably reliable software, perhaps using formal, mathematical approaches. At the other end of the spectrum, the analyst will not become extinct. Their role will be to guide users and an organization in making best use of the available packages.

The general trend, as illustrated by the particular case of data processing, is:

● the increasing scrutiny of the software development task

● systematization of software development

● the division of labor amongst specialists

● the automation of certain tasks using tools.

23.10 ● Summary

The software engineer is faced with a bewildering number of available methods, techniques, and tools. Before choosing, the first task is to carefully identify the specific goals of the project. Little hard data is currently available to allow comparison of methods. This is partly because of the difficulty in mounting experiments. Software metrics hold the promise for objective comparison of methods, but at the present time, evaluation of tools and methods is extremely difficult.

This book has presented a menu of techniques, and made some assessment of those techniques. But it is impossible to provide comprehensive guidance for selecting items from the menu; the evaluation and comparison of methods is currently the subject of research. However, often, the choice of method is based on rather mundane, practical considerations – like the expertise of the people that are available.

Software development methods have changed dramatically in the past and look set to do the same in the future. The trend is towards the increased use of packages, program generators, and automated tools.

Long-term, traditional procedural programming languages may vanish.

Generally, change may be seen as de-skilling large areas of software development work.

EXERCISES

23.1 List each of the goals of software engineering (see Chapter 1). List all the tools and techniques of software engineering. Draw up a table, with the goals as headings across the top of the page and with the tools and techniques down the left-hand-side. Place a tick at the places where a method contributes to a goal.

23.2 Draw up a list of criteria for assessing a software development method. Use it to evaluate:

- functional decomposition
- Object-oriented design
- the Michael Jackson method
- data flow design.

23.3 Different design approaches tend to model some important aspect of the problem domain. For each of the following design methods, identify what is modeled:

- functional decomposition
- Object-oriented design
- the Michael Jackson method
- data flow design.

23.4 What tools and methods would you use to develop each of the following:

(a) software to control a washing machine

(b) software to control a power station

(c) a system to calculate and print a company payroll

(d) a general-purpose operating system or data base management system.

23.5 Compare and contrast:

(a) procedural programming

(b) logic programming

(c) functional programming

(d) object-oriented programming

(e) parallel programming.

23.6 Compare and contrast the following approaches to software re-use:

(a) Unix filters

(b) libraries in a conventional programming language such as C

(c) OO classes.

23.7 Programming is easy. Discuss.

23.8 Software engineering is just programming, and programming is just hacking. Discuss.

23.9 The scrutiny of software development methods, together with the imposition of standards and procedures for quality assurance has taken all the fun out of it. Discuss.

23.10 The tasks involved in software engineering are going to dramatically change over the next 5–10 years. In particular, conventional programming will no longer exist. Discuss.

23.11 Predict the future of software engineering.

FURTHER READING

Read all about how Microsoft do it. A most comprehensive survey of the software development methods used by Microsoft is given in: Michael A. Cusumano and Richard W. Selby, *Microsoft Secrets*, The Free Press, 1995.

It is widely agreed that structured programming is a vital ingredient of software development. For a review of the (inconclusive) evidence about the effectiveness of structured programming, see: I. Vessey and R. Weber, Research on Structured Programming: An Empiricist's Evaluation. *IEEE Trans on Software Engineering*, 10 (4) pp. 397–407.

For a review of the (limited) evidence on the effectiveness of other software development methods, including object-oriented methods and formal methods, see: N. E. Fenton, How Effective are Software Engineering Methods? *Journal of Systems and Software*, 20 (1993), pp. 93–100.

Ed Yourdon is one of the gurus of software development. In this book he gives a very readable account of the problems that he perceives with software development today. The book continues by giving a survey of the possible remedies for the problems. It is altogether a very readable book, free of technicalities and free with opinions. The title reflects the author's opinion that American programmers are under threat from competition from programmers in Asia – who are paid less, but are better! Edward Yourdon, *Decline and Fall of the American Programmer*, PTR Prentice Hall, 1993.

The sequel to *Decline and Fall*, which is much more optimistic about the future of the American programmer, provided that they take the initiative and learn about new technologies, like Java: Edward Yourdon, *Rise and Resurrection of the American Programmer*, PTR Prentice Hall, 1995.

A possible future for software development is described in the following reference. Have the predictions turned out to be correct? A. I. Wassermann, The Future of Programming, *Communications of the ACM*, 25 (3), (March 1982).

An extensive treatment of the issue of de-skilling is given in: P. Kraft, *Programmers and Managers*, Springer-Verlag, 1977.

There have been several exciting accounts of the personal outlook and work methods of programmers. They give insights into how programming is actually done. They also contribute to the folklore of programming. The first, classic book is: G. Weinberg, *The Psychology of Computer Programming*, Van Nostrand Reinhold, 1971.

An example of a book on how programmers actually work. In the book, she reports on interviews with notable programmers. Susan Lammers, *Programmers at Work*, Microsoft, 1986.

Steven Levy, *Hackers, Heroes of the Computer Revolution*, Anchor Books, 1994.

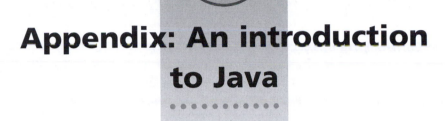

Appendix: An introduction to Java

This appendix presents an introduction to the non-object-oriented features of Java. It might be useful pre-reading for any of the chapters on:

The programming language, Chapter 13
Object-oriented programming, Chapter 14
Concurrent programming, Chapter 15.

This overview of the basic features of Java assumes that the reader has some familiarity with the general ideas of procedural programming, as exhibited by languages such as Basic, Fortran, Cobol, C, and Ada.

A.1 ● Variables and assignment

In Java, variables can be declared like this:

```
int i;
```

and values assigned to variables:

```
i = i + 23;
```

The primitive, built-in data types provided by the language are as follows.

`boolean`	true or false
`char`	16 bit Unicode character
`byte`	8 bit integer
`short`	16 bit integer
`int`	32 bit integer
`long`	64 bit integer
`float`	32 bit floating-point number
`double`	64 bit floating-point number

These data types are not themselves objects. All other data types (objects) are built from these primitive types. Character variables (`char`) are not much used in practice because a powerful string data type is provided and supported by a comprehensive library.

A.2 ● Control structures

Sequences of statements are, of course, common, as in any procedural language:

```
i = i + 23;
i = i + 1;
```

`if` statements provide selection. For example:

```
if (salary > 20000)
    tax = 10000;
else
    tax = 0;
```

You may notice that the syntax of Java – for example the use of semicolons – is very similar to that of C and C++ because of a deliberate policy to make a transition from these languages easy.

Loops are similar to those in most procedural languages. For example:

```
sum = 0;
i = 0;
while (table[i] > 0) {
    sum = sum + table[i];
    i = i + 1;
}
```

and as can be seen, arrays are supported by the language. Curly brackets group together a block of statements – in this case within the body of the loop to be repeated.

As in the languages C and C++, a loop such as the one above can be written more compactly using a `for` statement:

```
sum = 0;
for (i = 0; table[i] > 0; i = i + 1) {
    sum = sum + table[i];
}
```

A.3 ● Methods

Finally, like all other programming languages, Java supports procedures (subprograms, subroutines, functions) – called *methods*. The reason for calling these things methods arises from the history of OO languages and, in particular, Smalltalk. The way of understanding this terminology is to say that a method is simply a method for doing something. Unlike some languages, Java methods adopt a careful discipline:

● Information is communicated *to* a method as parameters.

● Any information communicated *from* the method as the value of the method.

Thus if we have a method called `add` that adds together the values of its two parameters, we would use it like this:

```
answer = add(x, y);
```

and the method itself is declared like this:

```
int add(int a, int b) {
    return(a + b);
}
```

in which the `int` before the method name describes the type of the data that is to be returned as the value of the method. The language word `return` signifies what is to be returned as the value of the method. If a method does not return a value (for example, a method to change the *x* coordinate of a graphical object on the screen), the method name is preceded by the word `void`:

```
void setX(int newX) {
    xCoord = newX;
}
```

A.4 ● Summary

The non-OO features of Java are:

● sequences of statements that are obeyed one after the other (as in any procedural language)

● control structures – `if` (for selection), `while` and `for` (for looping)

● methods with parameters

● built in, simple data types – `boolean`, `char`, `byte`, `short`, `int`, `long`, `float`, `double`

● arrays.

Index

abstract class 173
abstract data type 209, 227, 243, 244, 247
abstraction 80, 249
   control 221
   procedural 238
Ada 229, 235, 241, 246, 247, 248, 250, 251, 254, 255, 281
adversary team 383
animation 209
anthropomorphic programming 165
architectural design 23
assertion 401
assessing methods 450

backtracking 345
backward error recovery 405
beta testing 383
black box testing 375
bottom-up testing 386
boundary value 376
bounty hunter 383
browser 363
bug 13, 374, 396

C 232, 235, 255
C++ 232, 235, 247, 254, 255, 281
capability maturity model (CMM) 426
CASE 355
chief programmer team 437
class 267
class diagram 159, 272
class method 270

class-responsibility-collaborator cards 170
CMM 426
COCOMO 433
coding 23
cohesion 98
compile-time checking 399
complexity 90, 419
Computer Aided Software Engineering (CASE) 355
concurrency 286
concurrent programming 286
consistency 203
constructor 269
control abstraction 221
control structures 77, 464
correctness 207
cost 5, 8
cost estimation 432
coupling 95
CRC cards 170
currying 329

damage 405
dangling else 220
dangling pointer 235, 236
data flow design 141
data flow diagram 142
data hiding 92
data invariant 58
data refinement 200
data structure design 116
data type 227

deadlines 10
deadlock 313
declarative programming 321, 338
defensive programming 401
design patterns 176
desktop metaphor 186
destructor 270
detailed design 23
Dijkstra 383
dining philosophers 313
direct manipulation 186
dynamic binding 162
dynamic data structure 234
dynamic linking 274
dynamic typing 228

ego-less programming 379
encapsulation 92, 158, 265
environment 369
equivalence 218
equivalence partitioning 376
error 13
error recovery
    backward 405
    forward 405
errors 373, 379, 396
event-driven programs 275
evolutionary prototyping 31
exception handler 406
exceptions 406

failure 13
fault(s) 13, 383, 396, 422
    density 422
    detection 399, 402
    intolerance 397
    tolerance 396
filter 359
formal methods 36, 199
    role of 208
formal specification 55
    role of 64
Fortran 229, 237, 240
forward error recovery 405
function point analysis 433
functional decomposition 106
functional programming 321
    role of 333
functional requirements 51
functional team 434
functional testing 375
functions 239

garbage collection 236, 270
generics 248
global data 91, 96, 241
goto 72, 222
granularity 403
graphical user interface (GUI) 185, 274
guarded commands 208
GUI 185, 274

hacking 455
hardware costs 6
has-a analysis 175
Haskell 321
help system 194
higher-order function 327
Hope 331
human computer interaction/interface (HCI) 16,
    183

identifier 221
incremental testing 385
information hiding 92, 158, 241
inheritance 159, 271, 274
    multiple 160, 274
    single 160, 274
inspection 379, 381
instance 267
integration 23
integration testing 25, 385
Interlisp 360
invariant 59
is-a analysis 175

Java 229, 235, 246, 247, 252, 254, 255, 265, 286,
    463
JSP 116

Lambda expression 328
legacy systems 13
libraries 161, 169
lines of code (LOC) 419
Lisp 331, 360, 455
LOC 419
local data 241
logic programming 338
    role of 348

maintenance 12, 23
McCabe measure 420
mean time to failure (MTTF) 422
memory corruption 236
memory leaks 236

memory protection 402
mental model 186
methods
  assessing 450
  current state of 452
  new, introducing 442
  selecting 441
  use of 454
metrics 418
Michael Jackson method 116
Miranda 331
ML 331
modularity 85
module interconnection language 251
module size 88
monolithic testing 385
MTTF 422
multiple inheritance 160, 274
multithreading 286
mutation testing 382
mutual exclusion 293

n-version programming 413

object 265, 268
object-oriented design (OOD) 157
object-oriented programming (OOP) 102, 265
  role of 280
object-oriented project 439
OOD 157
OOP see object-oriented programming
open source 395
operation refinement 200, 208

packages 250
parameters 240
Pascal 229, 235
patterns, design 176
peopleware 443
performance 10
person months 433
pipes 359
planning 442
pointer 234
polymorphism 162, 274
portability 11
postcondition 60
precondition 60
private 246, 267
procedural abstraction 238
procedural programming 322
procedures 464

process 287
process improvement 426
process model 21
producer-consumer 301
productivity 6, 456
programmer tools see tools
programming by personification 165
programming in the large 216, 249
programming in the small 216
programming language 215, 256
  see also under different languages
project management 430, 431
project team 434
Prolog 338
proof obligations 203
prototyping 28, 190
  evolutionary 31
  throwaway 29
proximity 136
public 246, 267

quality 423, 456
quality assurance 418, 425
quality assurance plan 425
quality control 425

records 232
recovery block 410
recovery points 405
refactoring 169
referential transparency 323
refinement 200
reification 200
reliability 13
repetition 224
requirements analysis 45
requirements elicitation 47
requirements engineering 23, 45
requirements specification 23, 49, 200
re-usability 452
run-time checking 399

safety-critical system 15
scheduling 293
schema 58
scoping 241, 254
selection 222
separate compilation 253
Shaw and Garlan's classification 100
side effect 239, 323, 349
Simula 281
single inheritance 160, 274

skill 457
Smalltalk 281, 362
software engineering, future of 457
software fault tolerance 396
software metrics 418
software quality *see* quality
software tools *see* tools
specification 200
  formal 55
spiral model 37
S-shaped curve 6
static method 270
static typing 228
strong typing 227, 237
structural testing 377
structure chart 118, 144, 192
structure clash 131
structured programming 71
structured walkthrough 379, 380
syntax 218
system testing 25, 385

task 287
task analysis 191
teams 364, 383, 434
test bed 386
testing 374
thread 287
throwaway prototyping 29
tools 355, 357, 441, 452
top-down development 387
top-down testing 387
transform model 36

triple modular redundancy 413
types
  primitive 228
  structured 230, 232
  user defined 229
typing 227
  dynamic 228
  static 228
  strong 227, 237
  weak 227, 237

UML 154, 272
unit testing 24
Unified Modeling Language (UML) 154, 272
Unix 134, 358
use-case analysis 171
user interface design 183
user interface toolkits 195
users needs 4

validation 14, 24
VDM 200
verification 14, 24, 372
Visual Basic 366
voting 413

walkthrough 379, 380
waterfall model 25
weak typing 227, 237
white box testing 377

Z 57, 200